THE
PALESTINE
PROBLEM
IN INTERNATIONAL LAW AND WORLD ORDER

THE
PALESTINE
PROBLEM
IN INTERNATIONAL LAW AND WORLD ORDER

W. Thomas Mallison and Sally V. Mallison

W. Thomas Mallison is
Professor of Law and Director of the
International and Comparative Law Program at the
George Washington University,
Washington D.C., U.S.A.

Sally V. Mallison is
Research Associate of the
International and Comparative Law Program at the
George Washington University,
Washington D.C., U.S.A.

Longman

Longman Group Limited
Longman House, Burnt Mill, Harlow
Essex CM20 2JE, England
and Associated Companies throughout the world.

First published 1986

ISBN 0 582 78362 3

Set in Linotron 202 10/12 Palatino

Printed & bound by
Butler & Tanner Ltd, Frome & London

Acknowledgements

We are grateful to the American Educational Trust for permission to reproduce copyright maps which appear on pages 497 and 498.

ERRATA
p. 136 note 143 : should read 7 Israel Laws, in Appendix 5
   note 144 : should read Appendix 6
p. 137 note 145 : should read Appendix 7
p. 138 note 147 : should read Appendix 8

Contents

Preface

A deeper understanding throughout the world community of the facts and the law involved in the Palestine–Israel conflict situation is one of the most important steps in the achievement of peace in the Middle East. The primary purpose of the authors is to demonstrate that there is sound legal authority which is the indispensable basis for the achievement of such a peace. It is evident that a solution to the Palestine problem under the applicable principles of international law is essential if the world community is to be saved from the disaster of recurring wars in the Middle East and the danger of another world war in an era of weapons of mass destruction.

The world legal order with which this work is concerned is based on the customary and treaty law governing the activity of states and other international participants. The definitions of terms contained in the Introduction are essential to the understanding of the chapters which follow. The first two chapters analyze the background of the Zionist political objective of establishing "the Jewish state" for "the Jewish people" in Palestine. The next three chapters focus upon the partition of Palestine between Zionists and Palestinians and upon Palestinian national and individual legal rights in Palestine including Jerusalem. The two chapters which immediately precede the conclusion apply the legal criteria to two significant events in Palestine: the Israeli settlements in the post-1967 occupied territories and the major attack-invasion of 1982. The conclusion emphasizes the destructive consequences of the continuing violation of law in Palestine and outlines the value-conserving alternative of implementation of the world legal order with ensuing peace and as much justice as possible for both Israelis and Palestinians.

The Introduction is based in part upon a study entitled "The Zionist-Israel Juridical Claims to Constitute 'The Jewish

People' Nationality Entity and to Confer Membership in It: Appraisal in Public International Law" which was published in Volume 32, Number 5 of the *George Washington Law Review*. The second chapter is a revision and updating of an analysis entitled "The Legal Problems Concerning the Juridical Status and Political Activities of the Zionist Organization/Jewish Agency: A Study in International and United States Law" published in Volume 9, Number 3 of the *William and Mary Law Review*. Both law reviews have granted permission for the use of material which has been included in this book. Chapter 1 is an adaptation of material which originally appeared in *The Transformation of Palestine*, edited by Professor Ibrahim Abu-Lughod. The authors express their appreciation to Northwestern University Press for permission to use this material. An earlier version of Chapter 6 was printed as a monograph entitled *Settlements and the Law: A Juridical Analysis of the Israeli Settlements in the Occupied Territories* and distributed by the American Educational Trust of Washington, D.C. The same organization has published a version of Chapter 7 entitled *Armed Conflict in Lebanon, 1982: Humanitarian Law in a Real World Setting*.

The authors are indebted to many friends at home and abroad who have contributed to their understanding of the factual background of these chapters, and particularly to Rabbi Elmer Berger, Dr. John H. Davis, Dr. Harry N. Howard, Dr. Anis F. Kassim, and Mr. John Reddaway. Students, both American and foreign, at the Geroge Washington University Law Center have given much encouragement by their interest in the legal aspects of the Palestine problem. Ms. Nancy Jo Nelson and Mr. George W. Lindley Jnr. Juris Doctor candidates, have provided valuable research assistance. The authors also express appreciation to Robert G. Bidwell, Brian R. Dixon, Ved P. Gulatti and other members of the staff of the George Washington University Law Library. It has been a pleasure to work with the staff of Longman Group who have been helpful to the authors in many ways and who have efficiently prepared these materials for publication.

Introduction

The Palestine Problem in International Law and World Order is a collection of analyses of some of the main legal issues which have been raised as a result of the establishment of the State of Israel as a Zionist state. It is the conviction of the authors that international law must play a major role in achieving peace and justice in the Middle East in conformity with the world order system.

The first question which may be put to those who attempt to achieve objectives through international law is: What is meant by international law? In basic conception, international law consists of a common body of norms or principles which are used in the solution of diverse problems. It is essential that such norms or principles be applied consistently in order to promote the objectivity and uniformity associated with "law" as opposed to *ad hoc* or unprincipled decision-making in which a different rule is developed for each problem. Upon the basis of this premise, international law may be accurately regarded as a set of uniform principles which require at least minimum standards of reasonable and humane conduct in the world community.

It is also important to recognize that the principles of international law are established by consent and agreement. Express agreement is usually termed treaty or conventional law, and implicit agreement is usually termed customary law. Both are based primarily upon the consent of states as manifested by their governments, although other participants including international public bodies and individuals have a role to play. Among the public bodies which act in the development and acceptance of international law, the United Nations is particularly important. The United Nations Charter is a multilateral treaty agreed to by its members, as well as being the basic constitution for the world community.

A third element is indispensable to a practical conception of international law. Even the most just and widely accepted principles of law, such as those contained in the U.N. Charter, are ineffectual in protecting human rights unless they are actually enforced and sanctioned. International law involves a whole sanctioning process ranging from exclusive reliance upon persuasive procedures at one extreme to heavy reliance upon coercive measures at the other extreme, with many intermediate stages, including economic sanctions. Sanctions may be most constructively conceived as a continuous process rather than an isolated series of unrelated events. As a general approach, the more coercive sanctions should be increasingly used where the persuasive ones have been found to be ineffective. There are very few situations either in international or municipal law where enforcement procedures are either completely effective or totally ineffective. The most relevant questions concerning sanctions, consequently, are: How effective is the present sanctions process and what steps may be taken to improve it?

A fourth element which requires specification is that among the institutions created to serve mankind, the state is not above international law. Since states and their governments have the pre-eminent role in making international law, it is essential that they be held accountable for full compliance with it. As a practical matter this means the personal accountability of government officials which was established in international law by the *Nuremberg Trial* before the International Military Tribunal. The Nuremberg principles of the individual responsibility of government officials adopted by the United Nations General Assembly[1] are applicable to officials of all governments.

A second question may be asked concerning international law: Is it a relevant and practical means to achieve justice and peace in Palestine-Israel? The cynics may point to the actual decision-making process in the Middle East in general and in Palestine-Israel in particular. It may be stated with assurance that the great powers have used power

---

1.   *1 U.N. CAOR*, G. A. Res. 95(I), Doc. A/236 (1946). The principles also appear in 45 *Am. J. Int'l L.* 125 (1951).

politics, including a large measure of military methods, to deal with the problems of this area. From this accurate premise it may be erroneously deduced that international law has been a failure in the Middle East. It would be far more accurate to conclude that international law has not even been tried. The unprincipled power politics played in the Middle East have papered over the fundamental causes of the conflict situation and dealt, at best, with the results of injustice and violation of law.[2] Of course, when national officials are specialists in dealing with the overall context of great power relations and are distinct non-specialists in dealing with the Middle East, it is tempting for them to exercise their speciality. This technique requires no knowledge of, or even interest in, the human values which are involved in the Zionist-Palestinian and the Middle East conflict situations. The outcome of this approach to the problems of the area has been a further militarization accompanied by an indefinitely protracted conflict and the increasing destruction of human and material values.

Because of the dismal failure of the techniques which have been utilized, international law is no longer only an ideal alternative. It is also the only practical alternative to an indefinite continuation of the present situation.

It is useful at the outset to attempt to clarify the fundamental values which are involved in the legal problems concerning Palestine. This requires a consideration of the meaning which is given to particular word symbols. The subject matter dealt with here is in the domain of public international law. The task of public law, whether international or municipal, is conceived as providing an institutional framework in which the individual may achieve his fundamental values. These values[3] are:

---

2.   The United States Government materials which demonstrate this appear in [1947] *Foreign Rels. U.S.*, Vol. 5, pp. 999–1328 (1971).

3.   The eight value categories reflect the work of Professors Lasswell and McDougal of the Yale University Law School. Their classic introductory study, "Legal Education and Public Policy: Professional Training in the Public Interest," 52 *Yale L. J.* 203 (1943), makes explicit the relevance of value clarification to juridical analysis. See also McDougal & Associates, *Studies in World Public Order* (1960); McDougal, Lasswell & Chen, *Human Rights and World Public Order* (1980).

(1) *Respect for the dignity of the individual* – positively, this includes recognition of the general merit of all people as human beings and the particular merit of each person as an individual. Negatively, this precludes discrimination based upon religion, race, and all other factors which are irrelevant to individual worth.

(2) *Equality before the law and the sharing of governmental power* – this includes an opportunity for fair participation in the processes of government in the international, national, and local communities.

(3) *Enlightenment and information* – this includes freedom of inquiry and opinion, which are indispensable to rational decision-making.

(4) *Psychic and physical well-being* – positively, this includes the opportunity to develop individual abilities. Negatively, it requires freedom from arbitrary burdens, restrictions, and punishments.

(5) The opportunity to participate in *congenial and constructive inter-personal relationships*.

(6) *Goods and services* necessary to adequate standards of living.

(7) *Skills and "know-how"* necessary to achieve all values in a factual sense.

(8) Freedom to develop and apply *conceptions of morality and ethics* – this includes the freedom to worship God, or the freedom not to worship, depending upon individual choice.

A democratic conception of international and municipal law,[4] as opposed to totalitarian or authoritarian conceptions,[5] seeks to institutionalize the shaping and sharing of such values in a rational and peaceful context. At the minimum, such a democratic juridical conception must prohibit the coercion of individuals in their shaping and sharing of values where the coercion is exercised by public entities which are

---

4.   Democratic conceptions of law are set forth in each of the studies cited in *supra* note 3.

5.   For an analysis of Soviet Russian conceptions, see Ramundo, *The Socialist Theory of International Law* (George Washington University Institute for Sino-Soviet Studies No. 1, 1964).

foreign to the individuals coerced.[6]

Words without specified referents are highly ambiguous and are capable of having multiple and inconsistent meanings ascribed to them by writers and readers. In order to achieve clarity, it is desirable to set forth the general terms of reference which are connected with certain key word symbols appearing throughout this study.[7] It is recognized that these same word symbols are used by others with different terms of reference than those employed here.

Jew is used to refer to a voluntary adherent of the religion of Judaism. *Judaism* is used to refer to one of the monotheistic religions of universal moral values. The word "Jew" is used by the writers to refer to an adherent of Judaism in the same way that "Christian" refers to an adherent of Christianity.[8]

In setting forth a religious conception of "Jew" and "Judaism," the writers are adopting a basic tenet of traditional and contemporary Judaism. In 1878 Rabbi Her-

---

6. Even in democratic municipal juridical systems, individuals do not have effective means to protect themselves from foreign coercion and must seek governmental prohibition of such coercion.

7. See Ogden & Richards, *The Meaning of Meaning* (1936); Morris, *Signs, Language and Behavior* (1946); and Chafe, "The Disorderly Conduct of Words," 41 *Colum. L. Rev.* 381 (1941). A useful introduction to word symbols employed in the present study appears in Sussman, "'Jew,' 'Jewish People,' and 'Zionism,'" 20 Etc: *A Review of General Semantics* 372 (1963).

8. Professor Robert M. MacIver has written concerning the stated credo of the American Jewish Committee that, "A Jew in America can live a full and rich Jewish life as an integrated American":

> In the first place, what does it mean? Suppose we substitute another word in place of "Jewish"? We would then read, for example: "A Frenchman in America can live a full and rich life as an integrated American." A Frenchman in America, a Pole, an Englishman, a Chinese? The statement would not be very meaningful and might easily be resented. But if we said instead: "a Roman Catholic, a Mohammedan, a Lutheran can live" and so forth, then the expression would be acceptable, since all religions have equal rights and none involves any limitations on American citizenship.

National Community Relations Advisory Council, *Report on the Jewish Community Relations Agencies* 39 (1951). A thoughtful appraisal appears in Lasky, *An Analysis of the MacIver Report* (American Council for Judaism, undated).

mann Adler, then the Chief Rabbi in England, after stating that "Judaism has no political bearing whatever," continued:

> Ever since the conquest of Palestine by the Romans we have ceased to be a body politic. We are citizens of the country in which we dwell. We are simply Englishmen or Frenchmen or Germans, as the case may be, certainly holding particular theological tenets and practising special religious ordinances; but we stand in the same relation to our countrymen as any other religious sect, having the same stake in the national welfare and the same claim on the privileges and duties of citizens.[9]

The same religious concept of Judaism has been manifested in the United States. In 1883 Rabbi M. Wise, who had emigrated from Bavaria, wrote: "We, citizens of the United States who believe in Moses and the Prophets, are an integral element of this nation . . . with no earthly interests or aspirations different from those who believe in Jesus and his Apostles."[10]

In 1885 a group of Reform Rabbis met in Pittsburgh to enunciate basic principles of modern Judaism. Their Pittsburgh Platform included this statement:

> We consider ourselves no longer a nation but a religious community. And therefore expect neither a return to Palestine, nor a sacrificial worship under the administration of the sons of Aaron, nor the restoration of any of the laws concerning the Jewish state.[11]

The sole element in the present writers' use of the word "Jew" is the religious one. Some individuals, while acknow-

---

9. Quoted in Stein, *The Balfour Declaration* 75 (1961).
10. Quoted in Berger, *The Jewish Dilemma* 239 (1946).
11. *Id.* at 240. A contemporary conception of Judaism as a religion of universal moral values appears in American Council for Judaism, *An Approach to an American Judaism* (1953).

ledging the religious element, may regard Jewishness as involving other factors. The character of such additional factors may be cultural, racial, or national depending upon the preferred values of the individual. Some individuals regard themselves as Jews because their parents were Jews. Jews, like Christians or Moslems, are fully entitled to regard their religious identification as derived from that of their parents. Similarly, a Jew who regards his identification as involving a common cultural heritage with other Jews should be entirely free to adopt such a view. It should not be necessary to emphasize the fact that there is no empirical basis upon which Jews can be deemed to be members of a single racial group.[12]

Zionist is employed to refer to a member or supporter of the modern political movement of Zionism, which was started as an organized political movement at the First Zionist Congress in Basle, Switzerland, in 1897.[13] Though

---

12. The distinction between racial conceptions in anthropology and non-scientific racist ideologies is demonstrated in Benedict, *Race: Science and Politics* (1945).

> Jews are people who acknowledge the Jewish religion. They are of all races, even Negro and Mongolian. European Jews are of many different biological types; physically they resemble the populations among whom they live. The so-called "Jewish type" is a generalized type common in the Near East in countries bordering on the Mediterranean. Wherever Jews are persecuted or discriminated against, they cling to their old ways and keep apart from the rest of the population and develop so-called "Jewish" traits. But these are not racial or "Jewish"; they disappear under conditions where assimilation is easy.

Id. at 177. See also Comas, *Racial Myths* 27–32 (UNESCO 1958).

13. The Zionist Basle Program is examined in Chap. 1, Sec. 1.

many Zionists profess Judaism, there is no reason to limit an accurate functional conception of "Zionist" to those who claim to be Jews. Prime Minister David Lloyd George[14] and Foreign Secretary Arthur Balfour,[15] who were members of the British Government which issued the Balfour Declaration, did not claim to be Jews. Yet, in view of their political support for Zionism, they should be regarded as Zionists.

Zionist Organization is used to refer to the political entity constituted by the First Zionist Congress.[16] It is an instrumentality designed to achieve the political objectives of Zionism. Since the 1922 League of Nations Mandate for Palestine, the term "Zionist Organization" has been equivalent to the term "Jewish Agency."[17] Article 4 of the Mandate recognized the Zionist Organization as a Jewish agency and as a "public body."

Anti-Zionist is employed to refer to an opponent of the Zionist movement. Anti-Zionists include those who are identified as Jews, such as Edwin Montagu,[18] a member of the same British Government which issued the Balfour Declaration and who insisted upon the inclusion of the safeguard clauses in it. Anti-Zionists also include democratically oriented individuals of other faiths who reject the

---

14.   The consistency between anti-Semitism and pro-Zionism is described by the authoritative Zionist historian of the Balfour Declaration with reference to Lloyd George. See the text of Chap. 1 at note 45.

Stein describes the attitude of Field Marshal Smuts, another eminent political supporter of Zionism: "Smuts thought highly of Jews, but not so highly that he would not be glad to see some counterattraction provided for Jews who might otherwise be drawn to South Africa." Stein, *supra* note 9 at 478.

15.   See the text of Chap. 1 at note 38.

16.   The Constitution of the World Zionist Organization (as adopted by the Zionist General Council at its Session in Jerusalem, Israel, in December 1959–January 1960, in pursuance of the Resolution of the 24th Zionist Congress) demonstrates a high degree of centralized control over individual and group (such as the Zionist Organization of America) members. The writers, consequently, use the term "Zionist Organization," to refer to the World Zionist Organization, including its individual and group members, as a single public body.

17.   The Palestine Mandate which established the equivalency is examined in Chap. 1 in the text accompanying note 159.

18.   See the text of Chap. 1 at note 78.

juridical and secular separatism which Zionism attempts to impose upon Jews. From a democratic perspective, the term "anti-Zionist" is negative in form but positive in substance. In order to reject the political postulates of Zionism, an individual must have a set of political postulates and objectives inconsistent with Zionism. The most clearly inconsistent ones are those of democracy which are conceived as embracing the positive values of human dignity and individual freedom for all.[19] It should be recognized that some anti-Semites and other anti-democratic individuals may style themselves as anti-Zionists. The existence of such individuals, however, should not obfuscate the basic democratic character of most anti-Zionists.

Non-Zionist is a chameleon-like conception. Individuals who wish to support Zionism and the State of Israel financially, while attempting to disengage themselves from the juridical-political characteristics, may regard themselves as being "non-Zionists." Dr. Chaim Weizmann, the Zionist leader and first president of the State of Israel, has described non-Zionism in this way:

> [T]hose wealthy Jews who could not wholly divorce themselves from a feeling of responsibility toward their people, but at the same time could not identify themselves with the hopes of the masses, were prepared with a sort of left-handed generosity, on condition that their right hand did not know what their left hand was doing. To them the university-to-be in Jerusalem was philanthropy, which did not compromise them; to us it was nationalist renaissance. They would give –

---

19. See the studies cited in note 3 *supra* and Lasswell, "Democratic Character," in *The Political Writings of Harold D. Lasswell* 463–525 (1951).

For a specific rejection of the postulates of Zionism see M. R. Cohen, "Zionism: Tribalism or Liberalism" in *The Faith of a Liberal*, Chap. 39 (1942); and Berger, *Judaism or Jewish Nationalism: The Alternative to Zionism* (1957).

For uncritical approval of the postulates of Zionism, see Safran, *The United States and Israel* (1963); Halpern, *The Idea of the Jewish State* (1961).

with disclaimers; we would accept – with reservations.[20]

One of the most confusing aspects of non-Zionism is that non-Zionists, unlike Zionists and anti-Zionists, often appear to have no clarified political values of their own. Many anti-Zionists regard non-Zionists as being among the practical supporters of Zionism. If this is an accurate appraisal, it must be added, nevertheless, that non-Zionists often conceal from themselves (and perhaps from others) the extent to which their support is employed for the political purposes of Zionism.

Israel is used to refer to the present Near Eastern State of Israel.[21] It and the Zionist Organization are employed as the two principal political instruments of Zionist nationalism. It is recognized, however, that the word "Israel" has a deeply significant theological meaning to Jews. Thus, one of the traditional religious ways of referring to Jews is to employ the term, "the Children of Israel." Nevertheless, since this study is a juridical one, the term "Israel" is not used in its religious sense.

The State of Israel is sometimes termed the "Jewish" state. Such a label must be rejected if "Judaism" is to be regarded as a religion of universal moral values, rather than a religion of nationalism or tribalism, and if a "Jew" is to be regarded as a voluntary adherent of Judaism. From a functional standpoint there should be no hesitation in describing Israel as a "Zionist" state. Since 1948, when the State of Israel was established, the basic political objectives of Zionism and the State of Israel have been the same. This identity has been enunciated explicitly in claims advanced in

---

20. *Trial and Error: The Autobiography of Chaim Weizmann* 75 (1949). The Weizmann autobiography is cited hereafter as "Weizmann." It not only contains material of juridical significance but provides psychological insight into Zionist mentality. See generally Lasswell, *Power and Personality* (1948); Lasswell, "Psychopathology and Politics" in *The Political Writings of Harold D. Lasswell* 1–282 (1951).

21. For official information concerning Israel, see the annual *Israel Government Year Book*.

22. See Chap. 2 *infra*. For official justification of Zionist political objectives see Israel Office of Information (New York), *Israel's Struggle for Peace* (1960).

public international law.[22] Where it is not made explicit, a continuing common political program may be presumed to be the result of coordinated political planning rather than of a long continuing series of coincidences.

Zionist-Israel sovereignty is used to refer to the integral relationship between the State of Israel and the Zionist Organization. The public law character of this relationship between the State and the Organization is recognized explicitly in the Israeli Status Law of 1952 and the ensuing Covenant between the Government of Israel and the Zionist Executive of 1954.[23] The Status Law did not create the relationship between State and Organization, but rather recognized it.[24] The Covenant spells out an allocation and coordination of governmental functions as between State and Organization in furthering the Zionist political objectives of both.

The Jewish people is the most ambiguous concatenation of word symbols employed in the present study. Although the term, "the Jewish people," does not appear in Holy Writ, it was given an almost exclusively religious meaning until the founding of Zionism. Its most usual use was as a synonym for "Jews," "Israelites," "the Children of Israel," and "the people of the Book."[25] The Zionist movement has captured the term for its own juridical-political purposes and, consequently, the writers use "the Jewish people" to refer to the claimed constituency of Zionist nationalism. Even though the Zionists give a specific nationalistic meaning to the words, they have not rejected whatever political advantages accrue to them from the ambiguities of the words.[26] Thus, they accept the support of those who have found humanitarian or religious meanings in "the Jewish people."[27]

---

23. The Status Law and the Covenant are examined in the text of Chap. 3.

24. See Lasky, *Between Truth and Repose* 51 (1956).

25. Sussman *supra* note 7 at 373. See Chap. 2 note 2.

26. Sussman, *supra* note 7 at 374–75.

27. Weizmann 75 and *passim*.

In a fundamental sense, political Zionism is the reaction of Jews to ghetto life and the consequent denial to them of an opportunity to participate meaningfully in the secular life of the states of their regular nationalities.[28] The existence of ghetto life in some states reflected anti-Semitism. Zionism postulated that anti-Semitism was fundamental and ineradicable. Upon this postulate, the Zionists base their juridical objectives: that "the Jewish people" be constituted as a nationality entity and that membership in it be conferred upon Jews.[29]

In order to understand the Zionist views, it is useful to quote from the words of Dr. Theodor Herzl, the founder of political Zionism, in his classic Zionist statement entitled *The Jewish State:*[30]

> We naturally move to those places where we are not persecuted, and there our presence produces persecution. This is the case in every country, and will remain so, even in those highly civilized – for instance, France – till the Jewish question finds a solution on a political basis. The unfortunate Jews are now carrying Anti-Semitism into England; they have already introduced it into America.[31]

Herzl dealt with nationality status on the basis of Jewish identification as follows:

> But the distinctive nationality of Jews neither can, will, nor must be destroyed. It cannot be destroyed, because external enemies consolidate it. . . . Whole branches of Judaism may wither and fall, but the trunk remains.[32]

---

28. The same conclusion is reached in Taylor, *Prelude to Israel: An Analysis of Zionist Diplomacy, 1897–1947*, v, vi (1959), cited hereafter as *Zionist Diplomacy*.

29. See Chap. 1.

30. The book was published in German in 1896 as *Der Judenstaat*. The English translation from which the ensuing quotations in the text are taken is entitled *The Jewish State: An Attempt at a Modern Solution of the Jewish Question* (D'Avigdor and Israel Cohen transl. 1943).

31. *Id.* at 19, 20.

32. *Id.* at 24.

He stressed the desire for territory,[33] and he anticipated the opposition which Zionism would arouse among Jews:

> Perhaps we shall have to fight first of all against many an evil-disposed, narrow-hearted, short-sighted member of our own race.[34]

The most striking feature of Herzl's views is not that he stated a proposed political solution to the problem of anti-Semitism in 1896. Its deeper significance is that the juridical-political core of Zionism has not changed from Herzl's time to the present.[35] Today Zionist leaders stress the importance of saving Jews from the persecutions brought about by persistent anti-Semitism.[36] At the same time, they appear to be as afraid of religious freedom and secular integration as of persecution itself. Thus Nahum Goldmann, then president of the World Zionist Organization, stated: "The object of the Jewish State has been the preservation of the Jewish people, which was imperiled by emancipation and assimilation ... ."[37] On March 16, 1964, a Zionist Executive-Israeli Government Joint Communique referred to "the dangers of assimilation affecting Jewish communities ... ."[38] Zionism continues to manifest defensiveness to the threat of democratic systems based upon individual rights. On March 16, 1964 a commentary in the *Jerusalem Post* stated: "Today, Zionist leaders do not speak for the majority of Jewry, though all but a tiny proportion of the nation [i.e., "the Jewish people"] give their friendship and support to the State of Israel."[39]

---

33. See the text of Chap. 1 accompanying note 45.

34. *Id.* at 108.

35. Chaps. 1–3 demonstrate the consistency through time of the juridical objectives of Zionism.

36. Mallison, "The Zionist-Israel Juridical Claims to Constitute 'The Jewish People' Nationality Entity and to Confer Membership in it: Appraisal in Public International Law," *32 Geo. Wash. L. Rev.* 983 at 1046–1049 (1964).

37. Quoted in *Zionist Diplomacy* 2.

38. *Supra* note 36 at 1047.

39. Page 1, col. 1. The *Jerusalem Post* is regarded as a semi-official organ of the Israeli Government.

In addition to political Zionism, there also has been a movement known as "cultural" or "spiritual" Zionism. Achad Ha'am was the preeminent leader of this type of Zionism.[40] He accepted some of the aspects of political Zionism, provided that they were subordinated to the fundamental humanitarian principles of Judaism.[41] He participated in the negotiations leading to the issuance of the Balfour Declaration but attached an entirely different meaning to it than did the political Zionists. He believed that "a national home" for some Jews in Palestine would be consistent with the nationalistic aspirations of the Arabs. He regarded Palestine as an opportunity for creative collaboration with the Arabs for the common benefit of all of the inhabitants of the country, and he hoped that Palestine would become a center of Jewish religion and culture which would enrich Jews in other countries as well as those in Palestine.[42]

Achad Ha'am's central differences with the political Zionists concerned both the justification for the movement and its character. Whereas political Zionism thought of itself as the answer to negative and destructive anti-Semitism, Achad Ha'am regarded Zionism as an expression of the humanitarianism of Judaism and the creativity of Jews.[43] He valued individual rights and human dignity for all, including

---

40. 1 Esco Foundation for Palestine, *Palestine: A Study of Jewish, Arab, and British Policies* 18–22 (1947) contrasts the Zionism of Achad Ha'am with political Zionism. "Achad Ha'am" (also spelled Ahad Ha'am) was the pen name of Asher Ginsberg, whose work comprised a philosophy of Judaism. "Achad Ha'am" is translated as "One of the People."

The Esco work (comprising two volumes) is cited hereafter as *Esco Study*. The word "Esco" is an acronym of Ethel S. Cohen, who with her husband, was a founder of the Esco Foundation for Palestine. The *Esco Study* is a scholarly one written by several contributing authors. Its authors include such Zionists as: Rose G. Jacobs, Avraham Schenker, and Benjamin Shwadran. It uses the word "Jewish" in the title and in the text *passim* in contexts where "Zionist" would be more accurate.

41. Achad Ha'am, *Ten Essays on Zionism and Judaism, passim* (Simon transl. 1922), translator's introduction at 39.

42. *Supra* note 40; *Esco Study* 20.

43. *Esco Study* 19.

Arabs.[44] He believed that "a national home in Palestine" for some Jews did not conflict with the single nationality of other Jews. Thus, the humanitarian Zionism of Achad Ha'am was completely consistent with individual freedom for all, in Palestine and in other countries as well.

Professor Morris Raphael Cohen, the distinguished American scholar, has stated the basic conflict between Zionist nationalism and individual freedom:

> Though most of the leaders of Zionism in America are sincerely and profoundly convinced of the compatibility of Zionism and Americanism, they are none the less profoundly mistaken. Nationalistic Zionism demands not complete individual liberty for the Jew, but group autonomy.[45]

Jews, with other individuals, have the opportunity to expand and perfect existing democratic systems which include religious freedom and secular integration for all. The significant juridical features of such democratic systems are individual rights and equality. Such systems must be achieved in the broader context of domestic and world legal order.

The maintenance of public order is the most basic task of any legal system, whether domestic or international. The responsibility of a domestic order system is to exercise effective community control over private violence. In the same way, the responsibility of a world legal order is to exercise effective community control of violence and coercion exercised by national states.[46] The world legal order must, at

---

44. Professor Hans Kohn has described the last years of Achad Ha'am's life which were spent in Palestine at the start of the British Mandate. He died with the conviction that the ideals of cultural Zionism were being betrayed by the political Zionists. Kohn quotes one of Achad Ha'am's last letters which reflected his despair: "Is *this* the dream of a return to Zion which our people have dreamt for centuries: that we now come to Zion to slain its soil with innocent blood?" Kohn, "Zion and the Jewish National Idea," 46 *Menorah Journal* 17, 39 (1958).

45. Cohen, *supra* note 19 at 329.

46. The world legal order is considered systematically in McDougal and Associates, *Studies in World Public Order* (1960).

the very least, protect individuals and national states from coercion and aggression. Such an order, which may be characterized as a minimum order system, is prescribed by the United Nations Charter prohibition upon "the threat or use of force against the territorial integrity or political independence of any state, or in any other manner inconsistent with the purposes of the United Nations."[47] The Charter also contains a complementary provision which authorizes the use of force only for defensive purposes.[48] An optimum world legal order includes the basic elements of the minimum system and also embraces a context in which individuals and national states may seek their value objectives in a peaceful and nondiscriminatory environment. Optimum order will be achieved when the minimum order provisions of the Charter are effectively enforced and when the economic and social provisions,[49] including the key provisions on human rights,[50] are also achieved. It is clear that the Palestinians who have been the victims of organized Zionist terror since the time of the Balfour Declaration and who have been victimized by the Government of Israel's highly institutionalized state terror since 1948 have not received the benefits of a minimum order system. In the same way, those Israelis who have been the victims of the Palestinian responding violence have not received the benefits of such a system.[51] The great opportunity which a solution to the Palestine problem, including Jerusalem, presents to the world community is to provide Palestinians and Israelis alike with first the protection of minimum order and then the expanding benefits of optimum order. In this era of weapons of mass destruction, the effects of which fall

---

47. *U.N. Charter*, art. 2(4).

48. *Id.*, art. 51.

49. *Id.*, arts. 55–91.

50. *Id.*, arts. 55 and 56.

51. Both the Israeli state terror and the Palestinian responding violence are described and analyzed in Hirst, *The Gun and the Olive Branch: The Roots of Violence in the Middle East* (1977). The Zionist institutionalized terror before the establishment of the State of Israel is described in Begin, *The Revolt: Story of the Irgun* (1948, new ed. 1972).

upon the just and the unjust alike, the probable alternatives to the achievement of at least minimum order include a further destructive war in the Middle East and a world conflagration of mutual mass destruction as well.

Chapter 1

International Law Appraisal of the Balfour Declaration

> This right ["of the Jewish people to national rebirth in its own country"] was recognised in the Balfour Declaration of the 2nd November, 1917, and re-affirmed in the Mandate of the League of Nations which, in particular, gave international sanction to the historic connection between the Jewish people and Eretz–Israel and to the right of the Jewish people to rebuild its National Home.
>
> The Declaration of the Establishment of the State of Israel (1948)[1]

Introduction

The central legal issues of this chapter may be set forth briefly. Is the Balfour Declaration valid in public international law? If so, what is its juridical meaning? Is the Declaration consistent with the preeminent international law principle of the self-determination of peoples? As illustrated by the quoted portion of the Declaration of the Establishment of the State of Israel, the Zionists claim that it is valid and provides international authority for the Zionist State in Palestine.

It is important at the outset to reiterate that Zionism is both a political ideology and a blueprint for action for

---

1.   1 Laws of the State of Israel (Authorized Translation) 3 (1948) [hereafter cited as Israeli Laws. The quoted paragraph is the fifth; the wording in brackets is from the fourth paragraph.

"Jewish" nationalism.[2] Although some Zionists profess to be adherents of Judaism, it is clear that many Jews reject Zionism and regard it as an exploitation of their religion for political purposes.[3] Jews who have been aware of Zionist objectives have frequently taken different, and indeed inconsistent, positions from the Zionist ones on basic moral and juridical issues. This is illustrated by the negotiations leading to the Balfour Declaration where the Jews and the Zionists were the principal antagonists.[4]

I. Historical Background of the Central Zionist Objectives

The principal juridical objectives of Zionism were enunciated at the First Zionist Congress which met in Basle in 1897. This Congress was called by Dr. Theodor Herzl to provide political and juridical implementation for his basic assumption of ineradicable anti-Semitism and the consequent necessity of a "Jewish" state.[5] In the opening address Herzl stated the object of the meeting: "We are here to lay the foundation stone of the house which is to shelter the Jewish nation."[6] The Congress then proceeded to constitute the

---

2. Herzl, *Der Judenstaat* (1896). An English translation is: *The Jewish State: An Attempt at a Modern Solution of the Jewish Question* (D'Avigdor & Cohen transl. 1943) [hereafter cited as *The Jewish State*]. Further Zionist writings combining ideology and plans for action are collected in *The Zionist Idea: A Historical Analysis and Reader* (Hertzberg ed. 1959).

3. See *e.g.*, M. R. Cohen, *The Faith of a Liberal*, Chap. 39 entitled "Zionism: Tribalism or Liberalism" (1942); Berger, *Judaism or Jewish Nationalism: The Alternative to Zionism* (1957). The American Council for Judaism was the principal Jewish Anti-Zionist organization in the United States until the late 1960s. Since that time the main such organization has been American Jewish Alternatives to Zionism.

4. Sec. III *infra*.

5. *The Jewish State; Taylor, Prelude to Israel: An Analysis of Zionist Diplomacy, 1897 to 1947* 3–6 (1959) [cited hereafter as *Zionist Diplomacy*]; 1 Sokolow, *History of Zionism* 268–72 (1919) [cited hereafter as Sokolow]; 1 Esco Foundation for Palestine, *Palestine: A Study of Jewish, Arab, and British Policies* 40–42 (1947) [cited hereafter as *Esco Study*].

6. 1 *Esco Study* 40.

19

Zionist Organization,[7] and concluded with the adoption of a statement of Zionist purpose known as the Basle Program. The key provision stated: "The aim of Zionism is to create for the Jewish people a home in Palestine secured by public law."[8] Four means were formulated to obtain this objective: (1) the promotion of Zionist (termed "Jewish") immigration to Palestine; (2) the "organization and binding together of the whole of Jewry" through appropriate means; (3) "strengthening and fostering of Jewish national sentiment and consciousness"; (4) taking steps toward "obtaining government consent" for the objectives of Zionism.[9]

The present chapter analyzes the basic objective of the Basle Program, "to create for the Jewish people a home in Palestine secured by public law." Dr. Herzl, as the first president of the Zionist Organization, took energetic diplomatic steps to obtain public law authority for the Zionist national home enterprise in Palestine. During 1898 he met with Kaiser Wilhelm II who was visiting the Ottoman Empire. He suggested, as a first step, the creation of a land development company which would be operated under German protection in Palestine.[10] Herzl expected that the German Government would make appropriate arrangements to effectuate this enterprise with the Ottoman Government. As stated in a pro-Zionist historical study, the Kaiser's initial enthusiasm for the project was motivated, at least in part, by anti-Semitic considerations.[11] The Kaiser, nevertheless, shortly thereafter rejected the proposal.[12]

In 1901 Herzl attempted direct negotiations with the Sultan of Turkey. He proposed Zionist immigration to Palestine accompanied with the attractive offer of financial assistance for the development of the natural resources of the Ottoman Empire.[13] Humanitarian motives have been

---

7. *Id.* at 42; *Zionist Diplomacy, supra* note 5 at 6.

8. 1 Sokolow, *supra* note 5 at 268.

9. *Id.* at 268–69.

10. 1 *Esco Study, supra* note 5 at 43.

11. *Id.*

12. *Id.*

13. *Id.* at 44.

ascribed to the Sultan in allowing the immigration of Jewish refugees.[14] It was simultaneously made clear that the "national aspects" of immigration were to be rejected.[15]

In 1902 Herzl and his associates in the Zionist Executive entered into negotiations with the British Government to obtain the legal right to Zionist settlement in portions of the Sinai Peninsula. These negotiations came to nothing, although diplomatic contacts with the British Government were maintained.[16] The efforts bore fruit in 1903 when the British Government offered the Zionists the right to colonize a portion of East Africa, called Uganda.[17] While Herzl favored the Uganda offer, Dr. Chaim Weizmann, an able scientist and a brilliant politician of Russian origin, opposed it vehemently.[18] Because of the bitter conflict within the Zionist Organization, no practical steps were taken to implement the British offer and the Uganda proposal was dropped following Herzl's death in 1904.[19] This proposal, however, was significant in two respects. Its serious consideration by the Zionists as a substitute for Palestine provided indication of the secular character of the movement. It was also revealing in demonstrating British imperial sympathy and support for the territorial objectives of Zionist nationalism.

In 1904 Dr. Weizmann moved to England because of his conviction that, among the great powers, Great Britain was most likely to provide effective support for Zionism.[20] During the ensuing decade he and his associates painstakingly laid the foundations for what they hoped would be public international law authority for Zionist territorial objectives in Palestine.[21] British imperialists were readily interested in

---

14. *Id.*

15. *Id.*

16. *Zionist Diplomacy, supra* note 5 at 7.

17. 1 *Esco Study, supra* note 5 at 48; *Zionist Diplomacy* 7.

18. *Trial and Error: The Autobiography of Chaim Weizmann* 110–17 (East and West Library, London 1950) [cited hereafter as Weizmann].

19. *Id.* at 117.

20. *Id.* at 123–24.

21. *Id.* in Chaps. 7, 8, 12–15 and *passim*.

these objectives.[22] At the same time, the Zionist leaders were aware that no meaningful action could be taken until their friends came to political power.

II. Public Law Sources and Criteria of the Present Chapter

There is no doubt concerning the centrality of the Balfour Declaration in the Zionist-Israel juridical claims.[23] The issue of its accurate juridical interpretation is, therefore, one of very substantial importance. In view of these considerations, it is necessary to use the most reliable evidence, the primary public law source materials for interpretational purposes. Among these sources, the negotiating history of the Declaration including the various negotiating positions, as well as the final official text, are essential. Dr. Weizmann's autobiography[24] is of particular value in reflecting the successive positions of the Zionist negotiators and their interpretation. Mr. Leonard Stein, an English lawyer and leading Zionist, has provided a careful history of the negotiations leading to the Declaration.[25] His interpretations should be recognized as reflecting an authoritative Zionist perspective and be given thorough consideration.

The Balfour Declaration, originally a unilateral public law announcement of the British Cabinet, has been accorded the multilateral agreement of the member states of the League of Nations and the assent of the United States.[26] It must, accordingly, be interpreted under the same juridical criteria which are applicable to any other multilateral international agreement. The negotiations preliminary to an international

---

22. *Id.*

23. The primary authority for the textual statement is the continuing use of the Declaration as a juridical claim before and after the establishment of the State of Israel in 1948.

24. Note 18 *supra*.

25. Stein, *The Balfour Declaration* (Vallentine–Mitchell, London, 1961) [cited hereafter as Stein].

26. Sec. V of the present chapter.

agreement or treaty usually afford the greatest insight into the most accurate possible meaning. Elihu Root, a distinguished former Secretary of State of the United States, in a statement made when he was serving as a member of the United States Senate, emphasized the importance of negotiations. He stated with particular reference to the Hay–Pauncefote Treaty:

> If you would be sure of what a treaty means, if there be any doubt, if there are two interpretations suggested, learn out of what conflicting public policies the words of the treaty had their birth; what arguments were made for one side or the other, what concessions were yielded in the making of a treaty. Always, with rare exceptions, the birth and development of every important clause may be traced by the authentic records of the negotiators and of the countries which are reconciling their differences.[27]

There is a high degree of unanimity among the international law authorities concerning the basic importance of the negotiating history in ascertaining the most accurate interpretation of an international agreement.[28] It should be recognized that these authorities refer to a serious interpretative problem such as that involved in the Balfour Declaration. The suggestion is sometimes made that "the plain meaning rule" must be employed if the words under interpretation in a particular questioned agreement are "in

---

27. 5 Hackworth, *Digest of International Law* 259 (1943).

28. McDougal, Lasswell, & Miller, *The Interpretation of Agreements and World Public Order*, Chap. 4 (1967); McNair, *The Law of Treaties*, Chaps. 20–23 (1961); Harvard Research in International Law, "Draft Convention on the Law of Treaties," 29 *Am. J. Int'l L. Supp.* 653, 947 (1935). American Law Institute, *Restatement of the Foreign Relations Law of the United States*, Sec. 147 (1965) includes the context of the negotiations but accords it insufficient importance.

themselves clear and free from ambiguity."[29] For the purpose of completeness, therefore, this "rule" will be considered in interpretating the Balfour Declaration after it has been analyzed in the context of its negotiations.[30]

III. Analysis of the Negotiations Leading to the Declaration

The negotiations took place over a period of three years,[31] and the last months prior to the issuance of the Declaration involved careful examination of two preliminary drafts and four substantive ones as well as the final text itself.

A. NEGOTIATING OBJECTIVES

There were three direct participants in the negotiations. First, the British Government was actually or ostensibly concerned with advancing its national self-interest and in order to do this it had to serve as an arbitrator between the conflicting interests represented by the Jews and the Zionists. The second participant was the Zionist group who were represented by the most important Zionist leaders living in Great Britain during the First World War, Dr. Weizmann, the president of the English Zionist Federation, and Mr. Nahum Sokolow, a member of the Executive of the World Zionist Organization and consequently Weizmann's senior in the Zionist hierarchy. The third participating group was composed of British Jews. Edwin Montagu, the Secretary of State for India in the British Government at the time of the issuance of the Declaration, was the preeminent Jewish leader. Mr. Claude Montefiore, a private citizen, was another

---

29. The quoted words appear in the majority opinion in the case entitled, *Interpretation of the 1919 Convention Concerning the Employment of Women During the Night*, P.C.I.J., Ser. A/B, No. 50 at p. 373 (1922).

Article 31 of the Vienna Convention on the Law of Treaties, 8 Amer. Soc. of Int'l Law, *International Legal Materials* 679 at 691–92 (1969), reveals extraordinary faith in "the ordinary meaning" and then attempts to establish a rigid hierarchy of supplementary factors.

30. Sec. IV C of the present chapter.

eminent leader of the Jewish cause. At the beginning of the negotiations these Jews were deeply suspicious concerning Zionist political objectives. After the Zionist drafts of the Declaration were revealed, they became committed to an unequivocal anti-Zionist position in order to preserve basic Jewish values as well as the legal rights of the Palestinians.[32]

The Palestinians themselves constituted a group of major importance who could not be ignored in spite of the Zionist desire to do so.[33] Both the Jews and the British Government were aware that it was essential to recognize the existence of the Moslem and Christian Palestinians.[34] In 1918 there were approximately 700,000 Palestinians and only 56,000 of them were of Jewish religious identification.[35]

1. BRITISH OBJECTIVES

The British Government had two principal political objectives during the period of the negotiations. The first was to win the war, and the second was to maximize the British power position through the ensuing peace settlement.[36] In view of the increasing success of the German submarine war in 1917, the British Government was desperately searching for support from all sources. Dr. Weizmann, Mr. Sokolow, and their fellow Zionists offered the assistance of their claimed constituency of "the Jewish people" in return for a British public law declaration of support for Zionist national-

---

31. Stein, *supra* note 25 at 514; see the Weizmann–Rothschild memorandum quoted in the text accompanying note 95 *infra*.

32. The textual paragraph is based upon Stein, Weizmann, *supra* note 18, and *Zionist Diplomacy, supra* note 5, *passim*.

33. The text accompanying notes 147–49 *infra*.

34. The text accompanying notes 61, 62 *infra*.

35. Cattan, *Palestine, The Arabs and Israel: The Search for Justice* 21 (1969).

36. The text accompanying note 55 *infra* demonstrates Weizmann's awareness of the realities.

ism including, they hoped, the territorial objective in Palestine.[37]

The two principal proponents of a pro-Zionist declaration in the British Government were Prime Minister Lloyd George and Foreign Secretary Balfour. Mr. Stein introduces Balfour's attitudes this way: "If Balfour became an ardent pro-Zionist it was not simply out of a sentimental tenderness for Jews."[38] Then, after pointing out that Balfour regarded the Jews as possessing admirable qualities,[39] he proceeds to record Balfour's anti-Semitism. Balfour and Weizmann met briefly and discussed Zionism in 1906[40] and they became friendly during the First World War. In 1914 Balfour told Weizmann that he shared certain "anti-Semitic postulates."[41] Early in 1917 when British Jews appealed to him as Foreign Secretary for humanitarian assistance, he refused to intercede diplomatically with the Russian Government on behalf of the Jewish victims of persecution. While admitting the "abominable" treatment of Jews in Russia, he stated that "the persecutors had a case of their own."[42] The "case" was

---

37. 6 Temperley (ed.), *A History of the Peace Conference of Paris* 173–74 (1924) states:

> That it [the Balfour Declaration] is in purpose a definite contract between the British Government and Jewry represented by the Zionists is beyond question. In spirit it is a pledge that in return for services to be rendered by Jewry the British Government would "use their best endeavours" to secure the execution of a certain definite policy in Palestine.

Stein, *supra* note 5, states at 120:

> It is, on the face of it, nonsensical to imagine that the Declaration was handed to him [Weizmann] as a kind of good conduct prize. We shall see later how closely the case for the Declaration was considered before being finally approved by the War Cabinet as a deliberate act of policy.

Stein *passim* indicates the Zionist offer of "Jewish" political support in return for a public law declaration.

38. Stein 163–64.

39. *Id.* at 165.

40. Weizmann, *supra* note 18 at 142–45.

41. Stein 154, 163.

42. *Id.* at 164.

particularized by him as including Jews belonging to "a distinct race" and having a separate religion which was in Russia "an object of inherited hatred."[43]

Balfour's role as Prime Minister prior to the First World War in supporting legislation which reduced Jewish immigration to Great Britain is also revealing concerning his attitudes. In explaining the basis for his opposition to the immigration of Jews, he stated in the House of Commons:

> A state of things could easily be imagined in which it would not be to the advantage of the civilisation of this country that there should be an immense body of persons who, however patriotic, able and industrious, however much they threw themselves into the national life, remained a people apart, and not merely held a religion differing from the vast majority of their fellow-countrymen, but only intermarried among themselves.[44]

Stein introduces Lloyd George's perspective in this way:

> Like some other eminent pro-Zionists, Lloyd George had mixed feelings about Jews. In some of his speeches on the South African War and its aftermath there can be discerned a streak of ordinary vulgar anti-Semitism.[45]

So that there can be no ambiguity, specific examples of the anti-Semitic statements are provided. Stein recounts that Lloyd George stated in the House of Commons at the time of the Uganda offer: "There were a good many Jews they could well spare ... ."[46] He was also much impressed, it is added, by biblical history including "the prophecies which foretold the restoration of the Jews to the Holy Land."[47] The

---

43. *Id.*
44. *Id.*
45. *Id.* at 143.
46. *Id.*
47. *Id.*

reassuring statement is provided that Lloyd George "was sensitive to the Jewish Mystique."[48]

These facts, as documented by Mr. Stein, are significant in further explaining the objectives of some British Cabinet members during the negotiations. It is not possible to avoid the conclusion that anti-Semitism was an objective of considerable importance along with the expressed concern for British national interests.

2. ZIONIST OBJECTIVES

The consistent Zionist objectives before and during the negotiations were to obtain public law authority for their territorial ambitions. In the words of Dr. Herzl, writing in 1896 in *The Jewish State*:

> Let the sovereignty be granted us over a portion of the globe large enough to satisfy the rightful requirements of a nation; the rest we shall manage for ourselves.[49]

In the following year at the First Zionist Congress the territorial objective was reformulated as "a home in Palestine secured by public law."[50] The purpose of the change in terminology was to avoid antagonizing those Jews who had a religious or cultural attachment to Palestine but who opposed the concept of "Jewish" nationality and a Zionist state.[51] Herzl recognized, nevertheless, that the Zionists would continue to interpret it as meaning a "Jewish State."[52]

The Zionists entered the negotiations with the expectations of obtaining their full territorial demands.[53] These expectations, however, were necessarily limited by two

---

48. *Id*. Stein, *supra* note 25 *passim*, describes varying kinds of anti-Semitic support for Zionism. For example, Wickham Steed of *The Times* (of London) illustrated "the civilised type of anti-semitism ... ." *Id*. at 324.

49. *The Jewish State, supra* note 2 at 39.

50. The text preceding and accompanying note 5 *supra*; 1 *Esco Study, supra* note 5 at 41.

51. *Zionist Diplomacy, supra* note 5 at 5–6.

52. *Id*. at 6; 1 *Esco Study* 41.

53. *Zionist Diplomacy* 18–20; 1 *Esco Study* 87–92.

objective factors. The first was that the number of Jews in Palestine during the First World War was only a small fraction of the entire population of the country.[54] The second was that the Zionists could not expect anything from the British Government which did not accord with its actual or supposed imperial interests. Mr. Stein has summarized the situation this way:

> The Declaration [sought by the Zionists] itself presupposed that the Jewish people counted for something in the world and that the ideas bound up with the connection between the Jews and Palestine had not lost their potency. But the war years were not a time for sentimental gestures. The British Government's business was to win the War and to safeguard British interests in the post-war settlement. Fully realising that these must in the end be the decisive tests, Weizmann was never under the illusion that the Zionists could rely on an appeal *ad misericordiam*. Zionist aspirations must be shown to accord with British strategic and political interests.[55]

In seeking the territorial objective in Palestine, the Zionist negotiators regarded two points as crucial to their cause. First, the Zionist national home enterprise must be "reconstituted" in order to give a semblance of reality to the Zionist claim of a historic title to Palestine.[56] Second, it was regarded as essential that the British Government make an unequivocal commitment to carry out the Zionist territorial objective in Palestine.[57] In seeking these objectives, the Zionists ignored the existence of the Palestinians.[58]

---

54. The text accompanying note 35 *supra*.
55. Stein, *supra* note 25 at 126.
56. The text accompanying notes 70–72 *infra*.
57. Stein 552.
58. The text accompanying note 143 *infra*.

3. JEWISH OBJECTIVES

The Jewish objectives manifested in the negotiations were humanitarian. Montagu and his associates were, however, realists who recognized that humanitarian ends required juridical means. The immediate objective was to protect the existing equality of rights including the religious freedom of Jews in Great Britain. Zionism threatened the political rights of such Jews through their involuntary inclusion in the claimed "Jewish People" nationality constituency.[59] The leading British Jews, however, recognized that Zionist nationalism was directed not only at British Jews but at all Jews. One of their central objectives, consequently, was to maintain the existing legal rights of Jews in other states in addition to Great Britain. In their view, the victories won in obtaining emancipation and individual equality in many states could not be surrendered in return for the creation of a Zionist ghetto in Palestine.[60]

The Jews, in direct opposition to the Zionists, sought to maintain the existing rights of the Palestinians. Because of their full awareness of the historic persecution suffered by Jews, they believed it essential to protect Palestinians in the enjoyment of their rights. The Zionist position that the Palestinians were either a non-people or had no rights worthy of consideration imposed a moral obligation upon the Jews to attempt to protect these people, an obligation which they readily accepted.[61]

The British Government became willing to acknowledge the rights of the Palestinians because in addition to the moral factors there were basic military ones involved. In 1917 the British forces under General Allenby were seeking a major victory in Palestine against the Turkish armies. Arab military participation and civilian cooperation were essential for this

---

59. See Chap. 2 *infra*.

60. The textual paragraph is based, in part, upon Weizmann, *supra* note 18 at 199–208 and *passim; Esco Study, supra* note 5 at 104–05; *Zionist Diplomacy, supra* note 5 at 22–23. See Montagu's use of the word "Ghetto" in the text accompanying note 87 *infra*.

61. The objectives of the Jews are further particularized in the ensuing text describing their role in the negotiations.

military objective. The British could not expect to be welcomed as liberators unless they recognized the basic human rights of the inhabitants of the country.[62]

B. THE SIX DRAFTS AND THE FINAL TEXT

1. THE FOREIGN OFFICE PRELIMINARY DRAFT (JUNE OR JULY, 1917)

The key words, when drafting began at the Foreign Office, were "asylum" and "refuge."[63] The conception was that the British Government was to declare itself in favor of establishing in Palestine "a sanctuary for Jewish victims of persecution."[64] The late Sir Harold Nicolson wrote many years later with reference to the preliminary drafting: "We believed that we were founding a refuge for the disabled and did not foresee that it would become a nest of hornets."[65] This indicates that the working level personnel in the Foreign Office knew very little about the Zionist objectives. Mr. Sokolow protested that the language referred to "would by no means meet the case,"[66] and the Zionists then prepared a preliminary draft of their own.

2. THE ZIONIST PRELIMINARY DRAFT (JULY 12, 1917)

This draft, reflecting the work of Sokolow and others, included the central point that the British Government:

> [A]ccepts the principle of recognising Palestine as the National Home of the Jewish people and the right of the Jewish people to build up its national life in Palestine under a protection to be established at the conclusion of peace following upon the successful issue of the war ... .[67]

---

62. British objectives are described in 1 *Esco Study* 117–18.

63. Stein, *supra* note 25 at 468.

64. *Id.* Earlier informal Zionist drafting is described in *id.* at 466–67.

65. Stein 468, note 24.

66. *Id.* at 468.

67. *Id.* at 468–69.

It also referred to "the grant of internal autonomy to the Jewish nationality in Palestine, [and] freedom of immigration for Jews."[68]

Both Sokolow and Balfour found some objections to this draft and it was not submitted officially. Sokolow, in a letter of explanation to Lord Rothschild, stated that there should be two basic principles set forth in order to meet Zionist objectives: "(1) the recognition of Palestine as the national home of the Jewish people, (2) the recognition of the Zionist Organisation."[69]

3. THE ZIONIST DRAFT (JULY 18, 1917)

Sokolow's statement of basic principles was closely followed in the revised draft.

> 1. His Majesty's Government accepts the principle that Palestine should be reconstituted as the national home of the Jewish people.
> 2. His Majesty's Government will use its best endeavours to secure the achievement of this object and will discuss the necessary methods and means with the Zionist Organisation.[70]

This draft was accompanied by a letter from Lord Rothschild which asked for a message indicating formal governmental approval. Both were sent to Balfour about a month after he had invited the submission of an authoritative Zionist draft of a declaration.[71]

This draft contains the central objective that the Zionist enterprise in Palestine be "reconstituted." The word "reconstituted" was of particular importance to the Zionists since it implies establishment as a matter of legal right.[72] It is also important that the principle proposed for acceptance by

---

68. *Id.* at 469

69. *Id.*

70. *Id.* at 470.

71. *Id.*

72. The text accompanying notes 164–66 *infra*.

His Majesty's Government would apply to Palestine as a whole since no limitations are included which specify only a part of Palestine. The reference to "the Jewish people" involved the related claim of the transnational nationality entity alleged to comprise all Jews.

By the second paragraph the British Government would be obligated to employ "its best endeavours" to achieve the Zionist territorial objective. The reference to discussions with the Zionist Organization to achieve the objective would probably amount to British recognition of the Zionist Organization as a public body, at least *de facto.*

4. THE BALFOUR DRAFT (AUGUST 1917)

It is not surprising that the resultant Balfour draft accepted the Zionist objectives, without qualifications or limitations, since Balfour was a Zionist in the functional sense of supporting their juridical objectives.

His Majesty's Government accept the principle that Palestine should be reconstituted as the
national home of the Jewish people and will use
their best endeavours to secure the achievement
of this object and will be ready to consider any
suggestions on the subject which the Zionist
Organisation may desire to lay before them.[73]

It is apparent that some of the key words in this draft are taken directly from the Zionist Draft, and Mr. Stein accurately characterizes it as a "slightly amended version of the Zionist draft."[74] Since it was prepared by the Foreign Secretary, it was an official approval of the substance of the Zionist Draft of July 18, 1917, subject only to the approval of the Cabinet. There can be no doubt but that the governmental Zionists, including the Prime Minister himself, approved it. It represented, in summary, a very important tentative governmental acceptance of Zionist objectives including the comprehensive territorial objective of Palestine.

---

73. Stein, *supra* note 25 at 664.
74. *Id.* at 520.

5. THE MILNER DRAFT (AUGUST, 1917)

The contingent acceptance of Zionist aims in the Balfour Draft was not, however, submitted to the Cabinet. Apparently this draft was thought likely to be rejected. The Milner governmental draft was prepared in its place, and it provided:

> His Majesty's Government accepts the principle that every opportunity should be afforded for the establishment of a home for the Jewish people in Palestine and will use its best endeavours to facilitate the achievement of this object and will be ready to consider any suggestions on the subject which the Zionist organisations may desire to lay before them.[75]

This draft involved a substantial retreat from the acceptance of Zionist objectives. Apparently this was quite intentional since the new draft was designed to obtain the support of the Cabinet as a whole. In the changed draft it was now "a home" rather than "the national home." There was only expressed acceptance of "the principle that every opportunity should be afforded" for the creation of this home. Further, this "opportunity" would be afforded "in" Palestine and thus there was no implication that Palestine belonged to the Zionists or their claimed constituency of "the Jewish people." The wording "best endeavours" was repeated, but it now referred to a reduced set of objectives. The precatory wording concerning Zionist "suggestions" was repeated with minor variations. Stein accurately summarizes the new situation by referring to the Milner Draft as "a considerably watered down version of Balfour's [August] formula."[76] Even though this represented a marked retreat from the Zionist objectives, it was not as dangerous to them as subsequent developments. Specifically, it contained no direct statements that there were interests other than Zionist ones involved in Palestine.

---

75. *Id.* at 664.
76. *Id.* at 521.

In spite of the retreat from Zionist objectives manifested by the Milner Draft, the Jews were not prepared to accept it. Mr. Edwin Montagu, an eminent Jew and Englishman, was appointed to the Cabinet as Secretary of State for India and this was announced publicly on July 18, 1917.[77] He regarded Zionism as a repudiation of Judaism and as a nationalism designed to promote anti-Semitism. Stein states concerning the appointment:

> Thus, the question of a pro-Zionist declaration reached the War Cabinet at a time when the only Jew with direct access to the inner circle was an implacable anti-Zionist.[78]

Montagu was also disturbed concerning the Zionist impact upon his goal of obtaining reforms in the British Administration in India. As the Zionist historian reports Montagu's concern on this point:

> [N]or could anything better be calculated to prejudice his work in India, than a British declaration which, as he saw it, would imply that he belonged, as a Jew, to a people apart, with its home – the real focus of its loyalties – in Palestine.[79]

With characteristic directness, Montagu prepared a careful memorandum entitled "The Anti-Semitism of the Present Government"[80] and circulated it to his fellow Cabinet ministers. This remarkable document contains a concise but powerful statement of the Jewish case against Zionism. It was written in the face of tentative governmental approval of Zionist objectives and stated in the first paragraph:

---

77. *Id.* at 496, note 46.

78. *Id.* at 484.

79. *Id.* at 498–99.

80. United Kingdom Public Records Office, Cab. No. 24/24 (Aug. 23, 1917).

> I wish to place on record my view that the policy of
> His Majesty's Government is anti-Semitic in result
> and will prove a rallying ground for Anti-Semites
> in every country in the world.[81]

As to the objective of "the national home of the Jewish
people" set forth in the draft of July 18, 1917, he stated with a
manifestation of prescient insight into Zionist plans:

> I assume that it means that Mohammedans and
> Christians are to make way for the Jews, and that
> the Jews should be put in all positions of
> preference and should be peculiarly associated
> with Palestine in the same way that England is
> with the English ... .[82]

He added that:

> [Y]ou will find a population in Palestine driving
> out its present inhabitants, taking all the best in
> the country ... .[83]

Some of his comments, written decades before the Law
of Return[84] was enacted by the Knesset of Israel, point with
uncanny accuracy to this basic law of the State of Israel. He
stated:

> Perhaps also citizenship must be granted only as a
> result of a religious test.[85]

His own appraisal of such a test was unequivocal:

> [A] religious test of citizenship seems to me to be
> only admitted by those who take a bigoted and
> narrow view of one particular epoch of the history

---

81. *Id.*

82. *Id.*

83. *Id.*

84. 4 Israel Laws *supra* note 1 at 114 (1950). This statute is an immigration
law for Jews only.

85. Note 80 *supra.*

of Palestine, and claim for the Jews a position to which they are not entitled.[86]

In classic summary, Montagu stated: "Palestine will become the world's Ghetto."[87] His memorandum indicated that the Zionist and Balfour Drafts were not acceptable to the Jews. In addition, there was no reason to believe that the Milner Draft, although a blow to the Zionists, would satisfy him and the other Jews.

Mr. Montagu expanded on his memorandum orally at a War Cabinet meeting on September 3.[88] Although not a member of the War Cabinet (or inner cabinet), he had been specifically invited to be present to state his views.[89] It is not surprising that the result of his presentation was that no action was taken by the War Cabinet to support Zionist objectives.[90]

Montagu also had a far more formidable alternative course of action available to him than merely presenting the Jewish case to the Cabinet: he could resign from the Cabinet, of which he had so recently become a member, on the stated grounds of its anti-Semitism.[91] It would have been impossible for even such committed Zionists as Lloyd George and Balfour to represent a declaration as having pro-Jewish aspects following the resignation of the only Jewish member of the Cabinet in protest.

The Zionists, although deeply discouraged, were not yet prepared to accept defeat. Weizmann, who was fully aware of the situation at the time, later wrote that he "did not feel as desperate as Lord Rothschild ... ."[92] In planning their

---

86. Id.

87. Id.

88. Stein, supra note 25 at 502–03.

89. Id. at 502.

90. Id. at 503.

91. The near certainty of resignation, in the event of a Zionist victory, was implicit in his basic position. Dr. Weizmann has recognized "the implacability of his opposition." Weizmann, supra note 18 at 259.

92. Id. at 257.

counter-offensive, Weizmann and Mark Sykes, the pro-Zionist secretary of the War Cabinet, collaborated on a memorandum which was circulated to the Cabinet before the issues involved in a declaration were considered again. In their view it was essential to set forth exactly what the Zionists were asking for as well as what they were not asking for. This is the way their memorandum of about September 22, 1917 put it:

What the Zionists do not want is:

I. To have any special political hold on the old city of Jerusalem itself or any control over the Christian or Moslem Holy Places.
II. To set up a Jewish Republic or other form of State in Palestine or any part of Palestine.
III. To enjoy any special rights not enjoyed by other inhabitants of Palestine.

On the other hand, the Zionists do want:

I. Recognition of the Jewish inhabitants of Palestine as a national unit, federated with [? other] national units in Palestine.
II. The recognition of [the] right of bona fide Jewish settlers to be included in the Jewish national unit in Palestine.[93]

The retreat from the original Zionist objectives is striking. This not only renounced "a Jewish Republic," but also "other form of State in Palestine or any part of Palestine." It expressly claimed the desire of "recognition" as "a national unit" to be federated with other such units within Palestine. The reference to "bona fide Jewish settlers" suggests that Jews were to come to Palestine as individuals rather than as units of a Zionist organized and directed political entity

---

93. Stein 512. The material in brackets is supplied by Stein.

designed to infiltrate Palestine.[94] These drastic changes in the stated juridical objectives would most certainly facilitate the British Government agreeing to some kind of a declaration, but they could not ensure that the remaining Zionist objectives would not be abandoned in the process. If the purpose of the memorandum was to reassure Montagu and the other Jews so that they would accept a pro-Zionist declaration, it was a complete failure.

6. THE MILNER–AMERY DRAFT (OCTOBER 4, 1917)

Dr. Weizmann and Lord Rothschild, respectively the actual and nominal heads of the Zionist movement in the United Kingdom, were increasingly concerned about the impact which Montagu made upon the British Government and the inability of the pro-Zionist members of that Government to overcome his objections. Weizmann and Rothschild, consequently, prepared a further memorandum which they sent to Balfour on October 3 for transmission to the Government. It began with a deferential reference to Montagu as "a prominent Englishman of the Jewish Faith" and stated, in part:

> We must respectfully point out that in submitting our resolution [sic] we entrusted our national and Zionist destiny to the Foreign Office and the Imperial War Cabinet in the hope that the problem would be considered in the light of Imperial interests and the principles for which the Entente stands. We are reluctant to believe that the War

---

94. The facts concerning the Zionist infiltration are set forth in the Anglo-American Committee of Inquiry, *Report to the United States Government and His Majesty's Government in the United Kingdom, passim* and at 39 (1946):

> There thus exists a virtual Jewish nonterritorial State [through the Jewish Agency] with its own executive and legislative organs, parallel in many respects to the Mandatory Administration, and serving as the concrete symbol of the Jewish National Home. This Jewish shadow government has ceased to cooperate with the Adminstration in the maintenance of law and order, and in the suppression of terrorism.

See *The Jewish State, supra* note 2; Weizmann, *supra* note 18, *passim*; Sachar, *The Course of Modern Jewish History* 460–88 (Delta ed. 1963).

Cabinet would allow the divergence of views on Zionism existing in Jewry to be presented to them in a strikingly one-sided manner. . . . We have submitted it after three years of negotiations and conversations with prominent representatives of the British nation. We therefore humbly pray that this declaration may be granted to us.[95]

This was a basic change in strategy from presenting demands to a respectfully worded petition for help from British imperialism. It may be appraised as an indication of the position of weakness in which they had been placed by Montagu.

Leopold Amery, an assistant secretary of the Cabinet, has written that just before the War Cabinet meeting of October 4, he was asked by Lord Milner, a member of the Cabinet, to draft "something which would go a reasonable distance to meeting the objections, both Jewish and pro-Arab, without impairing the substance of the proposed Declaration."[96] The directions were obviously inconsistent because by meeting the Jewish and Arab objections the outcome would be further impairment of the substance of the Balfour Draft even as it had been diluted in the Milner Draft. The text of the Milner–Amery Draft demonstrates a further dimunition of the Zionist substance and the failure of the Weizmann–Rothschild petition.

His Majesty's Government views with favour the establishment in Palestine of a national home for the Jewish race and will use its best endeavours to facilitate the achievement of this object, it being clearly understood that nothing shall be done which may prejudice the civil and religious rights of existing non-Jewish communities in Palestine or the rights and political status enjoyed in any other country by such Jews who are fully con-

---

95. Stein, *supra* note 25 at 514.
96. *Id.* at 520.

tented with their existing nationality and citizenship.[97]

Mr. Stein states that in the Milner–Amery Draft "the main substance of the British undertaking, as expressed in Milner's August draft, remained unchanged."[98] He adds that Amery made "his main contribution" to the draft by adding "the two limiting provisos,"[99] that is, the safeguard clauses, and also that:

> [T]he progressive watering down of the formula submitted by Rothschild in July, and in substance accepted at the time by Balfour, was clearly a response, not only to the pressure of the Jewish anti-Zionists, but also to reminders that in dealing with the Palestine question there were other claims and interests to be considered besides those of the Jews.[100]

Dr. Weizmann's appraisal of the Milner–Amery Draft recognized the existence of a "compromise formula":

> Certain it was that Montagu's opposition, coupled with the sustained attacks which the tiny anti-Zionist group had been conducting for months – their letters to the press, the pamphlets, some of them written pseudonymously by Lucien Wolf, their feverish interviews with Government officials – was responsible for the compromise formula which the War Cabinet submitted to us a few days later.[101]

In a juridical analysis, it is significant that "the principle" which had been set forth in various forms in earlier drafts to

---

97. *Id.* at 521. The last two words in the text of the Draft were added two days later. *Id.* at 524, 525 note 31.

98. *Id.* at 521.

99. *Id.* at 522.

100. *Id.*

101. Weizmann, *supra* note 18 at 259.

meet the objectives of Zionist nationalism was now eliminated. It was replaced with nothing more than the vague statement that the Government viewed the Zionist national home enterprise "with favour" and "will use its best endeavours to facilitate" this object. This draft clause, in short, obligates the British Government to do nothing. Even if a very loose interpretation could somehow conclude that it was a kind of a political commitment, it was at most a very restricted one, and it was further limited by being expressly subordinated to the safeguard clauses.

The safeguard clauses set forth in the Milner–Amery Draft frustrated the Zionist negotiating objectives in the most direct manner. The first of these two clauses protected the existing rights of the overwhelming majority of the population of Palestine, that is, the Moslem and Christian Arabs. The second protected the rights of Jews in other countries than Palestine from inclusion within the Zionist claimed constituency of "the Jewish people." Both safeguards are given express priority over the favor clause.

The October 4 draft was sent by the Cabinet, with an invitation for comments upon it as a proposed declaration, "from Zionist leaders and from representative British Jews."[102] When it became apparent that the Cabinet was inviting the views of the Jews as well as the Zionists, Weizmann regarded this as an additional concession to Montagu and "did not conceal his indignation."[103] He, nevertheless, proceeded with great caution in expressing the Zionist position and apparently asked for nothing more than a change from "establishment" to "re-establishment" so that "the historical connection with the ancient tradition would be indicated."[104] Dr. Weizmann wrote in description of the retrenched Zionist position:

> We, on our part, examined and re-examined the formula, comparing the old text with the new.

---

102. Stein, *supra* note 25 at 524.

103. *Id.* at 518.

104. Weizmann 261. See the text accompanying note 72 *supra*.

We saw the differences only too clearly, but we did not dare to occasion further delay by pressing for the original formula, which represented not only our wishes, but the attitude of the [Zionist] members of the Government.[105]

Mr. Stein states that Claude Montefiore "was an important and impressive figure in Anglo-Jewish life and was recognized by the Zionists themselves as an opponent worthy of respect."[106] Montefiore expressed the Jewish views as follows:

The phrase "a national home for the Jewish race" appears to assume and imply that Jews generally constitute a nationality. Such an implication is extremely prejudicial to Jewish interests, as it is intensely obnoxious to an enormous number of Jews ... . [E]mancipation and liberty in the countries of the world are a thousand times more important than a "home." . . . It is very significant that anti-Semites are always very sympathetic to Zionism.[107]

The essential situation, however, was that since the safeguards and the "watered-down" favor clause met Mr. Montagu's requirements, they were also acceptable to the other Jews. Even those who would have preferred no declaration at all were willing to accept one which met Montagu's juridical objectives.[108] Weizmann was sufficiently resigned to the Milner–Amery Draft to telegraph it to Justice Brandeis in the United States for his approval.[109] Brandeis and his friends objected to

---

105. Weizmann 261.

106. Stein 175.

107. *Id.* at 525.

108. Montagu's power position and his confidence in maintaining the substantive gains of the Milner–Amery Draft in the final Declaration were reflected in his plans to depart for India. He left for India on Oct. 18, 1917. Stein, *supra* note 25 at 500.

109. *Id.* at 530.

it in two respects. They proposed eliminating the part of the second safeguard clause which read "by such Jews who are fully contented with their existing nationality and citizenship," and substituting for it "the rights and civil political status enjoyed by Jews in any other country."[110] Brandeis also apparently proposed the change of "Jewish race" to "Jewish people."[111] In both respects the final Balfour Declaration appeared to reflect his recommended changes.

Dr. Weizmann has provided an instructive comparison between the Balfour Draft and the Milner–Amery Draft characterizing the latter as "a painful recession." His analysis states:

> A comparison of the two texts – the one approved by the Foreign Office and the Prime Minister, and the one adopted on October 4, after Montagu's attack – shows a painful recession from what the Government itself was prepared to offer. The first [the Balfour Draft] declares that "Palestine should be reconstituted as the National Home of the Jewish people." The second [the Milner–Amery Draft] speaks of "the establishment in Palestine of a National Home for the Jewish people." The first adds only that the "Government will use its best endeavours to secure the achievement of this object and will discuss the necessary methods with the Zionist Organization"; the second introduces the subject of the "civil and religious rights of the existing non-Jewish communities" in such a fashion as to impute possible oppressive intentions to the Jews, and can be interpreted to mean such limitations on our work as completely to cripple it.[112]

---

110. *Id.* at 531.

111. *Id.*

112. Weizmann, *supra* note 18 at 260.

The Weizmann appraisal of the scope and breadth of the first safeguard clause is particularly candid and significant.[113]

7. THE FINAL TEXT (OCTOBER 31, 1917; ISSUED NOVEMBER 2, 1917)

As Dr. Weizmann expressly recognized, the Milner–Amery Draft could be interpreted to frustrate, or "cripple," their central political objectives. This draft of October 4 also demonstrated that the Zionist proclaimed limitations in the Weizmann–Sykes memorandum were being taken seriously in the sense of being acted upon, although they had not been effective in disarming the opposition and in producing a declaration consistent with the earlier Zionist objectives.

With considerable understatement, Mr. Stein refers to "the War Cabinet's sensitiveness to the protests of the anti-Zionists."[114] The ensuing actions taken by Weizmann and his associates demonstrate their deep concern that the Milner–Amery Draft, without substantial changes and retaining the safeguards, would become the final official Declaration. Their reaction was to shift their case from the negotiating forum to the political one. On October 11, the Council of the English Zionist Federation, with Dr. Weizmann presiding, decided on pressure group tactics to produce resolutions on behalf of "the Jewish people." Leonard Stein reports that: "Resolutions in these terms were passed, on October 21st, by some three hundred Zionist and other Jewish bodies all over the country and forwarded to the Foreign Office."[115]

Weizmann's other technique was to attempt an informal approach to the anti-Zionist Jews:

> So concerned was Weizmann about the situation which seemed to be developing that he considered the possibility of some understanding

---

113. It is also atypical since most Zionist analyses ignore the first safeguard.

114. Stein, *supra* note 25 at 519.

115. *Id.* at 520.

behind the scenes which would avert a head-on
collision with the anti-Zionists.[116]

Stein reports that the attempt to reach such an "understanding" came to nothing.[117] The inference which an observer
may draw is that the Jews were confident that they could
maintain their victory reflected in the Milner–Amery Draft
and, consequently, were not interested in participating in
such discussions.

Dr. Weizmann has described the Zionist dilemma:

> It is one of the "ifs" of history whether we should
> have been intransigent, and stood by our guns.
> Should we then have obtained a better
> statement? . . . Our judgment was to accept, to
> press for ratification.[118]

He thus concedes, after all attempts to change the substance
of the Milner–Amery Draft – or at least to remove or soften
the safeguards – had been defeated, that it was decided to
accept it as better than any alternative the Zionists had the
power to obtain.

It is significant that the letter from Balfour containing the
Declaration was sent to Lord Rothschild rather than to
Weizmann or Sokolow. This had the advantage of associat-
ing the Declaration with the prestige of the Rothschild name
even though the Rothschild family was bitterly divided upon
the subject of Zionism.[119] The use of their name was likely to
promote the propaganda aspects of the Declaration in
obtaining Jewish support, in addition to that of the Zionists,

---

116. *Id.* It is perhaps significant that the attempt was made in a letter to
Herbert Samuel of Oct. 18, 1917, the day Montagu sailed for India.

Weizmann referred to Sir Philip Magnus (an anti-Zionist) and Sir Stuart
Samuel (equivocal concerning Zionism) as those with whom "a satisfactory
arrangement" could be made. *Id.*

117. *Id.* at 520. Even if such an understanding could have been achieved, it
would have had no significance to the Cabinet without Montagu's
concurrence in it.

118. Weizmann, *supra* note 18 at 261.

119. Leopold de Rothschild and his wife were "furiously anti-Zionist." *Id.* at
205.

for the British Government.[120] The text was preceded by a short introductory sentence describing the Declaration as one "of sympathy with Jewish Zionist aspirations which has been submitted to, and approved by, the Cabinet." The statement of "sympathy," in contrast to any suggestion of a principle or a commitment, leads to a further diminution of the already "watered down" favor clause of the Declaration. It seems more accurate to view the first substantive clause of the text as merely a "favour" clause rather than as a political "promise" clause since it promised nothing.

The final text of the Declaration retained each of the substantive elements of the Milner–Amery Draft, including the safeguard clauses which made it so objectionable to the Zionists:

> His Majesty's Government view with favour the establishment in Palestine of a national home for the Jewish people and will use their best endeavours to facilitate the achievement of this object, it being clearly understood that nothing shall be done which may prejudice the civil and religious rights of existing non-Jewish communities in Palestine or the rights and political status enjoyed by Jews in any other country.[121]

IV. Interpretation of the Meaning of the Declaration.

The most accurate interpretation of the meaning of each clause of the Declaration requires an analysis in its context.

---

120. The propaganda aspects are considered in Lasswell, *Propaganda Technique in the World War* 176 (1927).

121. The quoted text is taken from the facsimile of the Declaration reproduced in Appendix 2.

A. THE FAVOR CLAUSE IN CONTEXT

1. THE ZIONIST INTERPRETATION

Mr. Stein provides this introduction to the Zionist interpretation:

> What, then, were the Zionists being promised? The language of the Declaration was studiously vague, and neither on the British nor on the Zionist side was there any disposition, at the time, to probe deeply into its meaning – still less was there any agreed interpretation.[122]

This description is typical of many Zionist interpretations since it ignores the safeguards and treats the Declaration as consisting only of the favor clause. There can be no reasonable doubt concerning the "studiously vague" character of this clause. It must be interpreted as even more vague when compared with the precise wording of the safeguards. It is interesting that Stein states that neither "the British" nor the Zionists wished to probe deeply into the meaning. This is eminently correct concerning the Zionists since any probing would reveal the Declaration to be a repudiation of their negotiating objectives. If by "the British" he refers to the Cabinet which issued the Declaration, he commits a profound error. The Cabinet, after careful consideration of six drafts and both Jewish and Zionist memoranda, issued a Declaration which met Jewish objectives, including the protection of the Palestinians, and repudiated Zionist ones.[123] This indicates that the Cabinet, probing far too deeply from the Zionist standpoint, rejected the Zionist juridical objectives with deliberation and precision.

Mr. Stein concedes that the Declaration also failed to provide direct British Government assumption of responsibility for the establishment of the Zionist national home enterprise in Palestine, although Weizmann and his associ-

---

122. Stein, *supra* note 25 at 552.

123. The Zionists and the British Government, nevertheless, received some propaganda benefits from the Declaration. These are emphasized in 2 Lloyd George, *The Truth About the Peace Treaties* 1118 (1938).

ates "had from the start regarded [this] as fundamental."[124]
He continues his analysis by stating:

> What the British Government did undertake
> was to use its best endeavours to "facilitate" (no
> more) "the establishment in Palestine of a national
> home for the Jewish people" – not, as it had been
> put in the Zionist draft and as Balfour would,
> apparently, have been prepared to concede, the
> reconstitution of Palestine as the national home of
> the Jews.[125]

Some of the words in the introductory paragraph of
Balfour's letter to Rothschild were interpreted by the Zionist
Organization/Jewish Agency in 1947:

> The phrase "Jewish Zionist aspirations" in the
> first paragraph of the Document referred to the
> age-old hope of Jews the world over that Palestine
> shall be restored to its ancient role as the "Land of
> Israel." These aspirations were formulated as a
> concrete aim at the first World Zionist Congress at
> Basle, Switzerland, in 1897, under the leadership
> of Dr. Theodor Herzl, in these words:
> "Zionism aims to create a publicly secured,
> legally assured home for the Jewish people in
> Palestine."[126]

The same Zionist source provides an interpretation of the
words "national home for the Jewish people":

---

124. Stein 552.

125. *Id.* at 552–53. Professor Sachar: "Montagu had done his work better
than he knew." *Supra* note 94 at 375.

In reporting by telegram upon the British official position concerning
Palestine to the Secretary of State, the American Ambassador in London
stated, *inter alia*, on December 21, 1917: "No discrimination shall be made
against them [the Jews in Palestine]. This is as far as the British Government
has yet gone." [1917] *Foreign Rels. U.S.*, Vol. 1, Supp. No. 2, p. 483 (1933).

126. Jewish Agency for Palestine, *Book of Documents Submitted to the General
Assembly of the United Nations Relating to the Establishment of the National Home
for the Jewish People* 1 (Tulin ed., 1947).

> The phrase "the establishment in Palestine of a National Home for the Jewish people" was intended and understood by all concerned to mean at the time of the Balfour Declaration that Palestine would ultimately become a "Jewish Commonwealth" or a "Jewish State", if only Jews came and settled there in sufficient numbers.[127]

The inaccuracy of the statement that this alleged meaning of an ultimate "Jewish State" was "intended and understood by all concerned" is obvious. Such an understanding could not be attributed accurately to the Jews, including Montagu, and to the British Cabinet which issued the final text of the Declaration.

Dr. Weizmann's views on the Declaration, expressed ten years after the event, are of particular importance because of his role as the preeminent Zionist negotiator.

> The Balfour Declaration of 1917 was built on air, and a foundation had to be laid for it through years of exacting work; every day and every hour of these last ten years, when opening the newspapers, I thought: Whence will the next blow come? I trembled lest the British Government would call me and ask: "Tell us, what is this Zionist Organisation? Where are they, your Zionists?" For these people think in terms different from ours. The Jews, they knew, were against us ... .[128]

The "foundation," which had to be laid after the event included attempted drastic changes in the meaning of the favor clause combined with a virtual elimination of the safeguards.[129] These are, of course, the same objectives which were rejected in the negotiations and the Declaration.

Consideration should also be given to Dr. Weizmann's

---

127. *Id.* at 5.

128. Weizmann, "Address at Czernowitz, Roumania (Dec. 12, 1927)" in *Chaim Weizmann: A Tribute on His Seventieth Birthday* 196, 199 (Goodman ed., 1945).

129. The text of the present section *passim.*

contemporaneous reaction which he recounts in his autobiography:

> While the cabinet was in session, approving
> the final text, I was waiting outside, this time
> within call. Sykes brought the document out to me
> with the exclamation: "Dr. Weizmann, it's a boy!"
> Well – I did not like the boy at first. He was not the one I
> had expected ... .[130]

In spite of his disappointment at that time, Dr. Weizmann
later developed a method of interpretation which satisfied
the Zionists: "It would mean exactly what we would make it
mean – neither more nor less."[131]

2. THE JURIDICAL INTERPRETATION

In a juridical interpretation it is necessary to consider the
views of the humanitarian Jews who supported the final text
of the Balfour Declaration. This support was, of course,
extremely welcome to the Zionists at the time since it tended
to identify them with the Jews. Later it became highly
embarrassing because of the basic divergencies in interpretations which arose. Justice Brandeis supported the Balfour
Declaration and suggested words to strengthen the second
safeguard.[132] Thereafter, "irreconcilable differences on questions of principle" developed between Brandeis and Weizmann which led "to an open breach."[133] The essential
difference between the two was that Brandeis insisted upon
interpreting the Declaration as the end of the political work of
Zionism. Dr. Weizmann wrote of the situation:

> What struck me as curious was that the
> American Zionists, under Justice Brandeis,

---

130. Weizmann, *supra* note 18 at 262.

131. *Id.* at 302.

132. See the text accompanying notes 110–11 *supra*.

133. Stein, *supra* note 25, at 581. See Berger, "Disenchantment of a Zionist,"
38 *Middle East Forum* No. 4, p. 21 (1962) concerning Brandeis' disillusionment
with Zionism.

though fully aware of what was going on in England and in Palestine, nonetheless shared the illusions of our Continental friends; they too assumed that all political problems had been settled once and for all [by the Balfour Declaration], and that the only important task before Zionists was the economic upbuilding of the Jewish National Home.[134]

Achad Ha'am provided considerable discomfiture to the Zionists. His interpretation of the Declaration emphasized that the Zionist objectives sought by Weizmann and Sokolow were frustrated and that the Declaration protected the interests of the Moslem and Christian Palestinians. He stated:

This position, then, makes Palestine common ground for different peoples, each of which tries to establish its national home there; and in this position it is impossible for the national home of either of them to be complete and to embrace all that is involved in the conception of a "national home." If you build your house not on untenanted ground, but in a place where there are other inhabited houses, you are sole master only as far as your front gate. Within you may arrange your effects as you please, but beyond the gate all the inhabitants are partners, and the general administration must be ordered in conformity with the good of all of them.[135]

The favor clause, as "watered down," was also a part of a bargain between the Zionists and the British Government. In return for this admittedly vague clause, the Zionists promised to deliver the political support of their world-wide alleged constituency of Jews ("the Jewish people") to the British Government during and after the war. Next to

---

134. Weizmann 301.

135. Achad Ha'am, *Ten Essays on Zionism and Judaism* xvi–xx (Simon transl. 1922).

Balfour, Prime Minister Lloyd George was the preeminent governmental Zionist. He described the *quid pro quo* in this way:

> The Zionist leaders gave us a definite promise that, if the Allies committed themselves to giving facilities for the establishment of a National Home for the Jews in Palestine, they would do their best to rally to the Allied cause Jewish sentiment and support throughout the world. They kept their word in the letter and the spirit ... .[136]

The British interest in the bargain also reflected concern with the power position following the war. A pro-Zionist study has stated: "The essential reason, accounts agree, was strategic and had to do with the need of strengthening Great Britain's lifeline to the East."[137] The same source adds: "Through the Balfour Declaration Great Britain ultimately strengthened and extended her position in the whole Near East."[138]

It was, of course, essential that the bargain involved not be reflected in the text of the Declaration. The danger for both the official Zionists, including Weizmann and Sokolow, and the British functional Zionists in the Government was that Jews, citizens of their respective national states, would have expressly repudiated the Zionist leaders' claim to act for them and to deliver their loyalties. In addition to it obviating this danger, the innocuous favor clause, when combined with the second safeguard clause to protect existing Jewish rights, would be juridically interpreted as a humanitarian measure on behalf of refugee Jews which should merit the support of men of good will. Thus the Zionists in and out of the Government were in a position to obtain credit for a humanitarian document,[139] and the Jews could support this

---

136. 2 Lloyd George, *The Truth About the Peace Treaties* 1139 (1938).

137. 1 *Esco Study, supra* note 5 at 117.

138. *Id.* at 118.

139. The propaganda aspects are mentioned in the text accompanying note 120 *supra*.

interpretation of the favor clause as restricted by the safeguards. In consequence, a persuasive juridical interpretation of the favor clause is that it is a humanitarian measure to allow Jewish refugees to emigrate to Palestine.

This is more reasonable than an alternative interpretation which contends that the favor clause was designed for the benefit of the Zionists rather than of refugee Jews. Even though the Zionist alleged constituency of "the Jewish people" is referred to in the favor clause, the purpose of the second safeguard is to prevent the involuntary inclusion of Jews in this claimed constituency. If the limited "Jewish people" of the Declaration had been frankly described as "Zionists," a humanitarian interpretation of the Declaration would not have been possible, and Montagu and the other Jews were prepared to accept only a Declaration which had humanitarian objectives rather than political ones. For this reason, the favor clause must be given a humanitarian interpretation. A further and even more compelling reason is that this is consistent with the first safeguard clause. Any interpretation which accorded legal authority for Zionist, as opposed to Jewish, immigration to Palestine could be understood to permit a direct attack upon the safeguarded rights which would far exceed mere "prejudice" to them.

In early 1918 an official of the British Government removed any doubts concerning the purpose of Jewish immigration to Palestine by informing the Sharif of Mecca that "Jewish settlement in Palestine would only be allowed in so far as would be consistent with the political and economic freedom of the Arab population."[140] The result was that the Sharif, as Professor Taylor has described it, "welcomed the Jews to the Arab lands on the understanding that a Jewish state in Palestine would not be in the offing."[141] This action was, of course, consistent with the humanitarian interpretaton of the favor clause of the Balfour Declaration which has just been described.

A contemporaneous Zionist writer concurred in upholding this view of the favor clause by ruling out the possibility

---

140. *Zionist Diplomacy, supra* note 5 at 32.

141. *Id.*

of a "Jewish State." Writing in the author's introduction to his semi-official history of Zionism, Sokolow stated:

It has been said, and is still being obstinately repeated by anti-Zionists again and again that Zionism aims at the creation of an independent "Jewish State." But this is wholly fallacious. The "Jewish State" was never a part of the Zionist programme.[142]

B. THE SAFEGUARD CLAUSES IN CONTEXT

1. THE FIRST SAFEGUARD: PALESTINIAN RIGHTS

In considering the Zionist interpretation of the first safeguard, it is necessary to examine briefly their attitude concerning the Palestinians. The Zionist slogan, "Give the land without a people to the people without a land,"[143] reflected the basic policy of studied indifference to the existence of the Palestinians. When their existence had, on occasion, to be recognized, the situation did not represent much of an improvement from a human rights standpoint. Leonard Stein wrote in 1923: "The fact has to be faced that so far as the great mass of the population [of Palestine] is concerned, the Arabs are immature and irresponsible to the point of childishness."[144] The consistency in the Zionist basic policy is reflected in the official statement of Mr. Galili, the Minister of Information of the Government of Israel in 1969: "We do not consider the Arabs of the land an ethnic group nor a people with a distinct nationalistic character."[145]

---

142. 1 Sokolow, *supra* note 9 at xxiv-xxv.

143. The slogan is widely attributed to Zangwill.

144. Stein, "The Problem of Self-Government" in Simon & Stein (eds.), *Awakening Palestine* 232, 235 (1923).

145. Talmon, "An Open Letter to Y. Galili," 15 *Arab World* No. 9, p. 3 (1969). Professor Talmon, an Israeli historian, provides strong criticism of the quoted words.

Goldmann, "True Neutrality for Israel," *Foreign Policy* No. 37, p. 133 (Winter 1979–80) and Avnery, *Israel Without Zionists: A Plea for Peace in the Middle East* (1968) demonstrate that the Zionist attitudes are inconsistent with Israeli national interests.

Dr. Frankenstein, a Zionist lawyer, provides a narrow analysis of the first safeguard clause:

> [I]t confines the protection of non-Jews to their civil and religious rights, omitting political status, while the immediately following words explicitly protect "the rights and political status enjoyed by Jews in any other country." There is a deliberate differentiation between the protection of the non-Jews in Palestine and of the Jews abroad.[146]

The purpose of the quoted analysis, since the Zionists failed to have this safeguard removed from the Declaration, is to interpret it in such a restrictive manner as to frustrate its protective purpose. It will be recalled that both the anti-Zionist Jews and the British Government believed it essential to protect the existing rights of the Palestinians. The more accurate interpretation, therefore, is that the wording "civil and religious rights" was intended to describe and protect the existing rights then possessed by the Palestinians.

A somewhat different interpretation, but equally narrow and restrictive as the Frankenstein one, is offered by Stein who states:

> It is not quite clear whether the rather curious expression "existing non-Jewish communities in Palestine" was meant to refer to the Arabs or whether this part of the proposed declaration was directed primarily to the position of the various Christian communities, whose traditional rights were of special concern to the French and Italian Governments and to the Roman Catholic and Orthodox Churches.[147]

This supposed choice between alternatives is quite inconsistent with the purposes of the first safeguard which was introduced in the Milner–Amery Draft. It will be recalled that

---

146. Frankenstein, "The Meaning of the Term 'National Home for the Jewish People'," *Jewish Yearbook of Int'l L.* 27, 29–30 (1948).

147. Stein, *supra* note 25 at 522.

the draft safeguard was written to meet "pro-Arab objections." There is not a scintilla of evidence to suggest that the existing rights of non-Jewish communities were to belong only to Moslem or Christian Palestinians. Such a false alternative would frustrate the comprehensive protective purpose by arbitrarily excluding some of the protected "non-Jewish communities" without warrant in either the negotiations or the final text of the safeguard.

There is persuasive judicial authority concerning the interpretation of an agreement in which the beneficiaries, like the Palestinians in the Balfour Declaration, have no direct negotiating or decisional role. In the famous *Cayuga Indians Case* (Great Britain v. United States)[148] the fact situation involved an agreement or covenant in which the covenantees, the Indian claimants, had no effective role. The tribunal referred to "universally admitted principles of justice and right dealing"[149] as being the applicable criteria in interpreting the covenant in favor of the Indians. The opinion emphasized the undesirable alternative method of applying "the harsh operation of the legal terminology of a covenant which the covenantees had no part in framing ... ."[150] In applying these judicial criteria, it should be recognized that the purpose of the Declaration including the first safeguard was protective rather than "harsh." It follows, *a fortiori*, that the entire document must be effectuated according to the "universally admitted principles" of elementary justice. If the Zionist interpretation were accepted, the document would then be one of "harsh operation."

In a juridical interpretation of the first safeguard protecting the "civil and religious rights" of the Palestinians, it must be recognized that it was inserted by the British Cabinet over the express objections of the Zionist negotiators. In this context, it appears that subsequent Zionist attempts to narrow the content of "civil and religious rights"

---

148. F. K. Nielsen (ed.), *Report of the Case Decided Under the Special Agreement Between the United States and Great Britain of August 18, 1910*, 203, 307 (1926).

149. *Id.* at 320.

150. *Id.*

are not very persuasive. The most reasonable interpretation is that the clause protected the rights which were possessed and exercised by the Palestinians when Palestine was a part of the Ottoman Empire. In addition to freedom of religion, these included the rights to livelihood, to own land, and to have an individual home as well as to maintain the integrity of the Palestinian community as a political entity.[151]

Professors Oppenheim and Lauterpacht, while recognizing that "many treaties stipulating immoral obligations have been concluded and executed," emphasize that "this does not alter the fact that such treaties were legally not binding upon the contracting parties."[152] The same scholars enunciate the doctrine applicable to "immoral obligations" in these unequivocal terms:

> It is a customarily recognised rule of the Law of Nations that immoral obligations cannot be the object of an international treaty. Thus, an alliance for the purpose of attacking a third State without provocation is, from the beginning, not binding.[153]

It must be obvious that the principal feature of the Declaration as interpreted by the Zionists is its immoral character in violating, *inter alia*, the rights protected by the first safeguard. There may be some borderline situations in which the legal scholars could properly engage in disputation as to whether or not a particular obligation is immoral. The Zionist interpretation of the Balfour Declaration does not put it in such a borderline category.

2. THE SECOND SAFEGUARD: JEWISH RIGHTS

This safeguard protected "the rights and political status enjoyed by Jews in any other country" than Palestine. It is

---

151. Cattan, *Palestine, The Arabs and Israel: The Search for Justice* 4–9 (1969) demonstrates that Palestinians, of whatever religion, enjoyed equality with other Turkish subjects in all categories of legal rights.

Some recognition of basic Palestinian political rights appears in Stein 621–51 (Chap. 41 entitled "The Arab Question").

152. 1 Oppenheim–Lauterpacht, *International Law: Peace* 896 (8th ed. 1955).

153. *Id.*

appropriate to recall that it also was placed in the Declaration over the strong objections of the Zionist negotiators. In particular, the Jews sought protection from the prejudice and injury to their existing political status which would be caused by their inclusion in the claimed "Jewish people" nationality entity.[154] There is no evidence which suggests that the word "political" was employed in the second safeguard to reduce the Palestinian rights which were protected in the first.

The differences between the wording of the second safeguard in the Milner–Amery Draft and that in the final Declaration have been considered. The important juridical consequence is a substantial strengthening of the protection afforded to the Jews. Rather than having the scope of the clause determined by the subjective test of ascertaining which individuals were "fully contented with their existing nationality," as the Milner–Amery Draft provided, the second safeguard was made broadly applicable to "Jews in any other country" than Palestine.

Many Zionist interpreters of the Declaration have simply ignored the second safeguard. In striking contrast, Professor Feinberg of the Law Faculty of the Hebrew University of Jerusalem has attempted a direct analysis. His highly original interpretation attempts to demonstrate that the second safeguard is intended to protect Zionist Jews in carrying out Zionist political objectives. In his words, it was necessary:

> [T]hat the grant of the National Home, and the ensuing right of all Jews to take part in the upbuilding of that home, did not in any way affect their status and allegiance as citizens of the countries to which they belonged.[155]

This interpretation of the second safeguard clause is completely inconsistent with the negotiating history of the Declaration including the unsuccessful Zionist attempts to eliminate the safeguards.

---

154. See Chap. 2 *passim.*

155. Feinberg, "The Recognition of the Jewish People in International Law," *Jewish Yearbook of Int'l L.* 1, 18 (1948).

It should be mentioned that any juridical interpretation of the Declaration must recognize that each of its three clauses is an integral part of the negotiated compromise. Even if there were no clear wording stressing the preeminence of the safeguards, they would have to be accorded priority over the favor clause since they protected existing rights which the British Government had no legal authority to change, or even to "prejudice," as provided in the Declaration.

C. THE DECLARATION IN "PLAIN MEANING" INTERPRETATION

Although the availability of the negotiating context affords an exceptionally high degree of accuracy in interpreting the Balfour Declaration, completeness in analysis requires that the "plain meaning" approach should also be considered. At the outset it is useful to recognize that this so-called rule is, in the thoughtful words of Lord McNair:

> [M]erely a starting-point, a prima facie guide, and cannot be allowed to obstruct the essential quest in the application of treaties, namely to search for the real intention of the contracting parties in using the language employed by them.[156]

Assuming, for purposes of analysis only, either that there is no negotiating history of the Declaration or that this history is unknown, it would then be necessary to use "a prima facie guide" to the interpretation of the final text of the Declaration as it would stand alone.

Such a textualistic interpretation would note that the British Government view "with favour" the national home enterprise which is restricted by the words "in Palestine," and that the Government "will use their best endeavours" to facilitate its achievement. In most usual legal usage such terms as "favour" and "best endeavours" are precatory or wishful words. They may be most obviously recognized as

---

156. McNair, *supra* note 28 at 366 (1961).

being in contrast to words of legal obligation or commitment which do not appear in the favor clause. It is clear that the favor clause, even if considered without the safeguards, specifies no legal obligation whatsoever, as is evidenced by the conspicuous absence of words such as "rights" or "obligations" or terms of similar meaning.

The first safeguard clause refers to the civil and religious "rights" of the Palestinians. In the same way, the second safeguard refers to the "rights and political status" of Jews in any other country than Palestine. The word "rights," set forth in each of the safeguards, specifies a clear juridical obligation concerning the stated rights. The particular rights enunciated in the safeguard clauses are, consistent with the "ordinary" meaning of the words used, the then existing rights of both Palestinians and Jews. This conclusion is further supported by the fact that the words in the text make no reference to some indeterminate or unspecified possible type of theoretical rights.

Without consideration of other words which are in the text of the Declaration, it is clear that the safeguard clauses are of a highly specific character and protect the stated "rights." When the safeguards are compared with the favor clause, the absence of any legal obligation in the favor clause becomes even more obvious. This leads to the conclusion that the safeguards set forth a legal requirement which must be given juridical priority over the favor clause since the latter lacks obligatory character.

It is not necessary, however, to rest the conclusion just stated upon the analysis made thus far because there are further words in the Declaration which compel the same conclusion. The safeguards are preceded by the unequivocal words which state "it being clearly understood that nothing shall be done which may prejudice" the safeguarded rights. The conclusion, therefore, must also be reached because of the specific priority accorded to the safeguards by the quoted words which introduce them. In addition, it is desirable to note that the preeminence of the safeguarded "rights" is not written in terms of prevention of injury to or violation of them. The words of the Declaration, with striking and clear choice of terminology, provide that nothing shall be done which would even "prejudice" the safeguarded rights.

Dr. Weizmann's expressed disappointment with the final text of the Declaration upon its issuance has been described. It is interesting that the "plain meaning" of the words of the Declaration presented an interpretive problem for him. He has written that "in spite of the phrasing, the intent was clear."[157] When Dr. Weizmann states that the "intent" was "clear," although inconsistent with, or "in spite of," "the phrasing," it is apparent that he is referring only to the Zionist intent. This intent, as analyzed above, has always been inconsistent with both the wording and the meaning of the Declaration.

V. Multilateral International Agreement to the Balfour Declaration

At the time of its issuance, the Balfour Declaration was only multilateral in the narrow sense that three distinct parties with different interests, the Jews, the Zionists, and the British Government, were participants in the negotiations. For this reason it is accurate to describe the Declaration as multipartite in terms of participants, but in form it was a unilateral declaration of the British Government. The legal authority of the British Government to make any changes in the juridical status of Palestine and the Palestinians would have been open to the gravest doubts if such changes had been attempted.[158] The actual Declaration of the British Government, however, containing safeguards protecting existing Palestinian and Jewish rights, stands upon a much more solid basis. It must be accurately construed, consequently, as a solemn promise by the British Government to recognize and support these existing rights.

In order to establish the three clauses of the Declaration as binding international law, it was necessary to obtain multilateral assent from other national states. This was

---

157. Weizmann, *supra* note 18 at 265.

158. The applicable limitations of international law are considered in Sec. VI *infra*.

accomplished mainly through the Mandate system provided for in the League of Nations Covenant.

A. THE LEAGUE OF NATIONS MANDATE FOR PALESTINE (1922)

The central objectives of the Mandate system are articulated in the League of Nations Covenant.

> To those colonies and territories which as a consequence of the late war have ceased to be under the sovereignty of the States which former-ly governed them and which are inhabited by peoples not yet able to stand by themselves under the strenuous conditions of the modern world, there should be applied the principle that the well-being and development of such peoples form a sacred trust of civilisation and that securities for the performance of this trust should be embodied in this Covenant.[159]

This basic principle of the Covenant indicates that the "sacred trust of civilisation" is to be exercised for the benefit of the peoples inhabiting the particular territories. The principle applies, *prima facie*, to the then existing inhabitants of Palestine of Moslem, Christian, and Jewish religious identifications. It would constitute a flagrant violation of this "sacred trust" to take Palestine from the Palestinians and allot it to the Zionists. The basic inconsistency involved is recognized by Dr. Stoyanovsky, a Zionist legal authority, who has written:

> The peculiarity of the national home policy seems to be the extension of this principle [protecting existing inhabitants] so as to include the Jewish people in the category of the above peoples.[160]

---

159. *League of Nations Covenant* art. 22(1).

160. Stoyanovsky, *The Mandate for Palestine: A Contribution to the Theory and Practice of International Mandates* 43 (1928).

The League of Nations Covenant also recognized provisionally the independence of territories formerly belonging to the Turkish Empire including Palestine. The applicable provision stated:

> Certain communities formerly belonging to the Turkish Empire have reached a stage of development where their existence as independent nations can be provisionally recognised subject to the rendering of administrative advice and assistance by a Mandatory until such time as they are able to stand alone. The wishes of these communities must be a principal consideration in the selection of the Mandatory.[161]

Great Britain was designated by the League of Nations as the Mandatory Power for Palestine and the Palestine Mandate became effective on September 29, 1923.[162] The second paragraph of the preamble to the Mandate for Palestine incorporated the Balfour Declaration with some changes in wording. It shortened the favor clause by omitting the wording concerning "best endeavours to facilitate this object." Only one word in the phrase introducing the safeguards was changed: the term "which might prejudice" was substituted for "which may prejudice." The safeguard clauses remained unchanged.[163]

In view of the frustration of the Zionist objectives in the final text of the Balfour Declaration, Dr. Weizmann attempted to have an unequivocal Zionist right to Palestine recognized in the preamble to the Mandate. He has written,

---

161. Note 159 *supra* at art. 22(4).

162. 1 *International Legislation* 109 (Hudson ed. 1931).

163. The text of the Palestine Mandate used herein is the official one taken from the Convention Between the United States and Great Britain Concerning Palestine of Dec. 3, 1924 (effectuated Dec. 5, 1925), 44 U.S. Stat. 2184. This Convention incorporated the entire Palestine Mandate including the Balfour Declaration with the changes described. The Mandate also appears in 2 UNSCOP, *Report to the General Assembly, 2 U.N. GAOR*, Supp. 11, pp. 18–22, U.N. Doc. A/364 Add. 1, (9 Sept. 1947) and in Stoyanovsky, note 160 *supra* at 355, and 2 *Diplomacy in the Near and Middle East* 106 (Hurewitz ed. 1956).

"Zionists wanted to have it read: 'recognizing the historic rights of the Jews to Palestine'."[164] Curzon had, however, replaced Balfour as the British Foreign Secretary and this provided no encouragement for the Zionists. It is apparent that both safeguard clauses of the Balfour Declaration as well as the "rights and political status" enjoyed by British Jews under British municipal law required Curzon to reject the claim of the alleged Zionist "rights," and he did so.[165] The third paragraph of the preamble to the Mandate provided:

> Whereas recognition has thereby [through the Balfour Declaration] been given to the historical connection of the Jewish people and to the grounds for reconstituting their national home in that country.[166]

It will be recalled that Weizmann attempted unsuccessfully to change the word "establishment" in the Milner–Amery Draft to "re-establishment."[167] Perhaps he found some solace in the word "reconstituting" quoted above. In view of the rejection of the Zionist claim of legal rights by Curzon combined with the retention of the safeguards in the Mandate for Palestine, it is not possible to interpret the Declaration as changed in meaning. The Zionists, of course, interpreted the Balfour Declaration as it was incorporated in the League of Nations Mandate the same way that they interpreted the original Declaration. Dr. Stoyanovsky, for example, wrote:

> There can hardly be any question now whether Jews constitute a distinct national entity in the eyes of international law. This seems to have been laid down, on the one hand, by the various treaties containing what is known as minority clauses, and on the other, by the

---

164. Weizmann, *supra* note 18 at 348.
165. *Id.*
166. 44 U.S. Stat. 2184.
167. The text accompanying note 104 *supra*.

mandate for Palestine providing for the establishment in that country of a *national* home for the
Jewish people.[168]

Such interpretations are fallacious because, *inter alia*, they
involve a violation of both safeguard clauses.

The Mandate for Palestine was, under the primary
authority of the League of Nations Covenant, the basic
constitutional document for the interim government of
Palestine agreed to by the League of Nations.[169] Its provisions, therefore, are of particular importance in implementing the juridical limitations imposed by the Balfour
Declaration as an integral part of the Mandate. It is
fundamental that no part of the Palestine Mandate could be
valid if it were in violation of any provisions of the League of
Nations Covenant. The Covenant was the preeminent
constitutional instrument of the organized world community
of the time and the Palestine Mandate was authorized by it
and subject to its limitations.[170] For example, the provisional
granting of independence to Palestine by the Covenant could
not be withdrawn or limited by the Palestine Mandate. In the
same way, the Mandate was juridically limited by "the sacred
trust of civilisation" for the benefit of the inhabitants of the
mandated territory.

Article 2 of the Mandate makes the Mandatory Government responsible for placing the country under such
conditions "as will secure the establishment of the Jewish
national home, as laid down in the preamble ... ."[171] The
word "the " in reference to the national home enterprise is
not significant juridically since it is specifically limited by the
terms "as laid down in the preamble" which refer to "a"
national home. It is of particular importance that this article

---

168. Note 160 *supra* at 55.

169. The British Government's Palestine Order in Council of Aug. 10, 1922
sets forth the municipal governmental structure under the Palestine
Mandate. It is in Stoyanovsky, *supra* note 160 at 363.

170. *League of Nations Covenant* art. 20(1) prohibited past or future
agreements by its members which were inconsistent with the Covenant.

171. Note 166 *supra* at 2185.

makes the Mandatory responsible for "the development of self-governing institutions"[172] for the existing inhabitants of Palestine. This basic provision appears to be both reasonable and necessary to implement the Palestinian independence provisionally recognized in the League Covenant. Article 2 also obligates the Mandatory, consistent with the safeguards of the Balfour Declaration, to protect "the civil and religious rights of all the inhabitants of Palestine, irrespective of race and religion."[173]

Article 4 recognizes the Zionist Organization/Jewish Agency "as a public body" and specifies that it is "subject always to the control of the administration, to assist and take part in the development of the country."[174] This public body status of the Zionist Organization was, of course, subject to each of the further express limitations of the Covenant and the Mandate.[175]

Article 5 is of particular relevance to ensuring the territorial integrity of Palestine and states in full:

> The Mandatory shall be responsible for seeing that no Palestine territory shall be ceded or leased to, or in any way placed under the control of, the Government of any foreign power.[176]

Article 6 considers "Jewish" immigration and, in relevant part, provides:

> The Administration of Palestine, while ensuring that the rights and position of other sections of the population are not prejudiced, shall facilitate Jewish immigration under suitable conditions ... .[177]

---

172. Id.
173. Id.
174. Id.
175. See Chap. 3.
176. Note 166 *supra* at 2185.
177. Id.

Such facilitation of Jewish immigration is consistent with the humanitarian interpretation of the favor clause of the Balfour Declaration. In addition, the facilitation is limited by the requirement that the rights of other sections of the population are not "prejudiced." This provision, with some of its wording taken from the safeguards of the Declaration, is consistent with both the Declaration and the Covenant. Only if Zionist national immigration were to be facilitated in violation of the expressly protected Palestinian rights would there be a violation of article 6.[178]

The first paragraph of article 15 is of particular importance and provides:

> The Mandatory shall see that complete free-dom of conscience and the free exercise of all forms of worship, subject only to the maintenance of public order and morals, are ensured to all. No discrimination of any kind shall be made between the inhabitants of Palestine on the ground of race, religion or language. No person shall be excluded from Palestine on the sole ground of his religious belief.[179]

This is consistent with article 6 concerning immigration and the two articles interpreted together permit the immigration of Jews, as well as adherents of other religions, on a basis of individual equality. The second sentence, which flatly prohibits "discrimination of any kind" between Palestinians, is, of course, entirely consistent with the first safeguard of the Declaration.

In summary, the Zionist "national home" enterprise referred to in the preamble of the Mandate was limited by the inclusion of both safeguards. The Zionist enterprise was also limited by each of the specific provisions of the Mandate for Palestine which has been considered. The Mandate is juridically significant because it involved the multilateral

---

178. Subsequent illegal Zionist immigration is described in *Zionist Diplomacy*, *supra* note 5 at 66–67; 2 *Esco Study, supra* note 5 at 942–55.

179. Note 166 *supra* at 2187.

approval and agreement of the League of Nations to the provisions of the Balfour Declaration. It does not change the juridical interpretation of the Declaration including the lack of legal obligation in the favor clause and the comprehensive and explicit character of the safeguard clauses.

B. THE ANGLO-AMERICAN CONVENTION ON PALESTINE (1924)

The entire League of Nations Mandate for Palestine, including the Balfour Declaration and its safeguards, was set forth in the preamble to the Anglo-American Convention on Palestine.[180] The full scope of United States agreement is enunciated in the first article of the Convention which expressly provides that the United States "consents" or agrees to the British administration of Palestine pursuant to the terms of the Mandate.[181] The United States thus added its authority to the existing agreement to the Mandate and thereby became a party to the Balfour Declaration as it was established as a multilateral agreement through the Palestine Mandate.

An additional purpose of this Convention was to put United States nationals in the same position as nationals of member states of the League of Nations in their business and other activities in Palestine. Article 7 of the Convention provided that no part of the Convention could "be affected by any modification which may be made in the terms of" the Palestine Mandate without the assent of the United States.[182]

C. CUSTOMARY INTERNATIONAL LAW AGREEMENT TO THE DECLARATION

The United Nations General Assembly resolution of November 29, 1947 recommended the partition of Palestine into an Arab state and a "Jewish" state.[183] As to both

---

180. Cited fully in note 163 *supra*.

181. Note 166 *supra* at 2191.

182. *Id.* at 2192.

183. 2 *U.N. GAOR* 131–50 (A/519) (1947).

proposed states, the resolution provided: "The State shall be bound by all the international agreements and conventions, both general and special, to which Palestine has become a party."[184] It is the position of the Government of Israel, however, that it is not bound by the limiting provisions of the Palestine Partition Resolution.[185] In addition, the same Government has enunciated the view that it is not a successor to the Palestine Mandatory Government in terms of being obligated by the international agreements which were applicable to the Palestine Mandate under the League of Nations. In 1949 this view was set forth in a memorandum prepared by the Government of Israel Foreign Ministry and sent to the United States Government. In relevant part it stated:

> It is the view of the Government of Israel that, generally speaking, treaties to which Palestine was a party, or which the Mandatory Government had applied to Palestine, are not in force in relation to the Government of Israel.[186]

It should be noted that this is formulated as a general and not an invariable rule. Thus the Government of Israel may, as an exception to the generalization, continue to rely upon the Balfour Declaration for claimed juridical authority for, *inter alia*, the Zionist territorial claims to Palestine.[187]

It is widely accepted that both the League of Nations Mandate for Palestine and the Anglo-American Convention on Palestine were terminated at the end of the British Mandate. There is no record, however, of any protest by the states which were parties to the Palestine Mandate and to the

---

184. *Id.* at 138.

185. This is illustrated by its seizure of territory in excess of that contemplated in the Resolution. Cattan, note 151 *supra* at 233 (1969) provides a map showing excess territory seized.

186. 2 Whiteman, *Digest of International Law* 972 (1963).

187. Other examples of the use of the Balfour Declaration as alleged authority for Zionist juridical claims before and after 1948 are provided in Chap. 2 *passim*.

Anglo-American Convention concerning the Zionist-Israel claims which rely upon the continuing validity of the Declaration. In particular, neither the United States nor Great Britain has protested.[188] The Declaration is thereby established as international law through the recognized customary law-making processes of the implicit agreement of states expressed by toleration, acquiescence and silence.[189]

There is no doubt that the proponents of the Zionist-Israel claims are no more interested in effectuating the safeguards in recent years than they have been at any earlier time.[190] The result, however, of the establishment of the Balfour Declaration as customary international law is its acceptance as a whole. This undoubtedly creates a very difficult situation for the State of Israel and its juridically linked Zionist Organization[191] because of the systematic and continuing character of the violation of both of the safeguard clauses.[192]

VI. International Law Limitations upon the Declaration

The Balfour Declaration, agreed to by the League of Nations and the United States and established in customary law, must be interpreted consistently with the basic limita-

---

188. Such protests would not be expected because of the protective purposes of the Declaration.

189. American Law Institute, *Restatement of the Foreign Relations Law of the United States* 3 (1965) emphasizes the law-making importance of failure of a state to object. Other authorities and examples concerning customary law-making appear in Chap. 2.

190. Jiryis, *The Arabs in Israel 1948–1966, passim* (Dobson transl., Inst. for Palestine Studies, Beirut, 1968) documents systematic violations of the first safeguard.

191. The juridical linking and subordination of the Organization as a political instrument of the Government of Israel is done through the Zionist Organization/Jewish Agency Status Law, 7 Israel Laws, *supra* note 1 at 3(1952), and the Covenant Between the Government of Israel and the Zionist Executive (1954). Both are appraised in Chap. 2 and printed in Appendices 5 and 6.

192. Note 190 *supra*.

tions of international law which apply to any international agreement. Professors McDougal, Lasswell, and Miller, with appropriate recognition of the necessity of according preeminence to the fundamental doctrines of international law over the subsidiary ones, have written: "The public order takes priority over particular agreements that contravene its fundamental values and institutions."[193] Unless this principle is implemented, the result could be the frustration of the fundamental values of the international public order by a plethora of destructive subsidiary agreements. This is merely a recognition in the international community of the same principle of constitutional priority which is established in the municipal order systems.

The twelfth of President Woodrow Wilson's fourteen points dealt specifically with the non-Turkish portions of the Ottoman Empire and provided:

> [T]he other [non-Turkish] nationalities which are now under Turkish rule should be assured an undoubted security of life and an absolutely unmolested opportunity of autonomous development ... .[194]

It need only be mentioned that Palestine was in no way excepted from this principle.

On February 11, 1918 President Wilson delivered a detailed address concerning the ultimate peace to be obtained to a Joint Session of the United States Congress. Of the four norms enunciated by the President, two have direct application to Palestine:

> Second, that peoples and provinces are not to be bartered about from sovereignty to sovereignty as if they were mere chattels and pawns in a game, even the great game, now forever discredited, of the balance of power; but that

---

193. McDougal, Lasswell, & Miller, *The Interpretation of Agreements and World Public Order* 261 (1967).

194. [1918] *Foreign Rels. U.S.*, Vol. 1, Supp. No. 1, at 12, 16 (1933).

> Third, every territorial settlement involved in this war must be made in the interest and for the benefit of the populations concerned, and not as a part of any mere adjustment or compromise of claims amongst rival states ... .[195]

The Balfour Declaration may only be upheld as valid under these criteria if the favor clause is interpreted as a humanitarian provision for refugee Jews. In the same way, the first safeguard must be given a sufficiently broad interpretation to make it consistent with "the benefit of the populations concerned."

President Wilson spelled out the juridical concept of self-determination of peoples with particularity in the same statement:

> Peoples are not to be handed about from one sovereignty to another by an international conference or an understanding between rivals and antagonists. National aspirations must be respected; peoples may now be dominated and governed only by their own consent. "Self-determination" is not a mere phrase. It is an imperative principle of action, which statesmen will henceforth ignore at their peril. We cannot have general peace for the asking, or by the mere arrangements of a peace conference. It cannot be pieced together out of individual understandings between powerful states.[196]

It would be difficult indeed, even with the advantage of the knowledge of Zionist objectives and practices revealed during the past five decades, to enunciate an "imperative principle" which would be more inconsistent with the territorial objectives of Zionism in Palestine.

The principles of the peace settlement promulgated by President Wilson and reflected in the League of Nations

---

195. *Id.* at 108, 112.
196. *Id.* at 110.

Covenant have been applied to Palestine by the King–Crane Commission. This Commission was sent to Palestine and the Near East by President Wilson to ascertain the facts and to make recommendations. Its recommendations are based upon a careful study and analysis of the relevant evidence.[197] The Report of the Commission refers particularly to the recognition of the provisional independence of "certain communities formerly belonging to the Turkish Empire" by the Covenant of the League of Nations.[198] The report states:

> In his address of July 4, 1918, President Wilson laid down the following principle as one of the four great "ends for which the associated peoples of the world were fighting": "The settlement of every question, whether of territory, of sovereignty, of economic arrangement, or of political relationship upon the basis of the free acceptance of that settlement by the people immediately concerned, and not upon the basis of the material interest or advantage of any other nation or people which may desire a different settlement for the sake of its own exterior influence or mastery". If that principle is to rule, and so the wishes of Palestine's population are to be decisive as to what is to be done with Palestine, then it is to be remembered that the non-Jewish population of Palestine – nearly nine-tenths of the whole – are emphatically against the entire Zionist program. The tables show that there was no one thing upon which the population of Palestine were more agreed than upon this. To subject a people so minded to unlimited Jewish immigration, and to steady financial and social pressure to

---

197. The authoritative study and evaluation of the importance of the King–Crane Commission is Howard, *The King–Crane Commission* (1963). Professor Howard appraises the recommendations made concerning Palestine as fair and involving a limited Jewish "national home" consistent with Palestinian rights. *Id.* at 320–21.

198. [1919] *Foreign Rels. U.S.*, Vol. 12 at 784 (1947).

surrender the land, would be a gross violation of the principle just quoted, and of the peoples' rights, though it kept within the forms of law.[199]

The Commission then quoted the relevant resolutions of the "General Syrian [including Palestinian] Congress" adopted on July 6, 1919 as an authentic manifestation of the views of the people inhabiting the country:

7. We oppose the pretentions of the Zionists to create a Jewish commonwealth in the southern part of Syria, known as Palestine, and oppose Zionist migration to any part of our country; for we do not acknowledge their title, but consider them a grave peril to our people from the national, economical, and political points of view. Our Jewish compatriots shall enjoy our common rights and assume the common responsibilities.

8. We ask that there should be no separation of the southern part of Syria known as Palestine nor of the littoral western zone which includes Lebanon from the Syrian country. We desire that the unity of the country should be guaranteed against partition under whatever circumstances.

10. The fundamental principles laid down by President Wilson in condemnation of secret treaties impel us to protest most emphatically against any treaty that stipulates the partition of our Syrian country and against any private engagement aiming at the establishment of Zionism in the southern part of Syria; therefore we ask the complete annulment of these conventions and agreements.[200]

199. *Id.* at 793.
200. *Id.*

The recommendations of the King–Crane Commission concerning Palestine include the following:

> We recommend, in the fifth place, serious modification of the extreme Zionist Program for Palestine of unlimited immigration of Jews, looking finally to making Palestine distinctly a Jewish State.
>
> (1) The Commissioners began their study of Zionism with minds predisposed in its favor, but the actual facts in Palestine, coupled with the force of the general principles proclaimed by the Allies and accepted by the Syrians have driven them to the recommendation here made.
>
> (3) The Commission recognized also that definite encouragement had been given to the Zionists by the Allies in Mr. Balfour's often quoted statement, in its approval by other representatives of the Allies. If, however, the strict terms of the Balfour Statement are adhered to – favoring "the establishment in Palestine of a national home for the Jewish people", "it being clearly understood that nothing shall be done which may prejudice the civil and religious rights of existing non-Jewish communities in Palestine" – it can hardly be doubted that the extreme Zionist Program must be greatly modified. For "a national home for the Jewish people" is not equivalent to making Palestine into a Jewish State; nor can the erection of such a Jewish State be accomplished without the gravest trespass upon the "civil and religious rights of existing non-Jewish communities in Palestine". The fact came out repeatedly in the Commission's conference with Jewish representatives, that the Zionists look forward to a practically complete dispossession of the present non-Jewish inhabitants of Palestine, by various forms of purchase.[201]

---

201. *Id.* at 792.

This analysis is, in the substance of its interpretation, the same as the one adopted in the present study.

The Commissioners also stated:

> The Peace Conference should not shut its eyes to the fact that the anti-Zionist feeling in Palestine and Syria is intense and not lightly to be flouted. No British officer, consulted by the Commissioners, believed that the Zionist program could be carried out except by force of arms. The officers generally thought that a force of not less than fifty thousand soldiers would be required even to initiate the program. That of itself is evidence of a strong sense of the injustice of the Zionist program, on the part of the non-Jewish populations of Palestine and Syria. Decisions, requiring armies to carry out, are sometimes necessary, but they are surely not gratuitously to be taken in the interests of a serious injustice. For the initial claim, often submitted by Zionist representatives, that they have a "right" to Palestine, based on an occupation of two thousand years ago, can hardly be seriously considered.[202]

Mr. Balfour, in a memorandum of August 11, 1919 to the British Government (intended for official use only) stated in relevant part:

> The contradiction between the letter of the Covenant and the policy of the Allies is even more flagrant in the case of the "independent nation" of Palestine than in that of the "independent nation" of Syria. For in Palestine we do not propose even to go through the form of consulting the wishes of the present inhabitants of the country, though the

---

202. *Id.* at 794. In the actual event the Zionist conquest of Palestine was accomplished by military force including the use of terror.

Concerning the Zionist alleged historic right to Palestine, it is significant that an Israeli legal writer does not even mention it in a book dealing with historic titles. Blum, *Historic Titles in International Law* (1965).

American [King–Crane] Commission has been going through the form of asking what they are. The four Great Powers are committed to Zionism. And Zionism, be it right or wrong, good or bad, is rooted in age-long traditions, in present needs, in future hopes, of far profounder import than the desires and prejudices of the 700,000 Arabs who now inhabit that ancient land.

In my opinion that is right. What I have never been able to understand is how it can be harmonised with the declaration, the Covenant, or the instructions to the Commission of Enquiry.

... In short, so far as Palestine is concerned, the Powers have made no statement of fact which is not admittedly wrong, and no declaration of policy which, at least in the letter, they have not always intended to violate.[203]

The fundamental inconsistencies between the Zionist territorial objectives in Palestine and both the Balfour Declaration and the League of Nations Covenant are among the major conclusions of the present study. It is important that scholars and others who value human dignity and equal rights for all address themselves to the task of enforcing the Balfour Declaration as now established in customary law and as interpreted consistently with the governing requirements of international law.

---

203. [1919] *Documents on British Foreign Policy 1919–1939*, First Series, Vol. 4 at 340, 345 (Woodward & Butler eds., 1952).

Chapter 2

The Juridical Status and Political Activities of the Zionist Organization/Jewish Agency

I. The Basic Juridical Issues

This inquiry considers two principal groups of issues. The first group concerns the present juridical status of the Zionist Organization. The historic claims to constitute the Zionist Organization as a public body will be considered also since they are indispensable to an understanding of the present legal status.

The second group of issues concerns the relationship in law of the Zionist Organization to certain national states. Its nexus to the British Government prior to and during the League of Nations Mandate for Palestine and its relation to the State of Israel from 1948 to the present must both be examined. Some examples of the relationship between the Zionist Organization and the United States Government are also provided.

II. The Context of the "Jewish People" Claims and Their Continuing Implementation

The "Jewish people" nationality claims are the core of Zionist public law.

A fundamental postulate of Zionism must be summarized at the beginning in order to provide clarity for the subsequent appraisal. Zionism is based upon an acceptance of anti-Semitism now and has been so based since its inception in 1897. Illustration may be provided from the words of Dr. Theodor Herzl:

We naturally move to those places where we are not persecuted, and there our presence produces persecution. This is the case in every country, and will remain so, even in those highly civilized – for instance, France – till the Jewish question finds a solution on a political basis. The unfortunate Jews are now carrying Anti-Semitism into England; they have already introduced it into America.[1]

Zionism and its "Jewish State" act upon the postulate that anti-Semitism is fundamental and ineradicable. The Zionist juridical objectives that "the Jewish people" be constituted as an additional nationality entity, membership in which is to be conferred upon all Jews, are based upon this postulate.[2] The "Jewish people" concept is used to recruit Jewish immigration to Israel and to achieve other Zionist political objectives. The Zionist "solution" to anti-Semitism is to "ingather" all Jews into the State of Israel.

A contemporary illustration of the importance of anti-Semitism as a guide to Zionist action is provided by Arthur Hertzberg, a leading proponent of Zionism in the United States:

> The assumption that anti-Semitism "makes sense" and that it can be put to constructive uses – this is at once the subtlest, most daring, and most optimistic conception to be found in political Zionism. . . . What is new in Herzl is that, assuming, as the heir of assimilation, that anti-Semitism is rational, he boldly turned this idea outward into the international arena.[3]

The "Jewish people" concept is consistently advanced as

---

1.   Herzl, *The Jewish State: An Attempt at a Modern Solution of the Jewish Question* 19, 20 (D'Avigdor & Cohen transl. 1943). The centrality of this concept is also stressed in the introduction in the text at note 31.

2.   Mallison, "The Zionist-Israel Juridical claims to Constitute 'The Jewish People' Nationality Entity and to Confer Membership in It: Appraisal in Public International Law," 32 Geo. Wash. L. Rev. 983–1075 (1964) [cited hereafter as The "Jewish People" Study].

3.   Hertzberg (ed.), *The Zionist Idea: A Historical Analysis and Reader*, Introduction at 49 (1966) [cited hereafter as Hertzberg, *Zionist Idea*].

a juridical claim in international law decision-making contexts. A particularly well known example involved the exploitation of the claim in the *Eichmann Case*.[4] The Nazi murder of millions of innocent men, women, and children is one of the most tragic events of the present century. All moral individuals of whatever national or religious identification share revulsion at those who perpetrated these crimes. A large group of victims was designated by the Nazis as "Jews." Other designated groups included, *inter alia,* "Poles," "Gypsies," and "Slavs." Many other civilians throughout Europe were also murdered by the Nazis even though they could not be included properly in even the most extended definitions of the specified victim groups. These crimes have been established by overwhelming evidence, including documents prepared by the Nazis themselves, in the forty-two volumes of *The Trial of the Major War Criminals Before the International Military Tribunal* at Nuremberg,[5] as well as in other post-war trials.

The juridical concept of crimes against humanity (as opposed to a concept of crimes against the victims and their co-religionists alone) was firmly established in international law by the principal *Nuremberg Trial* and other post-World War II trials.[6] The jurisdictional authority derived from crimes against humanity is a very extensive one which is usually termed universality of jurisdiction. "Universality," in this jurisdictional sense, authorizes any state having custody of the accused to try him without regard to the geographic location and time elements of the acts alleged to constitute the crime against humanity. In addition, the national state trying the accused may not discriminate upon

---

4. *The Attorney-General of the Government of Israel v. Adolf Eichmann*, 36 Int'l L. Reps. 18–276 (Dist. Ct. of Jerusalem, Israel, Dec. 11–12, 1961), aff'd 36 *id.* 277–342 (Sup. Ct. of Israel, May 29, 1962).

5. Official Text of the International Military Tribunal, Nuremberg (1947) [cited hereafter as I.M.T.]. See the Judgment of the Tribunal, 1 I.M.T. 171.

6. See *e.g. United States v. Ohlendorf* ("The Einsatzgruppen Case"), 4 Trials of War Criminals Before the Nuernberg Military Tribunals 1, 496–500 (1948).

the basis of the national identity of the accused or that of the alleged victim.[7]

The evidence produced before the Israeli trial court in the case against Adolph Eichmann appears to be ample to establish his guilt for crimes against humanity. If this had been the principal charge against Eichmann,[8] it seems probable that Israel would have been entitled to invoke universality of jurisdiction. It is particularly significant that the Israeli court in the *Eichmann Case*[9] paid only lip service to the concept of crimes against humanity.[10] Principal emphasis was placed upon the Zionist concept of "crimes against the Jewish people" nationality status of Eichmann's victims. Similarly, the Israeli court preferred to base its jurisdictional claim to try Eichmann principally upon the alleged link between the State of Israel and "the Jewish people" rather than upon the recognized authority of universality of jurisdiction.[11]

---

7. The requirements of universality of jurisdiction stated in the text are based upon the decisions of the post-Second World War trials conducted by the United States and its allies. The juridical formulation is reflected in Lauterpacht, *International Law* 753 (8th ed., 1955).
Israel 154 (Authorized Translation, 1950) [cited hereafter as Israel Laws, Lauterpacht, *International Law* 753 (8th ed. 1955).

8. Eichmann was also charged with crimes against humanity, but the principal charge was "crimes against the Jewish people." See the Israeli "Nazis and Nazi Collaborators (Punishment) Law," 4 Laws of the State of Israel 154 (Authorized Translation, 1950) [cited hereafter as *Israel Laws*], defining "crimes against the Jewish people." This Israeli statute was applied in the Eichmann Case cited *supra* note 4.

9. *Supra* note 5.

10. The Israeli trial court stated:

> It is superfluous to add that the "crime against the Jewish people", which constitutes the crime of "genocide", is nothing but the gravest type of "crime against humanity" (and all the more so because both under Israel law and under the Convention a special intention is requisite for its commission, an intention that is not required for the commission of a "crime against humanity").

Eichmann Trial Judgment cited *supra* note 4 at 41. In a conception of law based upon respect for the individual, "crimes against humanity" are of equal gravity without regard to the religious identification of the victim.

11. *Id.*

A sense of reality concerning the *Eichmann Case* can be achieved by examination of the following excerpts from it:

If an effective link (not necessarily an identity) existed between the State of Israel and the Jewish people, then a crime intended to exterminate the Jewish people has an indubitable connection with the State of Israel.

The connection between the State of Israel and the Jewish people needs no explanation. The State of Israel was established and recognised as the State of the Jews. . . . It would appear that there is hardly need for any further proof of the very obvious connection between the Jewish people and the State of Israel: this is the sovereign State of the Jewish people.

* * *

In view of the recognition by the United Nations of the right of the Jewish people to establish their State, and in the light of the recognition of the established Jewish State by the family of nations, the connection between the Jewish people and the State of Israel constitutes an integral part of the law of nations.[12]

It is significant that the claim of juridical connection between "the Jewish people" and the State of Israel is set forth not as a claim, but as though it were already established as "an integral part of the law of nations." The Zionist objection to basing the claim to jurisdictional authority upon the established concepts of crimes against humanity and ensuing universality of jurisdiction, as opposed to merely giving lip service to them, is that the established concepts recognize the membership of Jews in the common humanity of all. Such recognition is inconsistent with a purpose of "the

---

12.   *Eichmann Trial Judgment* cited *supra* note 4 at 52–53. Penetrating criticism of the Eichmann trial is provided in T. Taylor, "Large Questions in the Eichmann Case," *N.Y. Times Magazine* 11 (Jan. 22, 1961).

Jewish people" nationality claims which is to separate Jews from other individuals in public law. Thus, in the Zionist public law conception of the *Eichmann Case*, the regular nationality status of Jewish victims of the Nazis was ignored or minimized in favor of their alleged nationality status as members of "the Jewish people." The Zionist objective was to show that only the Zionist State of Israel seeks to protect the Jewish victims of the Nazis.[13] In contrast, the principal *Nuremberg Trial* and the subsequent war crimes trials employed the concepts of crimes against humanity and universality of jurisdiction without discrimination based upon the religious or national identity of the victims or the accused.[14]

The United States Department of State has responded to the "Jewish people" concept as follows:

> The Department of State recognizes the State of Israel as a sovereign State and citizenship of the State of Israel. It recognizes no other sovereignty or citizenship in connection therewith. It does not recognize a legal-political relationship based upon the religious identification of American citizens. It does not in any way discriminate among American citizens upon the basis of their religion.
>
> Accordingly, it should be clear that the Department of State does not regard the "Jewish people" concept as a concept of international law.[15]

Although this indicates official rejection of the "Jewish

---

13. The same conclusion is reached in Rogat, *The Eichmann Trial and the Rule of Law* 15–17 and *passim* (1961).

14. In addition, no discrimination was permitted where victim or accused either had or lacked religious or national identity or both. See *e.g.*, *United States v. Ohlendorf*, *supra* note 6 at 499 involving crimes against humanity where the victims were identified, factually but without juridical discrimination, as German Jews.

15. Letter from Assistant Secretary of State Talbot to Dr. Elmer Berger, Executive Vice President of the American Council for Judaism, April 20, 1964 in 8 Whiteman, *Digest of International Law* 35 (1967).

people" claim as "a concept of international law," there are interesting questions which remain concerning the efforts to implement the concept.

It is an error to regard the establishment of the State of Israel as the end of Zionism and its "Jewish people" concept. The establishment of the State is regarded by the Government of Israel and the Zionist Organization as only one step in obtaining assent to the "Jewish people" claims in law.[16] Another key step, consisting of a wide range of subordinate public law measures including municipal statutes, involves imposing "Jewish people" nationality law obligations upon Jews who are nationals of states other than Israel.[17] In addition, the working relationships between the Zionist Organization and the Government of Israel are based directly upon the "Jewish people" concept and, in particular, its implementation through the recruiting of Jewish immigrants.[18] This recruitment constitutes, in Zionist-Israel practice and law, both a national "right" of "the Jewish people" (and no other)[19] and the long range objective of "gathering in the exiles" (meaning all of "the Jewish people") into the State of Israel.[20]

The "Jewish people" nationality claims include the claim of collective political obligations from all Jews to the State of Israel. Former Prime Minister Ben Gurion has stated it in specific terms:

---

16. The continuing claims after the establishment of the State of Israel are examined in *The "Jewish People" Study, supra* note 2, 1036–49. The continuing use of the "Jewish people" claim is illustrated by Israeli representatives at the United Nations. See, *e.g.*, the statement of Ambassador Yehuda Blum, the Permanent Representative of Israel, on the floor of the General Assembly when the agenda item "Question of Palestine" was being considered on 2 Dec. 1980 in which he advanced the "Jewish people" claim five times. 35 *G.A. Provisional Verbatim Record,* A/35/PV.77 at 46.

17. The Israel Status Law (1952) examined *infra* in Sec. V B.

18. The Zionist-Israel Coordination Board examined *infra* in Sec. V C.

19. The Israel Law of Return provides in sec. 1: "Every Jew has the right to come to this country as an *oleh"* [Jewish immigrant]. 4 Israel Laws 114.

20. The Status Law, sec. 4, examined in Sec. V B *infra*.

> First of all there is the collective duty of the
> Zionist Organization and of the Zionist Move-
> ment to assist the State of Israel in all conditions
> and under any circumstances towards accomp-
> lishment of 4 central matters – the Ingathering of
> the Exiles, the building up of the country, security
> and the absorption and fusion of the Dispersions
> within the State.
>
> This signifies assisting the State whether the
> government to which the Jews in question owe
> allegiance desire [sic] it or not ... .[21]

The double loyalty issue is recognized by some of the Zionist
political elite and dealt with in apparent double talk. For
example, Mr. Berl Locker, speaking as chairman of the
Zionist Executive at a Session of the Zionist General Council,
stated as one of "the basic doctrines of Zionism in the present
day":

> The State of Israel lays no claim to the political
> loyalty of Jews resident in other countries. Jews
> are good citizens in all countries of their domicile
> and especially in the countries in which they enjoy
> equal rights. *But Jews as a community do possess a
> collective loyalty to the State of Israel, as Israel is the
> national home of the entire Jewish people.*[22]

On its face this statement is ambiguous since it can be
interpreted textually as meaning either single or double
loyalty. A Zionist statement, however, must usually be
interpreted in greater depth than "on its face." The italics in
the original indicate, of course, the relatively greater
significance of the italicized statement concerning the loyalty
of Jews to the State of Israel. Further analysis requires a basic
understanding of Zionist public law. Such law is concerned

---

21.   Article entitled "Tasks and Character of a Modern Zionist," based on a
speech delivered at the World Conference of Haichud Haolami on Aug. 8,
1951, *Jerusalem Post*, Aug. 17, 1951 at 5, cols. 3–8 at cols. 4–5.

22.   Organization Dept. of the Zionist Executive, *Session of the Zionist General
Council* 44 (July 21–29, 1954) [hereafter cited as *Zionist General Council*].

almost exclusively with collective rights and duties consistent with the collective "Jewish people" concept. From this perspective the statements which are not in italics have no Zionist significance since they are only concerned with individual Jews ("good citizens"). The italicized statement concerns the Zionist concept of the "entire Jewish people" as well as the lower level concept of "Jews as a community." Since Zionism is concerned with collective rights and duties, this is the only part of the quotation which has meaning to Zionists.[23]

III. The Subjects of International Law

Since the Zionist Organization has claimed status as a public body, a brief consideration of the subjects of international law is essential. It is widely recognized that the subjects of international law are no longer limited to national states.[24] A memorandum of the Secretary-General of the United Nations has described the current situation as follows: "Practice has abandoned the doctrine that States are the exclusive subjects of international rights and duties."[25] Among the subjects of international law other than states, international public bodies or organizations are of particular importance. In addition to the well known examples, a number of which are associated with the United Nations,

---

23. McDougal & Gardner, in "The Veto and the Charter: An Interpretation for Survival," 60 *Yale L. J.* 258, 263 (1951), state:

> For understanding any communication the relevant and indispensable questions are: Who, says What, to Whom, for what Objectives, How, under what Conditions, and with what Effects.

24. McDougal, Lasswell & Reisman, "The World Constitutive Process of Authoritative Decision," 19 *J. of Legal Ed.* 253, 263–67 (1967), describes five participants or subjects including national states.

25. Memorandum of the Secretary-General of the United Nations, *Survey of International Law in Relation to the Work of Codification of the International Law Commission*, A/cn.4/Rev.1, p. 19 (Feb. 10, 1949).

there are many less well known public bodies including the Sovereign Order of Malta.[26]

Public bodies are usually constituted as subjects of international law through the explicit multilateral agreement of states (conventional law),[27] and there is no authority for a state to constitute an international public body unilaterally. Such bodies may, on occasion, be constituted by necessary implication drawn from an appraisal of their substantive powers. The United Nations, in spite of its preeminent position as the principal general function public body, is not explicitly constituted as a public body by its Charter. The International Court of Justice in the *United Nations Reparation Opinion*,[28] however, determined that the United Nations enjoys international juridical status or "personality" as a necessary implication from the substantive powers which are granted to it by the Charter. It would have been unsound to allow the substantive grants of power to be frustrated through the failure to find the ancillary status or personality. The Court found the United Nations to be a "subject of international law and [a body] capable of possessing international rights and duties ... ." The present significance of the opinion is that it illustrates the empirical analysis which must be made in an inquiry concerning status as a public body-subject of international law.

In answering the question as to whether or not the Zionist Organization has been constituted as a public body the same empirical tests must be employed. Professor Lauterpacht has provided these succinct criteria:

> [I]n each particular case the question whether a
> person or a body is a subject of international law

---

26. See Farran, "The Sovereign Order of Malta in International Law," 3 *Int'l and Comp. L. Q.* 217 (1954); Farran, "The Sovereign Order of Malta: A Supplementary Note," 4 *id.* at 308 (1955).

27. See American Law Institute, *Restatement of the Foreign Relations Law of the United States* (1965) [cited hereafter as *Restatement*], sec. 5(a) of which defines an international organization, in part, as created by an international agreement.

28. *Advisory Opinion on Reparation for Injuries Suffered in the Service of the United Nations*, [1949] I.C.J. Reps. 174.

must be answered in a pragmatic manner by reference to actual experience and to the reason of the law as distinguished from a preconceived notion as to who can be subjects of international law.[29]

The principal juridical consequence of status as a public body, of course, is subjection to the law.[30] There can be no grant of powers and status as a public body without the accompanying legal obligations of a subject of the law. These obligations include, at the minimum, both the specific legal limitations imposed upon the public body and the general legal limitations which apply to all subjects of international law.

IV. The Claims to Constitute the Zionist Organization as a Public Body from the First Zionist Congress to the Termination of the League of Nations Mandate for Palestine (1897–1948)

A. THE EARLY CLAIMS TO CONSTITUTE THE ZIONIST ORGANIZATION AS A PUBLIC BODY (1897-1917)

The relevant activities of the First Zionist Congress, which met in Basle in 1897, have been summarized in Chapter 1. The analysis of the present chapter emphasizes the second point of the Basle Program (the "organization and binding together of the whole of Jewry" through appropriate means). It is clear that in Zionist conception the Zionist Organization was claimed to be a public body representing all Jews from its inception.[31] Such a claim standing alone is, however, not the equivalent of authoritative international decision. In order to constitute the claimant as a public

---

29. Lauterpacht, *International Law and Human Rights* 12 (1950).

30. *E.g.*, the *Mavrommatis Palestine Concessions Cases* considered and cited in Sec. IV D *infra*.

31. At Basle, Herzl described the Zionist Organization as "an agency for the Jewish people" intended to negotiate with governments. First Zionist Congress Address of Aug. 29, 1897 in Hertzberg, *Zionist Idea, supra* note 3 at 226. See particularly *id.* at 228, 230.

body-subject of international law, the assent of the community of states is required. Dr. Herzl, as the first president of the Zionist Organization, nevertheless conducted negotiations with the German Kaiser and the Turkish Sultan as if the Organization were a valid public body.[32] The results of these negotiations were negative. Herzl received no support either for the Zionist Organization or for Zionist immigration. In 1903 the Zionist Organization negotiated for and obtained a British proposal for Zionist colonization in Uganda. This was presented to the Sixth Zionist Congress and, although Herzl favored it, the proposal was not implemented.[33] Perhaps the mere conduct of these diplomatic negotiations resulted in a small measure of recognition of the Zionist Organization as a public body. If so, it did not amount to the international community assent required to constitute such a body in law.

The Balfour Declaration necessarily involved the implicit recognition by the British Government of the public body status of the Zionist Organization because Weizmann and his associates acted on behalf of organized Zionism and not as private individuals.[34] The Declaration manifested the British view that the Organization had the juridical status to receive the precatory clause as well as to be subjected to the legal limitations embodied in the safeguards. Although this still did not amount to the according of public body status by the community of states, it was a significant step toward this objective. The political "alliance"[35] between the Zionist Organization and the British Government allowed the former to participate in the Paris Peace Conference of 1919 where a further step to the objective could be taken.

---

32. 1 Esco Foundation for Palestine, *Palestine: A Study of Jewish, Arab, and British Policies* 42–45 (1947) [hereafter cited as *Esco Study*]; Taylor, *Prelude to Israel: An Analysis of Zionist Diplomacy 1897–1947* at 6–7 (1959) [cited hereafter as *Zionist Diplomacy*].

33. 1 *Esco Study* 48–49; *Zionist Diplomacy* 7.

34. See *supra* Chap. 1 *passim.*

35. The quoted term appears in 1 *Esco Study* 74.

B. THE ZIONIST ORGANIZATION AT THE PARIS PEACE CONFERENCE (1919)

Representatives of the Zionist Organization were invited to appear before the Supreme Council of the Peace Conference and on February 27, 1919 Dr. Weizmann and Nahum Sokolow addressed the Council and commented on several aspects of an official Zionist memorandum which had been sent to the Supreme Council on February 3, 1919.[36] Among the Zionist proposals was the creation of a "Jewish Council" which should have the status of "a legal entity" and which was designed, *inter alia*, to implement the Zionist "national home" project in Palestine.[37]

These events may be regarded as a tentative multilateral recognition of the Zionist Organization as a public body. Professor Feinberg, a leading Zionist legal scholar, suggests that the Zionist Organization "as the representative of the Jewish people" was probably granted a status "actually equivalent to that of the neutral States" at the Peace Conference.[38] Whether this view is accurate or not, the important point is that the status accorded to the Organization at the Peace Conference would lead shortly to unequivocal public body status.

C. THE ZIONIST ORGANIZATION AS A PUBLIC BODY CONSTITUTED BY THE MANDATE FOR PALESTINE

The Zionist Organization enjoyed a privileged position through its political alliance with the British Government and, as a result, participated in the drafting of the Mandate for Palestine.[39] Although the Zionists did not achieve all of their political objectives, a number were incorporated in the

---

36. *Zionist Diplomacy* 26.

37. The Zionist Memorandum appears in 2 *Diplomacy in the Near and Middle East* 45 (Hurewitz ed. 1956); 5 Miller, *My Diary at the Conference of Paris* 15 (1924).

38. Feinberg, "The Recognition of the Jewish People in International Law," *Jewish Yearbook of International Law 1948*, p. 14 (1949).

39. 1 *Esco Study*, cited *supra* note 32 at 151–77.

terms of the Mandate. Certain portions of it concern the functions and status of the Zionist Organization.

The preamble to the Mandate incorporated the substance of the Balfour Declaration and spelled out its safeguard clauses in full.[40] Thus it endeavored to protect the rights of the "existing non-Jewish communities in Palestine" and the rights "enjoyed by Jews in any other country" [than Palestine].

Article 4 is the most important provision concerning the Zionist Organization. It provides, in full:

> An appropriate Jewish agency shall be recognized as a public body for the purpose of advising and co-operating with the Administration of Palestine in such economic, social and other matters as may affect the establishment of the Jewish national home and the interests of the Jewish population in Palestine, and subject always to the control of the Administration, to assist and take part in the development of the country.
>
> The Zionist organisation, so long as its organisation and constitution are in the opinion of the Mandatory appropriate, shall be recognised as such agency. It shall take steps in consultation with His Britannic Majesty's Government to secure the cooperation of all Jews who are willing to assist in the establishment of the Jewish national home.[41]

---

40. The entire Mandate is set forth as the preamble to the Anglo-American Convention on Palestine, 44 U.S. Stat. 2184 (1925). It also appears in 2 UNSCOP, *Report to the General Assembly, 2 U.N. GAOR, Supp. 11*, pp. 18–22, U.N. Doc. A/364 Add. 1 (9 Sept. 1947), and in Stoyanovsky, *The Mandate for Palestine* 355 (1928), and 2 *Diplomacy in the Near and Middle East, supra* note 37 at 106.

41. *Id*. The future tense [*e.g.* "shall be recognized"] was used in the wording because the Mandate was drafted before it was approved by the Council of the League. Upon the effectuation of the Mandate on Sept. 29, 1922, the words, in the legal sense, were read as the present tense.

Thus the League of Nations, acting on behalf of the world community of the time, constituted the Zionist Organization as a public body. This was done without the participation of the United States which was not a member of the League.[42] The "Jewish agency" referred to is the "Jewish Council" requested in the Zionist memorandum to the Paris Conference.[43] From the time of the effectuation of the Palestine Mandate, the terms "Zionist Organization" and "Jewish Agency" have been simply different names for the same public body[44] which as a subject of international law possessed certain powers and was bound in law to observe the limitations on its powers.

Other provisions of article 4 concern the legal limitations which are imposed. The first paragraph describes the public body as having purposes which concern the "Jewish national home" and the "Jews in Palestine." The last portion of the same paragraph makes the Zionist Organization "subject always to the control of the Administration," thereby subordinating the public body to the British Government. Further explicit legal limitations appear in the second paragraph. The first sentence recognizes the Zionist public body status only while its "organisation and constitution are satisfactory to the Mandatory Government." Finally, the international activities of the Zionist Organization in behalf of the "national home" enterprise may be performed only in consultation with the British Government. In summary, article 4 constitutes the Zionist Organization as a public body

---

42. The United States agreed to the terms of the Mandate in the Anglo-American Convention on Palestine cited *supra* note 40.

43. See the text accompanying *supra* note 37.

44. The names quoted in the text, consistent with official Zionist sources, use a capital letter at the beginning of each word even though art. 4 of the Mandate uses a lower case letter at the beginning of the second word in each name.

while simultaneously imposing explicit legal limitations upon it.[45]

Other articles provide for further public functions of the Organization/Agency. Article 6 directs the Palestine Administration to promote "Jewish immigration" and, "in cooperation with the Jewish agency," to facilitate the settlement of Jews on the land. Article 11 concerns the development of "public works, services, and utilities," and provides that the administration of Palestine "subject to any international obligations accepted by the Mandatory, shall have full power to provide for public ownership or control of any of the natural resources of the country or of the public works, services and utilities ... ." A further provision of the same article states:

> The Administration may arrange with the Jewish agency mentioned in Article 4 to construct or operate upon fair and equitable terms, any public works services and utilities, and to develop any of the natural resources of the country, in so far as these matters are not directly undertaken by the Administration.

---

45. In 1930 the British Government recognized the "Jewish Agency for Palestine" as the appropriate Jewish agency under the terms of art. 4. Anglo-American Committee of Inquiry, *Report to the United States Government and His Majesty's Government in the United Kingdom* 20 (1946) [hereafter cited as *Anglo-American Report*]. The change was not a real one in substance since the "Jewish Agency for Palestine" was only an "enlarged" Jewish Agency in which "non-Zionists" were supposed to participate. Their participation was never effective and Zionist control continued. Mr. Lasky has written:

> While the Enlarged Agency professed to continue for a time, it was without non-Zionist participation, and the identity of the Zionist Organization and the Agency was at least de facto.

Lasky, *Between Truth and Repose* 70 (1956) [hereafter cited as Lasky]. The Lasky study is subtitled: "The World Zionist Organization, Its Agency for the State of Israel, The Means by Which It Raises Its Funds, and the Structure Through Which It Operates in the Diaspora: A Study in Organization."

D. DETERMINATION OF PUBLIC BODY STATUS BY THE PERMANENT COURT OF INTERNATIONAL JUSTICE IN THE *MAVROMMATIS PALESTINE CONCESSIONS CASES*

The issue of the juridical status of the Zionist Organization/Jewish Agency was considered by the Permanent Court of International Justice in the three cases which are collectively termed the *Mavrommatis Palestine Concessions Cases*.[46] While Palestine was a part of the Turkish Empire, the Turkish Government had granted certain public utility concessions in Jaffa and Jerusalem to Mr. Mavrommatis, a Greek subject. Thereafter the Mandatory Government, acting pursuant to articles 4 and 11 of the Mandate, arranged with the Zionist Organization to grant public works concessions to Mr. Rutenberg and these apparently overlapped the Mavrommatis concessions. Before asking the assistance of his government, Mr. Mavrommatis attempted to have his concessions recognized and honored through direct negotiations with the British Government. In doing this he relied upon the article 11 provision requiring that arrangements for "public works, services and utilities" shall be made "subject to any international obligations accepted by the Mandatory." As the successor government to the Turkish Government in Palestine, the Mandatory was bound by the international obligations of Turkey concerning Palestine.[47] In the course of his dealings with the British Government, the latter invited Mr. Mavrommatis "to come to an understanding with the Zionist Organization and with Mr. Rutenberg." Although no understanding was reached with either the British Government or the Zionist Organization, the British invitation to Mr. Mavrommatis to confer with the organization concerning a dispute in public international law provides further evidence of its public body status. Thereafter, the Greek Government took up Mr. Mavrommatis' claims and presented them

---

46. These cases are cited in notes 48, 52, and 55 *infra*.

47. "The Tinoco Claims Arbitration" (*Great Britain v. Costa Rica*) (Oct. 18, 1923), 18 *Am. J. Int'l L.* 147 (1924), is a leading case concerning the obligation of a successor government to honor the international undertakings of its predecessor.

against the British Government in the Permanent Court of International Justice. The Greek Government prevailed concerning the Mavrommatis concessions in Jerusalem but not concerning those at Jaffa.

If any reasonable doubts could exist concerning the public body status of the Zionist Organization under the Mandate, they were resolved by the decision in the first *Mavrommatis Case*.[48] The Court quoted from article 4 of the Mandate in substantial part and then stated:

> This clause shows that the Jewish agency is in reality a public body, closely connected with the Palestine Administration and that its task is to co-operate, with that Administration and under its control, in the development of the country.[49]

There is nothing in the dissenting opinions which is inconsistent with this holding of the Court.[50] The dissenting opinion of the British judge, Lord Finlay, employed wording very similar to that in the Court's judgment on this subject and stated that according to article 4 "a Jewish agency is to be recognized as a public body ... ."[51]

In the second *Mavrommatis Case*[52] the Court proceeded on the basis that the public body status had been adequately decided in the first case and referred in greater detail to the conversations which "took place with M. Rutenberg and with the president and other representatives of the Zionist Organization" and stated that the British Colonial Office was kept informed as to the status of these conversations.[53] The Court also considered "the influence of the Zionist Organiza-

---

48. "The Mavrommatis Palestine Concessions," (*Greece v. Great Britain*), [1924] P.C.I.J. ser. A, No.2.

49. *Id.* at 21.

50. The five dissents appear in *id.* at 38–93.

51. *Supra* note 48 at 38, 52.

52. "The Mavrommatis Jerusalem Concessions," [1925] P.C.I.J., ser. A, No. 5.

53. *Id.* at 18.

tion in the affairs of Palestine," and pointed out that provision is made for this influence in the terms of the Mandate.[54] In summary, the judgment in the second case does not reach any conclusions or make any findings inconsistent with the determination of the public body status of the Zionist Organization in the first case.

In the third *Mavrommatis Case*[55] the Zionist Organization/ Jewish Agency was again simply regarded as "a public body."[56] The dissenting judges again manifested no disagreement with the judgment of the Court concerning the public body status of the Organization. The dissenting opinion of Judge Altamira stated:

> But I think it necessary to point out, as regards the part played by the Jewish Agency in the economic policy of Palestine, that this very fact has the effect of excluding any action on the part of the public administration which would destroy the interests and character of the Organization. The recognition of that Organization as a true public body, with the rights conferred on it by Article 4 of the Mandate, implies that it must be accorded privileged or exceptional treatment which would disappear if the control exercised by the Administration were so extensive as to result in the substitution of the Administration itself for the Jewish Agency.[57]

Judge Caloyanni, in his dissenting opinion, recognized the close relation between the Organization and the Administration provided in the Mandate:

> From a study of these texts it clearly appears that the Zionist Organization is so closely con-

---

54. *Id.* at 43.

55. "Case of the Readaptation of the Mavrommatis Jerusalem Concessions (Jurisdiction)," [1927] P.C.I.J. ser. A, No. 11.

56. *Id.* at 17.

57. *Id.* at 33, 37.

nected with the Palestine Administration that for purposes of developing the country as regards economic questions and as regards works of public utility, it appears to be unable to do without this Organization, unless it consented.[58]

E. IMPLEMENTATION OF THE PUBLIC BODY STATUS

1. IMPLEMENTATION INSIDE PALESTINE: THE "SHADOW GOVERNMENT"

The provisions of the Mandate, and particularly those concerning the close relationship of the Zionist Organization/ Jewish Agency to the Palestine Administration, could lead to the conclusion that the Zionist Organization was an integral part of the governmental administration of Palestine. The dissenting opinions in the third *Mavrommatis Case* just considered could also be reasonably interpreted as leading to this conclusion. The British Government, nevertheless, took a different position shortly before the Palestine Mandate became effective. In the Churchill White Paper of July 1, 1922 the British Government stated:

> It is also necessary to point out that the Zionist Commission in Palestine, now termed the Palestine Zionist Executive, has not desired to possess, and does not possess, any share in the general administration of the country. Nor does the special position assigned to the Zionist Organisation in Article IV of the Draft Mandate for Palestine imply any such functions. That special position relates to the measures to be taken in Palestine affecting the Jewish population, and contemplates that the Organisation may assist in the general development of the country, but does

58.   *Id.* at 47, 50.

not entitle it to share in any degree in its Government.[59]

Almost a month earlier, on June 3, 1922, the British Colonial Office had written to the Zionist Organization including in the letter a pre-publication copy of the Churchill White Paper. The Colonial Office letter concluded with the statement that it would "be glad to receive from you a formal assurance that your Organisation accepts the policy as set out in the enclosed statement and is prepared to conduct its own activities in conformity therewith."[60] The enclosed White Paper included the paragraph barring the Zionist Organization from possessing "any share in the general administration of the country."

The Zionist Organization, in a letter to the Colonial Office of June 18, 1922 signed by Dr. Weizmann,[61] stated that the Executive of the Zionist Organization had considered the British statement of policy and had passed the following resolution concerning it:

> The Executive of the Zionist Organisation, having taken note of the statement relative to British policy in Palestine, transmitted to them by the Colonial Office under date June 3rd, 1922, assure His Majesty's Government that the activities of the Zionist Organisation will be conducted in conformity with the policy therein set forth.[62]

The same letter also stated:

> It [the Zionist Organization] has repeatedly made it clear both in word and deed that nothing is further from its purpose than to prejudice in the

---

59. Jewish Agency for Palestine, *Book of Documents Submitted to the General Assembly of the United Nations Relating to the Establishment of the National Home for the Jewish People,* 28, 29 (Tulin ed., 1947).

60. *Id.* at 27, 28.

61. *Id.* at 32.

62. *Id.* at 32–33.

smallest degree the civil or religious rights or the material interests of the non-Jewish population [of Palestine].[63]

For a short time the Zionist Organization/Jewish Agency observed these limitations on its authority. Thereafter, as its political and military power increased, it violated the express limitations in the Mandate and its undertakings to the British Government whenever the political objectives of Zionist nationalism and its claimed constituency of "the Jewish people" made this desirable. The 1946 report of a non-partisan and respected fact-finding committee, the Anglo-American Committee of Inquiry, provided a careful summary of the activities of the Jewish Agency in Palestine.

At first the Agency gave the Palestine Government effective cooperation. With its large revenue, its able administrators, advisors and staff, and its manifold activities, the Agency became finally and still remains the most potent non-governmental authority in Palestine and indeed in the Middle East. The Peel Commission described it as "a Government existing side by side with the Mandatory Government". The description is even more accurate today.[64]

The same committee also stated:

The Jews have developed, under the aegis of the Jewish Agency and the Vaad Leumi, a strong and tightly-woven community. There thus exists a virtual Jewish nonterritorial State with its own executive and legislative organs, parallel in many respects to the Mandatory Administration, and serving as the concrete symbol of the Jewish National Home. This Jewish shadow Government has ceased to cooperate with the Administration in the maintenance of law and order, and in the

---

63. *Id.* at 33.

64. *Anglo-American Report,* cited *supra* note 45 at 20.

suppression of terrorism.[65]

In summary, the Zionist Organization exercised the public body powers accorded to it by the Mandate but the limitations imposed upon it by the same authority were violated.

2. IMPLEMENTATION OUTSIDE PALESTINE: THE INTERNATIONAL PUBLIC BODY

The Zionist Organization acted in consultation with and under the control of the British Government in implementing the Zionist "national home" enterprise outside Palestine only so long as it was dependent upon that government. Thereafter, the Zionist Organization used its public body status and powers without regard to the legal limitations imposed upon it by the Balfour Declaration and the Mandate for Palestine. In particular, it advanced the "Jewish people" claims in opposition to the British Government before the Permanent Mandates Commission of the League of Nations.[66] In 1947 and 1948 it transferred its political pressure activities to the United Nations.[67] It advanced them there under the "Jewish Agency" name until it was formally replaced by the name of the State of Israel. Mr. Shertok (later Sharett), who was the principal Jewish Agency representative at the United Nations, became the first foreign minister of the State of Israel.[68]

The Zionist Organization also conducted its public body activities within national states including the United Kingdom, and diplomatic negotiations took place between the Organization and the British Government.[69] A basic negotiating and pressure objective of the Organization was to impose upon the British Government the principle that its basic legal obligation under the Mandate was not to the native

---

65. *Id.* at 39.

66. See *e.g.*, *supra* note 59 at 140–75.

67. See *supra* note 59 *passim.*

68. For a description of Israeli policy, see L. Rokach, *Israel's Sacred Terrorism: A Study Based on Moshe Sharett's Personal Diary and other Documents* (1980).

69. *Zionist Diplomacy, supra* note 33 at 50–52.

inhabitants of Palestine (composed of Moslems, Christians, and Jews), but to the Zionist claimed constituency of "the Jewish people."[70]

The principal focus of Zionist Organization public body activities shifted from the United Kingdom to the United States in the early part of the Second World War.[71] The Biltmore Declaration of May 11, 1942 provides illustration of Zionist Organization pressure group activities within the United States.[72] That Declaration demanded the establishment of a "Jewish Commonwealth" in Palestine without any reference to or regard for the safeguard clauses of the Balfour Declaration which were embodied in the Mandate for Palestine then in force.[73] Former President Truman described a part of this process with commendable candor after he left office.[74]

The Zionist Organization/Jewish Agency, and not the Government of Israel, undertook to negotiate a reparations agreement with the Federal Republic of Germany on behalf of "the Jewish people". The result was the Luxembourg Agreement of 1953[75] in which Germany paid to the Government of Israel a sum estimated at two billion dollars in reparations for Nazi confiscation of property belonging to Jews whether or not the particular Jews subsequently became Israeli nationals.

---

70. *Id.* at 51. See *supra* note 59 at 137–38.

71. *Zionist Diplomacy* 55; Stevens, *American Zionism and U.S. Foreign Policy 1942–1947* at 2–3 (1962).

72. The Biltmore Declaration appears in *supra* note 62 at 226–27.

73. Stevens, *supra* note 71, *passim.*

74. 2 Truman, *Memoirs: Years of Trial and Hope* 140, 153, 158 (1956).

75. It appears in Grossman, *Germany's Moral Debt: The German–Israel Agreement* 37 (1954).

V. The Claims to Continue the Public Body Status of the Zionist Organization from the Establishment of the State of Israel in 1948 to the Present

A. THE CONTINUATION OF ZIONIST ORGANIZATION PUBLIC BODY FUNCTIONS (1948–1951)

The end of the British Mandate and the establishment of the State of Israel on May 14, 1948 terminated the legal authority for the public body status of the Zionist Organization/Jewish Agency. No action taken by the United Nations provided a continuing juridical basis for the Organization. Since one of its principal political objectives had been the creation of the State of Israel, one might conclude that the Organization was now dissolved. The facts, however, indicate that it continued to function.

The Executive Reports submitted to the 23rd Zionist Congress at Jerusalem (1951) indicate in considerable detail the continuing functions of the Zionist Organization after the termination of the Palestine Mandate. According to these official records, a number of departments of the Organization ceased to function since the respective "activities were taken over by the Government."[76] The function of diplomatic negotiations, which had been done by the Organization

---

76. Zionist Organization and Jewish Agency, *Reports of the Executive Submitted to the 23rd Zionist Congress*, p. v (Aug. 1951) [hereafter cited as *Executive Reports*]. A secondary source has provided a brief summary:

> The new ministries of government were direct transformations of the bureaus of previously existing institutions. The Political Department of the Jewish Agency became the Foreign Ministry; the Social Welfare Department of the National Assembly became the Ministry of Social Welfare; the Haganah became the Israeli army. When the sovereignty of Israel was proclaimed, many officials simply moved their files from the Jewish Agency, the Histadrut, the Anglo-Palestine Bank, and other institutions, to their new desks. In some instances there was overlapping. For example, the Jewish Agency still shared with the government the responsibilities of immigration and housing, even as the Histadrut shared the responsibilities of public health and municipal transportation.

Sachar, *The Course of Modern Jewish History* 543 (Delta ed., 1963).

alone before 1948,[77] could probably now be shared by the Government and the Organization. The recruitment of Jewish immigrants into Israel, however, remained a preeminent function of the Zionist Organization.[78] In addition, the Zionist national funds continued their fund-raising efforts and according to these Executive Reports the Jewish Agency financed the war effort against the Arab states "during the early months of fighting as well as in the period preceding it."[79]

Problems remained, nevertheless, in terms of the allocation of public or governmental functions between the Government of Israel and the Organization. The concern of the Government lest the Zionist Organization perform a role for the State of Israel analogous to that which it had performed for the Mandatory Government was expressed by the Prime Minister. *The Jewish Agency's Digest* reported in 1949:

> Mr. Ben-Gurion said that during the British Mandatory regime, the Zionist Organization's function had been to shape the policy of the Palestine Government – insofar as the Mandatory had been faithful to the Mandate and to its international obligations, and to the promotion of immigration and settlement. The Jewish Agency had been to a certain extent "a state within a state, a government within a government."

> This would not be tolerated under the State of Israel, Mr. Ben-Gurion said.

> The Prime Minister warned against two misconceptions:

---

77. *Zionist Diplomacy, supra* note 33, *passim.*

78. The activities of the Immigration Department appear in *Executive Reports,* 23rd Zionist Congress 240–90 (Aug. 1951).

79. *Id.* at 822.

(1) That with the rise of the State, the Zionist Movement and the Zionist funds became obsolete.

(2) That notwithstanding the rise of the State the Zionist Movement would continue to function as though the State did not exist.[80]

It is clear that the functions performed by the Organization and the working relationships between it and the Government constituted a *de facto* status for the Organization and a juridical relation between it and the Government. If the Government of the new State had regarded the implementation of the "Jewish people" concept as completed by the establishment of the State, it could have performed necessary governmental functions itself without the Organization. "The Jewish people," however, was to be organized to support the State and to provide Jewish immigration for it,[81] and these continuing functions made the Organization indispensable.

By 1951 a "Co-ordinating Board," containing Organization and Government representation, was in existence.[82] This Board was concerned with, *inter alia*, "defining relationships between the two bodies."[83] In the performance of this task and in arranging further cooperation between Organization and Government, the Co-ordinating Board developed a series of working relationships which were later formalized in Zionist-Israel public law to define the relation between Organization and Government based on the preexisting working relationships.

---

80. 2 Information Dep't of Jewish Agency and World Zionist Organization, *The Jewish Agency's Digest of Press and Events* 318 (Nov. 18, 1949) [hereafter cited as *Jewish Agency Digest*].

81. *Executive Reports, 23rd Zionist Congress passim* (Aug. 1951).

82. 3 Information Dep't of Jewish Agency and World Zionist Organization, *Zionist Newsletter*, No. 19, "Zionist Problems Surveyed" 8, 10 (June 5, 1951).

83. *Id.*

B. THE ZIONIST ORGANIZATION/JEWISH AGENCY STATUS LAW (1952)

1. LEGISLATIVE HISTORY

For convenience in analysis the legislative history of the Status Law[84] will be examined in terms of its background in both the Zionist Organization and the Government of Israel. It should not be supposed, however, that this means that there are two distinct legislative histories. Since the Organization and the Government are both controlled by the same Zionist political elite, there is reason to believe that there was close cooperation between them. This is made explicit by the "Report by the Legal Adviser" which is included in the *Executive Reports* submitted to the 24th Zionist Congress in 1956. It is there stated that the "significant matters on which extensive services were rendered" by the Legal Adviser of the Zionist Organization/Jewish Agency included the preparation of drafts and negotiations with the Government concerning both the Status Law and the Covenant.[85] As to the Status Law, the Report by the Legal Adviser states: "Much of this work was done in close cooperation with the Legal Adviser to the Government of Israel."[86] As to the Covenant, "A great deal of work by the Legal Adviser was done in the closest cooperation with the Legal Adviser to the State of Israel."[87] The probable conclusion concerning the ensuing legislative history of the statute is that it is a common Zionist history whether performed within the Organization or the Government.

---

84. 7 Israel Laws 3 (1952).

85. *Executive Reports*, 24th Zionist Congress 23, 24 (1956).

86. *Id.* at 24.

87. Apparently the Legal Adviser of the Organization/Agency was the same Mr. Maurice M. Boukstein who appeared before the 1963 United States Senate Hearing mentioned in the text *infra* at note 128. This is indicated by the statements in the *Executive Reports* 24th Zionist Congress 23, 24 (1956) that the Legal Adviser also served as attorney for the United Jewish Appeal of Greater New York "in connection with various bank loans" and as attorney for the United Israel Appeal, Inc. and the Palestine Foundation Fund.

The 23rd Congress of the World Zionist Organization met in Jerusalem during August, 1951. This was a particularly important Congress since it was the first one held after the establishment of the State of Israel. One of the most significant items on the agenda was that concerning the juridical status of the Zionist Organization. The Congress produced the following important resolution entitled "Status for the Zionist Organisation":

(a) The Congress declares that the practical work of the World Zionist Organisation and its various bodies for the fulfilment of its historic tasks in Eretz Israel calls for the fullest degree of co-operation and co-ordination on its part with the State of Israel and its Government, in accordance with the laws of the land.

(b) The Congress considers it essential that the State of Israel shall grant, through appropriate legislative act, status to the World Zionist Organisation as the representative of the Jewish people in all matters relating to organised participation of the Jews of the Diaspora in the development and upbuilding of the country and the rapid absorption of the immigrants.

(c) In relation to all activities conducted in the interests of the State of Israel within the Diaspora it is essential that the Government of the State of Israel shall act in consultation and co-ordination with the World Zionist Organisation.

(d) In all matters regarding legislation by the State of Israel touching upon the activities of the World Zionist Organisation and the Jewish Agency, their property and their liabilities, it is essential that there shall be prior consultation between the Government and the Executive of the World Zionist Organisation and the Jewish Agency.

(e) (1) On the basis of the status to be granted to the World Zionist Organisation, the Executive of the World Zionist Organisation and the Jewish Agency shall be empowered to work within the

107

spheres defined from time to time by special agreement with the Israel Government.

(2) the following spheres of activity shall be fixed among others, for the forthcoming period:

(a) The organization of immigration, the transfer of immigrants and their property to Eretz Israel;
(b) Participation in the absorption of immigrants;
(c) Youth Aliyah;
(d) Development of agricultural settlement;
(e) Acquisition and amelioration of land by the Jewish National Fund;
(f) Participation in development projects.

(3) The Co-ordinating Body of the Israel Government and the Executive of the World Zionist Organisation and the Jewish Agency shall co-ordinate the above-mentioned spheres of activity.[88]

Paragraph (b) reflects the situation of the absence of formal juridical authority for the Organization since the termination of the Mandate. The requisite juridical status is to be obtained from the State of Israel but such status is not to make the Organization only a representative of the State. The Organization is to be recognized by the State "as the representative of the Jewish people," that is, the representative of Jews who are nationals of other states than Israel. There is no method consistent with international law whereby the State of Israel can make the Zionist Organization the representative of Jews who are not nationals of Israel.[89]

---

88. Organization Dep't of the Zionist Executive, *Fundamental Issues of Zionism at the 23rd Zionist Congress* 135–36 (1952). The term "Youth Aliyah" refers to youth immigration to Israel.

89. Concerning the closely related issue of functional subversion of nationality status see *The "Jewish People" Study, supra* note 2 at 1051.

Paragraph (c) also indicates that the activities involved include the advancement of Israel national interests among Jews in other national states. The balance of the paragraph concerns the tactical need of coordination in advancing Zionist nationalism among Jews who are not Israelis. Paragraph (d) requests special treatment through consultation for the Organization under Israel law in matters concerning it. The Organization, of course, enjoyed preferred treatment under the Mandatory Government in Palestine by virtue of its public body status.

The agreement device, referred to in the first subsection of paragraph (e) is important in giving the appearance of separate status and perhaps of equality of bargaining power to the Organization. The second subsection sets forth the public functions to be performed by the Zionist Organization with the consistent emphasis upon immigration. The "Co-ordinating Body" referred to in the final subsection is an important device because it, like the agreement, gives the Organization an appearance of equality with the Government. There was every reason to believe that the request for the "Co-ordinating Body" would be accepted since that body was actually operating in 1951.[90] In the same way, there was reason to believe that the other requests in the Resolution would be honored because of the close existing cooperation between Organization and Government in the implementation of Zionist objectives.

The Government of Israel was also interested in providing a formal juridical status for the Zionist Organization in view of the termination of the Mandate. In 1952 Prime Minister Ben Gurion stated in the Knesset concerning the proposed status legislation:

> This Bill differs generally from other laws not only in form but also in content. Usually a law is intended to change or improve something. This enactment is intended to maintain, to confirm, and to give legal force and State recognition, to a basic fact – the experience of the Jewish people, its

---

90. See the text accompanying *supra* notes 82–83.

historic continuity, unity, and aspiration. It will give the impress of the State and the law to the fact that the State of Israel is the creation of the Jewish people, indelible proof and faithful base of its existence, and primary instrument for its liberation.[91]

This official statement is particularly important in demonstrating that the Status Bill was intended to confirm or ratify the existing state of affairs. It also provides further indication of the centrality of the "Jewish people" concept. In the same statement, the Prime Minister also said:

But the advantage of the State is also a source of restriction. For the sovereign authority of the State is confined within its own borders, applying only to its own citizens, while over 80 per cent of the Jewish people are still to be found – and who knows for how long? – outside the borders of the State. The State of Israel cannot intervene in the internal life of the Jewish communities abroad, cannot direct them or make demands upon them. However unique is the State of Israel in the manner of its emergence and in its task, it is obliged to operate like every other state, and its capacity outside its borders is restricted. It is the Zionist Organization, built upon the voluntary association and activity, which is able to achieve what is beyond the power and competence of the State, and that is the advantage of the Zionist Organization over the State.

Hence the Zionist Organization has not been rendered useless by the establishment of the State but, on the contrary, its responsibility and mission have become incalculably greater. The State and the Zionist Movement complement each other, need each other and with joint effort can and must

---

91.   4 *Jewish Agency Digest, supra* note 80 at 1060, 1061 (May 16, 1952).

activate the Jewish people to realize the ideal of its redemption.[92]

The first of these two paragraphs seems to recognize the legal limitations which are imposed upon the State of Israel as a sovereign State since it is conceded that the State "cannot intervene in the internal life of the Jewish communities abroad." But it is then stated that the Zionist Organization can act in this area which is beyond the legal competence of the State. If the Zionist Organization is either closely linked in law to the State or is a part of the State, however, it is subject to the same legal limitations as the State. The "joint" character of the State and the Organization in implementing the "Jewish people" nationality claims is stressed in the second paragraph.

These official Government of Israel statements indicate two basic areas of agreement between the Organization and the Government: (1) the Zionist Organization is to continue to perform its preexisting functions including those which affect Jews in states other than Israel; (2) the Organization needs more formal juridical authority and status from the State in order to regularize its continued performance of these functions.

2   INTERPRETATION OF THE STATUTE
In the interpretation of a Zionist legal document it is essential to have a knowledge of Zionist ideology and to recognize that this ideology is a guide to action in public law. The "Jewish people" concept is basic to Zionist public law relations with Jews outside the State and to the recruitment of Jewish immigration to build up the manpower of the State.

The Status Law was enacted on November 24, 1952 and went into effect the following December 2.[93] A statement of its "constitutional" importance appeared in the *Israel Government Year-Book:*

---

92. *Id*. at 1069, 1070.

93. Note in 7 Israel Laws 3 (1952)

The World Zionist Organization-Jewish Agency for Eretz Israel Law 5713–1952 was of great constitutional importance. The Prime Minister, in submitting the Law to the Knesset, defined it as "one of the foremost basic laws." This Law completes the Law of the Return in determining the Zionist character of the State of Israel. The Law of the Return established the right of every Jew to settle in Israel, and the new Law established the bond between the State of Israel and the entire Jewish people and its authorized institutions in matters of immigration into and settlement in Israel.[94]

The State of Israel has no constitution as such, but its "basic laws" possess predominant constitutional characteristics including having considerably more importance than routine legislation.[95] Such constitutional laws include the statutes which implement Zionist ideology and those which establish the governmental structure. Both the Law of Return[96] and the Status Law qualify as constitutional laws in this sense.

In the ensuing analysis the sections of the Status Law are analyzed by subject even though this involves some departure from the numbered sequence.

(a) Introductory Provisions
The first three sections provide introduction and background to the entire statute. The first sets forth the consistent Zionist-Israel juridical claim of factual and legal connections between the State of Israel and the entire "Jewish people." This is the same "Jewish people" concept which the United States Department of State has rejected as a concept of international law.[97] This section also refers to the immigra-

---

94. State of Israel, *Government Year-Book* 57 (1953–54).

95. See generally Baker, *The Legal System of Israel* 14, *passim* (1961). See also *Fundamental Laws of the State of Israel* 3–5 (Badi ed. 1961).

96. 4 Israel Laws 114 (1950).

97. See the text accompanying *supra* note 15.

tion laws of the State of Israel which are discriminatory in terms of the religious identification of the immigrants.

The second section of the statute refers to the historic public body functions of the Zionist Organization in behalf of the claimed constituency of "the Jewish people." It also accurately recognizes the central role of the Organization in creating the State. This historical section is important in showing State recognition of the past functions of the Organization. Such deference is probably politic in view of the somewhat changed role of the Organization since the establishment of the State.

Section 3 is recognition in law that the Zionist Organization and Jewish Agency are simply different names for the same institution. It includes the phrase, "takes care as before of immigration," which indicates the consistent performance of the immigration function before and after the establishment of the State of Israel in 1948.

(b)   The Purview Concerning Status
The sections which directly concern status provide:

4. The State of Israel recognises the World Zionist Organisation as the authorised agency which will continue to operate in the State of Israel for the development and settlement of the country, the absorption of immigrants from the Diaspora and the coordination of the activities in Israel of Jewish institutions and organisations active in those fields.

11. The Executive is a juristic body and may enter into contracts, acquire, hold and relinquish property and be a party to any legal or other proceeding.

12. The Executive and its funds and other institutions shall be exempt from taxes and other compulsory Government charges, subject to such restrictions and conditions as may be laid down by the Covenant; the exemption shall come into force on the coming into force of the Covenant.

Section 4 provides State recognition of the Organization

113

not merely as an agency but as "the authorized agency." Since an agency relation necessarily involves a principal, the question arises as to the identity of the principal but the section does not answer this directly. The State, however, "recognizes" the agency status and this strongly suggests that the status is to act as agent for the State. In addition, the State has the legal authority to appoint an agent for itself but not for others such as Jews who are nationals of other states than Israel.[98] The State authorizes the Organization to coordinate activities of "Jewish institutions and organizations" within Israel. It is difficult to avoid the conclusion that the coordination is done on behalf of the State as principal. This appears to subject the organizations to effective governmental control even though they may prefer to regard themselves as both voluntary and philanthropic.

Section 11 provides that the Organization's Executive is "a juristic body." This is analagous to article 4 of the Palestine Mandate which constituted the Organization as "a public body." The question remains as to whether the juristic entity is a public or private one. Unless it performs usual private functions, it is highly improbable that it is a private "juristic body" such as a private corporation. Since the "central task" of the Organization, the recruitment of Jewish immigrants as provided in section 5, is a public function, it is reasonably clear that the "juristic body" must be a public one.[99] In addition, the broad grant of authority to the Executive to "be a party to any legal or other proceeding" cannot be accurately construed to exclude public proceedings and functions.

---

98. It will be recalled that paragraph (b) of the Status Resolution of the 23rd Zionist Congress requested status "as the representative of the Jewish people ... ." See the text accompanying *supra* note 88.

99. Even if it were somehow concluded that the Organization is a private juristic body, it would still be closely linked in law to the State. The United States Supreme Court has set forth a realistic approach to governmental activities in a case involving application of the U.S. Foreign Agents Registration Act of 1938, as Amended. Justice Goldberg stated for the Court in *Rabinowitz v. Kennedy*, 376 U.S. 605, 609–10 (1964):

> Furthermore, although the interest of the government in litigation might be labeled "financial or mercantile," it cannot be deemed only "private and nonpolitical."

Tax exemption is a typical attribute of governmental status and section 12 establishes the principle of exemption. This is probably done because the Executive and its branches and fronts are performing public functions which would otherwise be performed by the Government itself. In this respect, the Executive is simply treated as a part of the Government.

Sections 5 and 6 deal with Jewish immigration to Israel, the political unity required, and the role of the Zionist Organization in achieving it. Section 5 uses the broad term, "Zionist Movement," to refer to non-Zionist individuals and organizations who may be induced to cooperate with the Organization in recruiting Jewish immigrants. This interpretation is supported by the specific language concerning the State expecting the cooperation "of all Jews as individuals and groups." The only possible basis for this cooperation is the claimed nationality entity of "the Jewish people" comprising all Jews without regard to their democratic preferences. The purpose of this expected cooperation is frankly stated to be "building up the State" rather than merely assisting refugee Jews or performing other humanitarian activities.

Section 6 indicates that the Organization is the instrument to achieve the political unity of Jews. The provision concerning an "enlarged" Organization/Agency is a planned arrangement whereby non-Zionists may be involved more directly in Zionist activities at some future time. This same type of arrangement was previously effectuated through the "enlarged Jewish Agency" which was recognized in 1930 as the "public body" under the Mandate.[100] If the Organization decides to use this arrangement to "broaden its basis" of political support among Jews outside of Israel, it must obtain "the consent of the Government and the approval of the Knesset." This express limitation provides further indication of the subordination of the Organization to the State.

Section 7 of the Law authorizes the Organization to enter into a "covenant" or agreement with the State to arrange the

---

100. See *supra* note 45.

more specific details of the status of the Organization "and the juridical form of its cooperation with the Government." Although this section deals primarily with method and form, it also attempts to confer at least some status since it enables the Organization to make an agreement with the Government. Such an agreement might even give the appearance of equality of status as between Organization and State.

Section 8 manifests acceptance of the Status Resolution of the 23rd Zionist Congress as the basis of Zionist cooperation and employs the precise words, "the practical work of the World Zionist Organization and its various bodies,"[101] which appear in that Resolution. It would be surprising, in view of their identity of Zionist objectives, if there were differences other than minor tactical ones between State and Organization. The "full cooperation and coordination" is to be conducted, nevertheless, "in accordance with the laws of the State" (including the Status Law) to avoid any possibility of the Organization becoming a "shadow government" as it did under the Mandate.

Section 9 is of particular importance because it concerns the detailed cooperation which is to be effectuated through a committee. Although the statute provides that the committee is to be set up in the future, the committee is actually identical with the "Co-ordinating Board" which has been functioning since no later than 1951. At least this portion of the statute, therefore, is not law-making but only declaratory of the preexisting cooperation institution – whether termed "committee" or "Board." The statute, therefore, merely provides the opportunity through the Covenant device to make *de jure* an institution which was then functioning *de facto*.

---

101. See the text of the Resolution, paragraph (a) in the text accompanying *supra* note 88.

C. THE COVENANT BETWEEN THE GOVERNMENT OF ISRAEL AND THE ZIONIST EXECUTIVE (1954)

The Status Law provides a background for understanding the Covenant.

1. INTERPRETATION OF THE COVENANT

The preamble to the Covenant[102] states that it is entered into in accordance with the "Status Bill." It is clear that without the Status Law as enabling legislation the Organization would not have the authority to make a formal agreement with the State. There is, of course, nothing in Israel municipal law to prevent the enactment of legislation authorizing the Organization to make a "Covenant" with the Government. The question which must be raised, however, is to what extent an agreement in which one of the two parties participates by authorization of the other amounts to an actual negotiated agreement as opposed to a unilateral Government of Israel public law allocation of functions within a single sovereignty.[103] Whether it is a *bona fide* agreement or merely a unilateral allocation is not important to its effectiveness as Israel municipal law. The same issue may have, however, some juridical significance concerning the operations of the Organization outside Israel. If the Covenant is not a *bona fide* agreement, the Organization is apparently a part of the Government. If the Covenant is *bona fide*, the Organization is apparently a public body which is closely linked in law to the Government.

In the ensuing text the sections of the Covenant along with the annexes which are an integral part of it will be analyzed according to functional subjects. As in the analysis

---

102. The text of the Covenant appears in *Zionist General Council, supra* note 22 at 106–09 (July 21–29, 1954). The Covenant is set forth in full in Appendix A6 to this book.

103. The Balfour Declaration, in contrast, appears to be a unilateral British Government announcement but is actually a negotiated agreement. The negotiations are set forth in Chap. 1 *infra*. Lasky, *supra* note 45 at 40 states that the relation of the Organization to the State "stems out of an ideology born of Eastern European experiences and therefore not easy for a western or nonindoctrinated mind to grasp."

117

of the Status Law, this will involve some departure from the numbered sequence. Consistent with section 11 of the Status Law, the Zionist Organization is represented by its Executive in making this Covenant and the State is, of course, represented by its Government.

(a) Immigration and Other Functions of the Executive

The first section of the Covenant sets forth and accepts each of "the fields of activity" enumerated in paragraph (e) (2) of the Status Resolution of the 23rd Zionist Congress. In addition, the latter part of the section specifies further functions to be performed.[104] The adding of functions beyond those requested demonstrates the confidence of the Government in the Organization as an efficient tool for implementing the "Jewish people" concept. The first part of the section, by emphasizing functions concerning Jewish immigration and settlement, gives appropriate recognition in Zionist public law to what section 5 of the Status Law describes as "the central task of the State of Israel and the Zionist Movement in our days." Section 3 further emphasizes the importance of Jewish immigration to the State by requiring that the Executive shall "act on the basis of a plan" assented to by the Government or the Coordinating Board.

The characterization in the first section of the Keren Kayemeth Leisrael (the Jewish National Fund) and the Keren Hayesod (the United Israel Appeal) as "institutions of the Zionist Organization" is of considerable legal significance. It means that the conclusions of this chapter concerning the juridical status of the Zionist Organization apply equally to

---

104. Lasky 48, note 14 states, in part:

> The American Jewish Committee has expressed satisfaction that the Status Law did not give to the Agency as much as the Zionists, wished. Cf. Minutes A.J.C. Executive Committee October 23–4, 1954. The foregoing [evidence] would indicate that it gave more.

Since the Status Law gave the Organization/Agency more than it asked for, the interpretation of the American Jewish Committee is incorrect. It is not clear whether its interpretation is a serious one or merely a public relations indication that it as a "non-Zionist" group has not had its role of cooperation with the Government of Israel impaired by the Status Law.

the Jewish National Fund and the United Israel Appeal. Each of these engaged in supposed "charitable" solicitations outside Israel. The apparent assumption is that these institutions are voluntary and private associations. The Covenant indicates, however, that they are integral parts of the Zionist Organization.[105]

The last clause of section 1, consistent with section 4 of the Status Law, states that the Executive shall coordinate "the activities in Israel of Jewish institutions and organizations" which act within the scope of the functions carried out by the Zionist Organization. It adds that this is to be done "by means of public funds." The conclusion which follows is that coordination employing public funds is governmental coordination.[106] It is also clear that the Executive as the coordinator is acting on behalf of the Government or as part of it. Further support for the governmental character of the coordination is provided by section 4 which points up the importance of the coordination to the Government by providing expressly that it must be done "in agreement with the Government."[107] Such agreement was probably already required by necessary implication from the authorization in section 1 to use public funds.

(b) Juridical Subordination of the Organization to the State

Section 2 of the Covenant requires that the activities of the Organization within Israel be carried out consistently with law. At first glance this appears to be a routine provision but it also adds that such activities must be consistent with subordinate administrative orders which are applicable to governmental authorities. The result is another example of

---

105. The Jewish National Fund also has its "Covenant" with the Government of Israel which was signed on Nov. 28, 1961. *Executive Reports, supra* note 76, 26th Zionist Congress 345 (Dec. 1964). On the governmental functions of the Jewish National Fund see *id.* at 345–55.

106. The same conclusion is reached in Lasky, *supra* note 45 at 41.

107. The "Jewish institutions and organizations" coordinated are also apparently subject to Government of Israel audit control under the State Comptroller Law, 3 Israel Laws 23 (1949). Under sec. 7(d) of it such control is exercised over an "institution, fund, or other body . . . in the management of which the Government has a share."

119

treatment of the Organization as a part of the Government. Further, the background under the British Mandate when the Zionist Organization/Jewish Agency increasingly became the "shadow government" in opposition to the Mandatory Government must be recalled.[108] Because of this, it is essential that the subordination of the Organization to the public law of the State be made explicit.

Annex A, consisting of a note to the Zionist Executive from the Government, is dated the same day as the effective date of the Covenant and is appended to it. The first paragraph indicates that the Zionist Executive "and its institutions" are to be treated as parts of the Government of Israel in terms of administrative orders concerning "investigations, searches and detentions in Government offices." This is a specific implementation of section 2 of the Covenant. The second paragraph states that the Executive will not maintain, within Israel, "juridical or investigative machinery of its own" except consistent with Israel law and in cooperation with the Attorney General of Israel. It is apparent that the Zionist Organization/Jewish Agency conducted such activities in Palestine as the "shadow government" during the period of the Mandate for Palestine. The present arrangement is undoubtedly necessary to prevent duplication, overlapping, and perhaps competition, between Organization and Government investigative and judicial activities. The note does not outlaw such Organization functions but merely requires them to be consistent with Government law and policy. The note which appears as Annex C to the Covenant indicates Zionist Executive acquiescence in the legal limitations imposed on the Organization by Annex A.

Section 5 provides further evidence of the supremacy of the Government and the subordination of the Organization. The Organization may not delegate its "functions or rights under the Covenant" without the approval of the Government and may not authorize the performance of its functions by others except after notification to the Government.

---

108. See the text of Sec. IV E *supra*.

Section 6 imposes an obligation on the Organization to obtain "financial and material" support for its functions from *inter alia*, the United Israel Appeal and the Jewish National Fund. These functions are, of course, the various public and governmental ones specified in the first section.

Section 7 is another example of the supremacy of the Government over the Executive. The Government here agrees to "consult" with the Executive where proposed legislation would affect its functions. Nothing in the section, however, prohibits final determination by the Government of the content of the legislation following the consultation.

Section 11 provides directly and by further "special arrangement" to be added to the Covenant as another annex, for the Zionist Organization or "any of its institutions" to have the benefit of governmental status in tax law, and hence tax exemption, within the State of Israel. In a significant contrast, the same Zionist institutions are treated as private charitable funds for tax purposes outside Israel. The result is substantial tax benefits to these institutions in both cases but upon opposite juridical bases. It must be doubted that the same fund-raising institutions can be public and governmental in Israel and private and philanthropic in other countries.[109]

(c) Coordinating Board and Official Precedence

The Coordinating Board, which according to section 8 "shall be established," is the same one which has been in existence since 1951.[110] The Covenant, therefore, merely formalizes it. The importance of the Board is suggested by its inclusion in the Covenant, the Status Law, and the 23rd Zionist Congress Resolution on Status as well as by its composition. The Organization is represented by members of its policy-making Executive and the Government by "members of the Government," that is, by cabinet ministers.

---

109. See *e.g.*, Mallison, "The Legal Problems Concerning the Juridical Status and Political Activities of the Zionist Organization/Jewish Agency: A Study in International and United States Law," 9 *William & Mary L. Rev.* 554 at 600 (1968).

110. See the text accompanying *supra* note 82.

The provision for the Government and the Executive to each appoint half of the members of the Board establishes at least formal equality. The provision for the submission of the Board's deliberations and recommendations to both the Government and the Executive again maintains the formal equality of each of the Board's governmental superiors. The authority of the Board is as broad as "all spheres to which this Covenant applies." The real importance of the Board is, of course, determined by the functions it performs.[111]

In Annex B the Government establishes an "order of precedence at official ceremonies" which includes both Zionist Organization and Government officials. This does not refer to diplomatic precedence extended to officials of a foreign state by the Government of Israel. Diplomatic precedence is a matter of international custom and comity and cannot be determined by the host government alone. The present note is based on "the Government's decision" concerning internal Government of Israel ceremonies. Although this may be accurately termed a matter of ceremonial precedence, it is, nevertheless, a matter of substantive importance because it means that the Zionist Organization officials are recognized in the most direct manner as being a part of the structure of the Government. It is difficult to avoid the conclusion that the order of precedence reflects the prior Government acceptance of the Organization as a functional part of the Government.

Sections 10 and 12 through 14 concern merely the procedural implementation of the Covenant and need not be considered in detail. Section 12 provides that the Covenant is effectuated at the time of signature and it was signed on July 26, 1954 which is also the date of the Annexes. No further acceptance of it was necessary, but the Zionist General Council then in session in Israel did nevertheless unanimously adopt a resolution, thereby augmenting the appearance of a bargained agreement.[112]

---

111. See the text of Sec. V C *infra*.

112. *Zionist General Council, supra* note 22 at 211.

2. THE COORDINATION BOARD AS AN INSTRUMENT FOR
. IMPLEMENTATION OF "JEWISH PEOPLE" IMMIGRATION

There is no evidence of a lack of cooperation between Organization/Agency and Government in the immigration field at any time. This cooperation has been more formalized since the establishment of a Joint Government/Jewish Agency Immigration Authority by the Coordination Board in early 1967. It is described in the *Israel Digest*:

> The aim of the authority is to encourage immigration and to improve the absorption process by providing a single address for the immigrant, which will deal with all his problems.
>
> The authority, composed of four Ministers and four Members of the Agency Executive, will be headed by the Chairman of the Executive, with the Labor Minister as his deputy.
>
> It will be administered by a joint committee of senior Government and Agency officials, headed by a representative of the Labor Ministry, and will function within existing machinery, with no additional personnel.[113]

It would be a difficult task to draw the various lines between the roles of Jewish Agency and Government in the Joint Immigration Authority. Even if the task could be done, it would not be particularly meaningful if both Agency and Government are parts of and serve the same sovereign. The central point is that the roles of "Agency," "Government," and "Joint Immigration Authority" are all subordinate to the common plan of public law implementation of the "Jewish people" concept in immigration.[114] This involves a high level policy determination which is enunciated in both the Status

---

113. 10 *Israel Digest* (Amer. ed. published by the Jewish Agency-American Section) No. 3, p. 4, cols. 2, 3 (Feb. 10, 1967).

114. The functional identity of "Agency" and "Government" is indicated in a report on the establishment of the Joint Immigration Authority in the semi-official *Jerusalem Post*, March 7, 1967, p. 2, cols. 3, 4, at col. 4: "A decision adopted by a majority of either the Government or the Agency component [of the Joint Authority] will be binding on both."

Law and the Covenant. It also involves a day to day administrative process in terms of interviewing Jewish applicants for immigration to Israel. This is spelled out in the Zionist Executive Reports for 1963 as follows:

> We note with great satisfaction the fullest cooperation in the field of immigration between our offices and the Israel Consulates in the United States and Canada. According to a decision of the Coordination Committee of the Israel Government and the Jewish Agency, all cases of immigration applications made to an Israel Consulate are automatically referred to the Immigration Department of the Jewish Agency which makes its recommendations in each case.[115]

The application forms for immigration used by the Jewish Agency in the United States require information concerning the applicant's religious faith so that Jewish immigration may be promoted. This raises an issue concerning compliance with the First Amendment in the United States whether the Jewish Agency is appraised as a department of the Government of Israel or as its legally linked public body.[116]

If there are any humanitarian purposes involved in the solicitation of Jewish immigration to Israel, they are subordinate to the principal purpose of the Organization and the Government to build up the manpower of the State. This is spelled out in the official Executive Reports concerning the immigration regulations which were adopted by the Coordination Board in 1960:

---

115. *Executive Reports to the Zionist General Council* 192 (March, 1963).

116. The United States Government took unequivocal action as required by the First Amendment to the U.S. Constitution to deny the claimed authority of the Czarist Russian Government to question United States citizens concerning their religion. The issue arose when United States citizens applied to Czarist consulates in the United States for visas to travel to Russia. [1895] *Foreign Rels. U.S.* 1064, 1067 (1896).

In 1958 the need was felt to revise the regulations for immigration and for this purpose the Coordinating Board appointed a Committee composed of the Minister of Health, the Minister of Labour and the Heads of the Immigration and Absorption Departments. There was also a sub-committee consisting of the Directors of these Ministries and Departments. The sub-committee held nine meetings and proposed regulations designed to increase the proportion of immigrants of working capacity capable, from the health and social viewpoints, of becoming absorbed in the country, and to prevent the immigration of social welfare cases who could still be maintained abroad ... .

The sub-committee of the Coordination Board approved the Immigration Regulations unanimously, and they are now binding on all those engaged in immigration and absorption work.[117]

An evaluation of the importance of the Coordination Board has been provided by the late Moshe Sharett. Mr. Sharett was exceptionally well qualified to make such an evaluation because he had served on both sides of the Board. In 1954 he signed the Covenant as Prime Minister of Israel and in 1963 when he was chairman of the Zionist Executive he stated to the Zionist General Council:

I should like to place on record here the serious attitude of the Prime Minister towards the Coordinating Committee, at least in the period in which I have been participating in its meetings. Not only does he always respond to any demand to call a meeting of the Committee, but on his own initiative he calls meetings and places questions on the agenda for joint consideration.

Resolutions are faithfully respected and when

---

117. *Executive Reports, supra* note 76, 25th Zionist Congress at 75, 77 (Dec. 1960).

there is any matter liable to cause complications such as a clash of appeals or of financial projects, the Government always calls upon us to study the question. When we call upon the Government, there is always a response. A network of sub-committees of the Coordinating Committee has proliferated dealing with all sorts of questions.[118]

D. THE JURIDICAL EFFECTS OF THE CLAIMS TO CONTINUE THE PUBLIC BODY STATUS: THE CREATION OF A SINGLE ZIONIST-ISRAEL SOVEREIGNTY

It is not possible to understand the Status Resolution of the 23rd Zionist Congress, the Status Law, or the Covenant without an understanding of the core of Zionist ideology which is implemented in them. This ideology has been accurately described by Mr. Moses Lasky:

> All Jews of the world form one Nation, the State of Israel is the lawful representative of that portion of the Nation dwelling in Zion [Israel], and the Zionist Organization is the authorized representative of the Nation dwelling elsewhere throughout the world. The two are coordinate representatives of one nation and thus may make covenants and treaties and cooperate with each other to a common end.[119]

The "one Nation" is the claimed Zionist-Israel entity of "the Jewish people." The State and the Organization, although representatives of different portions of "the Jewish people," share the common juridical objective of implementing Zionist nationalism in law. In addition, the State and the Organization are controlled by a political elite which is dedicated to establishing in international law the claimed entity of "the Jewish people." When this single political elite with a common political program seeks to implement that program through public law, it should not be surprising that

---

118. *Zionist General Council, supra* note 22 at 210, 211 (March 18–26, 1963).

119. Lasky, *supra* note 45 at 49.

the substantive law employed embodies common juridical premises and objectives. [120] The details of juridical implementation are all consistent with the basic purpose of implementation of the "Jewish people" nationality claims. [121]

At the Zionist General Council meeting in Israel in 1954, at the time of the effectuation of the Covenant, the chairman of the committee on the "Status of the Zionist Organization (the Covenant)" stated concerning the juridical status provided for the Organization by the Covenant:

> From the letters attached to the Covenant you will see that the Government has granted the Jewish Agency and its institutions the status of Government institutions. In addition it has consented to give the Chairman and Members of the Zionist General Council official status in its official ceremonies. [122]

The governmental status of the Organization under the Covenant has not changed to the present time. One may expect, consequently, that the Zionist interpretation of the character of the Organization has remained consistent. This is indicated by a statement made by Dr. Goldmann, then president of the Zionist Organization, to a Zionist General Council meeting in 1966. His statement is also significant because it explains the relation between the Covenant and Zionist ideology:

> We have entered into a Covenant and are performing many tasks which in other countries are performed by Governments. The Covenant accordingly reflects an abnormal situation; but the

---

120. A different interpretation would have to postulate the existence of a long series of coincidences.

121. Even if the Covenant were interpreted as though it were an international agreement (the evidence shows it is not), its "general purpose" would still provide necessary context for its detailed interpretation. "Harvard Research in International Law," 29 Am. J. Int'l L. Supp. 937 (1935); Restatement, supra note 27, sec. 147.

122. Zionist General Council, supra note 22 at 105 (July 21–29, 1954).

situation of the State of Israel is still abnormal and the majority of the Jewish people still live outside the borders of the State, and there is need of a movement bringing thousands and tens of thousands of Jews to the State. This was the reason for the Covenant. At the same time it is clear that all this – settlement, absorption and immigration – can only be carried on in coopera- tion with the State.[123]

These quoted Zionist interpretations are working ones made in the course of administration of the Status Law and Covenant. As such, they are entitled to great deference under well known interpretational criteria.[124]

Although the negotiations which led to the Covenant took place over a period of time, there is no reason to believe that there were fundamental differences between the Organization and the State. The chairman of the Committee on the "Status of the Zionist Organization (the Covenant)" stated in the Zionist General Council Meeting at the time of the effectuation of the Covenant that "the Government of Israel had accepted most of the Amendments proposed by the Jewish Agency."[125] Because of the common Zionist ideology which was being implemented by Organization and State, it seems likely that the only differences which arose during the negotiations were concerned with the ascertain- ment of the best tactical methods to be employed. There is no reason to believe that there were differences concerning the common objective of implementation of the "Jewish people" concept. The Report of the Legal Adviser, examined above, supports this conclusion.[126]

Even though the Covenant is an agreement in form, it is a unilateral public law instrument in substance with the Zionist political elite represented on each side of the

---

123. *Id.* at 193, 194 (Jan. 11–18, 1966).

124. *Supra* note 121.

125. *Supra* note 122.

126. See the text accompanying *supra* notes 85–87.

supposed negotiations. In view of the basic identity of the public law views of both the representatives of the Organization and of the Government, why was the form of an agreement employed? More specifically, why were not all of the details embodied in the Covenant spelled out in the Status Law itself, thus avoiding the need for a subsequent agreement? Apparently, the covenant or agreement form was highly desirable as a matter of appearance since it indicates in both the title and the text that the Government of Israel and the Zionist Executive are two separate bodies. It further indicates that the Zionist Organization is such an important separate body that it is not appropriate to deal with it only through legislation, as in the Status Law, but that it is necessary to use the agreement device. The result is that the Status Law and the Covenant,[127] viewed together, give the appearance of at least some degree of status as a separate participant to the Zionist Organization. It would be difficult to achieve this appearance as effectively through a different device.

If it is stated that the Zionist Organization is a part of the Government of Israel, the existence of the Covenant provides a plausible response suggesting two independent bodies negotiating and agreeing with each other. The Covenant can be used more effectively to attempt to explain away the juridical connection of the Organization with the State than could a Status Law which included all of the specific provisions now covered in the Covenant. For example, in the United States Senate Foreign Relations Committee Hearing of 1963 concerning the Activities of Nondiplomatic Representatives of Foreign Principals in the United States, Mr. Boukstein, perhaps the preeminent Zionist lawyer in the United States at that time, stated:

> I take very great pride in the fact that I had a hand
> in negotiating with Prime Minister Ben Gurion

---

127. The word "Covenant" also has religious meanings. See Berger, "Community Covenant or 'Covenant Community': A Basis for Dialogue," 20 *Issues* [periodical of the American Council for Judaism] No. 4, p. 13 (Winter, 1967).

some years back the contractual arrangements between the Jewish Agency, which is a non-governmental body, and the Government of Israel in which arrangements were provided for the orderly administration of the enormous physical task of taking people in, going through their medical examinations, setting them on the land or in industry, and so forth.[128]

The "contractual arrangements" referred to are the Status Law and the Covenant.[129]

The juridical result of the Covenant standing alone is that there is some distinction in Zionist public law between the Government of Israel and the Zionist Organization. In terms of the central Zionist objective of recruiting Jewish immigrants for the State of Israel, the Organization/Agency is in most respects the Government. It must, nevertheless, act on the basis of agreement with the Government as provided by section 3 of the Covenant. In the same way, the Organization acts for, but "in agreement with the Government," according to section 4, in coordinating the activities within Israel of "Jewish institutions and organizations." The method employed in the Covenant is to separate the Organization from the Government for certain key purposes and then to ensure through specific requirements governing agreement and cooperation that the Organization faithfully executes the policies of the Government. Having given the appearance of separating the Organization from the Government, it is then necessary, as indicated in section 11 of the Covenant, to make special arrangements for its tax exemption.

---

128. *Hearing on Activities of Nondiplomatic Representatives of Foreign Principals in the United States* before the Senate Committee on Foreign Relations 88th Cong. 1st Sess. pt. 9, p. 1324 (May 23, 1963). Testimony and information by the Executive Branch of the U.S. Government concerning enforcement of the Foreign Agents Registration Act of 1938 as Amended, as well as the background to the Hearing, appears in pt. 1, pp. 1–167 (Feb. 4 and 6, 1963). The principal testimony and information concerning Zionist activities in the United States appears in pt. 9, pp. 1211–1424 (May 23, 1963) and pt. 12, pp. 1695–1782 (Aug. 1, 1963).

129. This conclusion is supported by the "Report of the Legal Adviser" considered in the text accompanying *supra* notes 85–87.

Annex A contains additional examples of apparent separation combined with effective government control. It indicates that the Organization may continue to carry on "judicial or investigative" activities of its own within Israel but this must be done only in compliance with law and "in constant coordination" with the Attorney General of the Government. In the same way, since the Organization has been separated from the Government for certain purposes, it is necessary to provide that the administrative orders concerning "investigations, searches, and detentions in Government offices" shall also apply to the Organization and its institutions including the United Israel Appeal and the Jewish National Fund.

In 1971 there was a "reorganization" of the Jewish Agency which resulted in changing its name, for at least some purposes, to the "Reconstituted Jewish Agency."[130] The apparent purpose of the "reorganization" was to put the Zionist political and the non-Zionist philanthropic operations on a plane of nominal equality with each of them having one-half of the control of the Jewish Agency as it was reconstituted.[131] This would result in the appearance of equal control of the disposition of the funds raised by the Jewish Agency and its subordinate institutions. One of the interesting aspects of this 1971 "reorganization" is that it was modeled upon an earlier reorganization which took place under the auspices of Dr. Chaim Weizmann, then the president of the Zionist Organization/Jewish Agency, in 1929.[132] Dr. Weizmann's stated purpose in creating the "Enlarged Jewish Agency" in 1929 was to bring non-Zionist

---

130. A comprehensive description and analysis of the "reorganization" is in the semi-official *Jerusalem Post*, "Special Supplement-Founding Assembly: The Reconstituted Jewish Agency," June 21, 1971.

131. The "Pincus Plan" (named for Mr. Arye Louis Pincus, the Chairman of the Zionist Organization/Jewish Agency Executive) providing for an equal number of "non-Zionist" and Zionist delegates to the Zionist Organization/Jewish Agency Assembly was implemented. *Id.* at 3 and 16. A large number of the named "non-Zionist" delegates are apparently committed Zionists. *Id.* at 16.

132. *Trial and Error: The Autobiography of Chaim Weizmann*, 376–89 (Chap. 27 entitled "The Jewish Agency") (East and West Library, London, 1950).

philanthropists into the work of the Zionist Organization/ Jewish Agency by creating the impression that they had a share of control of the use of the funds raised.[133] It was important then as in 1971 that the funds should not appear to be under political control because of the domestic laws which grant tax deductions for charitable purposes in a number of countries. In appraising the reality as opposed to the appearance of the 1971 "reorganization," however, it is essential to recognize that there was no concurrent or ensuing change in either the Status Law or the Covenant with the result that the character of the Zionist Organization/ Jewish Agency's relationship to the Government of Israel has remained unchanged.[134]

The provisions of the Covenant which distinguish between the Organization and the Government for certain purposes while ensuring the effective subordination of the Organization to the Government, distinguish only for efficiency and administrative convenience in pursuing the common juridical objectives of Zionist nationalism. When the Status Law is recognized as enabling legislation to empower the Organization to agree with the Government, this conclusion becomes even more persuasive. From this perspective it is clear that the Status Law and Covenant are only municipal law allocations of governmental authority in one aspect even though they are designed to have and do have an impact upon Jews who are nationals of other states than Israel.[135] As municipal law they are analogous to the separation of powers doctrine applicable to the United States Government. The main difference between the two is that the Zionist separation of powers is based only upon administrative expediency and can be changed easily at any time whereas the United States separation of powers is

---

133. *Id.* at 380–89. See also *supra* note 45.

134. A repeal or amendment of the Status Law or the Covenant could indicate a change in the relationship.

135. Application of the principles of the *Restatement*, cited *supra* note 21, p. 19, makes it clear that the claims against Jews who are not Israelis through the implementation of the "Jewish people" concept are an assertion of jurisdiction over them.

required by the Constitution. Explicit recognition of the Zionist allocation of authority as a "separation of powers" was made by Dr. Goldmann, speaking as president of the Zionist Organization, to a Session of the Zionist General Council in 1966:

> Since the foundation of the State and the separation of powers then decided upon one of the leading ministers of the Government has served as a Member of the [Zionist] Executive.[136]

A conclusion which is supported overwhelmingly by both the primary and secondary public law sources is that the Zionist Organization/Jewish Agency is a part, and a particularly important part, of the Government of Israel. This conclusion is based, *inter alia*, upon the Zionist working interpretations quoted above.[137] It is based also upon the specific provisions of the Status Law and Covenant as well as the actual governmental functions performed under them. Even though the Organization has a different name and other superficial indications of separate identity, it is subject to the overriding control of the Government of Israel as is any other part of the same Government. It is necessary, consequently, to recognize that there is only one Zionist-Israel sovereignty in fact and in law. In its internal separation of powers, provision may be made for the performance of particular governmental functions by the Zionist Organization as is done presently through the Coordination Board pursuant to the Status Law and the Covenant. In the same way, the substance of the present separation of powers may be provided for *de facto* as was done prior to the Covenant. The separation of powers may also be changed in any way including a performance of the Organization's governmental functions by another part of the Government which is given a name suggesting a separate identity. Further, any existing separation of powers may be abolished with the result that all

---

136. *Zionist General Council, supra* note 22 at 193 (Jan. 11–18, 1966).

137. See the text accompanying *supra* notes 122, 123.

functions are performed directly by the Government as such. In the event of any such changes, there could be no substitute for a juridical analysis which examines the governmental functions performed rather than the names employed.[138] An alternate conclusion which is also supported by both the primary and secondary public law sources is that the Organization/Agency is a public body closely linked in law to the Government and controlled by it. Even though section 11 of the Status Law designates the Zionist Executive as a "juristic body," this falls short of the multilateral state authority which is required to constitute a public body in international law.[139] However, when section 11 is combined with the other provisions of the Status Law and Covenant and the actual public body functions performed since 1948, it does provide some indication of the intent to continue public body status. If the conclusion of the public body status of the Organization/Agency should be appraised as more persuasive than the conclusion of its status as part of the Government of Israel, the same juridical effects would follow. It would then be clear that the public body is subject to all relevant legal limitations including those which bind its creator state. The Organization/Agency would still have to be recognized as an integral part of a single Zionist-Israel sovereignty because of the effective control the Government exerts over it.

The conclusion that the Organization/Agency is both a part of the Government and a public body is not a novel one. Writing in 1956 and utilizing the public law sources then available, Mr. Lasky stated concerning the status of the Organization upon the termination of the Mandate:

---

138.   "For it is not Names, that Constitute Governments, but the use and exercise of those Powers that were intended to accompany them. . .".

John Locke, *The Second Treatise of Government: An Essay Concerning the True Original, Extent, and End of Civil Government* sec. 215 (1698) in *John Locke: Two Treatises of Government* 427 (Laslett ed. 1960).

139. See the text accompanying *supra* note 27.

The rational conclusion is that the State of Israel stepped into the shoes of the mandatory power and that the Government of Israel is to be regarded as substituted for "Mandatory" or "administration of Palestine" or "his Majesty's Government" in all appropriate contexts. That being so, the Agency did continue as "a public body" whose function it now was "to advise and cooperate with the Government of Israel." In short, from a "recognized public instrument in the Administration of Palestine" under the Mandatory, it became an organ of the State of Israel.[140]

The most compelling conclusion is that the Zionist-Israel sovereignty contains an Organization/Agency component which is in some aspects part of the Government and in others its captive public body. Whichever aspects predominate at a particular time and for a particular purpose, the component is nevertheless subject to effective control by the Government of Israel. The juridical effects set forth in this chapter are not varied whether the Organization/Agency be appraised as government, public body, or both. In any or all three of these appraisals of status it remains a component of the single Zionist-Israel sovereignty.

VI. The Zionist Organization/Jewish Agency Under the United States Foreign Agents Registration Act

The purpose of the Foreign Agents Registration Act (F.A.R.A.)[141] is not to prevent the political activities, including propaganda, in the United States of the non-

---

140. Lasky, *supra* note 45 at 46.

141. 52 *U.S. Stat.* 63 (1938) as amended, 22 *U.S. Code* Sec. 611 (1964). Injunctive remedies were added to the F.A.R.A. in the 1966 amendments, sec. 8(f). These amendments greatly facilitated the administrative proceedings conducted before the Department of Justice during 1968–1970. See the text accompanying *infra* notes 142–145. The amendments were the main result of the Senate Hearings conducted under the chairmanship of Senator J. W. Fulbright. See *supra* note 128.

diplomatic agents of foreign governments, public bodies, and other principals. It is, in contrast, to describe completely the identity and characteristics of the foreign principal for which the agent acts and the particular political activities. To accomplish this purpose, such agents are required to register with the Department of Justice, to provide detailed information, and to file supplementary registration information every six months. Section 2(a) (2) of the F.A.R.A. requires each registrant to provide, *inter alia*:

> a true and complete copy of its charter, articles of incorporation, association, constitution, and bylaws, and amendments thereto a copy of every other instrument or document and a statement of the terms and conditions of every oral agreement relating to its organization, powers, and purposes; and a statement of its ownership and control.

Until 1971 the Zionist registrant under the F.A.R.A. was the "American Section of the Jewish Agency for Israel," Registrant No. 208. Its initial and supplementary registration statements did not meet the requirements of section 2(a) (2) quoted above. During the period 1968–1970 administrative proceedings were instituted before the Department of Justice to compel compliance. This was done initially on behalf of the American Council for Judaism, then the principal anti-Zionist Jewish organization in the United States, and subsequently on behalf of American Jewish Alternatives to Zionism.[142] In spite of the strenuous Zionist opposing arguments, Registrant No. 208 was compelled to file the World Zionist Organization-Jewish Agency Status Law (1952)[143] on October 25, 1968 and the Covenant Between the Government of Israel and the Zionist Executive Called Also the Executive of the Jewish Agency (1954)[144] on August 28, 1969. These two constitutive documents of the agent and its

---

142. A charitable organization dedicated to maintaining Judaism as a religion of universal moral values and exposing the basic inconsistency between Judaism and Zionism.
143. *7 Israel Laws* 3, in Appendix _____.
144. Appendix _____.

foreign principal (the Government of Israel or the Zionist Organization/Jewish Agency or both) created serious potential damage to each in that the documents demonstrated that neither the registrant nor its foreign principal were the voluntary private organizations which they claimed to be.

An even greater blow was dealt to the registrant and its foreign principal on June 9, 1970 when the Department of Justice required the filing of the tax annex to the Covenant. It is formally titled "Appendix to the Covenant Between the Government and the Executive of the Jewish Agency" and dated July 19, 1957.[145] Its first section provides in full:

> In this Appendix – "The Executive" – includes the Jewish National Fund and Keren Hayesod-United Israel Appeal.

The balance of the Tax Appendix provides comprehensive tax immunity for the funds on this premise that they are an integral part of the Zionist Executive. The juridical effect is that they are either a part of the Government of Israel or of its created and controlled public body.

Subsequent actions demonstrating the concern of the Zionist Organization/Jewish Agency included the purported 1971 "reorganization" of the Jewish Agency described above.[146] During the same year 1971, the American Section of the Jewish Agency, Registrant No. 208, de-registered under the F.A.R.A. on the alleged grounds that it was no longer engaged in political activities. In the same year the Zionist Organization/Jewish Agency registered under the name, "World Zionist Organization-American Section, Inc." as Registrant No. 2278. Registrant No. 208 had consistently listed its foreign principal as "The Executive of the Jewish Agency for Israel, Jerusalem, Israel," whereas Registrant No. 2278 has consistently listed its foreign principal as "The Executive of the World Zionist Organization, Jerusalem, Israel". In short, the foreign principal of the past and present registrants is identical although the wording is different. The

---

145. Appendix _____.
146. See the text accompanying *supra* notes 131–134. See also *supra* note 45.

striking change in the new registration is that neither the Status Law (1952), nor the Covenant (1954), nor the Tax Appendix (1957) has been filed initially or subsequently although the foreign principal is the same as the prior registrant and the specifics of the registration statements of the past and present registrants provide persuasive evidence that the foreign agents (the registrants) are the same or substantially the same.

In 1975 the Israeli Knesset enacted a law[147] which prescribed certain amendments to the Status Law (1952). One of its features included a new section 2A to be added to the earlier law (termed "the principal Law" in the amendment). This section provides in full:

> The Jewish Agency for Israel is an independent voluntary association consisting of the World Zionist Organisation and other organisations and bodies. It operates in the State of Israel in fields chosen by it with the consent of the Government.[148]

The juridical effect of this declaration that the Jewish Agency is "an independent voluntary association" amounts to no change at all in the existing basic Government of Israel control of the single Zionist Organization/Jewish Agency. The lack of change is emphasized by the provision that the Jewish Agency contains the Zionist Organization within it.

Section 3 of the principal law which stressed the identity of the Jewish Agency and the Zionist Organization is replaced by an amendment which states that they (identified separately by name) "take care of immigration as before". The "replaced" wording in section 3 of the principal law read that the single organization "takes case as before of immigration". Section 4 of the amendment changes section 4 of the principal law by making each of the separately named bodies "authorised agencies" for operation within the State of Israel by authority of its government. This, like the

---

147. World Zionist Organisation-Jewish Agency for Israel (Status) (Amendment) Law, 30 *Israel Laws* 43 (1975), in Appendix _____ .
148. 30 *Israel Laws* 43 at 44.

"change" in section 3, is not a change in substance since the added section 2A which makes the Zionist Organization part of the Jewish Agency remains in effect. In the same way, other provisions of the supposed amendments appear to be designed to produce changes in appearance without change in substance.

Sections 6, 7, and 8 of the amended law provide, *inter alia*, for two covenants to be entered into – one with the Agency and one with the Organization. Section 6 of the amendments provides that a new subsection shall be added to section 8 of the principal law and this subsection states in full:

> The Covenant with the Jewish Agency for Israel shall provide for full cooperation and coordination on its part with the State of Israel and its Government in accordance with the laws of the State.[149]

This significant section provides for continuing control of the Jewish Agency (and its stated sub-division the Zionist Organization) by "the laws of the State," and this is a specific enactment resulting in no change in the prior constitutive authority and documents of the Organization/Agency. Sections 8, 9, and 10 of the amended law provide some appearance of a separation between Organization and Agency but without change in meaning.

The name of the principal law is "World Zionist Organization–Jewish Agency (Status) Law", and section 11 of the amended law solemnly proclaims that the principal law shall be "renamed" the "World Zionist Organisation and Jewish Agency for Israel (Status) Law".

In many ways the most interesting part of the 1975 amendments is section 12 (the last section)[150] which states that the amendments shall be effective *ex post facto* from June 21, 1971 which is the date when the Jewish Agency was "reconstituted". As Israeli municipal law, the 1975 amendments are designed to give a semblance of reality to the alleged changes made by the "reconstitution" of the Jewish

---

149. *Id.*
150. *Id.* at 45.

Agency at that time. It is probable that the *ex post facto* aspect is also designed to lend credibility to the de-registration of a Zionist agent and the registration of a supposedly different Zionist agent in 1971. There is, however, no lawful method by which an Israeli law can be given *ex post facto* effect in so far as it has an impact on events in the United States. Even if the 1975 law could be given such effect, it would be without legal significance because of the lack of substantive change in it.

Careful searches of the initial and supplementary registration statements of the World Zionist Organization–American Section, Inc., Registrant No. 2278, do not reveal the filing of the 1975 amendments or of the two "covenants" referred to in section 5 of the amendments. Consequently, Registrant No. 2278 has not complied with the requirements of the F.A.R.A. and, thus far, the United States Department of Justice has not compelled it to do so. The 1975 amendments, its "covenants," if in existence, the 1952 "principal law," the Covenant of 1954, and its annexes including the Tax Appendix of 1957 remain its constitutive authority and their filing is required by section 2(a) (2). Among other sections of the F.A.R.A. which are violated is section 2(a) (3) which requires, *inter alia*, full information concerning:

> the extent, if any, to which each such foreign principal is supervised, directed, owned, controlled, financed, or subsidized, in whole or in part, by any government of a foreign country or foreign political party, or by any other foreign principal.

The conclusion of juridical status which follows from this evaluation of the 1975 "amendments" and the failure of the current Zionist Registrant No. 2278 to comply with the F.A.R.A. is the same as that based upon the pre-existing constitutive documents. It is that the Zionist Organization/ Jewish Agency and its fund raising institutions in the United States, including the Jewish National Fund, the United Israel Appeal, and its subsidiary the United Jewish Appeal, are either parts of the Government of Israel or they comprise a public body created and controlled by that government. The fund raising components of the Organization/Agency do not exercise effective domestic control over the allocation and use of funds raised in the United States and cannot do so under the constitutive authority which controls them. More specifically, the funds raised are disbursed under the direct control of the Government of Israel or under its indirect control through the Organization/Agency. This results in the mingling of the supposed philanthropic contributions with the other financial resources of the Government of Israel. Consequently, the funds do not meet the requirements of United States law[151] for tax exempt status and for the tax deductibility of contributions made to them. This conclusion is well known and was stated as long ago as 1963 by the authoritative Zionist scholar, Professor Nadav Safran:

> Moreover, the American government never seriously attempted to question the classification of the billion dollars of donations made by American Jews as tax-exempt "charity," though this money went, in effect, into the general development budget of Israel.[152]

In making a legal analysis of the Zionist Organization/ Jewish Agency and its political and financial activities, it is helpful to rely upon the wisdom of John Locke written almost three centuries ago:

> For it is not Names, that Constitute Governments, but the use and exercise of those Powers that were intended to accompany them ... .[153]

---

151. Internal Revenue Code, 26 *U.S. Code* Secs. 1–9, 601 and particularly Sec. 301 concerning the requirements for charitable organizations to receive tax deductible funds.
152. *The United States and Israel* 278 (Harvard, 1963).
153. John Locke, *The Second Treatise of Government: an Essay Concerning the True Original, Extent, and End of Civil Government* sec. 215 (1698) in *John Locke: Two Treatises of Government* 427 (Laslett ed. 1960).

Chapter 3

The United Nations and The Palestine Partition Resolution

I. The Development of International Law by the United Nations

An analysis of the United Nations' juridical competence concerning a particular subject requires an examination of the accepted methods of making international law. These methods are sometimes referred to as sources of law which are available to decision-makers for the resolution of particular controversies.

A. INTERNATIONAL LAW-MAKING

Article 38 of the Statute of the International Court of Justice specifies the sources of law which shall be applied by the Court. It is also widely accepted as describing the sources which are available generally in international law. The first paragraph of the article lists treaties, customs, and general principles as the main sources.[1] Custom is specified to be "international custom as evidence of a general practice accepted as law." It should be mentioned that this carefully worded provision does not require evidence of a universal practice. In the same way, the historic customary law-making process demonstrates that the rules which are regarded as legally established are based upon the assent of a substantial

---

1. I.C.J. Stat., art. 38(1) a, b, & c. Sub-section "d" lists judicial decisions and legal writings as subsidiary sources.

majority of states.[2] It has not been considered necessary that universal assent be obtained. General principles are specified as "the general principles of law recognized by civilized nations." The requirements here are not a combination of state practice and assent as in customary law, but rather a combination of state articulation or formulation along with assent.[3]

Customs are the more historic method of international law-making as compared with treaties. In 1625 when Grotius wrote his classic treatise,[4] custom stood as the almost unique method of prescribing international law. While conventions are created by the explicit agreement of states, customary law is based upon implicit agreement. In traditional legal analysis it is usually stated that customary law grows out of state usages or practices. A classic formulation of this view appears in Lauterpacht's Oppenheim:

> As usages have a tendency to become custom, the question presents itself: at what stage does a usage turn into a custom? This question is one of fact, not of theory. All that theory can say is this: Wherever and as soon as a line of international conduct frequently adopted by States is considered legally obligatory or legally right, the rule which may be abstracted from such conduct is a rule of customary International Law.[5]

This quotation also indicates with accuracy that it is not

---

2. In the famous case of *The Paquete Habana*, 175 U.S. 677 (1900) the U.S. Supreme Court based its holding concerning the immunity of coastal fishing boats from capture on such assent. The same point is made by legal writers. See *e.g.*, Professor Brierly who states: "It would hardly ever be practicable, and all but the strictest of positivists admit that it is not necessary, to show that every state has recognized a certain practice . . ." as creating customary law. Brierly, *The Law of Nations* 61 (6th ed., Waldock, 1963).

3. Professor Brierly has accurately characterized general principles as "a dynamic element in international law." Brierly, *supra* note 2 at 63. It has also been pointed out that international arbitral tribunals employed general principles of law before the establishment of the International Court of Justice. 1 Oppenheim, *International Law* 30 (8th ed., Lauterpacht, 1955).

4. *De Jure Belli ac Pacis* in J. B. Scott (ed.), *Classics of International Law* (Kelsey transl., Carnegie Endowment for International Peace, 1925).

5. Oppenheim, *supra* note 3 at 27.

necessary that the usage or practice be continued for a long time. The passage of time is only significant as to the existence of the practice which may also be evidenced in other ways.

Although much international law has grown out of state practice, it is an error to think that this is the only way that such law can be created or prescribed. An example may be drawn from the international humanitarian law of armed conflict. Article 9 of the Brussels Declaration of 1874[6] provided that irregular combatants who met certain specified criteria, not including governmental authorization but including adherence to the laws and customs of war,[7] were to be accorded the privileged status of prisoners of war upon capture. The practice of the Prussian Government during the Franco-Prussian War in which it summarily executed all *franc-tireurs* who could not produce a specific authorization of combatant status from the French Government was thereby rejected in the provisions drafted by the community of states represented at Brussels. Although the Brussels Declaration was intended to become a multilateral convention, it remained unratified. However, many of its provisions, including article 9, were widely accepted as embodying accurate formulations of the applicable international law on the subject. The substantive provisions of article 9 were set forth in *The Laws of War on Land* published by the Institute of International Law at Oxford in 1880.[8] The purpose of this manual was to reflect the existing law rather than to recommend innovations.[9] This provides evidence that the Brussels Declaration was then regarded as embodying the applicable principles of law concerning irregular combatants. There was little or no evidence of usage or practice applying

---

6. The Russian draft project, a summary of the discussions, and the final text of the Declaration are in 65 *Brit. & Foreign State Papers 1871–1874*, at 1067–1109 (1881). The text also is in Schindler & Toman (eds.), *The Laws of Armed Conflicts: a Collection of Conventions, Resolutions and Other Documents* 25–34 (1973).

7. The other criteria of article 9 are: military command, fixed distinctive emblem, and the open carrying of arms.

8. Art. 2(2) and art. 3. The text of this Oxford Manual is in Schindler & Toman, *supra* note 6 at 35–48.

9. Preface to the Oxford Manual, *supra* note 8.

article 9 during the decade and a half following 1874. Further evidence that these principles were accepted as law is provided by the fact that they were, without significant controversy, written into article 1 of the Annexed Regulations to Hague Convention II of 1899.[10] The same provisions were written into article 1 of the Annexed Regulations to Hague Convention IV of 1907,[11] and they also appear in the Geneva Prisoners of War Convention of 1949.[12] Each of these conventions was widely ratified and became a multilateral treaty in force. It is important that article 9 of the unratified Brussels Declaration was designed to change the pre-existing Prussian state practice.

B. THE UNITED NATIONS AS AN INTERNATIONAL LAW-MAKER

Although much international law is based upon pre-existing state practice, the community of states has the legal capacity and authority to formulate legal rules or principles through a multilateral conference, as at Brussels, or otherwise, even in the absence of pre-existing practice. The provisions of the United Nations Charter are designed to operate in the context of the contemporary international law decision-making process.[13] Following the ratification and the implementation of the Charter, states retain their pre-existing law-making competence. The Security Council (in subject matter restricted to international peace and security)

---

10. Hague Convention II With Respect to the Laws and Customs of War on Land, 29 July 1899, 32 U.S. Stat. 1803, U.S. Tr. Series No. 403; Gt. Brit. Tr. Series No. 11, Cmd. 800 (1901).

11. Hague Convention IV Respecting the Laws and Customs of War on Land, 18 October 1907, 36 U.S. Stat. 2227, U.S. Tr. Series No. 539; Gt. Brit. Tr. Series No. 9, Cmd. 5030 (1910).

12. Art. 4A(2), Geneva Convention Relative to the Treatment of Prisoners of War of August 12, 1949, 75 U.N. Tr. Series 135; [1956] 6 U.S. Trs. & Other Int'l Agrees. 3316; U.S. Trs. & Other Int'l Acts Series No. 3364; Gt. Brit. Tr. Series No. 39, Cmd. 550, p. 94 (1958).

13. The Charter, a constitutional document, requires that international peace and security be achieved in accordance with "the principles of justice and international law." Art. 1(1). Art. 51 incorporates "the inherent right" of self-defense which is the traditional international law on the subject. The Preamble refers to "the obligations arising from treaties and other sources of international law."

and the General Assembly (concerning a wide range of subjects) are institutions which facilitate the making of international law. The fact that the General Assembly, which is representative of the community of states, is a political body like a national legislature does not diminish its role as a prescriber of international law. The widespread use and reliance upon resolutions of the General Assembly and Security Council which are intended to have law-making effect provide convincing indication that the matters relied upon constitute, at the least, important evidence of the existence of particular rules or principles of international law.

In her treatise entitled *The Development of International Law Through the Political Organs of the United Nations*,[14] Dr. Rosalyn Higgins provides persuasive evidence, under several subject matter headings, of the law-making role of the General Assembly as a principal political organ of the United Nations. Dr. Higgins' analysis is much less innovative than it may appear to be at first glance, since traditional international law-making by multilateral treaty, custom, or general principle, has always been a highly political process which reflects the views of a substantial majority of states at any given time. In summary of her thesis, she states:

> With the development of international organiza-
> tions, the votes and views of states have come to
> have legal significance as evidence of customary
> law. Moreover, the practice of states comprises
> their collective acts as well as the total of their
> individual acts; and the number of occasions on
> which states see fit to act collectively has been
> greatly increased by the activities of international
> organizations. Collective acts of states, repeated
> by and acquiesced in by sufficient numbers with
> sufficient frequency, eventually attain the status
> of law. The existence of the United Nations – and
> especially its accelerated trend towards universal-
> ity of membership since 1955 – now provides a
> very clear, very concentrated, focal point for state
> practice.[15]

---

14. Oxford Press (1963).

15. Higgins treatise, *id.* at 2.

Dr. Higgins' analysis does not rely upon the law-making methods which are based upon the individual acts of states. She points out that customary law-making may be accomplished through the collective acts of states as now manifested preeminently by General Assembly resolutions. Although the outcome of this law-making method is usually characterized as "evidence of customary law"[16] rather than customary law itself, the effects of the two are very similar since either provides a legal basis for subsequent action taken in reliance upon it.

Judge Tanaka's distinguished dissenting opinion in the *South West Africa Cases* (1966)[17] differed with the holding of the International Court of Justice (decided by the narrow margin of the casting vote of the President) because he determined that there was a legal norm of equality which was violated by the South African Government's apartheid system. For present purposes the Tanaka opinion is important for the penetrating insight it provides into the collective customary law-making process:

> The appearance of organizations such as the League of Nations and the United Nations, with their agencies and affiliated institutions, replacing an important part of the traditional individualistic method of international negotiating by the method of "parliamentary diplomacy" . . . is bound to influence the mode of generation of customary international law. A State, instead of pronouncing its view to a few States directly concerned, has the opportunity, through the medium of an organization, to declare its position to all members of the organization and to know immediately their reaction on the same matter. In former days, practice, repetition and *opinio juris sive necessitatis*, which are the ingredients of customary law might be combined together in a very long and slow process extending over centuries. In the contemporary age of highly

---

16. *Id.* at 5.

17. *Ethiopia v. South Africa; Liberia v. South Africa, Second Phase* [1966] I.C.J. 6 at 248.

developed techniques of communication and information, the formation of a custom through the medium of international organization is greatly facilitated and accelerated; the establishment of such a custom would require no more than one generation or even far less than that.[18]

While the rather similar quoted analyses of Dr. Higgins and Judge Tanaka do not expressly refer to "the general principles of law recognized by civilized nations," it should be apparent that their arguments, *a fortiori*, may also lead to the conclusion that some resolutions of the General Assembly prescribe such general principles. In summary, the Higgins and Tanaka analyses find the state practice requirement for customary law-making in the collective acts of states (as in voting in favor of particular General Assembly resolutions) as well as in their individual acts.

The United Nations Charter is a multilateral treaty which creates the United Nations as a separate factual participant and legal subject of international law.[19] In addition, the Charter specifies particular purposes and principles including doctrines of international law which are to be effectuated. For example, article 1(1) provides that a main purpose of the United Nations is to maintain international peace and security, and this is to be done "by peaceful means, and in conformity with the principles of justice and international law." The basic Charter provisions must be interpreted and applied by the two main political organs of the United Nations. The Security Council must interpret the articles concerning international peace and security which confer authority upon it. In the same way, the General Assembly

---

18. *Id.* at 291.

19. *Advisory Opinion on Reparations for Injuries Suffered in the Service of the United Nations*, [1949] I.C.J. 174.

must interpret those articles which relate to its authority.[20] These interpretations are legally meaningful.

The main articles which empower the Security Council to carry out its functions concerning international peace and security appear in chapter VI (articles 33–38) and chapter VII (articles 39–51). The interpretation and exercise of these basic powers must be carried out in a manner consistent with the organizational and procedural rules of law specified in chapter V (articles 23–32). For example, the Security Council may make decisions on both procedural and substantive matters, but decisions on substantive matters must be made by a specified affirmative vote which includes "the concurring votes of the permanent members."[21] This provision has been interpreted by the Security Council to mean that the abstention or absence of a permanent member does not prevent the Council from making a decision on a substantive matter.[22]

The broad powers of the General Assembly are set forth in articles 10, 11, and 14, each of which empowers the General Assembly to act through "recommendations." Article 12(1) provides that the Assembly may not act when the Council is exercising the functions assigned to it "in respect of any dispute or situation" relating to the maintenance of international peace and security. Article 14 provides a comprehensive authority for the General Assembly and states:

> Subject to the provisions of Article 12, the General Assembly may recommend measures for the

---

20. This system of Charter interpretation is analagous to the "coordinate construction" of the United States Constitution, the prevailing system until after the Civil War, under which each of the three main branches of the Federal Government interpreted the Constitution for its own purposes. An example is provided by President Andrew Jackson's veto of the Second National Bank Bill on the ground of its unconstitutionality even though the Supreme Court had previously held the creation of a national bank to be constitutional. See C. B. Swisher, *American Constitutional Development* 178–85 (1943).

21. *U.N. Charter*, art 27(3).

22. An analysis of the Security Council's interpretation of art. 27(3), and the conclusion that it is legally sound, is in McDougal & Associates, *Studies in World Public Order*, Chap. 7 (1960).

peaceful adjustment of any situation, regardless of origin, which it deems likely to impair the general welfare or friendly relations among nations, including situations resulting from a violation of the provisions of the present Charter setting forth the Purposes and Principles of the United Nations.

Article 10 is even more comprehensive in subject matter scope and provides:

The General Assembly may discuss any questions or any matters within the scope of the present Charter or relating to the powers and functions of any organs provided for in the present Charter, and, except as provided in Article 12, may make recommendations to the Members of the United Nations or to the Security Council or to both on any such questions or matters.

Because of the considerations previously mentioned, "recommendations" of the General Assembly may in particular instances have significant legal import.[23] It is necessary to recognize that the General Assembly has two distinct functions. The first is as a major political organ of the United Nations with a separate legal identity.[24] The second is as a collective meeting of the states of the world community which comprise its membership. In this second function the legal authority of the Assembly is derived directly from the member states who have the same legal authority to develop and make international law in the General Assembly as they do outside of it. The advantageous feature of such activity in the Assembly is that it can be done more rapidly and efficiently than the same activity in a less institutionalized environment. The states of the world community since the

---

23. In addition to the examples analyzed *infra* in the present chapter, the Uniting for Peace Resolution. G, A. Res. 377A(V), of 3 November, 1950 (5 *U.N. GAOR, Supp. 20*, pp. 10–12, U.N. Doc. A/1775) should be considered. This resolution was adopted with the leadership of the United States Government following a Soviet Union veto in the Security Council which prevented the taking of enforcement measures there.

24. *Supra* note 20.

early years of the United Nations have in fact used the General Assembly as an instrument to express consensus on major international legal issues by majorities substantially in excess of the two-thirds vote required by the Charter for important questions. It is a matter of legal theory as to the precise allocation of authority between the powers derived directly from the Charter and those derived directly from the member states. The crucial point is that drawing on both sources of authority, the great majority of the member states have adopted the practice of expressing consensus on legal issues through the General Assembly. This practice is particularly evident in General Assembly resolutions concerning Palestine, Israel, and the Middle East.

II. The Palestine Partition Resolution 181(II)

A. THE BACKGROUND OF THE PARTITION RESOLUTION

1. THE GENERAL ASSEMBLY SPECIAL SESSION ON PALESTINE

It is not realistic to make a legal analysis of the Palestine Partition Resolution[25] without awareness of the circumstances which brought about United Nations action. The British Government policy of promoting Zionist immigration, at least until the White Paper of 1939,[26] had brought about the dangerous conflict situation in Palestine. This conflict arose from Palestinian resistance to the increasing determination of the European colonists under Zionist leadership to secure their overriding political objective of

---

25. G.A. Res. 181(II) Concerning the Future Government of Palestine (29 Nov. 1947), 2 *U.N. GAOR Resolutions*, 131–32, Doc. A/310 (16 Sept.–29 Nov. 1947). The resolution embodied a Plan of Partition with Economic Union and it is widely termed the Palestine Partition Resolution. It is referred to hereafter in this way and also as resolution 181. Parts IA, B and C of the resolution are reproduced in Appendix 10.

26. *Palestine: Statement by His Majesty's Government in the United Kingdom* (17 May 1939), Cmd. 6019 (1939). The rise of the Nazi tyranny to power in Germany in 1933 was also a significant factor in increasing the immigration of German refugees to Palestine and other places.

creating the "national home," which was later changed to a national state, for "the Jewish people."[27] This was to be done without regard to the rights of the native Palestinians, including the Palestinian Jews who opposed Zionism from the beginning.[28] After it was too late to control the effects of

---

27.   The earlier Zionist stated position is reflected in the official history by a member of the Executive of the World Zionist Organization:

> It has been said, and is still being obstinately repeated by anti-Zionists again and again that Zionism aims at the creation of an independent "Jewish State." But this is wholly fallacious. The "Jewish State" was never a part of the Zionist programme.

1 Sokolow, *History of Zionism*, intro. at xxiv-xxv (1919).
The later Zionist position is reflected in this official interpretation:

> The phrase [in the Balfour Declaration] "the establishment in Palestine of a National Home for the Jewish people" was intended and understood by all concerned to mean at the time of the Balfour Declaration that Palestine would ultimately become a "Jewish Commonwealth" or a "Jewish State", if only Jews came and settled there in sufficient numbers.

Jewish Agency for Palestine, *Book of Documents Submitted to the General Assembly of the United Nations Relating to the Establishment of the National Home for the Jewish People* 5 (Tulin ed., 1947).

28.   One of the preeminent leaders of the Palestinian Jewish community, Joseph Hayyim Sonnenfeld, wrote a criticism of the Zionists and their program in February, 1898, a short time after the meeting of the First Zionist Congress in Basle in 1897. After stating that "[t]he chief of these ruffians (*biryonim*) in our Holy Land has uttered terrible words, full of denial of the Most High . . .", he continued: "They [the Zionists] have also asserted their view that the whole difference and distinction between Israel and the nations lies in nationalism, blood, and race, and that the faith and the religion are superfluous." He concluded:

> For us in the Holy Land it is a sure sign that Dr. Herzl comes not from the Lord but from "the side of pollution", for we say, anyone who pleads in defence of Israel is exalted in the world by the Holy One, Blessed be He, while this evil man pleads in condemnation and multiplies accusation.

Quoted in Marmorstein, *Heaven at Bay: The Jewish Kulturkampf in the Holy Land* 79–80 (1969).
The Orthodox Jewish opposition to Zionism is continued in the State of Israel today by Naturei Karta and the Sephardic Community of Jerusalem. See for similar manifestations of opposition in the United States today *The Jewish Guardian*, which is the periodical publication of Naturei Karta of U.S.A., G.P.O. Box 2143, Brooklyn, N.Y. 11202.
It is not surprising that the Zionists apparently had little more liking for Palestinian Jews than for Palestinian Muslims and Christians. See Dr. Weizmann's criticisms of Palestinian Jews in the chapter of his autobiography entitled, "The Zionist Commission: Challukah Jewry." *Trial and*

Zionist policies, notwithstanding the provisions of the League of Nations Mandate for Palestine designed to protect Palestinian rights,[29] the British Government concluded that the Mandate was unworkable because of the irreconcilability of the native Palestinians' aspiration for self-determination with the political objectives of the Zionists.

In 1946 and 1947 the violence between the European immigrants and the native Palestinians was increasing sharply.[30] Great Britain indicated that it planned to terminate its role as the Mandatory Power and it requested a special meeting of the General Assembly. The First Special Session was convened in April, 1947.[31]

The Zionist case was presented at the Session by the Jewish Agency, which is the other name for the World Zionist Organization. Article 4 of the League of Nations Mandate for Palestine provided that the Zionist Organization was recognized as a public body and was designated as the Jewish Agency to cooperate with the Mandatory

---

Error: The Autobiography of Chaim Weizmann, Chap. 20 (East & West Library, London, 1950).

29. The text of the Mandate of 24 July 1922 is in 2 UNSCOP, *Report to the General Assembly, 2 U.N. GAOR Supp. 11* at 18–22, U.N. Doc. A/364, Add. 1 (9 Sept. 1947). The protective provisions include the Preamble and arts. 3, 5, 6, 9, 15 and 16.

30. See, *inter alia*, Anglo-American Committee of Inquiry, *Report to the United States Government and His Majesty's Government in the United Kingdom, passim* (1946).

> The Jews have developed, under the aegis of the Jewish Agency and the Vaad Leumi, a strong and tightly-woven community. There thus exists a virtual Jewish nonterritorial State with its own executive and legislative organs, parallel in many respects to the Mandatory Administration, and serving as the concrete symbol of the Jewish National Home. This Jewish shadow Government has ceased to cooperate with the Administration in the maintenance of law and order, and in the suppression of terrorism.

Id. at 39. See also [1947] 5 *Foreign Rels. U.S.* 999–1328 and *passim* (1971) and under following headings in index: Terrorism in Palestine, Irgun Zvai Leumi, Stern Gang.

31. *U.N. GAOR, First Spec. Sess. Plenary, Gen. Series,* U.N. Doc. A/286. The ensuing summary in the text is based primarily upon the cited *General Assembly Official Records.*

Government.[32] The Zionist arguments emphasized claimed "historic rights" as well as the Zionist interpretations of the Balfour Declaration and the Mandate for Palestine which were said to give primacy to the Zionist claims over the claims of the native Palestinians. The Zionists also claimed that "the Jewish problem" and the situation of Jewish refugees in Europe should be integrally linked to a resolution of the Palestine issue.

The Palestinian case was presented by the Arab Higher Committee of Palestine. It advanced the traditional view that the purpose of the League of Nations Mandate System, including the Palestine Mandate, was to bring self-determination and independence to the existing inhabitants of a country. It was pointed out that the Arab population numbered 1,200,000 while the Jewish population claimed by the Zionists was approximately 600,000. Of these, about 100,000 were native Palestinian Jews who were not supporters of Zionist nationalism.[33] The Higher Committee expressed sympathy for the European Jewish refugees but pointed out that the responsibility to provide for them was an international one. The view was that Palestine had already received far more than its fair share of these refugees. In summary, these claims postulated the natural right of the Arab majority in Palestine to remain in undisputed possession of the country and to receive recognition by the General Assembly of their right to self-determination and independence.

The General Assembly, in resolution 106 (S-I) of 15 May 1947,[34] created the United Nations Special Committee on Palestine (UNSCOP) to consist of the following eleven members: Australia, Canada, Czechoslovakia, Guatemala,

---

32. Jewish Agency and World Zionist Organization remain the official names for the same entity. The World Zionist Organization–Jewish Agency (Status) Law, 7 Laws of the State of Israel 3 (Authorized Translation, 1952) provides in sec. 3:

> The World Zionist Organisation, which is also the Jewish Agency, takes care as before of immigration and directs absorption and settlement projects in the State.

See the Zionist Organisation/Jewish Agency Status Law (1952) in Appendix 5 and the 1975 Amendment to it in Apendix 8.

33. See *supra* note 28.

34. 2 *U.N. GAOR, Resolutions*, 6–7 (16 Sept.–29 Nov. 1947).

India, Iran, Netherlands, Peru, Sweden, Uruguay, and Yugoslavia. This resolution permitted UNSCOP to link the problem of the European Jewish refugees to a solution of the Palestine problem by providing that the Special Committee "shall conduct investigations in Palestine and wherever it may deem useful."[35] Operative paragraph 6 of the resolution provided in full:

> The Special Committee shall prepare a report to the General Assembly and shall submit such proposals as it may consider appropriate for the solution of the problem of Palestine.

The fact that there was no reference in the resolution to independence for Palestine brought about protests by both the Arab Higher Committee and the Arab states.

2. THE UNITED NATIONS SPECIAL COMMITTEE ON PALESTINE (UNSCOP)

Before making its recommendations, UNSCOP examined "the Jewish case" and "the Arab case."[36] The Arab case as considered was principally that made by the Arab Higher Committee before the First Special Session of the General Assembly and summarized above.

In paragraph 126 of its report, UNSCOP stated:

> The Jewish case, as herein considered, is mainly the case advanced by the Jewish Agency which, by the terms of the Mandate, has a special status with regard to Jewish interests in Palestine.

Even though UNSCOP thereby recognized that "the Jewish case" was actually the Zionist case, it thereafter referred to the Zionist case as "the Jewish case"[37] and it gave scant attention to the views of distinguished anti-Zionist Jews such

---

35. Operative para. 4.

36. The findings and recommendations of UNSCOP which are examined in the ensuing text are in 1 UNSCOP, *Report to the General Assembly*, 2 U.N. GAOR, *Supp. 11*, pp. 29–35, U.N. Doc. A/364 (3 Sept. 1947).

37. The importance of labels should not be underestimated. Perspectives would have been different if the labels had been "the Zionist case" (or "the European case") and "the Palestinian case."

as Dr. Judah Magnes[38] in Palestine and Rabbi Elmer Berger[39] in the United States.

The UNSCOP Majority Report contained several inaccurate interpretations. For example, paragraph 146 states:

> Both the Balfour Declaration and the Mandate involved international commitments to the Jewish people as a whole. It was obvious that these commitments were not limited only to the Jewish population of Palestine, since at the time there were only some 80,000 Jews there.

Apparently the majority were somewhat aware of the untenable implications in the quoted paragraph since the ensuing paragraph states:

> This would imply that all Jews in the world who wish to go to Palestine would have the right to do so. This view, however, would seem to be unrealistic in the sense that a country as small and poor as Palestine could never accommodate all the Jews in the world.

The inaccuracies of paragraph 146, however, are much more fundamental than the qualifications raised by UNSCOP. It is difficult to find anything in either the Balfour Declaration (which was incorporated virtually unchanged in the Palestine Mandate) or in other provisions of the Palestine Mandate which involved "international commitments to the Jewish people as a whole." The only "rights" specified in the Balfour Declaration are those which appear in the two safeguard clauses.

Another example of inaccuracy in the UNCSOP Majority Report is provided by paragraph 164 of the report:

---

38. Then president of the Hebrew University of Jerusalem. See Magnes, "A Solution Through Force?" in Gary V. Smith (ed.), *Zionism – The Dream and the Reality: A Jewish Critique* 109 (1974).

39. Then executive director of the American Council for Judaism and now president of American Jewish Alternatives to Zionism. See Berger, "The Real Issues in the Arab–Israeli–Zionist Conflict" in *id.* at 218.

> The Arab population, despite the strenuous efforts of Jews to acquire land in Palestine, at present remains in possession of approximately 85 per cent of the land. The provisions of the land transfer regulations of 1940, which gave effect to the 1939 White Paper policy, have severely restricted the Jewish efforts to acquire new land.

The error of fact here involves the implication that Jews were making efforts to acquire land in Palestine. There is no evidence to support this statement other than isolated actions by individual Jews who, in the normal course of events, acquired land for their personal or business purposes and without regard to the Zionist political objectives.[40] In contrast to the quoted statement, the actual fact was that the Jewish National Fund, a principal Zionist institution then as now, was responsible for the acquisition of land for "the Jewish people" and land which was acquired by it was subjected to discriminatory restrictive covenants prohibiting the employment of Arabs on the land and indeed, any Arab connection with the land.[41] The quoted UNSCOP statement reveals a surprising ignorance of Zionist nationalism and an

---

40. See, *e.g.*, the reference to Jewish agriculturists who, contrary to Zionist policy and practice, spoke Arabic and employed Arabs on their farms, in Kirk, *A Short History of the Middle East* 152 (7th rev. ed. 1974).

41. The 1954 basic agreement between the State of Israel (represented by its government) and the World Zionist Organization (represented by its executive) was designed to regularize and institutionalize, but not to change, the working arrangements between the two. Section 1 of the agreement, which is formally entitled "Covenant between the Government of Israel (Hereafter the Government) and the Zionist Executive Called also the Executive of the Jewish Agency (Hereafter the Executive)," provides, *inter alia*, for "the acquisition and amelioration of land in Israel by the institutions of the Zionist Organization, the Keren Kayemeth Leisrael [Jewish National Fund] and the Keren Hayesod [United Israel Appeal]." The United Israel Appeal is the parent organization which receives most of the funds raised by the United Jewish Appeal. In brief, the United Israel Appeal receives the funds and the Jewish National Fund uses them in the acquisition and improvement of land. The Covenant appears in Appendix 6.

    The Jewish National Fund also has its own Covenant of 28 Nov. 1961 with the Government of Israel. *Executive Reports*, 26th Zionist Congress 345 (Dec. 1964). On the governmental and land acquisition functions of the Jewish National Fund see *id.* at 345–55.

    For the U.S. Senate investigation into Zionist activities in the United States see *Hearings on Activities of Nondiplomatic Representatives of Foreign Principals in the United States* before the Senate Committee on Foreign Relations, 88th Cong., 1st Sess., Part 9, pp. 1211–1424 (23 May 1963) and Part 12, pp. 1695–1782 (1 Aug. 1963).

inability to distinguish its acts from the acts of individual Jews.

UNSCOP unanimously recommended that the Palestine Mandate be terminated and that independence be granted "in Palestine" following a transitional period under United Nations responsibility.[42] It is significant that in spite of the factual and legal misconceptions, UNSCOP's Recommendation VII entitled "Democratic Principles and Protection of Minorities" sets forth basic requirements for human rights including full protection for the rights and interests of minorities, specifying "full equality of all citizens with regard to political, civil, and religious matters."[43] The Zionist objective of establishing an exclusivist Jewish state falls far short of this standard. Recommendation VI asked the General Assembly to immediately provide for an international arrangement to deal with "the problem of distressed European Jews" as "a matter of extreme urgency."[44] It was added that this would lessen immigration pressure on Palestine and create "a better climate" for solution of the Palestine question.[45]

The principal majority recommendations, supported by seven of the eleven members of UNSCOP, involved a plan of partition with economic union. The majority also proposed that the City of Jerusalem be placed under international trusteeship. In addition, it was recommended by the majority (with the dissent of two members and with one recording no opinion) that:

> In the appraisal of the Palestine question it be accepted as incontrovertible that any solution for Palestine cannot be considered as a solution of the Jewish problem in general.[46]

This reflects a clear rejection of the Zionist attempt to link the

---

42. The UNSCOP recommendations are in *supra* note 36 at 42–64.

43. *Id.* at 45.

44. *Id.* at 44.

45. *Id.*

46. *Id.* at 46.

solution of "the Jewish problem" with the proposed state in Palestine.

A minority of three (India, Iran, and Yugoslavia) recommended independence for Palestine as a federal state comprising, in internal structure, an Arab state and a Jewish state. One of the reasons advanced was that federation would create a situation where it would be in the interest of Arabs and Jews to work together. Under the heading of "Justification for the federal-state solution," the minority stated in paragraph 12:

> It is a fact of great significance that very few, if any, Arabs, are in favour of partition as a solution. On the other hand, a substantial number of Jews, backed by influential Jewish leaders and organizations, are strongly opposed to partition. Partition both in principle and in substance can only be regarded as an anti-Arab solution. The federal State, however, cannot be described as an anti-Jewish solution. To the contrary, it will best serve the interests of both Arabs and Jews.[47]

B. THE PLAN OF PARTITION WITH ECONOMIC UNION

Upon convening in September, 1947, the Second U.N. General Assembly constituted itself as the Ad Hoc Committee to Consider the Palestine Question, which was a committee of the whole Assembly.[48] The Ad Hoc Committee voted on 25 November 1947 in favor of the substance of the UNSCOP majority proposal for the Partition of Palestine by 25 votes to 13 with 17 abstentions. Prominent among the supporters of partition were both the United States and the Soviet Union.

Because a two-thirds majority was not required in the Ad Hoc Committee, the proposal in favor of partition was recommended to the General Assembly. On 29 November 1947 the General Assembly voted in favor of partition,

---

47. *Id.* at 59.

48. *2 U.N. GAOR, Ad Hoc Committee on the Palestine Question.*

adopting resolution 181(II)[49] by 33 votes in favor to 13 against with 10 abstentions. Haiti, Liberia, and the Philippines which had not previously supported partition voted in favor of it.

1. GENERAL PROVISIONS

General Assembly resolution 181, adopted with the full authority of a two-thirds vote as required for important questions, constitutes a recommendation by the General Assembly to Great Britain, as the Mandatory Power, and to all other members of the United Nations for the adoption and implementation of the Plan of Partition with Economic Union for Palestine. The Partition Resolution provided that "the Mandate for Palestine shall terminate as soon as possible but in any case not later than 1 August 1948."[50] It also provided that the armed forces of the Mandatory Power should be withdrawn from Palestine as soon as possible but in no event later than 1 August 1948. Two independent states, which were not specifically designated by name but were referred to as "the Jewish state" and "the Arab state," and the special International Regime for the City of Jerusalem should come into existence two months after the evacuation of the armed forces of the Mandatory Power but in no event later than 1 October 1948.

Among the steps preparatory to independence which were prescribed, a Commission on Palestine was to be established consisting of five member states to be elected by the General Assembly. The administration of Palestine should be progressively turned over to the Commission as the Mandatory Power withdrew its armed forces. The Mandatory Power was to cooperate with the Commission as the latter took over and administered areas which had been evacuated by the Mandatory Power. Upon its arrival in Palestine, the Commission should take measures to establish the frontiers of the "Arab" and "Jewish" states and the City of Jerusalem in accordance with the geographic boundaries spelled out in the Partition Plan except that the specified boundaries should be modified in such a way that, as a

---

49. *Supra* note 25.

50. The ensuing text is based upon the provisions of G.A. Res. 181.

general rule, villages should not be divided by state boundaries.

The Resolution provided that the Commission, after consultation with "democratic parties and other public organizations," should select and establish in each state a Provisional Council of Government. The activities of these councils should be carried out under the general direction of the Commission. During the transition period the Provisional Council should have authority in the areas under their control while acting under the overall authority of the Commission. The Council in each state should progressively receive full governmental authority and it should provide for the holding of elections "which shall be conducted on democratic lines" with Arabs and Jews entitled to vote in the state where they would become citizens. Other provisions of the Partition Plan specified freedom of transit, a customs union, a joint currency system, and other similar measures to bring about the economic union of Palestine.

The provisions to draw the boundaries of the two states were extremely complex. In over-simple summary, the territory of Palestine was divided into eight parts with three each allocated to the Jewish state and to the Arab state, while the seventh, Jaffa, was to form an Arab enclave in the Jewish state. The eighth part was to be the City of Jerusalem, established as a *corpus separatum* under a special international regime, which was to be administered by the U.N. Trusteeship Council for an initial period of ten years. There was not, however, compliance with the provisions of the Partition Resolution. The territorial boundaries were determined *de facto* by the outcome of the conflict situation in Palestine rather than by the provisions of the Partition Resolution.

One of the provisions of the Resolution which was shown to be impracticable was that which stated that the Provisional Council in each state should recruit an armed militia but that the ultimate control of the militia should remain in the Palestine Commission through the transition period.[51] The native Palestinians had had no significant

---

51. G.A. Res. 181, Part I B(8).

military force since the British Army had decisively defeated the Palestinian rebellion during 1936–1939. In striking contrast, the Jewish Agency/Zionist Organization had long had effective regular military forces in the Hagana and the Palmach.[52] In addition, although there were apparent disagreements on tactics, the Zionist terrorist organizations including the Irgun and the Stern Gang worked effectively with the Jewish Agency in achieving Zionist political and territorial objectives by military means.[53] The Palestine Commission was unable under these conditions to exert effective control.

2. HUMAN RIGHTS PROVISIONS

Among the most important human rights provisions of the Partition Plan is section 10(d) of Part I B which states:

> The Constituent Assembly of each State shall draft a democratic constitution for its State and choose a provisional government to succeed the Provisional Council of Government appointed by the Commission. The constitutions of the States shall embody chapters 1 and 2 of the Declaration provided for in section C below and include *inter alia* provisions for: ... .
>
> (d) Guaranteeing to all persons equal and non-discriminatory rights in civil, political, economic and religious matters and the enjoyment of human rights and fundamental freedoms, including freedom of religion, language, speech and publication, education, assembly, and association.

Part I C, entitled "Declaration," contains chapters 1 and 2 referred to above as well as the following two introductory paragraphs:

---

52. See in the Report of the *Anglo-American Committee of Inquiry, supra* note 30, the descriptions of the Hagana and the Palmach in Chap. 9 entitled "Public Security" at 45–46.

53. See the descriptions of the Irgun and the Stern Gang in *id.* at 47. Military cooperation between the Irgun and the Zionist regular forces is described in Begin, *The Revolt* Chap. 29 entitled "The Conquest of Jaffa," and *passim.* (1948, new ed. 1972).

> A declaration shall be made to the United
> Nations by the provisional government of each
> proposed State before independence. It shall
> contain *inter alia* the following clauses:
> The stipulations contained in the declaration
> are recognized as fundamental laws of the State
> and no law, regulation or official action shall
> conflict or interfere with these stipulations, nor
> shall any law, regulation or official action prevail
> over them.

Chapter 1, entitled "Holy Places, religious buildings and sites," makes detailed provisions for protection of the Holy Places and for the preservation of access to and rights concerning them. Chapter 2, entitled "Religious and minority rights," has the following provisions in its first three paragraphs:

> 1. Freedom of conscience and the free exercise
> of all forms of worship, subject only to the
> maintenance of public order and morals, shall be
> ensured to all.
> 2. No discrimination of any kind shall be
> made between the inhabitants on the ground of
> race, religion, language or sex.
> 3. All persons within the jurisdiction of the
> State shall be entitled to equal protection of the
> laws.

The Partition Resolution contains analogous human rights provisions for the inhabitants of the City of Jerusalem encompassing "the enjoyment of human rights and fundamental freedoms including freedom of conscience, religion, and worship ... ."[54] It was expressly provided that "[n]o discrimination of any kind shall be made between the inhabitants [of Jerusalem] on the grounds of race, religion,

---

54. G.A. Res. 181, Part III C 12(a).

language or sex."[55] Detailed provisions were also made for protection of the holy places including existing rights concerning them.[56]

The human rights provisions of the Partition Resolution qualify the authority to establish each of the two states by providing a reciprocal system of rights and obligations in which the exercise of the right to create a state is conditioned upon the obligation to implement human rights. The provisions for human rights in part I B section 10(b) are explicit and there cannot be any rational interpretation of the Partition Resolution which circumvents them. These provisions of the Partition Resolution are not surprising in view of the human rights provisions of the United Nations Charter. In addition to the basic provisions of articles 55 and 56, article 1(3) specifies as one of the major purposes of the United Nations, "promoting and encouraging respect for human rights and for fundamental freedoms for all without distinction as to race, sex, language, or religion."

The legal significance of the human rights provisions is that they do not concede the Zionist claims to establish an exclusivist state. The Declaration of Establishment of the State of Israel of 14 May, 1948 contains wording which is addressed to the maintenance of human rights. It provides that the State of Israel

> will ensure the complete equality of social and political rights to all its inhabitants irrespective of religion, race or sex; it will guarantee freedom of religion, conscience, language, education and culture.[57]

The test of compliance with the human rights provisions of the Partition Resolution is not, however, merely a verbal one. The test is whether or not the State which seeks to justify its legal authority under the Partition Resolution complies with the human rights provisions in fact. The State of Israel has no

---

55. *Id.* at Part III C 12(b).

56. *Id.* at Part III C 13, 14.

57. 1 Israel Laws, *supra* note 32, 3 at para. 12 (1948).

constitution as required by the Resolution.[58] It has made no attempt to enact and enforce nondiscriminatory human rights provisions. Its "basic laws" are a group of statutes of particular Zionist importance which provide for fundamental discriminations.[59] Among these "basic laws" of the State of Israel which are in violation of the Palestine Partition Resolution are the Law of Return[60] and the Nationality Law[61] under which a member of "the Jewish people" from anywhere in the world is entitled as a claimed legal right to come to the State of Israel and acquire citizenship. Under the same municipal laws a Palestinian Arab native is not entitled to return to his homeland.[62] This type of discrimination, and other analogous ones, are unequivocally prohibited under the human rights provisions of the Resolution.[63]

The same human rights provisions will constitute equally binding obligations upon a Palestinian Arab State established pursuant to the Partition Resolution and subsequent resolutions of the General Assembly.

---

58.   Some persons appeared to believe that a constitution would be drafted and adopted in spite of the difficulties which the human rights provisions of the Partition Resolution would present to the Government of Israel. See H. E. Baker, *The Legal System of Israel* 14 (1961).

59.   See generally *id*. at 31–49.

60.   4 Israel Laws, *supra* note 32 at 48 (1950) as amended.

61.   6 *id*. at 50 (1952) as amended.

62.   On its face the Nationality Law, *supra* note 61, is not so obviously discriminatory as the Law of Return, *supra* note 60. However, its substantive provisions, including the requirement of "lawful" pre-existing residence within the State of Israel, effectively bar the return of Palestinian Arab natives who are determined by these municipal laws not to have such residence.

63.   To the extent that the Partition Resolution human rights provisions represent the applicable international law on the subject, the existence of the Israeli discriminatory municipal statutes do not constitute a defense to the charge of violation of international law. It is one of the most basic principles of international law, which may be termed a world order principle, that municipal law can never be used as a defense to a charge of violation of international law. See, *inter alia, United Staes v. Guatemala* ("Shufeldt Claim," 1930), U.S. Dept. of State Arb. Series 3 at p. 851, 876–77; reprinted in relevant part in Bishop (ed.), *International Law: Cases and Materials* 83 (3rd ed., 1971).

C. THE JURIDICAL STATUS OF THE PARTITION RESOLUTION

1. CLAIMS OF INVALIDITY

There are a number of claims that the Partition Resolution is in violation of law. One such claim is that article 22 of the League of Nations Covenant was a decolonization provision which was conditioned only by a temporary period of Mandate status as a preparation for independence. This is particularly true of Palestine, it is claimed, because Palestine was provisionally recognized by the League of Nations Covenant as independent along with other parts of the former Turkish Empire.[64]

There is a single claim which underlies several of the charges of violation of particular articles of the Palestine Mandate. It is that the Palestine Mandate was in effect when the General Assembly acted in November, 1947 and that there was no authority to deprive the native Palestinians of rights and protections which were secured to them at the time by the Mandate.[65]

---

64. *League of Nations Covenant* art. 22 (4).

65. The League Mandate for Palestine is cited *supra* note 29. The ensuing text is based upon claimed violations of the provisions of the Partition Resolution, the terms of the League Mandate, and the terms of the United Nations Charter.

Ambassador Loy Henderson, then serving as Director of the Office of Near Eastern and African Affairs in the U.S. Department of State, made several basic criticisms of UNSCOP's Plan of Partition in a memorandum of 22 Sept. 1947 to the Secretary of State. For example, after stating that the UNSCOP plan violated both the U.N. Charter and American principles, he continued:

> These proposals, for instance, ignore such principles as self-determination and majority rule. They recognize the principle of a theocratic racial state and even go so far in several instances as to discriminate on grounds of religion and race against persons outside of Palestine. We have hitherto always held that in our foreign relations American citizens, regardless of race or religion, are entitled to uniform treatment. The stress on whether persons are Jews or non-Jews is certain to strengthen feelings among both Jews and Gentiles in the United States and elsewhere that Jewish citizens are not the same as other citizens.

[1947] 5 *Foreign Rels. U.S.* 1153 at 1157 (1971).

Additional claims concerning the invalidity of the Partition Resolution are in H. Cattan, *Palestine and International Law: The Legal Aspects of the Arab–Israeli Conflict,* Chap. 4 and *passim* (2nd ed., 1976).

Article 5 of the Mandate is one of several articles that placed obligations upon the Mandatory Power which made it a trustee for the Palestinians. It is contended that its provision against ceding Palestinian territory to "the control of the Government of any foreign Power" was violated by the General Assembly when it ceded the territory allocated to "the Jewish state" to the Jewish Agency/Zionist Organization. The view is that the Jewish Agency may have been a domestic power while it complied with the limitations placed upon it by article 4 of the Mandate which specified that it be "subject always to the control of the Mandatory Administration." However, at least from the time of the Anglo-American Committee of Inquiry of 1946 when it was characterized as a "shadow Government" which "has ceased to cooperate with the [Mandatory] Administration . . . in the suppression of terrorism,"[66] the Jewish Agency was a foreign power and the allocation of control of territory to it as the *de facto* government of "the Jewish state" in the Partition Resolution was a clear violation of article 5.

Article 6 of the Mandate required the Mandatory Administration to "facilitate Jewish immigration" providing "that the rights and position of other sections of the population are not prejudiced." There are three subsidiary claims involved. The first is that the immigration which took place was not a Jewish immigration, but that it was a politically motivated Zionist immigration. The second claim is that it was not an "immigration" at all as the term is commonly understood in both its factual and its legal aspects. It was rather an invasion by Zionist masses which subverted the Palestinian community under the guise of immigration. The third claim is that, whether it should be termed an immigration or an invasion, it resulted in flagrant violation of "the rights and position of other sections of the population" including depriving them of their homes and their livelihoods. The basic charge of illegality here is that the General Assembly compounded the illegalities of the Mandatory in this respect by acting upon and giving effect to the

---

66. *Supra* note 30.

Zionist "immigration" which was carried out in violation of the Mandate provisions.

Article 1 of the United Nations Charter, dealing with the Purposes and Principles of the United Nations, sets forth as the second of these the development of "friendly relations among nations based upon respect for the principle of equal rights and self-determination of peoples." Article 73 concerning non-self-governing territories provides that members of the U.N. which assume trusteeship responsibilities accept "a sacred trust" and are obligated "to develop self-government to take due account of the political aspirations of the peoples, and to assist them in the progressive development of their free political institutions." The claim is that, even though these Charter provisions do not explicitly apply to the Palestine Mandate, they are nevertheless a fortiori applicable. It would, so the argument goes, be totally beyond the powers of the General Assembly to deal with a League Mandate in disregard of the Charter principle of self-determination which binds the United Nations including, of course, the General Assembly.[67] The Partition Resolution, it is claimed, as a partition of the country against the will of the overwhelming majority of the native population, was a flagrant violation of the principle of self-determination and therefore illegal.

2. CLAIMS OF VALIDITY

Article 2(7) of the Charter prohibits the United Nations from intervening "in matters which are essentially within the domestic jurisdiction of any state." Palestine, however, had been regarded as a matter of international concern for some time prior to 1947. This is demonstrated by article 22(4) of the League Covenant as well as by the Palestine Mandate. In 1947 Palestine, although under a Mandate, was not a state. Consequently, there was no possibility of claiming Palestinian domestic jurisdiction as a bar to action by the General Assembly. In addition, the presence of a large number of recently arrived European immigrants tended to make

---

67. Self-determination is considered in more detail in the following chapter.

Palestine a continuing concern to the international community.

There can be no doubt but that the self-determination issue was a central one in the Palestine question. Self-determination is usually conceived as the right of the majority within an established political unit to determine its own future. There was strong evidence that Palestine was an established self-determination unit because of the provisions of the League Covenant[68] and of the Palestine Mandate.[69] The Palestinians and the Zionists in a sense were agreed upon what might be characterized broadly as self-determination for Palestine. The Palestinians' objective was self-determination for all the inhabitants of Palestine in a unitary state, whereas the Zionists' objective was self-determination for the European immigrant minority without regard to the rights of the majority population. The existence of the self-determination issue made the Palestine question a particularly appropriate one for action by the General Assembly. From a practical standpoint there was no alternative forum which could have dealt with the issue so authoritatively.

In 1947 the Zionist terror[70] along with the Palestinian responding violence[71] were creating a situation in which the most basic human rights were being denied including the right to life itself. This coercion situation made it essential for the United Nations to take immediate steps to protect human rights and it attempted to do so through the detailed human rights provisions of the Partition Resolution. The Charter treats the achievement of human rights as a basic principle and this provided additional authority for the General Assembly to act.

It should be recalled that Great Britain as the Mandatory Power addressed its request for United Nations assumption

---

68. Art. 22(4).

69. *Inter alia*, art. 2 (concerning "the development of self-governing institutions"), arts. 3, 5, and 6.

70. See Hirst, *The Gun and the Olive Branch: The Roots of Violence in the Middle East, passim* (1977). See also [1947] 5 *Foreign Rels. U.S., supra* note 30.

71. *Id.*

of responsibility concerning the future government of Palestine to the General Assembly. The General Assembly has comprehensive legal authority over the International Trusteeship system as provided in Chapter XII of the Charter. It also has supervisory authority in law over League of Nations Mandates as the successor to the Assembly of the League of Nations, as the International Court of Justice stated with particular reference to the South-West Africa Mandated Territory in the 1950 Advisory Opinion on the subject:

> [T]he Court has arrived at the conclusion that the General Assembly of the United Nations is legally qualified to exercise the supervisory functions previously exercised by the League of Nations with regard to the administration of the Territory, and that the Union of South Africa is under an obligation to submit to supervision and control of the General Assembly and to render annual reports to it.[72]

Article 80(1) of the U.N. Charter provides that, with the exception of provisions written into trusteeship agreements:

> [N]othing in this Charter shall be construed in or of itself to alter in any manner the rights whatsoever of any states or any peoples or the terms of existing international instruments to which Members of the United Nations may respectively be parties.

The comprehensive wording, "the rights whatsoever of any states or of any peoples," encompasses the rights which the native Palestinians had under the provisions of the Mandate for Palestine including the Balfour Declaration first safeguard clause. Upon the termination of the Palestine Mandate, the Partition Resolution constituted an undertaking to preserve human rights for all Palestinians on a non-discriminatory basis. The human rights provisions of the Partition Resolu-

---

72. *International Status of South-West Africa*, Advisory Opinion of 11 July 1950, [1950] I.C.J. 128 at 137. See also [1955] I.C.J. 67 at 76 and [1971] I.C.J. 16 at 43.

tion continue to bind the State of Israel because it does not have the legal authority to exercise rights under that resolution without complying with the correlative obligations.

3. THE CONTINUING VALIDITY OF THE PARTITION RESOLUTION
The adoption of the Partition Resolution by the two-thirds vote required for important questions gave it a high degree of legal authority. The representative of the Jewish Agency, Mr. Shertok (later the foreign minister and the prime minister of the Government of Israel), referred to its "binding force" on 27 April 1948:

> With regard to the status of Assembly resolutions in international law, it was admitted that any which touched the national sovereignty of the Members of the United Nations were mere recommendations and not binding. However, the Palestine resolution was essentially different for it concerned the future of a territory subject to an international trust. Only the United Nations as a whole was competent to determine the future of the territory, and its decision, therefore, had a binding force.[73]

The State of Israel has placed heavy reliance upon the Partition Resolution as providing legal authority.[74] Its Declaration of the Establishment of the State of Israel, after referring to General Assembly resolution 181 as "a resolution calling for the establishment of a Jewish state in Eretz-Israel," continues: "This recognition by the United Nations of the right of the Jewish people to establish their state is irrevocable."[75] Another paragraph of the Declaration pro-

---

73. U.N. Doc. A/C 1/SR. 127 at p. 7 (27 April 1948).

74. In addition to the primary sources considered in the text, it is significant that the authoritative Zionist lawyer, Professor N. Feinberg, has argued in favor of the validity of the Partition Resolution. *The Arab–Israel Conflict in International Law*, Chap. VI (1970).
   It is recognized that the Government of Israel has placed less reliance on the Partition Resolution since its extensive military conquests during the intense hostilities of June, 1967.

75. *Supra* note 57 at para. 9.

vides that the State is established "By Virtue of our Natural and Historic Right and on the Strength of the Resolution of the United Nations General Assembly."[76] Although the Preamble to the Palestine Mandate refers to "the historical connection of the Jewish people with Palestine,"[77] the negotiating history of this wording reveals that the Zionist claim of legal right on an historic basis was rejected.[78] Therefore, it appears that the Partition Resolution is the preeminent juridical basis for the State of Israel.

The Arab states not only voted against partition, but they initially took the position that it was invalid. It is, therefore, significant that they have subsequently relied upon it in presenting legal arguments on behalf of the Palestinians. The Arab states are now not only supporting the basic principles of the Partition Resolution, but subsequent General Assembly resolutions which are consistent with those principles as well.[79] The Arab states were deeply disturbed by what they initially regarded as the violation of the right of self-determination by the Partition Resolution. The self-determination issue may have been resolved in an unusual manner, but as a matter of law the particular method of self-determination in two states appears to have been accepted.

The Partition Resolution continues to provide legal authority, combined with restrictions upon that authority, for each of two states in Palestine. It is important to recognize that validity in law is not dependent upon subsequent effectuation. Even though there has been little effectuation of many of the specific provisions of the Partition Resolution, it

---

76. *Id.* at para. 10.

77. *Supra* note 29, Preamble para. 3.

78. Dr. Weizmann states:

> The most serious difficulty arose in connection with a paragraph in the Preamble – the phrase which now reads: "Recognizing the historical connection of the Jews with Palestine." Zionists wanted to have it read: "Recognizing the historic rights of the Jews to Palestine." But Curzon [the British Foreign Secretary] would have none of it ... .

Trial and Error, supra note 28 at 348.

79. See Chap. 4 *infra*.

is not possible to say that this demonstrates its invalidity. The subsequent resolutions of the General Assembly recognizing the right of return of individual Palestinians, as well as those recognizing the Palestinians as a people with national rights, are consistent with the basic conception of partition and two states in Palestine. The subsequent resolutions of the General Assembly are also consistent with the continued existence of the State of Israel, as one of the states authorized in the Partition Resolution, provided that it complies with the obligations which are conjoined with the authorization to establish the state.[80] The actions of the General Assembly concerning Palestine have been taken, it should be emphasized, with the affirmative participation of a substantial majority of the states of the world community which comprise the Assembly's membership and thereby constitute a worldwide consensus of support of the continuing validity of the basic principles of the Partition Resolution.

---

80. The International Court of Justice has considered the relationship between obligations and rights in connection with the then Mandated Territory of South-West Africa:

> The authority which the Union Government exercises over the Territory is based on the Mandate. If the Mandate lapsed, as the Union Government contends, the latter's authority would equally have lapsed. To retain the rights derived from the Mandate and to deny the obligations thereunder could not be justified.

Supra note 72, [1950] I.C.J. 128 at 133.

If the principle of reciprocal rights and obligations under the League Mandate for South-West Africa was lawfully applied to the Union of South Africa, there is no reason why the principle should not be equally applicable to the State of Israel under the Palestine Partition Resolution.

Chapter 4

The Fundamental Palestinian Rights in International Law

I. The Individual Right of Return

A. THE BACKGROUND OF THE RIGHT OF RETURN IN PRACTICE AND LAW

For most individuals the actual practice of returning to one's home or country is so commonplace a part of everyday living that the right of return as a legal concept is given little attention. The great majority of people in the world are able to exercise the customary right of return based upon state practice. This usual state practice is so uncontroversial that it is not the subject of diplomatic and juridical contention. The Palestinians, however, are in an unusual situation because their right of return has been systematically denied to them ever since the events of 1947 and 1948.

Historically, the right of return was so universally accepted and practiced that it was not deemed necessary to prescribe or codify it in a formal manner. In 1215, at a time when rights were being questioned in England, the Magna Carta was agreed to by King John. It provided that: "It shall be lawful in the future for anyone . . . to leave our kingdom and to return, safe and secure by land and water ... ."[1]

Particular provisions have been made to protect the right of return, termed "repatriation," in armed conflict and belligerent occupation situations. The four Geneva Conven-

---

1. *Magna Carta*, Chap. 42. The translation quoted is from S. E. Thorne et al, *The Great Charter: Four Essays on Magna Carta and the History of our Liberty* 133 (1965).

tions of 1949 concerning the protection of war victims[2] contain many provisions relating to the repatriation of such victims.[3] These Geneva Conventions have been ratified by almost as many states as have ratified the United Nations Charter, including all of the states which have been involved in the recurring hostilities in the Middle East. Among the most important common provisions which appear in each of the four Conventions is one which limits the effect of a denunciation of the Convention by a state party during a conflict or a belligerent occupation until after the repatriation of protected persons has been effectuated.[4] This provision is a recognition in multilateral treaty law of the importance of the right of return or repatriation. Its broad ambit applies to protected civilian persons[5] as well as to prisoners of war[6] and disabled military personnel.[7]

The Geneva Civilians Convention of 1949 also contains a significant law-making provision designed to prevent the removal of protected civilian persons so that they will not be in a position where they need to claim their right of return. The relevant article states:

> Individual or mass forcible transfers as well as deportations of protected persons from occupied territory to the territory of the Occupying Power or to that of any other country, occupied or not, are prohibited, regardless of their motive.[8]

---

2.   The following are the four Conventions of 1949: I. Geneva Convention for the Amelioration of the Condition of the Wounded and Sick in Armed Forces in the Field, 75 U.N.T.S. 31; II. Geneva Convention for the Amelioration of the Condition of Wounded, Sick and Shipwrecked Members of Armed Forces at Sea, 75 U.N.T.S. 85; III. Geneva Convention Relative to the Treatment of Prisoners of War, 75 U.N.T.S. 135; IV. Geneva Convention Relative to the Protection of Civilian Persons in Time of War, 75 U.N.T.S. 287.

3.   Conv. I: arts. 5, 63; Conv. II: arts. 6, 62; Conv. III: *inter alia*, arts. 5, 46–48, 109–119, 142; Conv. IV: *inter alia*, arts. 6, 36, 45(2), 134, 158.

4.   Conv. I: art. 63(3); Conv. II: art. 63(3); Conv. III: art. 142(3); Conv. IV: art. 158(3). See the text of Chap. 6 *infra* at note 20.

5.   Defined in Conv. IV, art. 4.

6.   Defined in Conv. III, art. 4.
7.   Defined in Conv. I, art. 13 and in Conv. II, art. 13.

8.   Art. 49(1).

This provision of the Convention is important for present purposes because it indicates that the state parties, including the State of Israel, were willing to go beyond the requirement of the right of return by prohibiting expulsions. Such a preventive approach can only be adopted by those who consider the less comprehensive right of return as being inadequate in belligerent occupation situations. The human values protected by the right of return and the prohibition of transfers and deportations are the same, although the advantage of effective prohibition is that it would make it unnecessary to exercise the right.

The Universal Declaration of Human Rights provides in relevant part: "Everyone has the right to leave any country, including his own, and to return to his country."[9] The broad ambit of the quoted language, including the terms "everyone" and "country" requires some emphasis. Unless the right of return is interpreted with appropriate breadth, it would require no more than a legalistic trick to expel certain inhabitants and then to deny them return on the false grounds that they are not nationals of the expelling state. There has been an attempt to justify the denial of the right of return of the Palestinians by arguing that the quoted provision of the Universal Declaration obligates states "to permit the return of their citizens or nationals only."[10] This argument would merely require discriminatory municipal statutes to bar the return of inhabitants to their country.[11]

The International Covenant on Civil and Political Rights contains a similar provision which states: "No one shall be arbitrarily deprived of the right to enter his own country."[12] Like the Universal Declaration, it avoids the use of narrow terms such as "nationals" and "state."

---

9. Art. 13(2). The Universal Declaration was approved by G.A. Res. 217A (III) (10 Dec. 1948).

10. Radley, "The Palestinian Refugees: The Right to Return in International Law," 72 Am. J. Int'l L. 586 at 613 (1978).

11. See the text of Chap. 3 accompanying notes 60, 61 and 62.

12. Art. 12(4). This International Covenant has been approved by G.A. Res. 2200(XI) (16 Dec. 1966).

Count Folke Bernadotte, the United Nations Mediator for Palestine, in his Progress Report of 16 September 1948,[13] set forth "seven basic premises" concerning the situation in Palestine. One of them, under the heading of the "Right of Repatriation," stated that:

> The right of innocent people, uprooted from their homes by the present terror and ravages of war, to return to their homes, should be affirmed and made effective, with assurance of adequate compensation for the property of those who may choose not to return.[14]

This basic premise was restated in the same Progress Report as a specific recommendation to the United Nations:

> The right of the Arab refugees to return to their homes in Jewish-controlled territory at the earliest possible date should be affirmed by the United Nations, and their repatriation, resettlement and economic and social rehabilitation, and payment of adequate compensation for the property of those choosing not to return, should be supervised and assisted by the United Nations conciliation commission ... .[15]

It is significant that Count Bernadotte did not recommend the creation of a new right, but instead recommended that the right to return "be affirmed by the United Nations." Consistent with this recommendation, subsequent resolutions of the General Assembly have sought to affirm and make effective an existing right. The right of return, based on state practice, was apparently regarded as an established part of customary international law as well as one of "the general principles of law recognized by civilized nations."

---

13. *3 U.N. GAOR, Supp. 11*, at 1–19, U.N. Doc. A/648 (21 Sept.–12 Dec. 1948).

14. *Id.* at 17, VIII 3(e).

15. *Id.* at 18, VIII 4(i).

B. GENERAL ASSEMBLY RESOLUTIONS APPLYING THE RIGHT OF RETURN

1. RESOLUTIONS 194(III) AND 513(VI) CONCERNING THE 1947–1948 REFUGEES

Count Bernadotte's mediation mission was ended on 17 September 1948 when he was assassinated by Israeli terrorists.[16] On 11 December 1948 the General Assembly adopted resolution 194(III)[17] entitled "Palestine – Progress Report of the United Nations Mediator." This Resolution was a comprehensive effort to deal with the ongoing conflict situation in Palestine and consisted of fifteen paragraphs. It established a Conciliation Commission for Palestine composed of three member states of the United Nations (France, Turkey, and the United States). The Commission was given broad authority to carry out the functions previously entrusted to the United Nations Mediator for Palestine and was instructed to assist the governments and authorities involved in the Palestine conflict with the purpose of achieving "a final settlement of all questions outstanding between them."[18] In the context of this major diplomatic and negotiating role assigned to the Conciliation Commission, paragraph 11 deals with the refugees by stating that the General Assembly:

> *Resolves* that the refugees wishing to return to their homes and live at peace with their neighbors should be permitted to do so at the earliest practicable date, and that compensation should be paid for the property of those choosing not to return and for the loss of or damage to property which, under principles of international law or in equity, should be made good by the Governments or authorities responsible.

---

16. The perpetrators were members of the Stern Gang. An account of the carefully planned murder appears in Hirst, *The Gun and the Olive Branch: The Roots of Violence in the Middle East* 147–55 (1977).

17. *3 U.N. GAOR, Resolutions* at 21–25, U.N. Doc. A/810, (21 Sept.–12 Dec. 1948).

18. *Id.*, para. 5.

> *Instructs* the Conciliation Commission to facilitate the repatriation, resettlement and economic and social rehabilitation of the refugees and the payment of compensation, and to maintain close relations with the Director of the United Nations Relief and Works Agency for Palestine Refugees and, through him, with the appropriate organs and agencies of the United Nations.

The text of paragraph 11 appears to have been written on the assumption that the principle of right of return was not in issue and that the central task was achieving practical implementation of repatriation. Therefore, it authorized the Conciliation Commission to deal with the Government of Israel on the subject. The conciliatory wording of the entire resolution was apparently based on the assumption that the Government of Israel would cooperate in good faith with the Conciliation Commission and "take all possible steps to assist in the implementation of the present resolution."[19] It was realized later that the efforts of the Conciliation Commission, like those of the United Nations Mediator before it, were a failure and did not effectuate the right of return of the Palestinian Arab refugees.

Paragraph 11 provides for two specifics concerning the implementation of the right of return. First, the refugees themselves are entitled to choose whether or not they wish to return to their homes within the *de facto* boundaries of the State of Israel. Second, the refugees are to be compensated for the loss of or damage to their property whether or not they choose to return. The specification that the refugees wishing to return should also wish to "live at peace with their neighbors" should be interpreted as a reassurance to the State of Israel that it would not be faced with an internal security problem following the return of the refugees. The additional provision that return should be carried out at the "earliest practicable date" is consistent with the approach that the Conciliation Commission was to use diplomatic and

---

19. *Id.*, para. 14.

mediation efforts to have the State of Israel comply with the terms of the resolution.

The Conciliation Commission for Palestine has given a careful interpretation to paragraph 11:

> The General Assembly had laid down the principle of the right of the refugees to exercise a free choice between returning to their homes and being compensated for the loss of or damage to their property on the one hand, or, on the other, of not returning to their homes and being adequately compensated for the value of the property abandoned by them.[20]

This interpretation is consistent with General Assembly Resolution 194(III) as well as subsequent resolutions.

The General Assembly again confronted the situation caused by the failure of repatriation on 26 January 1952 when it adopted resolution 513(VI)[21] which provided in paragraph 2 that its provisions were without prejudice to the repatriation provisions of resolution 194, paragraph 11. Paragraph 2 continued by endorsing a program proposed by the United Nations Relief and Works Agency for Palestine Refugees in the Near East (UNRWA) designed to expedite the reintegration of the displaced Arabs into the economic life of the area. It provides that this is to be accomplished either by repatriation, as enunciated in resolution 194, or through resettlement elsewhere. Resettlement was apparently offered as a practical alternative to the principle of repatriation which had thus far not been practically obtainable.

2. RESOLUTIONS 2452 (XXIII), 2535 (XXIV), AND 2963 (XXVII) CONCERNING THE 1947–1948 AND 1967 REFUGEES

In the years following the intense hostilities of June, 1967, the General Assembly adopted a series of resolutions which treat separately the right of return of the Palestinians displaced as a result of the 1947–1948 conflict and of those

---

20. *Historical Survey of Efforts of the U.N. Conciliation Commission for Palestine to Secure the Implementation of Paragraph 11 of G.A. resolution 194(III)*, para. 38; U.N. Doc. A/AC.25/W.81/Rev.2 at 20–21.

21. *6 U.N. GAOR, Supp.* 20 at 12–13 (6 Nov. 1951–5 Feb. 1952).

displaced as a result of the 1967 conflict. The dichotomy first appears in General Assembly resolution 2452 of 19 December 1968[22] which served as the functional paradigm for the significant substantive resolutions that followed, specifically resolutions 2535 and 2963.

The prefatory language of General Assembly resolution 2452B, dealing with the 1947–1948 refugees, after recalling both resolutions 194 and 513, further recalls those resolutions which affirm the principles of repatriation and resettlement stated in 194 and 513. Consistent with the tenor of the preceding resolutions, operative paragraph 1 of resolution 2452B provides that the General Assembly:

> *Notes with deep regret* that repatriation or compensation of the refugees as provided for in paragraph 11 of General Assembly resolution 194(III) has not been effected, that no substantial progress has been made in the programme endorsed in paragraph 2 of resolution 513(VI) for the reintegration of refugees either by repatriation or resettlement and that, therefore, the situation of the refugees continues to be a matter of serious concern.

Operative paragraph 4 of the same resolution states that the General Assembly:

> *Notes with regret* that the United Nations Conciliation Commission for Palestine was unable to find a means of achieving progress in the implementation of paragraph 11 of General Assembly resolution 194(III), and requests the Commission to exert continued efforts towards the implementation thereof.

In summary, in spite of past failure the General Assembly continued to rely upon diplomatic methods by the Conciliation Commission to obtain implementation of the right of return of the 1947–1948 refugees.

Resolution 2452A, dealing with the 1967 refugees, recalls

---

22.   *23 U.N. GAOR, Supp. 18* at 21–22.

Security Council resolution 237 of 14 June 1967 which calls upon the Government of Israel to facilitate their return. The prefatory wording of 2452A emphasizes the "requirement" of the refugees' "speedy return to their homes and to the camps which they formerly occupied." This wording indicates accurately that some of the 1947–1948 refugees who had fled to camps on the West Bank of the Jordan were again made refugees in 1967.

In resolution 2452A, the General Assembly bypasses the Conciliation Commission for Palestine, addresses the Government of Israel directly concerning the 1967 refugees, and asks the Secretary-General to follow and report upon "the effective implementation of the resolution."[23] Unlike resolution 194, there is no reassurance to the State of Israel that those returning desire to "live at peace with their neighbors." Israel is directly called upon to take "effective and immediate steps for the return without delay"[24] of the inhabitants who fled the area since the outbreak of hostilities. Like resolution 194(III), it appears to be written upon the assumption that the right of return is established and that the central task is to obtain its implementation.

On 10 December 1969, almost one year after the adoption of resolution 2452, the General Assembly adopted resolution 2535.[25] Resolution 2535A concerning the 1947–1948 refugees recalls, *inter alia*, resolutions 194, 513, and 2452. Like 2452B, resolution 2535A expresses regret over the fact that the refugees of the 1947–1948 conflict have not been repatriated or resettled pursuant to resolutions 194 and 513. As with earlier resolutions, it requests the Conciliation Commission to continue efforts towards implementation of the right of return of the 1947–1948 refugees.

Resolution 2535B deals with the 1967 refugees. Its first preambular paragraph states:

---

23. Operative para. 2.
24. Operative para. 1.
25. *24 U.N. GAOR, Supp. 30* at 25–26.

> *Recognizing* that the problem of the Palestine Arab refugees has arisen from the denial of their inalienable rights under the Charter of the United Nations and the Universal Declaration of Human Rights ... .

The resolution recalls Security Council resolution 237 (1967) and General Assembly resolutions 2252 and 2452A, all of which deal with the 1967 refugees. The operative paragraphs of resolution 2535B reaffirm "the inalienable rights of the people of Palestine,"[26] draw attention to the State of Israel's refusal to implement the resolutions concerning the 1967 refugees[27] and request the Security Council to take effective measures to ensure their implementation.[28]

General Assembly resolution 2963 of 13 December 1972[29] deals with several important matters including the national rights of the people of Palestine. It follows the general pattern of the resolutions just considered concerning the return of the refugees. Resolution 2963A recalls the relevant resolutions and notes with deep regret that resolution 194, paragraph 11 concerning the 1947–1948 refugees remains unimplemented. It requests the Conciliation Commission to continue efforts towards its implementation.

Resolution 2963D, in contrast, recalls the relevant resolutions dealing particularly with the 1967 refugees and in operative paragraph 1 affirms "the right of the displaced inhabitants to return to their homes and camps." Operative paragraph 4 states that the General Assembly *"Calls once more upon* Israel immediately to take steps for the return of the displaced inhabitants." Operative paragraph 6 requests the Secretary-General to report upon implementation. Resolution 2963C concerns the refugees expelled from the Gaza Strip, and operative paragraph 4 calls upon Israel "to take immediate and effective steps for the return of the refugees concerned to the camps from which they were removed ... ."

---

26. Para. 1.
27. Para. 2.
28. Para. 3.
29. *27 U.N. GAOR, Supp.* 30 at 27–29.

3. RESOLUTIONS 3089 (XXVIII), 3236(XXIX), AND SUBSEQUENT
   RESOLUTIONS CONCERNING THE INALIENABLE RIGHT TO
   RETURN TO THE AREA OF PALESTINE

Resolution 3089 of 7 December 1973[30] follows a somewhat similar pattern to resolution 2963 which has just been considered. The 1947–1948 refugees are dealt with in resolution 3089B in a manner like that employed in earlier resolutions requesting the Conciliation Commission "to exert continued efforts" to effectuate the right of return provided for in resolution 194. Resolution 3089C concerns the 1967 refugees and those expelled from the Gaza Strip and elsewhere during and after the intense hostilities of October 1973. It provides recognition and reaffirmation of their right of return in operative paragraph 1 which explicitly reaffirms "the right of the displaced inhabitants, including those displaced as a result of recent hostilities, to return to their homes and camps."

Operative paragraph 3 of resolution 3089D refers to "the inalienable rights of the people of Palestine" and states that "the enjoyment by the Palestine Arab refugees of their right to return to their homes and property, recognized by the General Assembly in resolution 194(III) of 11 December 1948, which has been repeatedly reaffirmed by the Assembly since that date" is indispensable for "a just settlement of the refugee problem." The broad reference to the right of the refugees "to return to their homes and property" should be interpreted as including return to the State of Israel as it existed with pre-June, 1967 *de facto* boundaries as well as to the Israeli-occupied Arab territories. It is clear that the right of return, as a right of individual Palestinians, may be exercised throughout Palestine including the State of Israel within whatever *de facto* boundaries it may have now or *de jure* boundaries that may be ultimately determined for that state.

Resolution 3236 of 22 November 1974[31] is one of the most fundamental actions of the General Assembly concerning the right of return and is notable in that it does not contain the dichotomy of separate provisions previously utilized for the

---

30. *28 U.N. GAOR, Supp. 30* at 26–28.

31. *29 U.N. GAOR, Supp. 31* at 4.

1947–1948 refugees and those of 1967 and 1973. After referring in operative paragraph 1 to the national inalienable rights of "the Palestinian people,"[32] this resolution provides in operative paragraph 2 that the General Assembly:

> *Reaffirms* also the inalienable rights of the Palestinians to return to their homes and property from which they have been displaced and uprooted, and calls for their return.

This paragraph emphasizes the significance of the right of return of the Palestinians by describing it as "inalienable." The characterization of rights as "inalienable" should be interpreted as meaning that they cannot be surrendered or otherwise terminated. Such fundamental rights may consequently be regarded as having unusual strength and permanence of a kind not associated with less important rights.

It should be mentioned that the right specified here, as in resolution 3089D, is of individual Palestinians to return, as distinguished from Palestinian national rights. The geographical reference of paragraph 2 is a comprehensive one. The term "their homes and property" covers areas of the State of Israel, whether as defined by the Palestine Partition Resolution or as it existed *de facto* prior to June 1967, and it also includes homes and property which are located in the territories occupied by Israel since 1967.

The present interpretation of resolution 3236 is not only required by the different wording of operative paragraph 1 dealing with national rights and operative paragraph 2 dealing with individual rights, but it is also required by the previous resolutions of the General Assembly including the Palestine Partition Resolution 181. There is nothing in resolution 3236 which derogates from resolution 181. Resolution 3236 is entirely consistent with the basic principle of two national states in Palestine which is embodied in resolution 181. It should also be mentioned that resolution 3236 is fully consistent with the provisions of the United Nations Charter including the principle of the sovereign equality of member

---

32. Such national rights are considered in Sec. II *infra*.

states. The sovereign equality of the State of Israel is not in question but, like other states, it must have its boundaries established in a lawful manner and honor the right of return as established in law and recognized by the world community through the General Assembly.

It may be suggested in opposition to the Palestinian right of return to the area within the lawful authority of the State of Israel that this would change "the Jewish character" of the State of Israel. It must be recognized that the term, "the Jewish character," is really a euphemism for the Zionist discriminatory statutes of the State of Israel which violate the human rights provisions of the Partition Resolution.[33] The matter was put directly by the then Israeli Defense Minister Dayan shortly after the intense hostilities of June 1967. He gave the following response to a reporter's question about Israel's ability to absorb the Arab population in the then recently occupied territories:

> Economically we can; but I think that is not in accord with our aims in the future. It would turn Israel into either a binational or poly-Arab-Jewish state instead of the Jewish State, and we want to have a Jewish state. We can absorb them, but then it won't be the same country.[34]

The United Nations is under no more of a legal obligation to maintain Zionism in Israel than it is to maintain apartheid in the Republic of South Africa.

Some subsequent resolutions concerning the right of return have reflected the earlier distinction between the 1947–1948 refugees and the 1967 and subsequent ones. For example, resolution 31/15A of 23 November 1976[35] dealing with the 1947–1948 refugees notes with deep regret that repatriation or compensation as provided for in paragraph 11 of General Assembly resolution 194 has not been achieved.

---

33. See *supra* Chap. 3, notes 60 and 61.

34. Quoted by I. F. Stone, "For a New Approach to the Israeli–Arab Conflict," in Gary V. Smith (ed.), *Zionism – The Dream and the Reality: A Jewish Critique* 197 at 209–210 (1974).

35. *31 U.N. GAOR, Supp. 39* at 48.

Resolution 31/15D dealing with the refugees displaced since 1967 reaffirms their right "to return to their homes and camps in the territory occupied by Israel since 1967." The same resolution calls upon Israel again to take "immediate steps" for the return of the displaced inhabitants and to desist from all measures obstructing their return.

Other subsequent resolutions, such as 3376(XXX) of 10 November 1975[36] have followed the pattern of resolution 3236 by referring to the exercise by the Palestinians of "their inalienable right to return to their homes and property from which they have been uprooted." Resolution 33/28A[37] of 7 December 1978 reaffirms that a just and lasting peace in the Middle East cannot be achieved without, *inter alia*, the attainment of "the inalienable rights of the Palestinian people, including the right of return ... ."

C. SECURITY COUNCIL RESOLUTIONS

The Security Council has had, at the most, a minor role in dealing with the Palestinian refugees. Its resolution 73 of 11 August 1949[38] expressed the hope that the "Governments and authorities concerned" in the 1947–1948 conflict would undertake to seek agreement "by negotiations conducted either with the Conciliation Commission or directly" to achieve agreement on "all questions outstanding between them"[39] including necessarily the refugee question, although it was not specifically mentioned. The parties did not achieve any agreement in spite of the efforts of the Conciliation Commission. The Palestinians were, of course, concerned with the crucial issues at stake in Palestine, but they had at that time neither a government nor a public body which could effectively represent their interests.

Following the intense hostilities of June, 1967, the

---

36. *30 U.N. GAOR, Supp. 34* at 3–4.
37. U.N. Doc. A/5942, 33rd Sess., (5 Feb. 1979).
38. *U.N. SCOR, Fourth Year* at 8–9.
39. Operative para. 1.

Security Council adopted resolution 237 of 14 June 1967.[40] The first operative paragraph of the resolution calls upon the Government of Israel "to facilitate the return of those inhabitants who have fled the areas since the outbreak of hostilities." In view of the time of the resolution and of the conflict fact situation, this should be taken to refer to the 1967 refugees. Other provisions of the resolution seek to obtain adherence to the obligations of the Geneva Prisoners of War and Civilians Conventions of 1949.

Security Council resolution 242 of November 22, 1967[41] attempts to establish a framework for "a just and lasting peace in the Middle East"[42] by enunciating certain principles. Among these, "the necessity" for "achieving a just settlement of the refugee problem"[43] is set forth. There are no elements of such a just settlement stated in the resolution and the only authoritative principles adopted by the United Nations on this subject remain the General Assembly resolutions which have been considered above.

Security Council resolution 338 of October 22, 1973[44] calls for a ceasefire in the then intense hostilities in the Middle East. It may also have some connection with the Palestinian refugees since operative paragraph 2 calls upon the parties concerned to start implementing all of the parts of Security Council resolution 242 immediately following the ceasefire. To the present time resolution 242, including its reference to the refugees, has not been implemented although it has been consistently referred to as the basis upon which peace must be established.

II. The National Rights of the People of Palestine

The United Nations Charter pertains to peoples as well as to states. Among the purposes of the United Nations

---

40. *U.N. SCOR, Twenty-second Year* at 5–6.

41. *Id.* at 8–9.

42. Preambular para. 2.

43. Operative para. 2(b).

44. *U.N. SCOR, Twenty-eighth Year* at 10.

specified in the first article of the Charter is:

> To develop friendly relations among nations
> based on respect for the principle of equal rights
> and self-determination of peoples ... .[45]

This marks a significant departure from the old legal theory that international law accords rights only to states and governments and not to groups or individuals.[46]

A. THE RECOGNITION OF THE PALESTINIANS AS A PEOPLE

The Palestinians, without distinction as to religion, were a people *de facto* as the inhabitants of the country named Palestine long before the twentieth century, and they had close connections with their fellow Arabs in adjoining Syria and Lebanon. The Palestinians, Syrians and Lebanese, along with other Arab peoples, were under the rule of the Ottoman Empire until the First World War. Following that conflict, Great Britain was designated as the Mandatory Power under the League of Nations Mandate for Palestine.[47] Because the Mandate, consistent with the requirements of article 22 of the League of Nations Covenant, was designed to lead the people of the country to independence, it contained an implicit recognition of Palestinian national identity.[48] The United Nations accorded the Palestinians *de jure* recognition of their status as a people with national rights in the

---

45. Art. 1(2). The Preamble to the Charter states that "We the Peoples of the United Nations" acting through governments agree to the Charter and establish the United Nations". The human rights provisions of the Charter, arts. 55 and 56, encompass the rights of peoples and individuals. Art. 80(1) refers to the rights of "any peoples." See Goodrich, Hambro & Simons, *Charter of the United Nations: Commentary and Documents* 494–500 (3rd rev. ed., 1969).

46. The contrast between the contemporary and older theories of international law is pointed out in McDougal, "Perspectives for an International Law of Human Dignity," 53 *Proc. Am. Soc. Int'l L.* 107 (1959) [Address as president of the American Society of International Law].

47. *Supra* note 36.

48. Art. 2 of the League Mandate for Palestine, Chap. 3, *supra* note 29, obligated the Mandatory Power to secure, *inter alia*, "the development of self-governing institutions."

provisions of the Palestine Partition Resolution authorizing them to establish "the Arab State."[49] From the time of that resolution in 1947 until 1969, however, the United Nations emphasized the Palestinians' *de facto* role as individuals who were refugees and war victims. The United Nations actions of that period were designed to implement their right of return[50] and achieve their other elementary human rights.

In 1969 the General Assembly shifted its perspective to acknowledge again the status of the Palestinians as a people having rights under the United Nations Charter. The first preambular paragraph of General Assembly resolution 2535B (XXIV) of 10 December 1969[51] recognizes "that the problem of the Palestine Arab refugees has arisen from the denial of their inalienable rights under the Charter of the United Nations and the Universal Declaration of Human Rights." The first operative paragraph provides recognition by the United Nations of the Palestinians as a people with a national identity by reaffirming "the inalienable rights of the people of Palestine." This recognition of juridical status has been reaffirmed by all subsequent resolutions of the General Assembly which deal with the subject.

General Assembly resolution 2672C (XXV) of 8 December 1970[52] follows the pattern of the resolution just considered. A preambular paragraph reaffirms the inalienable rights of "the people of Palestine" and the first operative paragraph uses the same words in referring to the people's national rights. The second operative paragraph repeats the identical words in declaring that full respect for the people's inalienable rights is indispensable for the achievement of a just and lasting peace. General Assembly resolution 3210 (XXIX)[53] concerns the status of the people by providing that "the Palestinian people is a principal party to the question of Palestine." It also concerns the status of its representative by

---

49. G.A. Res. 181(II), Part IA(3) and *passim.*

50. *Supra* Sec. I.

51. *Supra* note 25 at 25–26.

52. *29 U.N. GAOR, Supp. 31* at 4.

53. *Id.* at 3.

inviting the Palestine Liberation Organization as "the representative of the Palestinian people" to participate in plenary meetings of the General Assembly concerning the question of Palestine. This status is further augmented by the seventh operative paragraph of resolution 3236[54] which "*Requests* the Secretary-General to establish contacts with the Palestine Liberation Organization on all matters concerning the question of Palestine." In resolution 3237 (XXIX) of 22 November 1974[55] the General Assembly invites the Palestine Liberation Organization to participate in the sessions and work of the General Assembly and of all international conferences convened under the auspices of the General Assembly in the capacity of observer. The people of Palestine have a relationship to the Palestine Liberation Organization similar to the French people's relationship to the Free French organization (later known as the Fighting French) when France was under military occupation during the Second World War.

The United Nations Charter provides that "the United Nations shall promote," *inter alia*:

> universal respect for, and observance of, human rights and fundamental freedoms for all without distinction as to race, sex, language, or religion.[56]

Consistent with this requirement, "the Palestinian people" must comprise all Palestinians on a non-discriminatory basis. If it did not do so, it could not be recognized by the General Assembly without violation of the Charter provisions concerning human rights. In summary, "the Palestinian people" includes individuals of diverse religious identification today as it did before the rise of Zionist nationalism. It also would be essential to maintain this characteristic in the establishment of the Palestinian state in order to comply with the human rights requirements for each of the two states authorized by the Palestine Partition Resolution as well as

---

54. *Id.* at 4.
55. *Id.*
56. Art. 55c.

with the human rights provisions of the United Nations Charter.

B. THE RIGHT OF SELF-DETERMINATION IN INTERNATIONAL LAW

The practice of self-determination preceded the development of the principle or right of self-determination in international law. The American Revolution and the subsequent Latin American revolutions against European colonialism provide preeminent historic examples. The idea of self-determination was present in President Woodrow Wilson's Fourteen Points.[57] Professor Kissinger has accurately described the situation as it existed at the post-First World War peace settlement:

> In 1919, the Austro-Hungarian Empire disintegrated not so much from the impact of the war as from the nature of the peace, because its continued existence was incompatible with national self-determination, the legitimizing principle of the new international order.[58]

It is important to note that the principle of self-determination was reflected in the provisions of the League of Nations Covenant through the mandates system with the mandatory powers assuming "a sacred trust" to promote "the well being and development of such peoples."[59] At the present time the only examples of peoples who were placed under the mandates system who have not achieved self-determination are the people of Palestine and the people of Namibia

---

57. Point V concerning "colonial claims" provided that "the interests of the populations concerned must have equal weight with the equitable claims of the government whose title is to be determined." Point XII provided that "the other [non-Turkish] nationalities which are now under Turkish rule should be assured an undoubted security of life and an absolutely unmolested opportunity of autonomous development . . . ." [1918] *Foreign Rels. of U.S.*, Vol. 1, Supp. 1 at 15–16 (1933).

58. Kissinger, *A World Restored: Metternich, Castlereagh and the Problems of Peace 1812–1822*, 145 (Sentry ed., undated).

59. Art. 22(1).

(Southwest Africa). The widespread implementation of self-determination since the end of the Second World War is reflected directly in the membership of the United Nations. One of the major purposes of the United Nations, which has been set forth above, is the development of friendly relations based upon respect for "the principle of equal rights and self-determination of peoples ... ."[60] It is sometimes contended by those who oppose self-determination for others that the Charter only states that self-determination is a principle and not a right. This view lacks merit since the carefully drafted and equally authentic French text states, "du principe de l'égalité de droits des peuples et de leur droit à disposer d'eux-mêmes ... ." By using the word "droit" in connection with self-determination, the French text removes any possible ambiguity. Article 55 of the Charter emphasizes the importance of self-determination by stating that peaceful and friendly relations are based on respect for it. Article 73 of Chapter XI concerning non-self-governing territories provides that members assuming responsibility for such territories are required to "develop self-government, to take due account of the political aspirations of the people, and to assist them in the progressive development of their free political institutions ... ."[61]

The General Assembly has performed the task of interpreting and developing these principles from the early history of the organization to the present time. It should be recalled that the Palestine Partition Resolution 181 provides authority for two distinct national self-determinations in Palestine. General Assembly resolution 1514 (XV) of 14 December 1960,[62] entitled "Declaration on the Granting of Independence to Colonial Countries and Territories," is an important statement of basic principles and rights. The first two operative paragraphs of this resolution provide:

---

60. *U.N. Charter*, art. 2(1).
61. Art. 73b.
62. *15 U.N. GAOR, Supp. 16* at 66–67.

       1. The subjection of peoples to alien subjuga-
tion, domination and exploitation constitutes a
denial of fundamental human rights, is contrary to
the Charter of the United Nations and is an
impediment to the promotion of world peace and
co-operation.

       2. All peoples have the right to self-
determination; by virtue of that right they freely
determine their political status and freely pursue
their economic, social and cultural development.

The vote on this resolution was 90 votes in favor to none
opposed, with 9 abstentions. Since there were no opposing
votes, this resolution must be interpreted as reflecting the
stated legal views of the membership of the United Nations at
that time. In view of the increasing implementation of
self-determination since 1960, there can be no doubt but that
the present membership of the United Nations provides full
support for the views expressed in the 1960 resolution.
Subsequent applications of the self-determination principle
of resolution 1514 to Algeria, Angola, and to Zimbabwe
(Rhodesia) indicate the position of the General Assembly that
a right of self-determination is established in law,[63] and the
entire course of action taken by the United Nations since 1960
is consistent with this basic principle.

General Assembly resolution 2625 (XXV) of October 24,
1970,[64] entitled "Declaration on Principles of International
Law Concerning Friendly Relations and Co-Operation
Among States in accordance with the Charter of the United
Nations,"[65] provides further development of the right of
self-determination. There are four principal bases for the
authoritativeness of this resolution.[66] First, it is based on the
Charter, and therefore its principles were already binding on

---

63.   G.A. Res. 1573 (XV) re Algeria; G.A. Res. 1603(XV) re Angola; G.A. Res.
1747(XVI) re Zimbabwe (Rhodesia).

64.   *25 U.N. GAOR, Supp. 28* at 121–24.

65.   *Id.*

66.   The first three of these bases are set forth in J. A. Perkins, *The Prudent
Peace: Law as Foreign Policy* 66 (1981).

the member nations through their adherence to the Charter. Second, it was developed and adopted by consensus and the negotiating history indicates that a number of governments regard it as binding international law on the theory that the unanimity of acceptance gives it authority as law either under Article 38(1) (c) of the Statute of the International Court of Justice concerning "general principles of law recognized by civilized nations," or as a "subsequent agreement between the parties regarding the interpretation of the treaty or the application of its provisions" in accordance with Article 31 (3) (a) of the Vienna Convention on the Law of Treaties.[67] The third basis for the authority of resolution 2625 is that it was developed to provide a statement of law, not merely one of policy or aspirations. The title itself and the final paragraph which provides that "[t]he principles of the Charter which are embodied in this Declaration constitute basic principles of international law," are further indication of the intent of the member states that this resolution be a binding statement of international law.

The Declaration considers a number of principles. Under the heading of the "principle of equal rights and self-determination of peoples" the first paragraph states:

> By virtue of the principle of equal rights and self-determination of peoples enshrined in the Charter of the United Nations, all peoples have the right freely to determine, without external interference, their political status and to pursue their economic, social and cultural development, and every state has the duty to respect this right in accordance with the provisions of the Charter.

The conjoining of "equal rights" and "self-determination" both in the Charter and in the Declaration means that the peoples who have not yet achieved self-determination have the same equal right to it as did those who exercised it previously.

There is a further significant basis for the high degree of

---

67. U.N. Doc. A/CONF. 39/27, 8 *Int'l Legal Mats.* 679 (1969).

legal authority of both the 1960 Declaration on Decolonization and the 1970 Declaration on International Law and
Friendly Relations. It is that their substantive provisions
concerning self-determination and independence have been
implemented in the practise of states. This practise is
manifested by the exercise of self-determination since the
establishment of the United Nations which has resulted in
more than tripling its membership. The practise of states is
the same requisite element in making customary law which
has existed for centuries prior to the establishment of the
United Nations.[68] It is probable, therefore, that if the legal
formulations of self-determination had not been developed
beyond those in the Charter, the practise of states would
have made self-determination a doctrine of customary law
without either the 1960 or 1970 resolutions.[69] In the present
situation, self-determination is law because of the Charter,
the development of the Charter in the subsequent resolutions, and the assent and practise of states which have made
it customary law.

The opponents of self-determination usually contrast the
law of the Charter, including the relevant resolutions of the
General Assembly, with the traditional law which existed
prior to 1945.[70] General Assembly resolutions concerning the
right of self-determination which have been adopted by
consensus or by large majorities have been subjected to
particular criticism as being politically motivated.[71] One of
the main weaknesses of their arguments is that the law of
self-determination has been developed and implemented by
precisely the same methods of assent and practise which
characterized law-making in the pre-1945 traditional law.
The making of customary international law has always been

---

68. See *e.g.*, *The Paquete Habana*, 175 U.S. 677 (1900) and *Filártiga v.
Peña-Irala*, 630 Fed. 2d 876 (C.A. 2d, 1980).

69. G. Arangio-Riuz, *The United Nations Declaration on Friendly Relations and
the System of the Sources of International Law* (1979) considers several theoretical
bases for G.A. Res. 2625 but gives inadequate attention to the practice of
states in implementing self-determination and independence.

70. See *e.g.*, J. Stone, *Israel and Palestine: Assault on the Law of Nations* (1981).

71. *Id.* at 27–44, 69–75, and *passim*.

based upon the political consensus of a substantial majority of the community of states. Professor Higgins has stated: "Customary international law is therefore perhaps the most 'political' form of international law, reflecting the consensus of the great majority of states."[72] Such political decision was the basis for the abolition of the slave trade in the nineteenth Century.[73]

C. THE APPLICATION OF THE RIGHT OF SELF-DETERMINATION TO THE PEOPLE OF PALESTINE: GENERAL ASSEMBLY RESOLUTIONS 2649 (XXV), 2672C (XXV), 3089D (XXVIII), AND 3236 (XXIX) AND SUBSEQUENT ONES

Critics of the right of self-determination as enunciated in the Charter and in the 1960 and 1970 resolutions point out the imprecision in these formulations. In particular, they emphasize that there is no precise definition of the "self" which qualifies as a national group of people entitled to self-determination. One such critic has written:

> If, indeed, the references to "self-determination" in the Charter and in General Assembly declarations have established some legal (as distinct from political) principle, the legal criteria for identifying a "people" having this entitlement – the "self" entitled to "determine" itself – remain at best speculative.[74]

It seems probable that this difficulty arises from the confusion of the basic legal doctrines of the Charter and the 1960 and 1970 resolutions with the subsequent legal instruments which specify the identity of the people qualifying for

---

72. R. Higgins, *The Development of International Law Through the Political Organs of the United Nations* 1 (1963).

73. 1 Oppenheim, *International Law: Peace* 732–35 (8th ed., Lauterpacht, 1955).

74. J. Stone, "Hopes and Loopholes in the 1979 Definition of Aggression," 71 *Am. J. Int'l L.* 224 at 235 (1977).

self-determination. It is as much of a mistake to look for specifications in these general constitutional formulations as it is to look for specifics in the constitution of a state. The general principles of the constitutional doctrines are made specific by the subsequent legislative and judicial application of them.

The provisions of the Palestine Partition Resolution which provide authority for the establishment of "the Arab State" constitute the first direct specification or recognition of the Palestinian national right of self-determination.[75] The second such recognition is provided by General Assembly resolution 2649 of November 30, 1970.[76] This resolution expresses concern that, because of alien domination, many peoples were being denied the right to self-determination. It then condemns those governments which deny the right to peoples "recognized as being entitled to it, especially the peoples of southern Africa and Palestine."[77] The legal effect of this significant resolution is that the prior resolutions setting forth the basic right of self-determination, resolutions 1514 and 2625 considered above, are now specifically applicable to the Palestinian people.

With the adoption of resolution 2672C on 8 December 1970,[78] the General Assembly moved toward acknowledging the correlation between the right of self-determination and other inalienable rights. The second preambular paragraph recalls resolution 2535B and the first such paragraph reiterates the language contained in that resolution providing that the Palestine Arab refugee problem had arisen from the denial of their inalienable rights. The two operative paragraphs of resolution 2672C state that the General Assembly:

1. *Recognizes* that the people of Palestine are entitled to equal rights and self-determination, in

---

75. *Supra* note 49.
76. *Supra* note 64 at 73–74.
77. Operative para. 5.
78. *Supra* note 64 at 36.

accordance with the Charter of the United Nations;

2. *Declares* that full respect for the inalienable rights of the people of Palestine is an indispensable element in the establishment of a just and lasting peace in the Middle East.

In addition to reiterating the specific Palestinian national right of self-determination, this resolution links the achievement of Palestinian inalienable rights to the achievement of peace in the Middle East. It should be recalled that article 1 of the Charter requires the United Nations to bring about peace "in conformity with the principles of justice and international law." It should be clear that neither of these principles is honored unless Palestinian rights are implemented.

General Assembly resolution 3089D of 7 December 1973,[79] which has been considered concerning the right of return, enunciates the relationship between the rights of self-determination and return by providing in its third operative paragraph that the General Assembly:

> *Declares* that full respect for and realization of the inalienable rights of the people of Palestine, particularly its right to self-determination, are indispensable for the establishment of a just and lasting peace in the Middle East, and that the enjoyment by the Palestine Arab refugees of their right to return to their homes and property . . . is indispensable . . . for the exercise by the people of Palestine of its right to self-determination.

The necessary legal linkage of return and self-determination is designed to assure Palestinians the practical exercise of national self-determination as a "people." It is based on the common sense conception that there can be no self-determination without return to the areas where self-determination may be exercised.

An analysis of operative paragraph 3 reveals that while the General Assembly understandably views the achieve-

---

79. *28 U.N. GAOR, Supp. 30* at 78.

ment of return as a necessary prerequisite to the effective exercise of self-determination, the right of self-determination of Palestinians as a national group was apparently not intended to follow invariably from the return of individual Palestinians. The pertinent wording provides that the "Palestine Arab refugees" are entitled to enjoy "their right to return to their homes and property," while the "people of Palestine" is entitled to exercise "its right to self-determination." The use of "Palestine Arab refugees" when referring to return is apparently meant to stand in contradistinction to the use of "people of Palestine" when reference is made to self-determination.

General Assembly resolution 3236 of 22 November 1974 has been considered in connection with the right of return.[80] It also has preeminent importance concerning the right of self-determination. Its fifth preambular paragraph recognizes that "the Palestinian people is entitled to self-determination in accordance with the Charter of the United Nations." The first operative paragraph provides that the General Assembly:

> *Reaffirms* the inalienable rights of the Palestinian people in Palestine, including:
> (a) The right to self-determination without external interference;
> (b) The right to national independence and sovereignty.

The exact boundaries of the area in Palestine in which these inalienable rights apply must be settled *de jure*.[81] The language of the resolution quoted above includes the "right to national independence and sovereignty" as a particularization of the self-determination right.

In operative paragraph 5, resolution 3236 refers to methods by which rights may be regained. It provides that the General Assembly:

---

80. *Supra* Sec. I B(3).
81. See *infra*, sec. II D.

> *Further recognizes* the right of the Palestinian
> people to regain its rights by all means in
> accordance with the purposes and principles of
> the Charter of the United Nations.

Further specification concerning methods is provided in General Assembly resolution 3070 of 30 November 1973[82] which, after reaffirming the inalienable right to self-determination of all peoples under alien subjugation,[83] provides that the General Assembly:

> *Also reaffirms* the legitimacy of the peoples
> struggle for liberation from . . . alien subjugation
> by all means including armed struggle.[84]

Since the American Revolution relied upon armed struggle to achieve self-determination about a century and a third before the principle of self-determination was used in the post-First World War peace settlement,[85] it is not surprising that the General Assembly specifies it as a permissible method now. Its permissibility is legally significant as an authoritative General Assembly assertion that armed struggle for self-determination is consistent with the purposes and principles of the United Nations Charter. In a situation such as Palestine where the people has been denied its right of self-determination by armed force, the right to regain it by armed struggle is considered permissible under article 51 of the Charter concerning self-defense.

D. THE GEOGRAPHICAL AREA TO WHICH PALESTINIAN SELF-DETERMINATION APPLIES

Where "in Palestine," to use the wording of resolution 3236, may Palestinian national self-determination including independence and sovereignty be exercised? General Assembly resolution 2625 (XXV) dealing with "Principles of

---

82. *Supra* note 79.
83. Operative para. 1.
84. Operative para. 2.
85. See the text accompanying *supra* note 58.

International Law Concerning Friendly Relations," which has been considered concerning the right of self-determination,[86] also provides basic legal interpretation concerning areas where self-determination may be exercised. Under the heading of the "principle of equal rights and self-determination of peoples" the penultimate paragraph provides:

> Nothing in the foregoing paragraphs shall be construed as authorizing or encouraging any action which would dismember or impair, totally or in part, the territorial integrity or political unity of sovereign and independent states conducting themselves in compliance with the principle of equal rights and self-determination of peoples as described above and thus possessed of a government representing the whole people belonging to the territory without distinction as to race, creed or colour.

The quoted wording is of particular importance since it is designed to preserve the territorial integrity or political unity of non-discriminatory states which have a government "representing the whole people belonging to the territory." The State of Israel cannot qualify as such a state as long as its discriminatory Zionist features, including the denial of the right of return of Palestinians to their homes and property, are maintained in municipal law and practice. Pursuant to this provision of resolution 2625, the General Assembly may provide for lawful *de jure* boundaries for the State of Israel which do not preserve its "territorial integrity or political unity" as they may exist *de facto* at a particular time as a result of military conquest and of illegal annexation.[87] The prohibi-

---

86. See the text accompanying *supra* note 64.

87. Art. 47 of the Geneva Civilians Convention, 75 U.N.T.S. 135, provides that protected persons in occupied territory shall not be deprived of the benefits of the Convention if the occupying power annexes "the whole or part of the occupied territory." This provision was written to avoid a repetition of the Nazi practice of using the annexation device to attempt to avoid the application of the law concerning occupation.

tion on the acquisition of territory by military conquest is regarded as fundamental in the United Nations Charter[88] and in resolutions of both the General Assembly and the Security Council.

The only *de jure* boundaries which the State of Israel has ever had are those which were specified for "the Jewish State" in the Palestine Partition Resolution.[89] Following the Armistice Agreements of 1949, which did not fix *de jure* boundaries, the State of Israel existed within *de facto* boundaries until June 1967. It is possible that those pre-1967 boundaries may have received some international assent. Security Council resolution 242 of 22 November 1967, after emphasizing "the inadmissibility of the acquisition of territory by war,"[90] refers in the first operative paragraph to the principle of "withdrawal of Israel armed forces from territories occupied in the recent conflict." Since there is no statement of withdrawal from territories occupied at a time before 1967, this may amount to an indirect recognition of the pre-June 1967 boundaries. Operative paragraph 1 also refers to the principle of the "territorial integrity and political independence of every State in the area and their right to live in peace within secure and recognized boundaries."

It is clear that two different national exercises of the right of self-determination cannot take place simultaneously upon precisely the same territory, and the careful wording of resolution 3236 is consistent with this reality. Consequently, those Palestinians who choose to exercise their right of return within the State of Israel cannot exercise Palestinian national self-determination within that state. Since resolution 181 established the principle of two states in the area and subsequent resolutions have not departed from this concept, it is clear that it is not the intent of the General Assembly to authorize Palestinian self-determination within the State of Israel. The Palestinian national right of self-determination as recognized in General Assembly resolutions may be ex-

---

88. It is based, in part, on art. 2(3) and (4).

89. G.A. Res. 181(II), Part II B.

90. Preambular para. 2.

ercised "in Palestine" within the *de jure* boundaries of the Palestinian state which are yet to be determined, and outside the *de jure* boundaries of the State of Israel as ultimately determined.

III. The Rights and Obligations for Each of Two States in Palestine

In the Palestine Partition Resolution[91] the General Assembly acted to resolve a situation of conflict and crisis by authorizing the establishment of two democratic states in the territory of the Palestine Mandate. The rights to establish the states were balanced by concomitant obligations to do so in accordance with the United Nations Charter and the terms of the Partition Resolution. The ensuing resolutions of the General Assembly adhere to the basic elements of the Partition Resolution.

The General Assembly established its Committee on the Exercise of the Inalienable Rights of the Palestinian People, composed of twenty member states, in resolution 3376 (XXX)[92] of 10 November 1975. In General Assembly resolution 32/40B[93] of 2 December 1977 effective staff assistance was provided for the Committee by the establishment within the United Nations Secretariat of the Special Unit on Palestinian Rights. The Committee on the Exercise of the Inalienable Rights has made recommendations designed to implement the established rights of individual Palestinians and of the Palestinian people. The General Assembly has adopted the recommendations, but the Security Council has not because of the threat or use of its negative vote (sometimes termed the "veto") by the United States. Following the failure of the Security Council to make a decision on the recommendations of the Committee on 30 April 1980, the Seventh Emergency Special Session of the General Assembly was called under the

---

91. Chap. 3 *supra*, note 25.

92. *30 U.N. GAOR, Supp. 34* at 3–4.

93. *32 U.N. GAOR, Supp. 45* at 24–25. G.A. Res. 32/40 A, *inter alia*, endorses further recommendations of the Committee on the Exercise of the Inalienable Rights of the Palestinian People.

Uniting for Peace procedure.[94] In the principal resolution of that Special Session adopted on 29 July 1980,[95] the Assembly reaffirmed its prior resolutions on Palestine including the individual right of return and the national right of self-determination. A key operative paragraph of the resolution provided that the Assembly:

> *Reaffirms,* in particular, that a comprehensive, just and lasting peace in the Middle East cannot be established, in accordance with the Charter of the United Nations and the relevant United Nations resolutions, without the withdrawal of Israel from all the occupied Palestinian and other Arab territories, including Jerusalem, and without the achievement of a just solution of the problem of Palestine on the basis of the attainment of the inalienable rights of the Palestinian people in Palestine.[96]

This resolution was adopted by a vote of 112 in favor, 7 against (including the United States and Israel), and 24 abstentions. At its Thirty-Fifth Regular Session in the Autumn of 1980 the General Assembly reaffirmed its earlier resolutions on Palestine including those adopted by the Seventh Emergency Session.[97]

Security Council resolution 242 of 22 November 1967[98] concerning "a just and lasting peace in the Middle East" has been supplemented by the resolutions of the General

---

94. The General Assembly first used its authority to act on a matter concerning international peace and security when the Security Council was unable to act due to a negative vote by a permanent member during the Korean conflict on 3 November 1950. The Uniting for Peace Resolution, G.A. Res. 377(V), *5 U.N. GAOR, Supp. 20* at 10–12, was adopted under the leadership of the United States Government following a Soviet Union negative vote.

95. A/RES/ES–7/2 entitled Question of Palestine.

96. Para. 2.

97. G.A. Res. 35/169A of 15 Dec. 1980. This resolution contains an annex which sets forth the basic recommendations of the Committee on the Exercise of the Inalienable Rights of the Palestinian People which were endorsed by the General Assembly at its thirty-first session.

98. *U.N. SCOR, Twenty-second Year* at 8–9.

Assembly which have been considered here. In particular, resolution 242's undefined "just settlement of the refugee problem" is made specific by the General Assembly's recognition of the right of return for individual Palestinians. In addition, the General Assembly has recognized the national rights of the Palestinian people in carefully formulated terms which do not infringe upon the legitimate rights of the State of Israel. These Israeli national rights which remain inviolate include, among others, the rights to self-determination and to national independence and sovereign equality with other states consistent with international law including the pertinent United Nations resolutions. The Israeli rights do not include, among others, supposed rights to deny self-determination and independence to the Palestinian people and a supposed right to establish Israeli borders on the basis of military conquest and illegal annexations.

The outcome of the United Nations resolutions is that there is continuing authority for the establishment of two states in Palestine. The authority to provide for a state carries with it the authority to impose limitations including those based upon the human rights provisions of the Charter. A limitation which is inherent in the authorization of the two states is that each may exercise its national rights conditioned on, at the least, the requirement of non-obstruction of the national rights of the other. The member states of the United Nations which have authorized the two states in the international forum of the General Assembly are now required by the Charter to "fulfill in good faith the obligations assumed by them in accordance with the present Charter."[99] Among the Charter obligations is the requirement that:

> All Members shall give the United Nations every assistance in any action it takes in accordance with the present Charter, and shall refrain from giving assistance to any state against which the United Nations is taking preventive or enforcement action.[100]

---

99. Art. 2(2).

100. Art. 2(5).

Chapter 5

The Juridical Status of Jerusalem

I. Jerusalem: Religion and Sovereignty

It is well known that each of the great monotheistic religions of universal moral values regards Jerusalem as a Holy City. The religious claims of Judaism, Islam and Christianity are each unique in the sense that they contain doctrinal differences and they each accord different significance to particular places in Jerusalem. In the same way that Palestine is the Holy Land of the three religious faiths, Jerusalem is their Holy City. An example of the overlapping of the Holy Places in a single small location is the place where Solomon built his temple, Jesus Christ taught in the synagogue, and Mohammed was transported to Heaven. This one spot, not larger than four square blocks, known as the Temple Mount, or Mount Moriah, or the Haram al-Sharif, depending upon the religious perspective, illustrates in a microcosm the problem of Jerusalem. The religious claims are not exclusive, however, in the practical sense that if each is to be respected, the claimants must also respect the claims of the others. In this fundamental sense the religious claims are shared or inclusive. Although it is important to distinguish religious claims from claims to political control or sovereignty, the religious claims may properly receive recognition and protection from the law which is to be applied in Jerusalem.

If the religious claims were to be treated as a sound basis for political control, it is apparent that each of the religions could advance a case for sovereignty over Jerusalem with the inevitable result of political conflict. In addition, it should be recognized that some of the religious claimants specifically reject political claims. For example, at the end of the nineteenth century the newly born Zionist Organization made territorial claims on behalf of "the Jewish people."[1] Palestinian Jews, however, including those living in Jerusalem, were among the first to oppose the Zionists and their political and territorial claims.[2] There are religious Jews living in Jerusalem today who regard political Zionism and its State of Israel as inconsistent with the religious precepts of Judaism.[3] The State of Israel claim of political right based upon religious connection is, however, consistent with the Zionist ideology which attempts to incorporate the religion of Judaism and make it an instrument of Zionist nationalism.[4]

A brief summary of the background of the area including Jerusalem indicates the relative status of the claims to the City based on history. The Canaanites were the first known inhabitants of Palestine.[5] In about 1000 B.C. David, who had temporarily united a number of tribes, conquered Jerusalem from the Jebusites. David's son, Solomon, built the first Jewish Temple there. After Solomon's death the kingdom was divided into Israel and Judah with Jerusalem as the capital of the latter. These two kingdoms were frequently at war with each other and soon both were defeated by the Assyrians. Thereafter, Assyrian, Babylonian, and Macedonian conquerors, in sequence, ruled Palestine. The Roman Conquest took place in 73 B.C., and in 135 A.D. Hadrian expelled the Jews from Palestine including Jerusalem. From about 400 A.D. until the Islamic Conquest in 637 A.D., Palestine was part of the Byzantine Empire. The rule of the Crusaders in Jerusalem began in 1099 and lasted only until

---

1.   Israel Cohen, *The Zionist Movement* 77 (1946). The Basle Program is reproduced in Appendix 1 *infra*.

2.   Chap. 3 *supra*, note 28.

3.   *E.g.*, the Naturei Karta.

4.   See *e.g.*, the criticism by Achad Ha'am, *Ten Essays on Zionism and Judaism*. *passim* (L. Simon transl., 1922); *supra* Chap. 1, note 3.

5.   See George Adam Smith, *Jerusalem: The Topography, Economics, and History From Earliest Times to A.D. 70* (2 vols., London, 1908) and Gaius Glenn Atkins, *Jerusalem Past and Present* (London, 1918). Henry Cattan, *Jerusalem* (1981) although primarily a legal analysis, provides an excellent historical account in Chap. 2. Aamiry, *Jerusalem: Arab Origin and Heritage* (London, 1978) is a useful short history. Salah-El-Din's humanitarianism when he captured Jerusalem from the Crusaders is described in Lane-Poole, *Saladin and the Fall of the Kingdom of Jerusalem* 224–34 (Beirut, 1964).

1187. In that year Jerusalem came under Arab rule following the conquest by Salah-El-Din who allowed Jews to return and to worship in their own way. Palestine, including Jerusalem, remained under Arab domination until it was conquered by the Turks in 1517 and became a part of the Ottoman Empire. Both the Arabs and the Turks professed the religion of Islam. In all, Jerusalem was under the control of rulers who professed Islam for more than eleven centuries, broken only by the Crusader rule of less than a century. Jerusalem was under the control of rulers who professed Judaism for a much shorter time period and in a more remote historical epoch. If the religious identification of its historic rulers provides authority for contemporary sovereignty, the adherents of Islam clearly have a far better claim than the adherents of Judaism or Christianity. It is also important to be aware that Jerusalem is not only a center of religious interests. Both its historical and its archeological roles make it a city of world-wide concern.

II. The United Nations and Jerusalem

It is particularly significant for the present analysis that Jerusalem was not specifically mentioned in the League of Nations Mandate for Palestine,[6] with the juridical result that it was simply treated as an integral part of Palestine. The inhabitants of Jerusalem, like other Palestinians, were to receive the protection of the first safeguard in the Balfour Declaration as incorporated in the Mandate. The Palestine Mandate also provided for a single Palestinian citizenship without discrimination concerning religious identification.[7] In addition, the Mandate contained provisions concerning the responsibility of the Mandatory to protect the Holy Places of the three religions, most of which are located in Jerusalem.[8]

---

6. The text of the Mandate of 24 July 1922 is in 2 UNSCOP, *Report to the General Assembly, 2 U.N. GAOR, Supp. 11*, 18–22, U.N. Doc. A/364, Add. I (9 Sept. 1947).

7. *Id.*, arts. 7 and 15. See Chap. 1, Sec. IV B(1) *supra* concerning the first safeguard clause, and Sec. V A concerning the Mandate.

8. *Supra* note 6, arts. 13–16.

The Palestine Partition Resolution 181(II) of November 29, 1947[9] provided for the establishment of two states in Palestine and thereby recognized both Israeli and Palestinian national rights. This was the first statement in which the General Assembly enunciated principles concerning a separate international status for Jerusalem. Its terms provided that "the Mandate for Palestine shall terminate as soon as possible but in any case not later than August 1, 1948,"[10] and the *corpus separatum* for Jerusalem was then to go into effect. In the actual event, as one result of the intense hostilities of 1947–1948, Jerusalem was divided on a *de facto* basis between Israel and Jordan.

At the time when Israel was seeking admission to the United Nations, Mr. Abba Eban, then the foreign minister, implicitly recognized the international status of Jerusalem when he stated, *inter alia*:

> I do not think that article 2, paragraph 7, of the Charter, which relates to domestic jurisdiction, could possibly affect the Jerusalem problem since the legal status of Jerusalem is different from that of the territory in which Israel is sovereign ... .[11]

On admission to membership in 1949 Israel, like other members of the United Nations, accepted obligations under the Charter. Among the most basic of these obligations is the requirement that international disputes be resolved "by peaceful means in such a manner that international peace and security, and justice, are not endangered."[12] Article 25 of the Charter states that: "The Members of the United Nations agree to accept and carry out the decisions of the Security Council in accordance with the present Charter." These

---

9.   G.A. Res. 181 (II) concerning the Future Government of Palestine (29 November 1947), 2 *U.N. GAOR, Resolutions*, 131–32, U.N. Doc. A/519 (16 Sept.–29 Nov. 1947). See Chap. 3. Sec. II *supra*.

10.   *Id.* Res. 181 at Part I, Sec. A (1).

11.   3 *U.N. GAOR*, Part II, Ad Hoc Political Com. at 286–87, U.N. Doc. A/818 (1949).

12.   Art. 1 (1).

obligations, among others, apply as much to Jerusalem as to any other dispute.

A. GENERAL ASSEMBLY RESOLUTIONS

Part III of resolution 181, the Plan of Partition with Economic Union, concerns Jerusalem and provides in relevant part:

A. Special Regime
The City of Jerusalem shall be established as a *corpus separatum* under a special international regime and shall be administered by the United Nations. The Trusteeship Council shall be designated to discharge the responsibilities of the Administering Authority on behalf of the United Nations.

B. Boundaries of the City
The City of Jerusalem shall include the present municipality of Jerusalem plus the surrounding villages and towns … .

The Partition Resolution provisions, including those concerning Jerusalem, remained unimplemented and Jerusalem was divided between Israel and Jordan as a result of military operations. On April 26, 1948 the General Assembly, fully aware of the conflict situation, adopted resolution 185 (S-II)[13] concerning the protection of the City of Jerusalem and its inhabitants, asking the Trusteeship Council to study "suitable measures for the protection of the city and its inhabitants, and to submit within the shortest possible time proposals to the General Assembly to that effect." The report from the Trusteeship Council contained conclusions and recommendations which were approved by the General Assembly in resolution 187 adopted on May 6, 1948.[14] This resolution also called for the appointment of a special

---

13.   *3 U.N. GAOR, Supp.* 2, 2nd Spec. Sess., 5, U.N. Doc. A/555 (16 April–14 May 1948).

14.   *Id.* at 7–8.

municipal commissioner. The appointment was made, but the commissioner was not able to function effectively.

Resolution 186 of May 14, 1948[15] provided for a United Nations Mediator for Palestine and Count Folke Bernadotte took this position on May 20. On September 16, just before he was assassinated, he submitted a progress report which, *inter alia,* stated as one of his basic premises that:

> The City of Jerusalem, because of its religious and international significance and the complexity of interests involved, should be accorded special and separate treatment.[16]

Among his specific conclusions was that:

> The City of Jerusalem, which should be understood as covering the area defined in the resolution of the General Assembly of 29 November, should be treated separately and should be placed under effective United Nations control with maximum feasible local autonomy for its Arab and Jewish communities, with full safeguards for the protection of the Holy Places and sites and free access to them, and for religious freedom.[17]

On December 11, 1948 the General Assembly adopted resolution 194 based on Count Bernadotte's recommendations.[18] It established the Conciliation Commission for Palestine in paragraph 2 and stated in paragraph 8 that the General Assembly:

---

15. *Id.* at 5–6.

16. *Progress Report of the United Nations Mediator on Palestine Submitted to the Secretary-General for Transmission to the Members of the United Nations, 3 U.N. GAOR, Supp.* 11 at 17–19, U.N. Doc. A/648 (1948); reprinted in 3 *The Arab–Israeli Conflict: Documents* 367–72 at 369 (J. N. Moore, ed., 1974).

17. *Id., id.* at 371.

18. *3 U.N. GAOR, Resolutions,* 21–25, U.N. Doc. A/810 (21 Sept.–12 Dec. 1948).

> *Resolves* that . . . the Jerusalem area . . . should be accorded special and separate treatment from the rest of Palestine and should be placed under effective United Nations control.

The basic consistency between this resolution and the Palestine Partition Resolution is that both set forth a separate status for Jerusalem and place it under United Nations control.

In resolution 303 of December 9, 1949,[19] the General Assembly refers to both resolutions 181 and 194 in the first prefatory paragraph. The first operative paragraph provides that the General Assembly decides concerning Jerusalem:

> To restate, therefore, its intention that Jerusalem should be placed under a permanent international regime, which should envisage appropriate guarantees for the protection of the Holy Places, both within and outside Jerusalem, and to confirm specifically the following provisions of General Assembly resolution 181(II):

> (1) the City of Jerusalem shall be established as a *corpus separatum* under a special international regime and shall be administered by the United Nations; (2) the Trusteeship Council shall be designated to discharge the responsibilities of the Administering Authority . . .; and (3) the City of Jerusalem shall include the present municipality of Jerusalem plus the surrounding villages and towns.

The second operative paragraph of this resolution requests the Trusteeship Council to complete preparation of the Statute of Jerusalem considering "the fundamental principles of the international regime for Jerusalem set forth in General Assembly resolution 181(II)" and to "proceed immediately with its implementation." The Statute, approved by the Trusteeship Council on April 4, 1950,

---

19. *4 U.N. GAOR, Resolutions*, 25, U.N. Doc. A/1251 (20 Sept.–12 Dec. 1948).

provided for, *inter alia*, protection for the Holy Places and for human rights and fundamental freedoms for all persons in the City.[20]

By this time Palestine and Jerusalem were already partitioned as a result of the armed conflict. While the United Nations continued to advocate internationalization of the City, the Governments of Israel and Jordan continued to strengthen their holds upon their separate portions of it. Before the end of 1949 Israel moved the Knesset, the Supreme Court, and most of its ministries to West Jerusalem, and on January 23, 1950 Israel had proclaimed West Jerusalem as its capital.[21] Neither the Security Council nor the General Assembly protested this action.

The Conciliation Commission did attempt, however, to implement the policies of the United Nations including the internationalization of Jerusalem. In its Report of September 2, 1950 the Commission set forth the Israeli and Arab positions on internationalization:

> During the Commission's conversations in Beirut with the Arab delegations, the latter showed themselves, in general, prepared to accept the principle of an international regime for the Jerusalem area, on condition that the United Nations should be in a position to offer the necessary guarantees regarding the stability and permanence of such a regime.
>
> From the beginning, however, the Government of Israel, while recognizing that the Commission was bound by General Assembly resolution 194(III), declared itself unable to accept the establishment of an international regime for the City of Jerusalem; it did, however, accept without reservation an international regime for, or the

---

20. *U.N. Trusteeship Council Off. Recs., 2nd Sess.*, 3rd Part, Annex 4–24, U.N Doc. T/118, Rev. 2 (1948).

21. *Israel Parliamentary Protocol*, 1st Knesset, 2nd Sess., 108th mtg. 602, 60 (1950) (in Hebrew).

international control of, the Holy Places in the City.[22]

The opposition of Israel prevented the implementation of the proposed plan for internationalization.

In summary, while there was no change in the basic international juridical status envisaged for Jerusalem in the General Assembly resolutions just considered, the *de facto* partition between Israel and Jordan which had been established following the 1947–1948 hostilities continued until 1967.

Following the intense hostilities of June 1967, the Government of Israel incorporated into its municipal law that portion of Jerusalem previously controlled by Jordan.[23] On July 4, 1967 the General Assembly, meeting in emergency special session, adopted resolution 2253[24] which provided that the General Assembly:

> *Deeply concerned* at the situation prevailing in Jerusalem as a result of the measures taken by Israel to change the status of the City,
>
> 1. *Considers* that these measures are invalid;
>
> 2. *Calls upon* Israel to rescind all measures already taken and to desist forthwith from taking any action which would alter the status of Jerusalem.

Ten days later the General Assembly adopted resolution 2254.[25] After recalling and noting non-compliance with resolution 2253, it stated that the General Assembly:

> 1. *Deplores* the failure of Israel to implement General Assembly resolution 2253 (ES–V);

---

22. *Progress Report of the United Nations Conciliation Commission for Palestine December 11, 1949–October 23, 1950*, 5 U.N. GAOR, Supp. 18 at 121 (Sept. 2, 1950 Report) and 30–31 (Oct. 23, 1950 Supplementary Report), U.N. Doc. A/1367, Rev. 1 (1951); reprinted in Moore *supra* note 16 at 515.

23. 21 Israel Laws (auth. trans.) 75 (1967).

24. *22 U.N. GAOR (ES–V), Supp. 1* at 4, U.N. Doc. A/6798 (July 1967).

25. *Id.*

2. *Reiterates* its call to Israel in that resolution to rescind all measures already taken and to desist forthwith from taking any action which would alter the status of Jerusalem.

There is an apparent ambiguity in these two resolutions. The preambular paragraph of resolution 2253 refers to "the status of the City" and the second operative paragraph of each of the two resolutions refers to "the status of Jerusalem." These terms may be interpreted as referring either to the juridical status of Jerusalem as a *corpus separatum* or, since there is no mention in these post-1967 resolutions of resolutions 181, 194, or 303, to the *de facto* status of the City as it existed under partial Jordanian and partial Israeli control prior to the intense hostilities of June, 1967. The broad phrase "all measures already taken" which appears in the second operative paragraph of each of the foregoing resolutions may be interpreted as meaning that the State of Israel is called upon to rescind its measures without a specific reference to the time when the measures were taken. If this interpretation is adopted, the Israeli measures to be rescinded would include those taken after the 1948 conquest of the Western part of Jerusalem.

In spite of these ambiguities, it is appropriate to suggest that one of the alternative interpretations which exist is more likely to be accurate than the other. Both resolutions were adopted following the intense hostilities of June, 1967 and the municipal measures designed to bring the eastern portion of the City under effective Israeli domination. On the same day in which resolution 2253 was adopted, the General Assembly also adopted resolution 2252[26] which focused only on the situation brought about by the hostilities of June 1967 and the urgent need for humanitarian assistance to victims of the conflict and adherence to the requirements of international law in order to protect such victims. In addition, if the intention of the General Assembly had been to demand a return to the *corpus separatum* it could have done so in clear

---

26. *Id.* at 3.

and unequivocal wording. In the statements of representatives on the floor of the General Assembly prior to the adoption of resolutions 2253 and 2254 some reference was made to the international status of Jerusalem but the primary emphasis was upon the new situation brought about by the Israeli occupation of East Jerusalem.[27] For these reasons, the interpretation which probably reflects the intention of the General Assembly is that "the status of the City" in resolution 2253 and "the status of Jerusalem" in resolution 2254 refer to the status which existed from 1948 until June 5, 1967.

There were no resolutions primarily concerned with Jerusalem between 2254 in July 1967 and 1980. In May, 1980 a so-called "Basic Law" was introduced in the Israeli Knesset. It declared the united Jerusalem to be the capital of Israel and contained specific provisions concerning the Holy Places and the "development and prosperity of Jerusalem." Following this, the Seventh Emergency Session of the General Assembly met during the summer of 1980 pursuant to the 1950 Uniting for Peace Resolution[28] of the Assembly. This resolution had been initiated and adopted under the leadership of the United States when the Security Council was unable to act during the Korean War because of the Soviet negative vote. It provides for action by the General Assembly to maintain international peace and security when the Security Council is prevented from acting on the subject because of a negative Great Power vote.[29] The prefatory paragraph of resolution ES-7/2, which was adopted on July 29, 1980,[30] explains the circumstances in which the General Assembly was meeting:

---

27. 22 U.N. GAOR, (ES–V), P.V. 1548 (4 July 1967) 1–18; 22 U.N. GAOR, (ES–V), P.V. 1554 (14 July 1967) 1–11.

28. G.A. Res. 377A (V), 3 Nov. 1950, 5 U.N. GAOR, Supp. 20, 10–12, U.N. Doc. A/1775.

29. U.N. Charter, art. 12 (1) prohibits the General Assembly from acting on matters concerning international peace and security while the Security Council is functioning effectively.

30. 35 U.N. GAOR, Supp. 1 at 3, U.N. Doc. A/ES– 7/14.

> *Noting with regret and concern* that the Security Council, at its 2220th meeting on 30 April 1980, failed to take a decision, as a result of the negative vote of the United States of America ... .

In the seventh operative paragraph, the General Assembly stated that it:

> *Calls upon* Israel to withdraw completely and unconditionally from all the Palestinian and other Arab territories occupied since June 1967, including Jerusalem, with all property and services intact, and urges that such withdrawal from all the occupied territories should start before 15 November 1980.

This provision for Israeli withdrawal from Jerusalem and the other territories occupied in 1967 may be interpreted as a first step which does not prejudice the long-range efficacy of the *corpus separatum* concept. However, it must be recognized that the time specification set forth requires only prompt withdrawal from East Jerusalem.

The "Basic Law" was formally enacted by the Knesset on July 30, 1980.[31] At its Thirty-Fifth Session the General Assembly responded to this event by passing resolution 35/169E on December 15, 1980[32] with only the State of Israel voting against it. In preambular paragraphs it reaffirmed that "the acquisition of territory by force is inadmissible" and expressed satisfaction at the actions of several states in withdrawing their diplomatic representatives from Jerusalem pursuant to Security Council resolution 478 (1980).[33] In the operative paragraphs the General Assembly, *inter alia*, condemned "in the strongest terms the enactment by Israel of the 'basic law' on Jerusalem" and affirmed in operative paragraph 2:

---

31. Embassy of Israel, Wash. D.C., *Information Background* p. 8 (Aug. 27, 1980).

32. *Supra* note 30.

33. *U.N. SCOR, Thirty-fifth Year* at 14.

that the enactment of the "Basic Law" by Israel constitutes a violation of international law and does not affect the continued application of the Geneva Convention relative to the Protection of Civilian Persons in Time of War of 12 August 1949, in the Palestinian and other Arab territories occupied since June 1967, including Jerusalem ... .

Operative paragraph 5 stated the decision that the "Basic Law" was not recognized.

The actions of the Thirty-Sixth General Assembly remained consistent. Resolution 36/120E adopted on December 10, 1981[34] reaffirmed the previous basic principles concerning Jerusalem and provided in the first operative paragraph that the General Assembly:

> *Determines once again* that all legislative and administrative measures and actions taken by Israel, the Occupying Power, which have altered or purport to alter the character and status of the Holy City of Jerusalem, and, in particular, the so-called "Basic Law" on Jerusalem and the proclamation of Jerusalem as the capital of Israel, are null and void and must be rescinded forthwith.

Although the position of the General Assembly was unchanged, the United States under the Reagan Administration changed its position with the result that it joined Israel in providing two votes against the resolution.

There are some differences among the authorities concerning the legal effect of General Assembly resolutions. There is, however, a broad consensus that while most resolutions may not immediately make law, there is a cumulative effect over a period of time and frequently repeated resolutions adopted by large majorities are one way

---

34. *36 U.N. GAOR*, Supp. 51 at 28, U.N. Doc. A/36/51.

of creating customary law.[35] The agreement of states may be manifested through such resolutions of the General Assembly as well as in the more traditional ways. On this basis it is clear that the world community has rejected decisively the Israeli actions involving East Jerusalem. In addition, the community of states has not explicitly abandoned the principle of the *corpus separatum* through General Assembly resolutions or in any other manner.

B. SECURITY COUNCIL RESOLUTIONS

The famous Security Council resolution 242 of November 22, 1967,[36] which is sometimes referred to as the widely accepted basis for peace in Palestine and in the Middle East,[37] does not mention Jerusalem by name. A key preambular paragraph, however, emphasizes "the inadmissibility of the acquisition of territory by war ... ."[38] This basic principle is as applicable to Jerusalem as to any other part of Palestine. The first operative paragraph of this resolution sets forth other basic principles which should be applied in order to establish "a just and lasting peace in the Middle East." The first of these is stated as: "Withdrawal of Israel armed forces from territories occupied in the recent conflict ... ." This clearly includes Jerusalem and was so understood by Lord Carradon, the principal author of the resolution.[39] The balancing principle was the establishment of "secure and recognized boundaries" which meant minor modifications in the borders.[40]

In 1968 the focus of attention on Jerusalem shifted from the General Assembly to the Security Council with the latter

---

35. See Higgins, *The Development of International Law Through the Political Organs of the United Nations* 1–10 and *passim* (1963). See the text of Chap. 3 Sec. B *supra*.

36. *U.N. SCOR, Twenty-second Year* 8–9.

37. Lord Carradon in *U.N. Security Council Resolution 242: A Case Study in Diplomatic Ambiguity* 6 (School of Foreign Service, Georgetown Univ., 1981).

38. *Id.* at 17.

39. *Id.* at 14.

40. *Id.* at 9.

stressing the principles previously enunciated by the former. Security Council resolution 252 of May 21, 1968,[41] after recalling General Assembly resolutions 2253 and 2254, provides in its first three operative paragraphs that the Security Council:

> 1. *Deplores* the failure of Israel to comply with the General Assembly resolutions mentioned above;
> 2. *Considers* that all legislative and administrative measures and actions taken by Israel, including expropriation of land and properties thereon, which tend to change the legal status of Jerusalem are invalid and cannot change that status;
> 3. *Urgently calls upon* Israel to rescind all such measures already taken and to desist forthwith from taking any further action which tends to change the status of Jerusalem.

The first quoted paragraph manifests Security Council concurrence with the broad terms of General Assembly resolutions 2253 and 2254. The second refers to the invalidity of "all legislative and administrative measures and actions taken by Israel" without limitation of time. The most significant feature of the second paragraph is the setting forth of "the legal status of Jerusalem" as the standard and providing that actions which tend to change it are invalid. Probably the most definitive legal status that has been provided for Jerusalem is the one establishing it as a *corpus separatum*. There may also be another legal status based upon the possibility that the post-1967 resolutions of both the General Assembly and the Security Council show community acquiescence in the Israeli control over West Jerusalem. These resolutions can be interpreted to refer to the territorially divided City, with East Jerusalem being considered as occupied territory.

The State of Israel failed to comply with the terms of

---

41. *U.N. SCOR, Twenty-third Year* 9–10.

resolution 252, and on July 3, 1969 the Security Council adopted resolution 267[42] which recalled its resolution 252 and General Assembly resolutions 2253 and 2254. Its first five operative paragraphs provide that the Council:

1. *Reaffirms* its resolution 252 (1968);
2. *Deplores* the failure of Israel to show any regard for the resolutions of the General Assembly and the Security Council mentioned above;
3. *Censures* in the strongest terms all measures taken to change the status of the City of Jerusalem;
4. *Confirms* that all legislative and administrative measures and actions taken by Israel which purport to alter the status of Jerusalem, including expropriation of land and properties thereon, are invalid and cannot change that status.
5. *Urgently calls* once more upon Israel to rescind forthwith all measures taken by it which may tend to change the status of the City of Jerusalem, and in future to refrain from all actions likely to have such an effect.

The first quoted paragraph reaffirming resolution 252 thereby includes the norm of "the legal status of Jerusalem." The fourth confirms the invalidity of "all" Israeli measures and actions "which purport to alter the status of Jerusalem," again without reference to time.

Although resolutions 252 and 267 reflect similar legal principles, the latter contains some particularly strict language. For instance, paragraph 3 of resolution 252 simply urges that the State of Israel "rescind all such measures already taken," whereas paragraph 5 of resolution 267 explicitly states that such rescission must be made "forthwith." Moreover, paragraph 5 of resolution 267 urges Israel not only to rescind measures which may tend to change the status, but also to refrain comprehensively "from all actions likely to have such an effect."

---

42. *Id., Twenty-fourth Year* 3–4.

Security Council resolution 271 of September 15, 1969[43] was adopted in response to the damage caused by arson to the Al Aqsa Mosque in Jerusalem on August 21, 1969. The first operative paragraph of the resolution reaffirms resolutions 252 (1968) and 267 (1969). The third operative paragraph provides that the Security Council:

> *Determines* that the execrable act of desecration and profanation of the Holy Al Aqsa Mosque emphasizes the immediate necessity of Israel's desisting from acting in violation of the aforesaid resolutions and rescinding forthwith all measures and actions taken by it designed to alter the status of Jerusalem ... .

Operative paragraph 4 calls upon Israel to adhere to the provisions of the Geneva Conventions of 1949 for the Protection of War Victims and the international law "governing military occupation."[44]

There is a suggestion of further action by the Security Council in the sixth operative paragraph in which it:

> *Reiterates* the determination in paragraph 7 of resolution 267 (1969) that, in the event of a negative response or no response, the Security Council shall convene without delay to consider what further action should be taken in this matter ... .

Security Council resolution 298 was adopted on September 25, 1971.[45] Its first preambular paragraph recalls Security Council resolutions 252 and 267 as well as General Assembly resolutions 2253 and 2254 and describes them as "concerning measures and actions by Israel designed to change the status of the Israeli-occupied section of Jerusalem." It appears to be the intention of the Security Council to restrict by this language the scope of the recalled resolutions to the

---

43. *Id.* at 5.
44. *Id., Twenty-sixth Year* 6.
45. *Id., Thirty-fourth Year* 4.

post-1967 situation. However, while it is within the authority of the Council to interpret its own resolutions, it is beyond its power to impose limitations on the meaning of General Assembly resolutions. If the General Assembly is retaining the principle of the *corpus separatum*, it may do so even if it is assumed that the Security Council is doing otherwise. The third preambular paragraph of resolution 298 reaffirms "the principle that acquisition of territory by military conquest is inadmissible," and no time limitation is imposed upon the application of this principle.

The first four operative paragraphs of resolution 298 provide that the Security Council:

1. *Reaffirms* its resolutions 252 (1968) and 267 (1969);

2. *Deplores* the failure of Israel to respect the previous resolutions adopted by the United Nations concerning measures and actions by Israel purporting to affect the status of the City of Jerusalem;

3. *Confirms* in the clearest possible terms that all legislative and administrative actions taken by Israel to change the status of the City of Jerusalem, including expropriation of land and properties, transfer of population and legislation aimed at the incorporation of the occupied section, are totally invalid and cannot change that status;

4. *Urgently calls upon* Israel to rescind all previous measures and actions and to take no further steps in the occupied section of Jerusalem which may purport to change the status of the City or which would prejudice the rights of the inhabitants and the interests of the international community, or a just and lasting peace.

The second of these paragraphs deplores the failure of Israel to respect the prior resolutions of the United Nations, thereby including both General Assembly and Security Council resolutions. The second and fourth quoted paragraphs refer to "the status of the City." The third in comprehensive terms states that "all legislative and administrative actions taken by Israel" aimed at "the incorporation of the occupied section" are "totally invalid" and ineffective in changing the status of the City. This wording is particularly severe, including the phrase "totally invalid." However, no enforcement action was taken in the face of continued non-compliance by the Government of Israel. The fourth paragraph calls upon Israel to rescind "all previous measures and actions" and not to take further steps "in the occupied section of Jerusalem" to change the City's status and prejudice other important interests. The references in these operative paragraphs, as well as in the first and last paragraphs of the Preamble, to the "occupied section" apparently refer only to East Jerusalem. These references also raise the implication that in the view of the Security Council there is an unoccupied section of Jerusalem.

In resolution 446 of March 22, 1979,[46] the Security Council established a commission consisting of three members of the Council to examine the situation relating to the settlements in the Arab territories occupied since 1967 including Jerusalem. The Government of Israel refused to cooperate with the commission. In the unanimous resolution 465 of March 1, 1980[47] the Security Council commended the work done by the commission and called upon the Government of Israel to cooperate with it. In the fifth operative paragraph, the Security Council stated that it:

> *Determines* that all measures taken by Israel to change the physical character, demographic composition, institutional structure or status of the Palestinian and other Arab territories occupied since 1967, including Jerusalem, or any part thereof, have no legal validity and that Israel's policy and practices of settling parts of its population and new immigrants in those territories constitutes a flagrant violation of the Fourth Geneva Convention relative to the Protection of

---

46. *Id.*
47. *Id., Thirty-fifth Year* 5.

Civilian Persons in Time of War and also constitutes a serious obstruction to achieving a comprehensive, just and lasting peace in the Middle East.

This key provision, like each of the other provisions of resolution 465, is entirely consistent with prior positions of the United States Government manifested both inside and outside the United Nations. Subsequent to President Carter's statement, made more than forty-eight hours later, that the United States' affirmative vote was a mistake resulting from a "failure to communicate" and should have been an abstention, the Department of State submitted forty official documents to the House of Representatives Foreign Affairs Committee which demonstrate the consistency of resolution 465 with prior positions of the U.S. Government.[48] Even if the United States had abstained on resolution 465, however, the legal result in the Security Council would not be changed. The United States could have cast a negative vote and blocked the resolution, but this course of action was apparently not even contemplated.

In resolution 476 of June 30, 1980,[49] following the introduction of the "Basic Law" concerning East Jerusalem in the Knesset, the Security Council again considered the situation in Jerusalem. In the third operative paragraph the Council stated that it:

> *Reconfirms* that all legislative and administrative measures and actions taken by Israel, the occupying Power, which purport to alter the character and status of the Holy City of Jerusalem have no legal validity and constitute a flagrant

---

48. The 40 documents and two other items were enclosures with the undated letter from Asst. Sec. of State Atwood to Chairman Zablocki of the U.S. House of Representatives Committee, received on March 12, 1980. Sec. Atwood's letter and the documents appear in *Resolution of Inquiry Concerning the U.S. Vote in the Security Council on Israeli Settlements in the Occupied Territories,* Hearings before the Committee on Foreign Affairs, House of Representatives, 96th Cong., 2nd Sess. on H. Res. 598, pp. 81–192 (March 12, 21, and 26, 1980).

49. *Supra* note 47 at 13.

violation of the Fourth Geneva Convention relative to the Protection of Civilian Persons in Time of War and also constitute a serious obstruction to achieving a comprehensive just and lasting peace in the Middle East.

Security Council resolution 478 of August 20, 1980[50] dealt with the situation brought about by the enactment of this "Basic Law" by the Knesset.[51] In the first three operative paragraphs of resolution 478 the Council stated that it:

1. *Censures* in the strongest terms the enactment by Israel of the "basic law" on Jerusalem and the refusal to comply with the relevant Security Council resolutions;

2. *Affirms* that the enactment of the "basic law" by Israel constitutes a violation of international law and does not affect the continued application of the Fourth Geneva Convention of 12 August 1949 Relative to the Protection of Civilian Persons in Time of War in the Palestinian and other Arab territories occupied since June 1967, including Jerusalem;

3. *Determines* that all legislative and administrative measures and actions taken by Israel, the occupying Power, which have altered or purport to alter the character and status of the Holy City of Jerusalem and, in particular, the recent "basic law" on Jerusalem are null and void and must be rescinded forthwith ... .

Although the Security Council, unlike the General Assembly, is not directly representative of the world community of states, it is important to recall that it cannot adopt a resolution in the face of a negative vote by one or more of the five Great Powers which have permanent seats. The Security Council, therefore, typically reflects a consen-

---

50. *U.N. SCOR, Thirty-fifth Year* 14.

51. *Supra* note 31.

sus of the Great Powers in its resolutions. Such a consensus can have a significant legal effect.[52]

C. BASIC JURIDICAL PRINCIPLES OF THE UNITED NATIONS CONCERNING JERUSALEM

In summary, although the pre-1967 resolutions of the General Assembly were very specific in prescribing the *corpus separatum* status for Jerusalem, there is a lack of clarity in those of 1967 concerning its status. In contrast, the 1980 and 1981 resolutions of the General Assembly and those of the Security Council following the 1967 intense hostilities appear to accept the concept of the divided City. The result of these actions of the General Assembly and Security Council concerning Jerusalem is that while the principle of the *corpus separatum* remains valid, emphasis since 1967 is placed upon the illegality of the Israeli attempt to annex East Jerusalem. The continuing relevance of Jerusalem as an international *corpus separatum* is indicated by the actions of a number of governments demonstrating their refusal to recognize Jerusalem as the capital of Israel.[53]

Although the Government of Israel, through its "Basic Law," has attempted to separate East Jerusalem from the occupied territory of the West Bank, the status of the eastern portion of the City is still that of occupied territory under the applicable humanitarian law.[54] The mandatory applicability of this law, and particularly the Geneva Civilians Convention of 1949,[55] has been stressed in some of the resolutions of both the General Assembly and the Security Council.[56] The Civilians Convention provides, *inter alia*, that civilian

---

52. *Supra* note 35 at 5.

53. See Sec. III C *infra*.

54. See Chap. 6 *infra, passim*. Israeli violation of art. 64 of the Geneva Civilians Convention as a basis for the illegality of the "Basic Law" is stated in Crane, "Middle East: Status of Jerusalem," 21 *Harvard Int'l L. J.* 784 at 792 (1980).

55. 75 U.N.T.S. 287 [1955] 6 U.S.T. 3516, T.I.A.S. No. 3365.

56. See, *inter alia*, the following resolutions considered *supra*: G.A. Res. 2252 and 35/169E; S.C. Res. 271, 465, 476, and 478.

protected persons in occupied territory are not to be deprived of the benefits of the Convention by changes introduced "into the institutions or government of the said territory" or "by any annexation by the latter [the occupying power] of the whole or part of the occupied territory."[57]

III. A Survey of Proposed Solutions for Jerusalem

A. ISRAELI DOMINATION OF THE ENTIRE CITY

The maintenance of the status quo since 1967 involves a continuation of the comprehensive Israeli political and military control of all Jerusalem including the adjacent villages. At least so far as East Jerusalem is concerned, this is in opposition to the determinations of both the United Nations General Assembly and the Security Council, and it is in direct violation of the basic principle of the "inadmissibility of the acquisition of territory by war" which is specified in Security Council resolution 242. It is a form of "enforced solution" but one which is enforced unilaterally by the Government of Israel rather than by consensus of the authorized organs of the world community. The practical effect of this plan for Jerusalem would be to further embitter the Palestinians as well as others who have a legitimate interest in the City.

It is appropriate to examine the Israeli claims to West Jerusalem and, more recently, the eastern portion as well.[58] The claim of title to West Jerusalem, rather than a mere status as military occupant, is apparently based upon the same

---

57. *Supra* note 55, art. 47.

58. Although the Israeli presence in both western and eastern Jerusalem has been brought about by military conquest, there are Zionist legal writings which attempt justification in terms of international law. Among those are Elihu Lauterpacht [the son of the late Professor Hersch Lauterpacht], *Jerusalem and the Holy Places* (London, 1968) [cited hereafter as Lauterpacht]; Yehuda Z. Blum, *The Juridical Status of Jerusalem* (Hebrew Univ. of Jerusalem, 1974) [cited hereafter as Blum]; and Julius Stone, *Israel and Palestine: Assault on the Law of Nations* at 98–123 (1981) [cited hereafter as Stone]. Of these three, the most detailed arguments appear in Lauterpacht.

grounds as claims to other portions of Palestine beyond the boundaries specified in the Partition Resolution.[59] Heavy emphasis is placed upon the allegation that the Arab role in the 1947–1948 hostilities was that of the aggressor, but little, if any, evidence is offered to support this thesis.[60] It is simply assumed that the Zionist role, both before and after the establishment of the State of Israel, was defensive in spite of the evidence of the systematic attacks upon the indigenous Palestinians which led to the expulsion and dispossession of the great majority of them.[61] The Zionist legal writers at the present time give little or no weight to the Partition Resolution[62] and they give no consideration at all to the concept that the title, or sovereignty, to Jerusalem remained in the Palestinians[63] or, in the alternative, that the title to Jerusalem as a *corpus separatum* was in the community of states represented by the United Nations. Their central argument is that with the withdrawal of the British forces there was a "vacuum in sovereignty" in Jerusalem which could be filled in any lawful manner.[64] Then the conclusion is reached that since Israel acted defensively, it acquired West Jerusalem lawfully and thus filled the previous vacuum in sovereignty. Mr. Elihu Lauterpacht has put it this way:

It is on this basis – the legitimate filling of the sovereignty vacuum – that the legality of Israeli presence in the New City of Jerusalem in the

---

59. See Chap. 6 *infra, passim.*

60. Lauterpacht at 21, 43, 47; Blum at 8–14, 19–21; repeated allegations of Arab "aggression" appear in Stone, *passim.*

61. The basic Zionist plan to expel the Palestinians and its implementation are considered in Childers, "The Wordless Wish: From Citizens to Refugees" in *The Transformation of Palestine* 165 (I. Abu-Lughod ed., 1971). Plan Dalet, proposed by the Haganah High Command in March, 1948 and implemented immediately, emphasized military attacks on Palestinian population centers located outside the boundaries of "the Jewish state" specified in the Palestine Partition Resolution 181. Plan Dalet is described in Lt.-Col. Netanel Lorch, *The Edge of the Sword: Israel's War of Independence, 1947–1949* at 87–89 (1961).

62. *E.g.*, Lauterpacht 15–16, 42.

63. Cattan, *Jerusalem* 107–08 (1981).

64. Lauterpacht 41; Stone 117–18.

period prior to the fighting of June 1967 may be seen as resting.[65]

He has attempted to buttress this conclusion by also stating that in addition to acquiring a valid title to those parts of Palestine allotted to it by the Partition Resolution, it also has such a title or sovereignty in "those parts of Palestine *outside* the area allotted to the Jewish State"[66] which Israel was compelled to take in self-defense.

The entire argument which has been set forth fails for one crucial reason. It is a basic doctrine of international law, including the United Nations Charter, that defensive measures may only be authorized to conserve existing values, and there is no authority whatsoever to extend values as by acquiring title to territory.[67] The development of a contrary legal doctrine[68] would prove to be an irresistible temptation to any militaristic and expansionist state. Even if it should be assumed, contrary to the overwhelming evidence including authoritative Zionist sources,[69] that the Israeli military measures in 1948–1949 and in 1967 were defensive, it provides no basis for a legitimate title claim. The other

---

65. Lauterpacht 45.

66. *Id.* at 46.

67. The basic doctrine appears in, *inter alia*, R. Y. Jennings, *The Acquisition of Territory in International Law* 55–56 (1963); McDougal & Feliciano, *Law and Minimum World Public Order* 222–24 (1961); and in Professor G.I.A.D. Draper, "The Status of Jerusalem as a Question of International Law," in *The Legal Aspects of the Palestine Problem with Special Regard to the Question of Jerusalem* 154, 163 (Hans Koechler, ed., 1981). [This book contains the papers presented at the International Progress Organization Conference in Vienna, 5–7 Nov. 1980.]

68. The principal attempt to develop such a contrary doctrine is Schwebel, "What Weight to Conquest?", 64 *Am. J. Int'l L.* 344 (1970). His argument that this contrary doctrine has been established in law is readily accepted by other Zionist writers. Lauterpacht 51–52; Blum 20–21; Stone 120–21.

69. *Supra* note 61. A description of the elaborate Israeli military planning leading up to the massive air attacks of June 5, 1967 appears in R. S. Churchill & W. S. Churchill, *The Six Day War* 53–77 (1967). The authors attribute to General Hod, then the commander of the Israeli Air Force, the statement that sixteen years of planning went into the attack and that, "We lived with the plan, we slept on the plan, we ate the plan. Constantly we perfected it." *Id.* at 91.

assumption, that there was a vacuum in sovereignty, is also inadequately supported.

The Zionist arguments designed to establish an Israeli title to East Jerusalem following the intense hostilities of 1967 are quite similar to those concerning West Jerusalem. It is alleged that Jordan was again an aggressor in 1967 (the same arguments are advanced concerning the other Arab states) with the legal consequence that when it was forced out, a vacuum of sovereignty existed which was filled lawfully by Israel.[70] This argument must be rejected because of the known facts concerning the Israeli surprise attack of June 5, 1967 as well as for the other reasons that the Israeli title claims to West Jerusalem fail. During the period 1948–1967 Jordan, whether acting for itself or for the Palestinian people, received at the least as much community acquiescence concerning its position in East Jerusalem as Israel did concerning the western portion. In addition, all of the 1967 and subsequent resolutions of the United Nations, including Security Council resolution 242, reject the Israeli claim to East Jerusalem. These authoritative community determinations permit East Jerusalem to be a part of a community planned solution which is free of a legitimate Israeli claim. In the same way, the failure of the legal claim to West Jerusalem made by Israel also permits it to be allocated by the community rather than by unilateral Israeli dictation. It is important to recognize that even though Israel cannot claim a legitimate title to West Jerusalem under the international law concerning aggression and self-defense,[71] it is possible that the community of states could give such a title through silence and acquiescence.

Functional internationalization of Jerusalem has been suggested by some Zionist writers.[72] It would involve a measure of international religious supervision and control of

---

70. Lauterpacht 46–48; Blum 16–20; Stone 116 (all cited *supra* note 58). It is also argued that Jordan as an "aggressor" had no "reversionary rights" in East Jerusalem. Lauterpacht 18–19; Stone 118–20.

71. See the analysis of aggression and self-defense in Chap. 7.

72. Lauterpacht 55–75; Blum 26–32; Stone 108–10.

the Holy Places only, and it would not involve any change in the fundamental governmental control of the geographical areas in which they are situated. Thus functional internationalization is a minor variation upon Israeli domination of the entire City which is apparently viewed by the Government of Israel as a method for making its continuing political control more acceptable to the world community.[73]

B. A DIVIDED ARAB–ISRAELI CITY

This plan involves a re-division of Jerusalem substantially along the lines that obtained from 1948 to 1967, with the western section remaining under Israeli control and the eastern section returned to Arab control.[74] East Jerusalem could be returned to Arab control directly or through an interim United Nations regime to act as trustee for the Palestinians pending the full implementation of Palestinian self-determination. Self-determination for the present City of Jerusalem alone would not be just in view of the Israeli practice of systematic displacement of the Arab inhabitants and bringing in of Zionist Jews. As stated in a study prepared by the Congressional Research Service of the Library of Congress in Washington:

> The Israeli census taken after the war showed an Arab population of 70,000, which would mean that some 60,000 Arabs left the Jerusalem region either during the war or immediately afterward.[75]

Any attempt to utilize the divided City plan becomes

---

73. Functional internationalization is criticized in Evan M. Wilson, *Jerusalem: Key to Peace* 135 (1970).

74. See *id.* at 133; S. V. Mallison & W. T. Mallison, "The Jerusalem Problem in Public International Law: Juridical Status and a Start Towards Solution," in Hans Koechler (ed.) *supra* note 67, p. 98 at 108–09; R. H. Pfaff, *Jerusalem: Keystone of an Arab–Israeli Settlement* 54 (Amer. Enterprise Inst., 1969); M. Kerr, "The Changing Political Status of Jerusalem" in Abu-Lughod (ed.) *supra* note 61, p. 355 at 368–71.

75. *Jerusalem: The Future of the Holy City for Three Monotheisms,* Hearing Before the Subcommittee on the Near East of the Committee on Foreign Affairs of the U.S. House of Representatives, 92nd Cong., 1st Sess., Appendix III, p. 145 at 159 (July 28, 1971).

increasingly difficult with the passage of time. The situation has been complicated by the extensive construction of concrete block housing for Israeli settlers surrounding the eastern portion of the City, thereby changing the demographic distribution of population and making it impossible to effectuate the division of the sectors through a process of local area self-determination.[76] The Commission appointed in accordance with Security Council resolution 446 of March 22, 1979 "to examine the situation relating to settlements in the Arab territories occupied since 1967, including Jerusalem" reported that as of that time the number of Israeli settlers in Jerusalem and the West Bank had reached 90,000 and that the largest number of these settlers (estimated by some authorities at 80,000[77]) are in the eastern part of Jerusalem.[78] The Commission stated that "those changes are of such a profound nature that they constitute a violation of the Fourth Geneva Convention relative to the Protection of Civilian Persons."[79] This Israeli settlement policy has been used to ensure that there will not be an Arab majority in East Jerusalem and also to segregate the Arab population of the City from the remainder of the West Bank.

In the event that arrangements could be made to redistribute the recently added Israeli population and make appropriate population adjustments for the division of the City, some of the undesirable practices which were associated with the 1948 to 1967 division between Jordan and Israel would need to be corrected. Among these were the facts of the inaccessibility of the Wailing Wall to Israeli Jews and the desecration of the Armenian Church of St. Savior on Mt. Zion by the Israeli Army.[80] As in any workable plan, there must be

---

76. Cattan, *supra* note 63, Chap. 7 entitled, "The Massive Colonization of Jerusalem and its Surroundings" 79–89 (1981). See Ned Temko, "What's Behind Israel's Extension of Jewish Control over Holy City," Christian Science Monitor, Aug. 5, 1980, p. 1, cols. 1–2, and p. 12, cols. 2–4. See also "Survey of Israeli expansion in Jerusalem" with accompanying map in *id.* at p. 12, col. 2.

77. *Supra* note 63 at 82.

78. *Id.*

79. *Id.* at 83.

80. Kerr, *supra* note 74 at 374.

protection of and access to all the Holy Places. In addition, a change should be made from the former situation of division by barbed wire and machine gun emplacements. There is no doubt but that a peaceful border here would require detailed administrative arrangements and a considerable measure of good faith on both sides, but the importance of the results would fully justify the efforts involved in achieving them.

Insofar as legal authority for this plan is concerned, the community of states, acting through the United Nations and in many cases individually, has never specifically recognized the unilateral claims of Israel and Jordan to the sections of Jerusalem which they occupied before 1967. It may be argued, however, that the failure to protest these claims as well as the silence on the subject manifested in the post-1967 United Nations resolutions may constitute sufficient community acquiescence to give some implied measure of legal authority. Implementation of the plan for the divided City would have the advantage to the State of Israel of providing for the first time explicit international legal authority for its presence in West Jerusalem.

C. INTERNATIONALIZATION

Suggestions that internationalization was the proper status for Jerusalem were heard well before the United Nations Partition Resolution with its *corpus separatum*. Among them, the Peel Commission recommended in 1937 a sovereign Jewish state and a sovereign Arab state with a permanent British mandatory zone including Jerusalem, Bethlehem, and a narrow corridor to the sea.[81]

United Nations General Assembly resolution 181 specified in considerable detail the plan for internationalization of the City of Jerusalem.[82] Under this plan, the City would be given a separate international status quite apart from the State of Israel and the General Assembly specifications for a Palestinian State, and neither the capital of Israel nor the

---

81. *Report of the Palestine Royal Commission*, Cmd. 5479 (June 22, 1937) reprinted in part in Moore, *supra* note 16 at 150.

82. The text *supra* accompanying notes 12–13.

capital of the Palestinian State could be located within Jerusalem. This plan was referred to in succeeding General Assembly resolutions as the *corpus separatum* or as "the legal status of the City." This often repeated formulation by the world community provides a measure of legal authority for the status of internationalization. A number of states have taken positions which are consistent with this status. For example, the United States specifically stated this position in its refusal, in a note of July 9, 1952, to move its embassy from Tel Aviv to West Jerusalem:

> The Government of the United States has adhered to and continues to adhere to the policy that there should be a special international regime for Jerusalem ... .[83]

In a dispatch to the Secretary of State on December 30, 1958 the United States Consul-General at Jerusalem stated:

> Many other countries mark their respect for the internationalization resolutions by establishing embassies in Tel Aviv, thus avoiding recognition of Jerusalem as the capital of Israel and, by implication, as Israel's *de jure* sovereign territory.[84]

To date the United States has not moved its embassy to either portion of Jerusalem.

In the summer of 1979, the then recently-elected Prime Minister Clark of Canada announced that his government would move its embassy from Tel Aviv to Jerusalem.[85] Over a period of the next few months there was a strong surge of feeling in Canada as well as pressure from the United States against this move, and in October 1979 it was announced that the planned move had been abandoned.[86] Following the

---

83. 1 Whiteman, *Digest of International Law* 595 (1963).

84. *Id.* at 594.

85. *New York Times*, June 6, 1979, p. 8, col. 3.

86. *Id.*, June 10, 1979, p. 7, col. 1; *id.*, June 24, 1979, p. 8, col. 1; *id.*, June 25, 979, p. 6, col. 4; *id.*, Oct. 30, 1979, p. 3, col. 1.

Israeli municipal annexation of East Jerusalem in July, 1980 and the subsequent actions of the United Nations, the Netherlands,[87] Turkey,[88] and the ten Latin American States[89] which had their embassies in Jerusalem closed them and moved them to Tel Aviv. Further strength was added to the international refusal to recognize Israel's claims to the City when President Mubarak of Egypt refused to include a visit to Jerusalem in his proposed but subsequently cancelled trip to Israel in March or April of 1982.[90]

The plan of internationalization has the advantages of providing for a unified open City and for effective international protection of the Holy Places of each of the religions. It would also be based upon a centralized United Nations administration rather than hoped-for Arab–Israeli cooperation. A practical consideration is that it would not require the moving and resettling of people as would be necessary to effectuate the divided City. The disadvantage is that international administration is both theoretically complicated and practically difficult.[91]

D. PARTIAL INTERNATIONALIZATION

The plan for a limited or partial international enclave of Jerusalem has been proposed by Evan M. Wilson[92] who was formerly the Consul-General of the United States in Jerusalem. It is distinct from the functional internationalization favored by the State of Israel in that it involves complete political control of the geographical area rather than merely a limited religious control of the Holy Sites.[93] Mr. Wilson's plan involves the recommendation that Jerusalem be divided, as it

---

87. *Id.*, Aug. 27, 1980, p. 7, col. 1.

88. *Id.*, Aug. 29, 1980, p. 2, col. 6.

89. *Id.*, Sept. 8, 1980, p. 7, col. 2.

90. A. Rabinovich, "Mubarak's 'No' to Jerusalem Worries Israel," *Christian Science Monitor*, Mar. 2, 1982, p. 3, cols. 1–2.

91. See *supra* note 73 at 134.

92. *Id.* at 134–38.

93. See the text accompanying *supra* note 72.

was before 1967, between Arab and Israeli authorities but that there be a small international area comprising the old Walled City plus a few specified places outside of the Wall. The enclave would be under the authority of a United Nations administrator assisted by a consultative council equally composed of Arabs and Israelis. The plan would involve the demilitarization of the entire City and the provision of measures to secure protection for and access to the religious shrines. The United Nations administrator would have an effective police power to insure the sanctity of the Holy Places.

It should be remembered that Mr. Wilson proposed this plan in 1970 and that with the passage of time it has the disadvantages, pointed out in the plan for the divided City, resulting from the Israeli actions to change the demographic character of the City. The advantage of the plan for partial internationalization, as Mr. Wilson has pointed out, is that it would have positive aspects from both Arab and Israeli perspectives and that it would be sufficiently limited in scope to be capable of efficient administration.[94] From the Israeli standpoint, it would provide international legal authority for their presence in West Jerusalem. Foreign embassies which now, contrary to the often expressed desire of the Government of Israel, remain rooted in Tel Aviv could be moved to West Jerusalem without ensuing difficulties. In the same way, the proposed Palestinian State in the West Bank and the Gaza Strip could locate its capital in East Jerusalem. For Jews, Christians, and Muslims, without discrimination in terms of their national identity, it would provide protection and access to the Holy Places of the Walled City, and it would be consistent with peace and justice in the remainder of Palestine for both Israelis and Palestinians. In addition, it would protect the significant interests of the international community.

E. CONCLUSION

The Jerusalem problem has too often been regarded as so difficult that it should be delayed until it can be made part of a

---

94. *Supra* note 73 at 137–38.

comprehensive settlement. The fact is that delay makes the problem much harder to solve. If the world community had reacted with vigor in 1967 by using the available economic and military sanctions provided for in the United Nations Charter,[95] the solution of the problem of Jerusalem would have been much easier and would have greatly facilitated the solution of the Palestine problem as a whole. The wasted years of good intentions including General Assembly and Security Council resolutions based upon sound and just premises but without enforcement cannot now be retrieved, but the opportunity for a responsible world community decision combined with adequate enforcement still exists. The decision should be reached and implemented at the earliest possible time.[96]

The solution for Jerusalem must also be seen in the context of the comprehensive solution of the Palestine problem as a totality. The Palestinian population of Jerusalem is an integral part of the population of the occupied territory of the West Bank.[97] Therefore, whatever solution for the City may be undertaken separately must take this fact into consideration and be understood to be a temporary one designed to prevent further severe damage to the demographic, archeological, and other aspects of the City until such time as it can become a part of the comprehensive solution of the problem as a whole.

---

95. Arts. 39–42.

96. The harm done by delay and the urgent need for early enforcement were presented convincingly by Mr. John Reddaway in a paper entitled, "Jerusalem and International Organizations," at the International Seminar on Jerusalem in London (3–5 December 1979).

97. See A. E. Shapiro, "Does 'Al-Fajr' Endanger Israel's Security?", *Jerusalem Post*, Nov. 2, 1982 reproduced in *Israeli Mirror* (London), March 9, 1982 at pp. 3–4 which points out that the suspension of a newspaper published in East Jerusalem because of its effect on the West Bank is contrary to the Government of Israel position that there is no connection between East Jerusalem and the West Bank. "After Al-Fajr, is it possible to continue to maintain that there is no linkage between Judea and Samaria and the Arab population in East Jerusalem?" *Id.* at 4.

Chapter 6

A Juridical analysis of the Israeli Settlements in the Occupied Territories

I. The International Law Applicable in Occupied Territories

The customary international humanitarian law concerning the protection of civilians in territories under belligerent occupation was developed largely in the nineteenth century. Following the War of 1812 when parts of the United States came under British occupation, the United States Supreme Court defined some of the legal effects of occupation.[1] One of the clearest features of the customary law as developed in the nineteenth century was the rule that the occupant had no authority to disturb private property rights as opposed to property belonging to the state. As early as 1833, Chief Justice Marshall stated in *United States v. Percheman:*

> [I]t is very unusual, even in cases of conquest [which was then a lawful method of acquiring territory], for the conqueror to do more than to displace the sovereign and assume dominion over the country. The modern usage of nations, which has become law, would be violated, that sense of justice and of right which is acknowledged and

---

1. *U.S. v. Rice*, 17 U.S. (4 Wheat.) 253 (1819) held that the laws of the United States were only suspended in the portion of the United States under British occupation during the War of 1812. *Shanks v. DuPont*, 28 U.S. (3 Pet.) 243 (1830) held that the capture of Charleston, South Carolina by the British during the Revolutionary War did not permanently change the allegiance or national character of the inhabitants.

felt by the whole civilized world would be outraged, if private property should be generally confiscated, and private rights annulled.[2]

The outcome of the customary law-making process was that the belligerent occupant no longer had the sovereign powers which it had under the earlier law. It was regarded as having only a temporary and *de facto* authority to protect its security interest and it was subject to various substantive limitations designed to protect the inhabitants.[3]

The Hague Conferences of 1899[4] and 1907[5] codified some aspects of existing customary law, including several provisions of the unratified but widely accepted Brussels Declaration of 1874,[6] and added new provisions which were designed to provide more protection for both the lives and the property of the indigenous civilian population of occupied territory. Article 46 of the Regulations annexed to each Convention is declaratory of the pre-existing customary law. It provides:

Family honour and rights, the lives of persons, and private property, as well as religious convictions and practice, must be respected.
Private property cannot be confiscated.

---

2.   32 U.S. (7 Pet.) 82 at 86–87 (1833).

3.   Art. 3 of *Instructions for the Government of Armies of the United States in the Field* (24 April 1863), U.S. Army General Order 100, codified the customary law rule that the pre-existing domestic law may only be suspended and provides further that the existing "civil and penal law" may be continued in force. These *Instructions* are also known as "Lieber's Code" for their principal author, Professor Francis Lieber of Columbia college, New York. It is reprinted in *The Laws of Armed Conflicts: A Collection of Conventions, Resolutions and Other Documents* 3 (Schindler and Toman eds., 1981). See D. Graber, *The Development of the Law of Belligerent Occupation 1863–1914* pp. 192–216 (1949); G. von Glahn, *The Occupation of Enemy Territory: A Commentary on the Law and Practice of Belligerent Occupation* 45–80 (1957).

4.   Hague Convention II with Respect to the Laws and Customs of War on Land and Annexed Regulations of 18 October 1907, 36 U.S. Stat. 2227, Gt. Brit. For. St. Papers 1898–1899, p. 988.

5.   Hague Convention IV Respecting the Laws and Customs of War on Land and Annexed Regulations of 18 October 1907, 36 US Stat. 2227, Gt. Brit. Tr. Ser. No. 9, Cmd. 5030 (1910).

6.   Schindler & Toman, *supra* note 3 at 25.

Article 56 of both Annexed Regulations is another provision which reflects the pre-existing law. It states that:

> The property of municipalities, that of institutions dedicated to religion, charity and education, the arts and sciences, even when State property, shall be treated as private property.
>
> All seizure or destruction of, or wilful damage to, institutions of this character, historic monuments, works of art and science, is forbidden, and should be made the subject of legal proceedings.

Those provisions which were regarded by some as law-making when written are regarded today as having become so widely accepted by the community of states that they also now reflect existing customary law.[7]

During the Second World War the Nazis in Europe and the Japanese militarists in Asia flagrantly violated the then-existing customary and treaty law concerning the elementary human and property rights of the civilian populations under their control.[8] In particular, these regimes attempted to evade the application of the law by annexing territory or bringing it under the rule of puppet regimes. In the post-Second World War crimes trials, Nazi defendants argued that they were not bound by the law of belligerent occupation since the formerly occupied territories had been annexed to Germany. The International Military Tribunal at Nuremberg, as well as other war crimes tribunals, rejected this argument and held that the purported annexations were invalid and that the provisions of Hague Convention IV of 1907 continued to be applicable.[9] A notorious practice

---

7.   2 Oppenheim, *International Law: Disputes, War and Neutrality* 229 (7th ed., Lauterpacht ed., 1952).

8.   The textual paragraph is based upon *Trial of the Major War Criminals Before the International Military Tribunal at Nuremberg* (42 vols., 1947–1949) [cited hereafter as I.M.T.], and *Law Reports of Trials of War Criminals* (U.N. War Crimes Comm., 15 vols., 1947–1949) [cited hereafter as Reps. U.N. Comm.].

9.   Judgment, 1 I.M.T. 171 at 254 (1947); *Trial of Gauleiter Artur Greiser*, 13 Reps. U.N. Comm. 70 at 112–14 (Supreme National Tribunal of Poland, 1946).

particularly associated with the Nazis was the establishment of "Aryan" or "racial German" civilian settlements in the occupied territories. Sometimes the indigenous civilian populations were allowed to remain, and in other situations they were displaced by the German civilian settlers.[10]

The Geneva Diplomatic Conference of 1949 met in the shadow of these grim events with the determination to prevent their repetition. In addition to three Conventions dealing with the subjects of protection of war victims in land warfare,[11] naval warfare,[12] and in prisoner of war status,[13] it produced a Convention which for the first time was devoted exclusively to the protection of civilian populations.[14] Since the main abuses of elementary civilian human rights had taken place in occupied territories, the new Civilians Convention is primarily concerned with civilians in occupied territories. Its article 47 provides that the inhabitants of occupied territory are not to be deprived of the benefits of the Convention during a belligerent occupation by any changes made in the institutions or government of the territory, or by agreements between the local authorities and the occupying power, or by any annexation of "the whole or part of the occupied territory." The provision concerning annexation simply codifies the holding of the war crimes tribunals on this subject.[15] Article 49(6) prohibits in broad and unequivocal terms the establishment by the occupant of civilian settlements without regard to the purported purpose of the settlements.[16]

---

10.   1 I.M.T. 171 at 243–47 (1947).

11.   75 U.N.T.S. 31, Geneva Convention (I) for the Amelioration of the Condition of the Wounded and Sick in Armed Forces in the Field.

12.   75 *id.* 85, Geneva Convention (II) for the Amelioration of the Condition of Wounded, Sick and Shipwrecked Members of Armed Forces at Sea.

13.   75 *id.* 135, Geneva Convention (III) Relative to the Treatment of Prisoners of War reproduced in part in Appendix 34.

14.   75 *id.* 287, Geneva Convention (IV) Relative to the Protection of Civilian Persons in Time of War. The date of each of the 4 Geneva Conventions is 12 August 1949. Reproduced in part in Appendix 35.

15.   *Supra* note 9.

16.   See the text accompanying *infra* note 78.

The law of the United Nations Charter is also relevant to a legal analysis of settlements in occupied territories. Article 2(4) of the Charter is the basic prohibition upon the use or threat of force otherwise than in self-defense or with the lawful authority of the United Nations.[17] This Charter principle is specified in Security Council Resolution 242 of 22 November 1967 as "the inadmissibility of the acquisition of territory by war." In addition, the principle of self-determination, which is the right of the indigenous population of a territory to determine its own political future in its own way, is a basic right of peoples under the United Nations Charter.[18]

II. Appraisal of the Claims of the Government of Israel Under the Criteria of International Law

A. INTRODUCTION TO THE CLAIMS

Shortly after the then newly-elected Prime Minister Begin returned to Israel following his July, 1977 visit to the United States, the *Israel Digest* (American Edition) published an article which included some of his views on the Israeli settlements in the territories occupied in the 1967 armed conflict. It stated:

> Israel's Prime Minister asked why Jews should not live side by side with Arabs in Judea and Samaria just as they did in Israel. He affirmed that he had made his position categorically clear in the United States, namely, that Jews have the right to live in every part of the Land of Israel.
>
> Replying to American questioners on this point, Israel's Prime Minister had told them that there are several dozen Bethlehems, Hebrons,

---

17. *U.N. Charter* art. 51 authorizes the use of force in self-defense.

18. *Id.* arts. 1(2) and 73. See W. T. Mallison & S. V. Mallison, *An International Law Analysis of the Major United Nations Resolutions Concerning the Palestine Question* 42–48 (U.N. Doc. ST/SG/SER.F/4, 1979).

Shilohs and Beth-els in the United States. "Imagine if the Governors of some states were to ban Jews from settling in these towns. What an outcry there would be against such racial discrimination!

"How can we, a Jewish government, prevent the Jews of Eretz Yisrael from buying land or building their homes in the original Bethlehem, Hebron, Shiloh and Beth-el?"[19]

The analogy Mr. Begin draws between "Jews" moving into towns in the United States and into towns in the occupied territories is a false one. "Jews" moving into any town in the United States do so as individuals with the same domestic law rights and obligations as any other Americans.[20] In contrast, "Jews" moving into any place in the occupied territories do so as members of "the Jewish people"[21] with claimed national rights to initially establish exclusivist "Jewish" settlements and later make the claim to sovereignty on behalf of Israel. The meaning of "Jew" is entirely different in the United States law from the meaning of the same word in Israeli law. In United States law a Jew is a private individual who, like the adherent of any other religion, is entitled to practice his religion and is protected from the imposition of a state religion.[22] In Israeli law a Jew is a member of a legally defined nationality group who is entitled to special rights and benefits which are denied to other

---

19. 20 *Israel Digest* (Amer. Ed.) No. 16, p. 5, col. 2 (Aug. 12, 1977) [published by the World Zionist Organization-Amer. Sec.].

20. Amendment 1 to the U.S. Constitution prohibits the government from making any distinctions between individuals on the basis of their religious identification.

21. Chap. 2, Sec. IIA *supra*. The Zionist "Jewish people" concept has been rejected by the U.S. Government as a concept of international law in the letter of April 20, 1964 from Asst. Sec. of State Talbot to Dr. Elmer Berger, Exec. Vice Pres. of the Amer. Council for Judaism, printed in 8 Whiteman, *Digest of Int'l Law* 35 (U.S. Dept. State, 1967). This Zionist juridical concept is appraised in W. T. Mallison, "The Zionist–Israel Juridical Claims to Constitute 'The Jewish People' Nationality Entity and to Confer Membership in It," 32 *Geo. Wash. L. Rev.* 983 (1964).

22. *U.S. Constitution,* Amendment 1.

Israelis.[23] The two situations are also not analogous in that the acquisition of property within the borders of the United States is governed solely by domestic law. In contrast, the acquisition of property in the occupied territory by any Israeli of any religious persuasion is limited by the international law of the Geneva Civilians Convention.[24]

In early 1980 Mr. Niall MacDermot, the Secretary-General of the International Commission of Jurists, visited Israel and the occupied territories and met with Prime Minister Begin. He has reported on a portion of this meeting in these terms:

> I said I understood the Israeli concern for secure frontiers, but I was not clear what frontiers they were wishing to secure, particularly in view of the increasing number of settlements in the occupied territories which were universally condemned as a violation of international law. What hope had the Palestinians before them?
>
> The position taken by Mr. Begin in reply to these questions was an extreme one. He relied on the Balfour Declaration as establishing the right of the Jewish people to the whole of the British mandated territories of Palestine. It was not correct, therefore, to talk of occupied territories, even though they were subject to a military government. The settlements were settlements in their own land and were therefore not illegal. There had been few Arabs in Palestine at the end of the British mandate. They were, as the PLO Charter itself proclaimed, part of the Arab Homeland, which stretched from the Persian Gulf to the Atlantic. There was, therefore, plenty of room for

---

23. *E.g*, The Law of Return, as amended, 4 Israel Laws (auth. transl.) 11‹ (1950). *Rufeisen v. Minister of Interior (Brother Daniel Case)*, 16 P.D. 2428 (1962) Selected Judgments of Sup. Ct. Israel: Spec. Vol., p. 1 (1971) and *Shalit v Minister of Interior*, 23 PD (II) 477 (1969), *id.* at p. 35 apply the statute t‹ determine membership in "the Jewish people."

24. *Supra* note 14.

them elsewhere. As to the Arabs now living within the area, they would benefit from the "autonomy" proposals under the peace treaty with Egypt, and after 5 years time further developments could be expected.[25]

The position is not only "extreme" as characterized by Mr. MacDermot, but it has no basis in law. The Balfour Declaration as incorporated in the League of Nations Mandate for Palestine contains no promise of legal right to "the Jewish people."[26] Its first safeguard clause prohibits anything which "may prejudice" both "the civil and religious rights" of the Palestinians.[27] In addition, the claim that there were "few Arabs in Palestine at the end of the British mandate" is false. There were at least twice as many Arabs in Palestine as there were Jewish supporters of Zionism in early 1948.[28]

There is no question but that the overwhelming population of the West Bank and Gaza is still comprised of Palestinian Arabs in spite of the increasing numbers of Israeli civilian settlements which are being implanted there. Two reporters of the *Washington Post*, following their on-site investigations on the West Bank, wrote in 1980:

> Since the accords were signed nearly two years ago, the physical landscape of the West Bank has changed with the addition of 39 new Jewish civilian communities, bringing the total number of settlements operating there, under construction or approved by the government, to 72. They now have a population of about 14,000.
>
> In all, since the West Bank was captured by Israel in 1967, nearly one-third of its 2,200-square-

---

25. International Commission of Jurists, *Newsletter: Quarterly Report #4*, p. 29 at 33 (January–March 1980).

26. Chap. 1, Sec. 4A *supra*.

27. *Id.*, Sec. 4B.

28. J. Abu-Lughod, "The Demographic Transformation of Palestine" in *The Transformation of Palestine* 139 at 153–61 (I. Abu-Lughod ed., 1971).

mile area has been bought, expropriated, "closed" or otherwise seized for Israeli civilian and military purposes. The settlements alone cover 28,000 acres.[29]

There have been consistent pronouncements by authorized Israeli leaders that the settlements are permanent and that Israel intends to retain control of the occupied territories. Among these, the following statements are typical. In May, 1981 Prime Minister Begin, speaking before a crowd of 35,000 at the West Bank settlement of Ariel, stated:

I, Menahem, the son of Ze'ev and Hasia Begin, do solemnly swear that as long as I serve the nation as Prime Minister, we will not leave any part of Judea, Samaria, the Gaza Strip and the Golan Heights.[30]

On April 25, 1982 Mr. Begin stated on the National Broadcasting Company's program "Meet the Press," that:

You can annex foreign land. You cannot annex your own country. Judea and Samaria [the biblical names for the West Bank] are part of the land of Israel, where the nation was born.[31]

---

29. W. Claiborne & E. Cody, *The West Bank: Hostage of History* 1 (Foundation for Middle East Peace, Nov. 1980). This book is a reprint of articles originally published in the *Washington Post*. The figures cited in the text were updated in W. Claiborne, "Israel Opens 11 Settlements in Bid to Offset Sinai Withdrawal," *Washington Post*, Apr. 29, 1982, p. A21, cols 1–6 at col. 1:

> The new outposts bring to 94 the number of Israeli settlements in the West Bank, or 29 more than two years ago, when Begin publicly declared that only 10 more new settlements were planned for the West Bank and Gaza Strip. The population of the settlements is estimated to be about 20,000.

30. *Israeli Mirror*, SUNI News Service, London, #558, p. 3, May 21, 1981 (reprint from the *Jerusalem Post*, May 10, 1981).

31. W. Claiborne, "Israel Turns to West Bank: Israel Says Pullout [from Sinai] Was Last Concession," *Washington Post*, April 26, 1982, p. A1, col. 2 at p. A19, col. 1.

Yitzhak Shamir, then foreign minister of Israel, stated in January of 1982:

> We want peace, but only in conditions that will enable us to continue our existence, and this means the Golan Heights, Judea and Samaria within the boundaries of the land of Israel.[32]

Overwhelming primary evidence of the Zionist intention to acquire the territories under military occupation is contained in the World Zionist Organization's "Master Plan for the Development and Settlement in Judea and Samaria, 1979–1983," also known as the "Drobles Plan" for its author.[33] In its desire to acquire the land without also acquiring its Palestinian population, Israel has used a systematic campaign to force the native Palestinians to leave the area.[34] There has been the approach through legislation, with various devices used to create a "legal" condition of absenteeism in order to confiscate privately owned Palestinian land under the 1948 Absentee Property Law[35] and assign it to Israeli Jews.[36] There has also been deliberately created economic pressure to make it increasingly difficult for the Arab population to remain in the area.[37] Along with this there has been the setting up of Israeli settlements in a carefully planned pattern to isolate Palestinian communities. The Drobles Plan makes clear the fact that the settlements have a military purpose and that their chosen locations are part of an overall strategic consideration. Paragraph 1 states:

> Settlement throughout the entire Land of Israel is for security and by right. A strip of settlements at strategic sites enhances both internal and external

---

32. *New York Times*, Jan. 25, 1982, p. 6, col. 2.

33. U.N. Doc. A/34/605 Annex and U.N. Doc. S/13582 Annex (22 Oct. 1979). The Drobles Plan is printed in Appendix 9 *infra*.

34. J. Abu-Lughod, "Israeli Settlements in Occupied Arab Lands: Conquest to Colony," 11 *J. Palestine Studies*, No. 2, p. 16 at 45 (Winter 1982).

35. 4 Israel Laws (auth. transl.) 68 (1948).

36. *Supra* note 34 at 22–24.

37. *Supra* note 29 at 2; *supra* note 34 at 50.

security alike, as well as making concrete and realizing our right to Eretz Israel.

As implemented by the actions of the World Zionist Organization and the State of Israel, the Drobles Plan belies any claim that the civilian settlements are the result of private or spontaneous acts by Israeli private citizens. The acceleration of the building of settlements following the Camp David accords demonstrates clearly the Israeli intention to "create facts" forestalling any possibility of meaningful self-determination for the Palestine people.[38]

B. THE ZIONIST IDEOLOGICAL CLAIMS BASED UPON POLITICO-RELIGIOUS GROUNDS

The ideological claims to title to the territories occupied in 1967 are frequently formulated in terms of an alleged "divine" or "eternal" right. They apparently seek uncritical acceptance or belief and are not intended to be subject to the criteria of international law. An official version of the claims appeared in the "Guidelines" of the Likud Party as it was approved by majority vote of the Israeli legislature in the process of installing the government of Prime Minister Menahem Begin in June, 1977. These Government of Israel "Guidelines" state:

> The Jewish people have an eternal, historic right to the Land of Israel, the inalienable inheritance of its forefathers.
> The Government will plan, establish and encourage urban and rural settlement on the soil of the homeland.[39]

"The Jewish people," a term which does not appear in biblical text, refers to the world-wide constituency of Jews claimed by Israel in the implementation of its Zionist ideology.[40] To the extent that this claim has a supposed

---

38. *Supra* note 29.

39. *Jerusalem Post*, Int'l Edition, June 21, 1977, p. 2, cols. 1–4 at col. 3.

40. *Supra* note 21.

religious basis, it postulates the existence of a type of deity who would promote the expulsion of the remaining Palestinians from their homes in the West Bank and the Gaza Strip because this is part of the historic "Land of Israel." For present purposes it is sufficient to point out that these politico-religious claims are not made by Jews who regard their religious identity as primary, but by Zionist Jews for political purposes.

In the *Elon Moreh Case*[41] the Supreme Court of Israel described the affidavit submitted on behalf of the Elon Moreh settlers as based upon the Biblical text of Numbers 33:53. This verse and the preceding one provide in the King James version:

> Then ye shall drive out all the inhabitants of
> the land from before you, and destroy all their
> stone idols, and destroy all their molten images,
> and demolish all their high places;
> And ye shall dispossess the inhabitants of the
> land, and dwell therein; for I have given you the
> land to possess.

While stating that it had to apply the law of Israel in the situation, the Court quoted Leviticus 19:34.
This verse states:

> But the stranger who dwelleth with you shall
> be unto you as one born among you, and thou
> shalt love him as thyself; for ye were strangers in
> the land of Egypt.

Although not mentioned by the Court, Leviticus 24:22 is also relevant. It states:

> Ye shall have one manner of law, as well for
> the stranger as for one of your own country; for I
> am the Lord your God.

---

41. *Seventeen Residents of the Village of Rujerib v. Gov't of Israel et al.*, (*The Elon Moreh Case*). H.C.J. 390/79, at pp. 6–8 (Sup. Ct. Israel, 22 October 1979). The citation to this case is from the English translation prepared by the Government of Israel and circulated at the United Nations Headquarters.

It is clear that Zionists and Jews have differing interpretations of the scriptures which are used as the basis of the State of Israel's politico-religious claims. [42]

C. THE CLAIMS THAT THE GENEVA CIVILIANS CONVENTION IS NOT APPLICABLE IN THE TERRITORIES OCCUPIED SINCE JUNE 1967

All of the state participants in the recurring hostilities in the Middle East are parties to the four Geneva Conventions of 1949[43] which are multilateral treaties with almost as broad a membership as that of the United Nations. As of March 1, 1982 there were only 17 states which were not state-parties to these Conventions. [44] Article 158 (3) of the Civilians Convention provides that during an armed conflict, including an occupation, a denunciation of the Convention:

> shall not take effect until peace has been concluded, and until after operations connected with the release, repatriation and re-establishment of the persons protected by the present Convention have been terminated.

Since termination by denunciation is thereby prohibited, the State of Israel has used various theories attempting to avoid the application of the Convention. Dr. Yehuda Z. Blum, then a lecturer in international law at the Hebrew University of Jerusalem and later the Permanent Representative of Israel at the United Nations, made such an attempt in an article

---

42. For Jewish religious perspectives see E. Berger, "An Examination of the Claim of Zionism to Divine Authorization for Establishing Settlements," 1 Arab Perspectives No. 3, p. 24 (May 1980). See also E. Marmorstein, *Heaven at Bay: The Jewish Kulturkampf in the Holy Land, passim* (Oxford, 1969) in which the author emphasizes the thesis that Zionism and the religion of Judaism are incompatible.

43. *Supra* notes 11–14.

44. The states are: Angola, Belize, Bhutan, Burma, Cape Verde, Comoros, Equatorial Guinea, Guinea, Maldives, Mozambique, Samoa, Seychelles, Vanuatu, Zimbabwe (all United Nations members), and Antigua and Barbuda, Kiribati, and Nauru (not United Nations members). I.C.R.C., INFO/DIF Nr. 1/1, 01.03.82 – JJS/DE, p. 15.

entitled, "The Missing Reversioner: Reflections on the Status of Judea and Samaria" in 1968.[45] The significance of this article is that the Government of Israel has acted upon each of the arguments advanced by Dr. Blum.[46] The balance of the present inquiry will examine the Israeli juridical claims and appraise them under the criteria of international law.

1. THE CLAIM POSTULATING THE NECESSITY THAT THE "LEGITI-MATE SOVEREIGN" BE DISPLACED BY THE OCCUPANT

A major Israeli claim originated by Dr. Blum uses the thesis that the application of the law of belligerent occupation in general, and the Geneva Civilians Convention in particular, is based upon the presupposition that the "legitimate sovereign" of the occupied territory must have been displaced by the occupant.[47] This argument maintains that Jordan and Egypt were not "legitimate sovereigns" in the West Bank of the River Jordan and in the Gaza Strip respectively because they were there as a result of their alleged acts of aggression.[48] Therefore, the Government of Israel is not required to apply the humanitarian law of the Civilians Convention for the benefit of the inhabitants of the occupied territory. The Israeli argument recognizes that article 2 of the Convention in relevant part provides: "The Convention shall also apply to all cases of partial or total occupation of the territory of a High Contracting Party ... ." However, it assumes, without an identifiable basis in law, that the word "territory" in article 2 must be narrowly construed as only including the territory over which the

---

45. 3 *Israel L. Rev.* 279 (1968).

46. The then Attorney General of Israel, Mr. Meir Shamgar, set forth the same arguments used by Dr. Blum, including the inapplicability of the Civilians Convention in the occupied territories, in "The Observance of International Law in the Administered Territories," 1 *Israel Y.B. Human Rights* 262, 263–64 (1971). A memorandum circulated by the Israeli Embassy in Washington, D.C. entitled "Jewish Settlement in Areas Administered by Israel" (Oct. 25, 1977) also repeats Dr. Blum's arguments.

47. *Supra* note 45 at 292–93.

48. *Id.* at 283–88.

displaced government has *de jure* title.[49] There are several compelling legal reasons which require that this claim be rejected.

First, Dr. Blum and the Government of Israel use an obscure method of treaty interpretation which is not known in international law, or indeed in any civilized legal system. It places no reliance upon either the text of the Convention or its negotiating history, which are the accepted primary sources for ascertaining meaning,[50] because there is nothing in either to support the claim.

Second, the claim assumes without supporting evidence that the word "territory" in article 2 of the Civilians Convention must be interpreted as being restricted to territory where the displaced government had the complete formal title as the "legitimate sovereign." Even if the claim that Jordan annexed the West Bank unlawfully should be accepted for purposes of legal argument, this does not mean that this territory is not "the territory of a High Contracting Party" within the meaning of article 2. It has never been previously doubted that the word "territory" as used here included, in addition to *de jure* title, a mere *de facto* title to the territory. The words "legitimate sovereign" upon which so much emphasis is placed do not appear in the convention or

---

49. The same arguments which appear in Dr. Blum's article, *supra* note 45, were repeated by him in *The Colonization of the West Bank Territories by Israel*, Hearings Before the Subcommittee on Immigration and Naturalization of the U.S. Senate Committee on the Judiciary, 95th Cong., 1st. Sess., p. 24 (Oct. 17, 1977). Dr. Blum also stated:

> Coming now to the question of sovereignty, I would have to say this. Yes, indeed, I consider Israel as the potential sovereign over Judea and Samaria.

Id. at 36.

Dr. W. T. Mallison presented a different legal analysis in the same Hearings. *Id.* at 46.

50. It appears unnecessary to cite legal authority to demonstrate the relevance of the text of an international agreement to the interpretation of that agreement. The negotiating history is useful as a means of providing context and background for the text. The importance of context is emphasized in McDougal, Lasswell, and Miller, *The Interpretation of Agreements and World Public Order*, 119 *et seq.* and *passim* (1967).

its negotiating history.[51] Dr. Blum's only authority for his key point that the law of belligerent occupation is not applicable unless the legitimate sovereign has been displaced by the occupant is a treatise entitled *The Occupation of Enemy Territory* by Dr. Gerhard von Glahn.[52] He quotes this authority as stating:

> [B]elligerent occupation . . . as regulated by customary and conventional international law, presupposes a state of affairs in which the sovereign, the legitimate government of the occupied territory, is at war with the government of the occupying forces.[53]

Dr. Blum interprets this as meaning that "the legitimate sovereign" must have a perfect title or complete *de jure* sovereignty. There is, however, no suggestion to this effect in the source quoted. On the contrary, Dr. von Glahn uses the terms "the legitimate government" or "the legitimate sovereign" throughout his book merely to distinguish it from the government of the occupying state.[54]

Third, the idea that in order to apply the law of belligerent occupation it is necessary for the belligerent occupant to accept the validity of the title of the displaced government to the territory finds no support in either the text of the Convention or its negotiating history. In addition, it is contrary to the well established customary law based upon state practice. For example, during the American Civil War, the United States treated territory which it claimed as the "legitimate sovereign" but which the Confederate States had held as the *de facto* possessor as being subject to the law concerning belligerent occupation when it was recovered by

---

51. The negotiating history of the Civilians Convention is in 4 volumes (numbered I, IIA, IIB and III) of the *Final Record of the Diplomatic Conference of Geneva of 1949* (Swiss Federal Political Department, undated).

52. *The Occupation of Enemy Territory: A Commentary on the Law and Practice of Belligerent Occupation* (1957).

53. Blum, *supra* note 45 at 293, appearing in von Glahn, *supra* note 52 at 273.

54. *Supra* note 52 at 31–37 under the sub-heading "The Problem of Sovereignty over Occupied Territory" and *passim*.

the United States armed forces.[55] This customary international law was widely observed up until the Nazi and the Japanese militarist practices of the Second World War, and there is nothing in the Geneva Civilians Convention which changes it.

An interesting aspect of this claim regarding the inadequacy of the Jordanian title is that much emphasis is placed upon the allegation that only two states, Great Britain and Pakistan, recognized Jordanian sovereignty over the West Bank, and this is deemed to demonstrate its invalidity.[56] Dr. Nathan Feinberg, who is Professor Emeritus of International Law at the Hebrew University of Jerusalem, has pointed out that this is a vulnerable argument since no states have recognized the Israeli annexation of Jerusalem – and he refers specifically to West Jerusalem.[57]

Fourth, Dr. Blum's argument appears to attempt to resurrect the discredited "just war" theory upon the basis of the maxim "*ex injuria jus non oritur.*"[58] He and the Government of Israel claim the right to unilaterally categorize the opponent's title to land as being the result of aggression and to determine that the effect of this is that civilians in the territory do not receive the protection of the international humanitarian law.[59] If accepted, this Israeli agrument would have astonishing consequences. The argument contends that the inhabitants of the West Bank were the victims of Jordanian aggression in 1948. It is then concluded that

---

55. Lieber's Code, *supra* note 3, contained arts. 1–10 concerning belligerent occupation which were applied by the United States Government. The U.S. Supreme Court stated in *The Grapeshot Case*:

> The duty of the national government in this respect [during the Civil War] was no other than that which devolves upon the government of a regular belligerent occupying during war the territory of another belligerent.

9 Wall. (76 US) 129, 132 (1870).

56. *Supra* note 45 at 290.

57. "The West Bank's Legal Status," 20 *New Outlook,* No. 7, p. 60 (Oct.–Nov. 1977).

58. *Supra* note 45 at 283.

59. *Id.* at 288, 292–93.

because of this, these civilians must be victimized further by being denied the humanitarian protections of the Civilians Convention under Israeli occupation. If the humanitarian law were to be interpreted so that its application were made contingent upon acceptance by the belligerent occupant of the justness and the non-aggressive character of the war aims of its opponent, it is clear that this law would never be applied. The modern legal interpretation, however, requires application of the humanitarian law without regard to the question of justness or aggression.[60]

The fifth legal block to the acceptance of the Israeli thesis is that it frustrates the entire humanitarian purpose of the Civilians Convention. The Convention, and indeed the entire humanitarian law, is interpreted in the claim as designed to protect governmental rights and particularly the right to claim disputed territory.[61] In contrast, the governments represented at the Geneva Diplomatic Conference of 1949, including the Government of Israel, stated in the preamble to the Civilians Convention that they met "for the purpose of establishing a Convention for the Protection of Civilian Persons in Time of War." To attempt to avoid humanitarian protections for civilians by alleging the existence of governmental rights not specified in the Convention is to turn the entire Convention upside down.[62] Since the Convention was written by governments, it is clear that the governmental rights which the Israeli claim alleges to exist would have been specified in the Convention if the governments at Geneva had accepted their validity. An aspect of this claim emphasized by Dr. Blum is his insistence

---

60. *The Trial of Wilhelm List and Others*, 8 Reps. U.N. Comm. 34 at 59 (U.S. Military Tribunal, 1948).

61. Dr. Blum states:

> The legal standing of Israel in the territories in question is thus that of a State which is lawfully in control of territory in respect of which no other States can show a better title.

Supra note 45 at 294.

62. The basic humanitarian purpose of the Civilians Convention is pointed out in "Israeli Settlements in Occupied Territories," *Int'l Comm. Jurists Rev.* No. 19, p. 27, *passim* (Dec. 1977).

that the purpose of the humanitarian law is to protect the "reversionary rights" of the "legitimate sovereign."[63] Once again, this governmental rights claim using the term "reversionary rights" employs words which do not appear in either the text or the negotiating history of the Civilians Convention. In contrast, the official International Committee of the Red Cross *Commentary* upon the Civilians Convention characterizes it this way:

> [I]t is the first time that a set of international regulations has been devoted not to State interests, but solely to the protection of the individual.[64]

In addition to the preamble to the Convention, its text demonstrates the unambiguous intention of the states which wrote it to confer rights directly upon protected persons. A recent expression concerning its applicability to the occupied territories came from the Twenty-fourth International Red Cross Conference which was held in Manila November 7–14, 1981. This Conference passed a resolution which in paragraph 2 *"reaffirms* the applicability of the Fourth Geneva Convention [Civilians Convention] to the occupied territories in the Middle East," and in paragraph 5 *"affirms* that the settlements in the occupied territories are incompatible with articles 27 and 49 of the Fourth Geneva Convention."[65]

---

63. *Supra* note 45 at 293, 301. It is surprising to note that Dr. Blum, after demonstrating to his satisfaction that the humanitarian law does not apply in the occupied territories, then states: "[T]hat part of the law of occupation applies which is intended to safeguard the *humanitarian* rights of the population." *Id.* at 294. He does not, however, identify that part of the humanitarian law which is designed to protect "humanitarian rights" or distinguish it from the part alleged to protect "reversionary rights."

64. 4 *I.C.R.C. Commentary on the Civilians Convention* 77 (Pictet ed. 1958).

65. *Int'l Rev. of Red Cross* No. 225, pp. 320–21 (Nov.–Dec. 1981).

2. THE CLAIM OF TITLE TO TERRITORY BASED ON "DEFENSIVE CONQUEST"

After contending that the titles of the Arab sovereigns are deficient in one way or another, the Government of Israel then claims to be in the territories occupied since June 1967 as a result of its "defensive conquest"[66] and this premise quickly leads to the conclusion stated by Dr. Blum that Israel has "a better title" in the territory of Palestine, including the whole of Jerusalem, than do Jordan and Egypt.[67] The premise assumes, without evidence or legal reasoning, that the Israeli role in the intense hostilities of June, 1967 was defensive.

Assuming, for purposes of analysis only, that the claim of Israeli defensive action could be said to be accurate, the validity of the conclusion that title to territory may be obtained by "defensive conquest" should be examined. The customary law of self-defense as incorporated in article 51 of the United Nations Charter gives clear indication that national self-defense is limited to the conservation of existing values or interests and does not provide any basis for an extension of values by the acquisition of title to enemy territory.[68] A state exercising national defense may go beyond its national boundaries to repel an attack, but it may not go beyond its national boundaries to acquire territory. Article 2(4) of the United Nations Charter specifically prohibits "the threat or use of force against the territorial integrity of any state … ." If international law provided for an exception to this basic rule under the heading of "defensive conquest," it would prove to be an irresistible attraction for a militaristic and expansionist state.[69]

---

66. In the Senate Hearing *supra* note 49 at 34, Dr. Blum cited only one authority for this argument: Schwebel, "What Weight to Conquest?", 64 *Am. J. Int'l L.* 344 (1970) which attempts to develop a concept of "defensive conquest."

67. *Supra* note 49 at 34–35.

68. R. Y. Jennings, *The Acquisition of Territory in International Law* 55 (1963).

69. *Id.* at 55–56.

3. THE CLAIM OF UNUSUAL CIRCUMSTANCES: *SUI GENERIS*

An auxiliary claim made by Israel is that the Civilians Convention is intended only for short-term belligerent occupations and is not relevant to the unusual circumstances, termed the *sui generis* situation, in the occupied territories. Dr. Blum stated in the Hearing before a subcommittee of the U.S. Senate Judiciary Committee:

> Belligerent occupation exceeding a long period of time simply cannot work under the same constraints as the normal belligerent occupation, if the term "normal" can be applied to a situation of this kind. Obviously the Red Cross Convention and other international instruments have in view the "normal" situation under which the hostilities are ceased or terminated and you have an interim period of a few weeks or months of belligerent occupation followed by peace negotiations which finally dispose of the territory.[70]

This Israeli argument amounts to a plea for an exception from the generally recognized criteria of the Civilians Convention on the ground of claimed special circumstances which, if accepted, would leave the belligerent occupant in effective control of the territories but without the applicable legal limitations. On the contrary, the provisions of the Civilians Convention were adopted in advance by all the parties, including the State of Israel, in order to be applied to all later situations of occupation. The comprehensive wording of the Convention concerning applicability specifies "all cases of partial or total occupation"[71] and thereby eliminates the possibility of exceptions.

4. THE CLAIM THAT THE CIVILIANS CONVENTION HAS NOT BEEN PREVIOUSLY APPLIED

This claim assumes as a fact that the Civilians Convention has never been applied anywhere else and appears to

---

70. *Supra* note 49 at 42.
71. Art. 2, para. 2.

conclude that, therefore, it should not be applied by the State of Israel.[72] The short answer is that as a matter of both logic and law there is no reason to assume that the first application is not required by the binding law of the Convention. There is, of course, no suggestion in the text or the negotiating history of the Convention that it is not applicable for the first time.

5. THE IMPLICIT CLAIM THAT THE CIVILIANS CONVENTION IS THE ONLY LAW ON THE SUBJECT

Neither Dr. Blum nor the Government of Israel has addressed the possibility that even if they were successful in demonstrating the inapplicability of the Civilians Convention they would continue to be bound by, at the least, its customary law provisions. Although the Convention was law-making in many respects in 1949, it has now been accepted as law by the overwhelming majority of states for a period of decades. This leads to the possibility that the entire Civilians Convention has become binding customary law. There is no doubt whatsoever that its provisions which were declaratory of the existing customary law when they were written in 1949 have retained their binding status.[73] Such provisions, like other customary law, are binding upon the few states which are not parties to the Geneva Conventions of 1949 as well as to the state parties.

The heavy Israeli emphasis upon attempting to avoid the application of the Civilians Convention has resulted in a lack of attention to Hague Convention IV of 1907 and its Annexed Regulations.[74] The character of this Convention and its

---

72. This claim is set forth in *supra* note 62 at 33 and answered at 35.

73. See generally J. L. Brierly, *The Law of Nations* 59–62 (6th ed. Waldock, 1963) concerning the making of customary law. *Supra* note 7 at 451 characterizes, *inter alia*, article 47 of the Civilians Convention as "to a large extent declaratory of existing International Law." Article 47 is summarized in the text accompanying *supra* notes 14, 15.

74. *Supra* note 5.

Regulations as binding customary law has been accepted by, *inter alia,* the Supreme Court of Israel.[75] Article 46 of the Hague Regulations prohibits the confiscation of private property including land.[76] Its effect makes the utilization of confiscated private property for the occupant's settlements illegal. Article 55 of the Hague Regulations applies to, *inter alia,* public real estate and provides:

> The occupying State shall be regarded only as administrator and usufructuary of public buildings, real estate, forests, and agricultural estates belonging to the hostile State, and situated in the occupied country. It must safeguard the capital of these properties, and administer them in accordance with the rules of usufruct.

Since the status of the occupant is "only" that of "Administrator and usufructuary," it has limited and temporary rights concerning public real estate during the period of occupation. One of the clearest features of the civilian settlements is that they are not intended to be temporary.[77] Since they are usually placed upon confiscated land, whether public or private, they are prohibited by the binding customary law of the Hague Regulations as well as by the Geneva Civilians Convention.

D. THE CLAIM THAT ASSUMES THE APPLICABILITY OF THE CIVILIANS CONVENTION BUT CONTENDS THAT ITS SPECIFIC PROVISION CONCERNING THE SETTLEMENTS HAS NOT BEEN VIOLATED

Dr. Blum has also advanced an alternative argument focusing upon the sixth paragraph of article 49 of the Civilians Convention. This paragraph provides:

---

75. *The Elon Moreh Case, supra* note 41 at 10–15 tested the validity of Israeli municipal law under the Hague Regulations although the State of Israel is not a party to Hague Convention IV of 1907. The I.M.T. at Nuremberg had previously held that the Hague Regulations were declaratory of the existing law. Judgment, 1 I.M.T. 171 at 254 (1947).

76. See the text accompanying *supra* note 5.

77. *Supra* notes 30–33.

The Occupying Power shall not deport or transfer parts of its own civilian population into the territory it occupies.

Almost identical wording, making no exceptions, appeared in the draft Civilians Convention prepared by the International Committee of the Red Cross which was used as a working paper in the Geneva Diplomatic Conference of 1949.[78] It was originally written as article 45(5) of the Draft Civilians Convention which was approved by the XVIIth International Red Cross Conference meeting in Stockholm in August, 1948.[79] The Geneva Diplomatic Conference of 1949 made substantive changes in other paragraphs of the draft article as well as adding a paragraph to it. The only change made in article 49(6) as adopted is that the word "civil" in the Stockholm draft was changed to "civilian" in the text. This final broadly worded text was adopted by Committee III of the Diplomatic Conference on July 6, 1949 without a dissenting vote being recorded.[80] At the Twenty-Sixth Plenary Meeting of the Diplomatic Conference on August 3, 1949 the same text of article 49(6) was adopted, again without dissenting vote.[81] There is no suggestion throughout the four volumes of negotiating history of the 1949 Conference that article 49(6) should be given a narrow or restrictive meaning.

The State of Israel has made a reservation concerning the Civilians Convention but it only pertains to the Israeli intention to use the Red Shield of David as its distinctive sign rather than one of the distinctive signs authorized by article 38 of the Geneva Convention Concerning Wounded and Sick in the Field and incorporated by reference in articles 21 and 22 of the Civilians Convention.[82] It is also possible for a state to make a declaration concerning an interpretation which it gives to a particular article of a treaty, but Israel has made no

---

78. I *Final Record, supra* note 51, p. 113 at 121.
79. *Id.*
80. IIA *id.* at 760.
81. IIB *id.* at 416.
82. I *id.* at 348.

such declaration concerning article 49(6). In summary, the State of Israel had ample opportunity to object to article 49(6) during the negotiations leading to its adoption and it had the further opportunity to make a reservation or declaration concerning the narrow interpretation it now advances at the time it ratified the Convention, but it did neither.[83] The negotiating history at Geneva provided no indication of concern by any state about the comprehensive wording of article 49(6). It is significant that no suggestions were made, much less action taken, to either narrow the wording or to read exceptions into the broad wording.

Dr. Blum, nevertheless, has contended that article 49(6) applies to only one situation, that is, the particular situation where the civilian settlements displace the population of the occupied territory.[84] He argues that this was the only Nazi practice that the article is aimed at. His contention raises a factual question since there is persuasive evidence that substantial numbers of Palestinians have been displaced from their property by the Israeli settlements.[85] Assuming for purposes of argument, however, that the Israeli settlements do not displace the indigenous population, it is appropriate to appraise the claim. At the outset, there is no possibility of arguing an exception from the text, since it provides for none and no suggestion of support for exceptions exists in the negotiating history. Dr. Blum has therefore cited the most recent edition of Professor Oppenheim's text edited by Professor Lauterpacht. This text, after summarizing the terms of article 49(6), states that it is:

---

83.   The Government of Israel ratified the four Geneva Conventions of 1949 for the Protection of War Victims (including the Civilians Convention) on July 6, 1951. Schindler & Toman, *supra* note 3 at 491.

84.   *Supra* note 49 at 25–26.

85.   See the testimony of Mrs. Ann M. Lesch in *Israeli Settlements in Occupied Territories*, Hearings Before the Subcommittees on Int'l Orgs., and Europe and the Middle East of the U.S. House of Representatives Comm. on Int'l Rels., 95th Cong., 1st Sess., pp. 7–42 (including appendices) (Sept. 12, 1977). Mrs. Lesch's testimony indicates the displacement of Palestinians and the permanence of the settlements.

a prohibition intended to cover cases of the occupant bringing in its nationals for the purpose of displacing the population of the occupied territory.[86]

There can be no doubt but that this is one of the several fact situations covered by article 49(6). The Nazi practices, however, were not limited to the displacement of the civilian population since it was often retained to provide cheap labor or slave labor.[87] Dr. Blum interprets the inherent ambiguity in the quoted text as if it read that the prohibition was intended only to cover cases of the occupant displacing the indigenous population, but that is quite different from the quoted text as well as from article 49(6) itself which is not limited to any single purpose. The International Committee of the Red Cross *Commentary* on the Civilians Convention states in its analysis of article 49(6):

> It is intended to prevent a practice adopted during the Second World War by certain Powers, which transferred portions of their own population to occupied territory for political and racial reasons or in order, as they claimed, to colonize those territories. Such transfers worsened the economic situation of the native population and endangered their separate existence as a race.[88]

Nothing in the analysis mentions or suggests a possible limitation of the application of the article to a situation where the civilian population is displaced.

Dr. Blum does not consider article 49(1) which, as a general rule, prohibits forcible transfers or deportations from the occupied territory whether on an individual or mass basis. The fact that this provision stands apart from article 49(6) is a clear indication that the two are not connected or

---

86. *Supra* note 7 at 452.
87. Judgment, 1 I.M.T. 171 at 243–47 (1947).
88. *Supra* note 64 at 283.

contingent upon one another.[89] In addition, article 49(1) deals with "forcible" transfers, whereas there is no such limitation in article 49(6). Therefore, it is not possible to read article 49(1) as stating the only situation in which article 49(6) is to be applied. The International Committee of the Red Cross *Commentary* confirms this interpretation by treating each paragraph as separate and distinct.[90]

Professor Eugene V. Rostow, like Dr. Blum, has argued the legality of the settlements. Writing in 1979, he begins his analysis by stating:

> [I]t is impossible seriously to contend, as the United States government does, that Israeli settlements in the West Bank are illegal.[91]

He criticizes the often repeated position of the U.S. State Department, and its accompanying legal analysis, that the settlements are in violation of the Civilians Convention.[92] On this point he states:

> The Department's position is in error; the provision was drafted to deal with "individual or mass forcible transfers of population," like those in Czechoslovakia, Poland, and Hungary before and after the Second World War. Israeli administration of the areas has involved no forced transfers of population or deportations.[93]

---

89. S. V. Mallison, *Israeli Settlements Under International Law* 15 (Amers. for Middle East Understanding, 1981).

90. *Supra* note 64 at 278–80, 283.

91. "'Palestinian Self-Determination': Possible Futures for the Unallocated Territories of the Palestine Mandate," 5 *Yale Studies in World Public Order* 147 at 159 (1979).

92. Opinion of the Legal Adviser of the U.S. Department of State [1978] *Digest U.S. Prac. in Int'l L.* 1575 (1980).

93. *Supra* note 91 at 160. Professor Rostow's last quoted sentence concerning "no forced transfers" or "deportations" is factually in error. *Supra* note 85 *passim.* See J. Yemma, "The Tightening Grip on Gaza: Israel's Quest for a Secure Border," Christian Science Monitor, April 20, 1982, p. 3, cols. 2–3. "[T]he situation on the ground here indicates Israel is intent on keeping Gaza under its control and pressuring Palestinians to emigrate." *Id.* at col. 2.

By citation of authority, he makes it clear that his reliance is upon the views previously expressed by Dr. Blum.[94] The conclusion of Professor Rostow's brief analysis is that:

[I]t suffices simply to conclude that Israel's legal position with regard to its right of settlement in the West Bank is impregnable.[95]

Professor Rostow's consideration of the phrase in article 49(1) which deals with "forcible" transfers, like that of Dr. Blum, does not take into account the fact that article 49(6) does not contain such a limitation and is not contingent upon article 49(1). President Reagan appears to have accepted Professor Rostow's conclusion. He stated in a press interview, shortly after assuming office as President, without any consideration of the long-term prior position of the United States, that the settlements are not illegal.[96] Since that time the United States Government has emphasized the character of the settlements as a major obstacle to the peace process.[97]

Professor Julius Stone has also argued the legality of the settlements by repeating Professor Rostow's arguments and adding a new point of his own.[98] In his view:

The issue is rather whether the Government of Israel has any obligation under international law to use force to prevent the voluntary (often the fanatically voluntary) movement of these [Gush Emunim] individuals.

On that issue, the terms of Article 49(6), however they are interpreted, are submitted to be totally irrelevant. To render them relevant, we would have to say that the effect of Article 49(6) is

---

94. *Supra* note 91 at notes 34, 35, p. 160.

95. *Id.* at 162.

96. Press interview, Christian Science Monitor, Feb. 4, 1981, p. 22, col. 3. Professor Rostow has been appointed director of the U.S. Arms Control and Disarmament Agency by President Reagan.

97. *E.g., Christian Science Monitor,* Nov. 10, 1942, p. 1, col. 1, cont. p. 9, cols. 2–3, at col. 2.

98. *Israel and Palestine: Assault on the Law of Nations* 177–81 (1981).

to impose an obligation on the state of Israel to ensure (by force if necessary) that these areas, despite their millennial association with Jewish life, shall be forever *judenrein*.[99]

III. The Objective of the Israeli Settlement Policy

It should be emphasized that the text of article 49(6), contrary to Dr. Blum's interpretation,[100] contains no limitation in terms of one or more particular purposes of the prohibited settlements. If the purpose of the settlements is to be regarded as relevant, however, the basic aim of the Israeli settlements, like that of the Nazi ones, is to "create facts" which facilitate the acquisition of territory.[101] This conclusion has been amply documented.

During the period of the League of Nations Mandate for Palestine, the Zionist settlements became the significant power base which was used to transform "the Jewish national home" into the Zionist State of Israel. Dr. Weizmann's autobiography emphasizes the crucial importance of Zionist settlement in Palestine to the achievement of the political objectives.[102] The ensuing settlement policy was described in a statement made by the late General Moshe Dayan in 1969:

> We came to this country which was already populated by Arabs, and we are establishing a Hebrew, that is a Jewish state here. In considerable areas of the country [the total area was about 6 percent] we bought the lands from the Arabs. Jewish villages were built in the place of Arab villages. You do not even know the names of these Arab villages, and I do not blame you,

---

99. *Id*. at 180.

100. The text accompanying *supra* note 84.

101. Dr. Blum's statement, *supra* note 49, of Israel as "the potential sovereign" over the West Bank; the Drobles Plan in the text accompanying *supra* note 33.

102. *Trial and Error: The Autobiography of Chaim Weizmann* 405 and *passim* (East and West Library, 1950).

> because these geography books no longer exist:
> not only do the books not exist, the Arab villages
> are not there either ... . There is not one place
> built in this country that did not have a former
> Arab population.[103]

Dr. Janet Abu Lughod has set forth and analyzed the process which has resulted in the demographic transformation of Palestine from a land inhabited by a settled Arabic-speaking community (largely Moslem but with significant Christian and Jewish minorities) to one now inhabited overwhelmingly by European, Asian, and African Jews.[104] This transformation has resulted in the displacement of a great proportion of the Palestinian Arab population.

A more recent carefully documented study by Dr. W. W. Harris, entitled *Taking Root: Israeli Settlement in the West Bank, the Golan, and Gaza-Sinai, 1967–1980*,[105] deals with the systematic settlement policies in the post-1967 occupied territories. It emphasizes the importance of the "Allon Plan" which was based upon the conception of settlement for "security" purposes when it was originated under the Labor Party and was gradually modified under the pressure of the forces of politico-religious nationalism in Israeli domestic politics.[106] This plan was discarded by the Likud Party when it came to power in 1977 and replaced by a new emphasis on establishing a large civilian presence in the more densely populated areas of the West Bank.[107] The study also contains documentation of official and unofficial government support for the creation of new settlements and increasing the population of existing ones.[108]

---

103. Ha-Aretz, April 4, 1969, quoted in E. Said, *The Question of Palestine* 14 (Vintage Books, 1979).

104. *Supra* note 28 *passim*.

105. *Taking Root* is published by the Research Studies Press of John Wiley & Sons (1980).

106. *Id.* at 138–39.

107. *Id.* at 147.

108. *Id.* at 149–51 and *passim*.

Dr. Meron Benvenisti, a former deputy mayor of Jerusalem, has recently completed an in-depth study of settlement entitled *West Bank and Gaza Data Base Project*.[109] It refers to the more recent developments in the plan to implement Israel's version of "autonomy" (for the Palestinian inhabitants but not for the territory) which involves the creation of a dual society where all the rights and benefits of Israeli law and services will be in effect in the "Jewish areas."[110] The Arab areas will remain under the domination of an Israeli military or civil administration.[111] The domestic legal bases for this dual society were laid in two military orders which were published only in Hebrew at first and later translated into Arabic. Order Number 783[112] created and determined boundaries of the areas for Jewish administration, and Order Number 947[113] established the civil administration for the Arab areas. The "Jewish areas" are now treated administratively as if they were parts of Israel under this elaborate political arrangement.

Dr. Benvenisti points out the various methods used to seize land and shows that the land now made available by the Begin Government for settlement amounts to more than 55 percent of the entire West Bank.[114] In addition to the land seized under such devices as the Absentee Property Law[115] and that claimed for security or military requirements, the

---

109. This study, sub-captioned "Pilot Study Report," was published in photo-copied typescript in 1982. The study was supported financially by the Graduate School of the City University of New York and the International Center for Peace in the Middle East, Tel Aviv.

110. *Id.* at 42–43.

111. *Id.* at 104–05.

112. *Id.* at 43–47.

113. *Id.* at 48–49. J. Kuttab and R. Shehadeh, *Civilian Administration in the Occupied West Bank: Analysis of Israeli Military Government Order No. 947, passim* (Law in the Service of Man, an Affiliate of the International Commission of Jurists, Geneva, 1982) demonstrates that Order 947 is solely in the interest of the belligerent occupant and in violation of international law.

114. *Taking Root, supra* note 105 at 35.

115. *Supra* note 35. See also *supra* note 109 at 29.

Begin Government has turned to the pre-existing Turkish land law under which much of the land was not privately owned.[116] The Israeli Government now claims that all Jewish settlements are "built on state land."[117] Even if this were assumed to be accurate, since under the customary law reflected in article 55 of the Hague Regulations the legal status of the occupying power is only that of a usufructary or trustee of public real estate, the settlements would still be in violation of law.[118] The Military Government Order Number 291 of 1968[119] halted the issuance of new title deeds to Arabs on the so-called "unsettled land." According to Dr. Benvenisti, the Labor Party froze Arab building outside the limits of Arab towns and cities, and the Begin Government has left these restrictions in effect, thereby making most of the West Bank unavailable for further Arab residential or business development.[120]

The Benvenisti study stresses the point that the type of settlement being built is more significant than the number of settlements. The emphasis now is upon urban settlements which are suburbs of major Israeli cities.[121] It was estimated in 1982 that the current budget for development and building of such settlements was $160 million.[122] The housing in these suburb communities is being offered to Israelis on such terms that it is drawing large numbers of young middle income people into the area.[123] Financing is made so attractive, and the price of services is so low, that people can afford a far higher quality of life here than in the cities inside the pre-June 1967 boundaries. The result of this will be the creation of a significant political lobby of 100,000 people which would

---

116. *Supra* note 109 at 32. See also I. Lustick, *Arabs in the Jewish State: Israel's Control of a National Minority* 170–82 (1980).

117. *Id.* at 34.

118. See the text accompanying *supra* notes 76 and 77.

119. *Supra* note 109 at 33.

120. *Id.* at 35–37.

121. *Id.* at 62.

122. *Id.* at 66.

123. *Id.* at 64.

prevent any Israeli political party from considering the return of this territory.[124]

In an interview published in the *Jerusalem Post*, Dr. Benvenisti stated:

> When President Reagan talks of "freezing settlements" he displays an anachronistic approach to the problem. It is not the announcement or creation of eight more dots on the map but the increasing shift of Israel's urban population into areas which guarantees Israeli control over the West Bank and which creates perhaps an insurmountable political problem for any concession-oriented political party in the country.[125]

IV. Conclusions

The present inquiry and its conclusions apply equally to all of the settlements beyond the pre-June 1967 boundaries of the State of Israel. There are three basic conclusions which necessarily follow from the legal analysis that has been made. The first is that the Geneva Civilians Convention is applicable in all of the territories occupied by Israel since the intense hostilities of June 1967. The second is that the Israel civilian settlements in the occupied territories are in violation of the Convention. The third is that the Government of Israel has violated the customary law of belligerent occupation as it was developed in the nineteenth century and codified in the Hague Regulations of 1907 by its actions in the occupied territories.[126] Even if the attempts to evade the application of the Civilians Convention were successful, there is no way that the customary law could be avoided.

---

124. *Id.* at 66.

125. "Creating Facts on the West Bank" (interview with Dr. Benvenisti), *Jerusalem Post*, Int'l Ed., Sept. 19–25, 1982, pp. 14–15 at 15, col. 3.

126. The Israeli violations of private property rights as detailed by Mrs. Lesch, *supra* note 85, *passim*, constitute violations of the customary law of belligerent occupation as it was developed in the nineteenth century. See *supra* notes 1–3 and accompanying text.

Because the Civilians Convention concerns people and is a humanitarian convention, it should be interpreted liberally to effectuate its protective purposes.[127] In view of the universal humanitarian interests which are protected, destroying its effectiveness could be disastrous for all peoples. Those Israelis who are concerned with legitimate national interests rather than with the Zionist policy of territorial expansion are aware of this protective function of the international humanitarian law. Among them, Professor Emeritus Nathan Feinberg, writing in *New Outlook*, has decisively rejected the legal arguments of the present Government of Israel as fundamentally inconsistent with international law.[128] Professor Feinberg refers to Mr. Begin's reference to the Israeli Law and Administration Ordinance of 1967[129] in his speech of July 27 in which he presented his cabinet to the Knesset, and his statement that:

With this law we announced to all the nations that no single part of the Land of Israel is occupied or conquered territory.[130]

Professor Feinberg comments:

This assertion totally contradicts a basic principle of international law, recognizing the primacy of international law over local laws passed by state legislatures. Thus, a state which wants to regulate a certain matter which must be done in accordance with international law is not allowed to base its acts on internal legislation.[131]

---

127. Probably the most fundamental principle of interpretation is that a treaty must be interpreted so as to effectuate its basic purpose. See, *e.g.*, Harvard Research, *Draft Convention on Treaties*, 29 Am. J. Int'l L. Supp. 937 *et seq.* and especially art. 19.

128. *Supra* note 57.

129. 21 Israel Laws (auth. transl.) 131 (1967).

130. Quoted in *supra* note 57 at p. 60.

131. *Id.*

His overall conclusion is that international law governs the situation on the West Bank.

Article 1 of the Geneva Civilians Convention provides in full:

> The High Contracting Parties undertake to respect and to ensure respect for the present Convention in all circumstances.[132]

The obligation to respect a convention is, of course, commonplace. The obligation "to ensure respect," which was added at Geneva in 1949, was a significant new common provision designed to enhance enforcement of each of the four Geneva Conventions for the Protection of War Victims. It means that if any one of the parties to each Convention violates it, the other state parties are also in violation until they take necessary measures to ensure that the violating party respects it.[133] This is an obligation of all of the parties to the Convention, but as a practical matter, it is a particular obligation of the Great Powers including the United States and the Soviet Union.

On November 3, 1980, while the Carter Administration was still in office, the United States voted affirmatively in the roll call vote on resolution 35/122A.[134] The last preambular paragraph of this resolution reads:

> *Taking into account* that States parties to that Convention undertake, in accordance with article 1 thereof, not only to respect but also to ensure respect for the Convention in all circumstances.

The first operative paragraph provides that the General Assembly:

> *Reaffirms* that the Geneva Convention relative to the Protection of Civilian Persons in Time of War, of 12 August 1949, is applicable to Palestinian and other Arab territories occupied by Israel since 1967, including Jerusalem.

---

132. *Supra* note 14.

133. *Supra* note 64 at 16.

134. Only the State of Israel voted against this resolution.

In 1981, during the first year of the Reagan Administration the same subject matter was dealt with in General Assembly resolution 36/147A of December 16, 1981. The last preambular paragraph and the first operative paragraph of this resolution are identical with those of the 1980 resolution quoted above. On the roll call vote on this 1981 resolution the United States changed from its prior affirmative position and abstained.[135] This abstention indicates that it has not complied with its obligation under article 1 of the Civilians Convention "to ensure respect for the present Convention in all circumstances." One of the legal consequences of this position is that while Israel is in violation of the Convention because of its violation, *inter alia*, of article 49(6), the United States is in violation of its obligation to ensure respect for the Convention. The consistent resolutions of the General Assembly calling upon the State of Israel to apply the Civilians Convention and to carry out its terms in the occupied territories[136] are a reflection of the member-states' obligation as parties to the Geneva Civilians Convention of 1949 and a start toward enforcement. Much more needs to be done to develop a fully effective sanctioning process.[137] If such a process is developed and used to compel withdrawal from the remaining occupied territories (the West Bank, Gaza, and the Golan), the State of Israel has the bright prospect of being accepted within its pre-June 1967 boundaries as specified in Security Council Resolution 242 of 22 November 1967. If the settlement policy initiated under the leadership of the Israeli Labor Party and intensified by Prime Minister Begin's Likud Party is continued, it will result in the further destruction of human and material values for Israelis and Palestinians alike.

---

135. *Id.*

136. See *e.g.*, G.A. Res. 34/90B (12 December 1979) which calls upon Israel to apply the Geneva Civilians Convention in the Palestinian and other Arab territories under occupation (operative para. 1). Only Israel voted against this resolution.

137. The sanctioning authority authorized by the U.N. Charter appears in Chap. VII (arts. 39–51). McDougal & Feliciano, *Law and Minimum World Public Order*, (1961), Chap. 4, "Community Sanctioning Process and Minimum Order," analyzes the existing sanctions process.

Chapter 7

The 1982 Israeli Attack on the Palestine Liberation Organization and Invasion of Lebanon: Appraisal under International Law

Publisher's Note: Chapter 7

Chapter 7 is a specific application of the international humanitarian law. The regulation of coercion is an integral part of the world legal order, and it has been a major subject of both customary and treaty law. The authors believe that the events of the summer of 1982 in Lebanon are a development of historical trends, including violations of the applicable international law, which are analyzed in earlier chapters. If the law is to be applied and its violation to be considered, a detailed compilation of the relevant specific facts is necessary. Although these may appear unpleasantly graphic, the authors have in all cases endeavored to use only sources, newspaper and other, which are considered to be the most accurate and reliable available. In this respect the authors have been gratified to note that reliable Israeli sources buttress the basic facts reported by the media in Great Britain and the United States.

276

I. The Factual Situation

A. THE BACKGROUND: THE LEBANESE INTERNAL CONFLICT

A comprehensive examination of the relevant background is beyond the scope of the present inquiry. It is necessary, however, to mention some of its aspects. Entirely apart from the problem of the displaced Palestinians who have taken refuge there, Lebanon has basic internal causes of strife resulting from socio-economic tension, intra-elite authority conflict, sectarian hostility, and the clash of identities and priorities.[1] This has resulted in a persistent authority problem as the various groups struggle for domination.

Particularly since 1967, Lebanon has been a natural, although sometimes somewhat reluctant, sanctuary for Palestinians who have fled or been driven from their homes in what is today Israel, the West Bank, and Gaza.[2] It has also been the location of the Palestine Liberation Organization (PLO) political leadership and infrastructure. The latter includes both military and civilian components. Its civilian structure places emphasis upon schools (predominantly at the elementary level), other academic and research activities, and medical facilities, although there are some handicraft, manufacturing, and financial operations.[3]

This Palestinian functional state-within-a-state was a further divisive factor in a Lebanon where the traditional pluralist order was already unravelling in the face of regional as well as internal pressures. Initial support given the Palestinians by many Lebanese reflected a common commitment to the Arab cause and the cultural perception of the

---

1.   Hudson, "The Palestinian Factor in the Lebanese Civil War," 32 *Mid. E. J.* 270 (1978).

2.   Cooley, "The Palestinians" in *Lebanon in Crisis* at 21–29 (Haley and Snider, eds., 1979).

3.   *Wall Street J.*, Oct. 22, 1979, p. 1, col. 1, cont. p. 21, cols. 1–3.

4.   *Supra* note 1 at 264.

Palestinians as brothers.[4] Inevitably, however, the long-term presence and increasing organization of the Palestinian community, and the accompanying and virtually routine Israeli military assaults on south Lebanon and Beirut which the Palestinian presence occasioned, led to a split in the ranks of Lebanese tolerance. In particular, the right-wing, largely Christian factions whose dominant political and economic status depended upon the maintenance of the mechanistically apportioned confessional system of government, became hostile to the threatening presence of the largely Muslim Palestinian refugee population. The presence of the organized Palestinian military forces added to the friction.[5]

Serious confrontation between the right-wing dominated Lebanese Government and Army and the Palestinians began in 1969 and led to the renowned Cairo Agreement of that year which attempted to regulate the armed Palestinian presence and reconcile it with Lebanese sovereignty.[6] The agreement was amended in 1970 and affirmed in 1973 following renewed Lebanese–Palestinian violence.[7]

The inevitable collapse of order occurred in 1975 with the outbreak of the Civil War. Palestinians, allied with largely Muslim, leftist Lebanese forces seeking reforms in the Lebanese political system, confronted right-wing Lebanese forces seeking to maintain their political and economic dominance. Thousands of civilian casualties resulted, the Lebanese economy was wrecked, and the constitutional system created at the termination of the French Mandate was in shambles.[8] Fearing a leftist victory in the spring of 1976, substantial units of the Syrian Army began moving into Lebanon in April with the stated objective of stopping, or at least reducing, the internal conflict.[9] In a move to stem

---

5. *Id.* at 267.

6. *Supra* note 2 at 29–30.

7. *Id.* at 31–32.

8. See generally M. Deeb, *The Lebanese Civil War* (1980).

9. Syrian intervention was with "tacit approval" by the United States (*New York Times*, June 2, 1976, p. 1, col. 2), Israeli acquiescence (*Wash. Star*, Apr 11, 1976, p. 1, col. 6), and right-wing Lebanese support (*New York Times*, Jun 6, 1976, p. 1, col. 8).

divisions in Arab ranks over the Syrian military intervention, the League of Arab States met in emergency session in Cairo on June 9th, called for a cease-fire, and agreed to establish a token Arab peacekeeping force to be sent to Lebanon.[10] Large scale fighting continued, however, until October 18 when representatives of Saudi Arabia, Kuwait, Syria, Lebanon, Egypt and the PLO met in Riyadh and agreed to a cease-fire and an expanded 30,000-man Arab peacekeeping force.[11] Interpreted in Beirut as an Arab mandate for continued Syrian political and military intervention in Lebanon,[12] the Riyadh Accord was affirmed by 19 of 21 representatives of Arab nations and the PLO at a meeting of the League of Arab States in Cairo on October 25.[13] The enlarged Arab peacekeeping force was to consist mainly of Syrian troops already in place and was to be financed by the League of Arab States.[14] It was specified that it would act under the overall command of President Sarkis of Lebanon.[15] Since that time the mandate has been renewed periodically at the request of the Lebanese Government and the forces continued to operate under the multilateral authority of the League of Arab States until the mandate expired July 27, 1982 during the Israeli seige of Beirut.[16]

B. THE INTERNATIONAL CONFLICT AND THE JULY 24, 1981 CEASE-FIRE

There has also been a continuing international conflict situation in southern Lebanon for many years before the intense hostilities of June, 1982. Professor Michael Hudson has described a part of it in these terms:

---

10. *New York Times*, June 9, 1976, p. 14, col. 6.

11. *Id*. Oct. 19, 1976, p. 1, col. 6, cont. p. 3, cols. 1–2.

12. *Id.*, Oct. 20, 1976, p. 4, cols. 1–4 at col. 1.

13. *Id.*, Oct. 26, 1976, p. 11, cols. 1–6 at cols. 1–2.

14. *Id.*, Oct. 27, 1976, p. 1, col. 1, cont. p. 3, cols. 3–4 at p. 1, col. 1.

15. *Id*. at p. 3, col. 3.

16. *Wash. Post*, July 28, 1982, p. A16, cols. 3–4.

[T]he PLO was unable to eliminate cross-border operations altogether, because rejectionist Palestinian groups were still operating independently. Israeli reprisals grew ever fiercer so that by mid-1974 much of life in south Lebanon was disrupted. For example, after the PFLP-GC [Popular Front for the Liberation of Palestine-General Command] attack on Maalot on May 15 Israeli air force squadrons attacked a number of Lebanese towns and Palestinian refugee camps killing at least 50 civilians and wounding 200. Altogether, in the 44 major Israeli attacks into Lebanon between mid-1968 and mid-1974, approximately 880 Lebanese and Palestinian civilians had been killed, according to Lebanese government sources.[17]

Israeli plans for an attack-invasion of Lebanon were made a considerable time before they were implemented. Among the early references to such an operation was the entry in the diary of Israel's first Prime Minister, David Ben Gurion, for May 21, 1948 where he wrote:

The Achilles heel of the Arab coalition is the Lebanon. Muslim supremacy in this country is artificial and can easily be overthrown. A Christian State ought to be set up here, with its southern frontier on the river Litani. We would sign a treaty of alliance with this State ... .[18]

The *Personal Diary* of Mr. Moshe Sharett, when he was serving as Prime Minister as well as Foreign Minister of Israel, includes a letter from Mr. Ben Gurion dated February 27, 1954 which reads in part:

It is clear that Lebanon is the weakest link in the Arab League ... . The creation of a Christian State is therefore a natural act; it has historical roots and it will find support in wide circles in

---

17. *Supra* note 1 at 267.

18. Quoted in Bar Zohar, *The Armed Prophet* 139 (London, 1967).

the Christian world, both Catholic and Protestant ... . [N]ow is the time to bring about the creation of a Christian State in our neighborhood. Without our initiative and our vigorous aid this will not be done. It seems to me that this is the *central duty,* or at least one of the central duties, of our foreign policy.[19]

Mr. Sharett's *Diary* also records a meeting of senior officials on May 16, 1954 where Mr. Ben Gurion stated that the time was propitious for action concerning Lebanon because of tensions between Syria and Iraq as well as internal trouble in Syria. Major General Dayan, then the Chief of Staff, expressed enthusiastic support. In the words of Mr. Sharett:

According to him [Dayan] the only thing that's necessary is to find an officer, even just a Major. We should either win his heart or buy him with money to make him agree to declare himself the savior of the Maronite population. Then the Israeli army will enter Lebanon, will occupy the necessary territory, and will create a Christian regime which will ally itself with Israel.[20]

The Ben Gurion–Dayan approach was not implemented at that time.

Although there were many relatively minor Israeli ground incursions into Lebanon (in addition to repeated aerial attacks) the first major invasion did not take place until 1978. The March 1978 Israeli invasion of southern Lebanon up to the Litani River was a "watershed" event. On March 11, 1978, 11 Palestinians seized two buses filled with sightseers on the Tel Aviv–Haifa Road and attempted to drive to the city. A gun battle erupted at a road block and 36 Israelis and nine of the Palestinians were killed.[21] On March

---

19. Quoted in L. Rokach, *Israel's Sacred Terrorism: A Study Based on Moshe Sharett's Personal Diary and Other Documents* 25 (1980).

20. *Id.* at 28.

21. *Wash. Post,* Mar. 15, 1978, p. A1, cols. 1–6 at col. 3.

14, in alleged retaliation for the incident, the Israelis attacked across the international border and continued north until they reached the Litani River. The ground operations were preceded by heavy aerial and artillery bombardments which resulted in substantial civilian casualties.[22] Israeli Defense Minister Weizmann stated on March 15:

> This is an operation attempting to – and I think it will succeed – destroy and liquidate as best as possible concentrations of terrorists in southern Lebanon.[23]

The Security Council of the United Nations acted on the matter on March 19, 1978 by adopting resolution 425.[24] The first two operative paragraphs called for respect for Lebanese territorial integrity, and Israeli cessation of military action and withdrawal "forthwith" of its armed forces from Lebanon. The third operative paragraph established what was subsequently termed the United Nations Interim Force in Lebanon (UNIFIL) in these words:

> Decides, in the light of the request of the Government of Lebanon, to establish immediately under its authority a United Nations interim force for Southern Lebanon for the purpose of confirming the withdrawal of Israeli forces, restoring international peace and security and assisting the Government of Lebanon in ensuring the return of its effective authority in the area, the force to be composed of personnel drawn from Member States.

Before Israeli armed forces withdrew from Lebanon on

---

22. According to the U.S. Congressional Research Service, by March 22, 1978 approximately 700 Lebanese and Palestinian civilians had been killed and more than 250,000 were made homeless. *Palestine and the Palestinians* 29 (Issue Brief No. IB76048, Oct. 23, 1979).

23. Press conference, *The Search for Peace in the Middle East: Documents and Statements, 1967–1979*, 340 (U.S. Congressional Research Service, 1979).

24. *33 U.N. SCOR* at 5, Doc. S/INS/34 (1978).

June 13, 1978 they established a zone across southern Lebanon, and the first stage of the Ben Gurion plan for Lebanon recorded in Mr. Sharett's *Personal Diary* was put into operation almost three decades later.[25] The zone was placed under the authority of a renegade Lebanese military faction headed by Saad Haddad, formerly a major in the Lebanese Army. Thereafter, Major Haddad's forces were supplied, paid, and controlled by the Government of Israel.[26] UNIFIL subsequently was established in a zone to the north and west of the Haddad forces (termed the *de facto* forces by UNIFIL), but has not been able to carry out its functions in the zone controlled by the Government of Israel through Major Haddad.[27]

On June 17, 1981 the Government of Israel conducted a massive aerial bombing of Beirut which caused 300 civilian deaths and a much larger number of civilians wounded.[28] Following the adoption of Security Council resolution 490 on July 21, 1981, which called "for an immediate cessation of all armed attacks," the United States and Saudi Arabian

---

25. *Supra* note 20.

26. *The Middle East* 178 (Cong. Quarterly Inc., 5th Edition, 1981).

27. The Reports of the Secretary-General on UNIFIL consistently set forth particulars concerning harassment and incursions including the use of weapons by the *de facto* forces against UNIFIL. In addition, the *de facto* forces have murdered captured UNIFIL soldiers. See, e.g., *Report of the Secretary-General on the United Nations Interim Force in Lebanon* [hereafter cited as *Report*] (for the period 11 Dec. 1979 to 12 June 1980) at 10–15, Doc. S/13994 (12 June 1980); *id.* (for the period 13 June to 11 Dec. 1980) at 13–17, Doc. S/14295 (12 Dec. 1980).

In *Special Report of the Secretary-General on the United Nations Interim Force in Lebanon* [hereafter cited as *Special Report*], Doc. S/13888 (11 April 1980) a summary appears at p. 5:

> In the present situation, far too much of UNIFIL's energy is distracted by efforts to resist the harassment and violence to which it is daily exposed, while its capacity to carry out its functions is greatly reduced by the fact that it cannot operate in a vital part of its area of operations which is at present controlled by the *de facto* forces.

28. Cong. Res. Service, *Lebanon: Israeli–Palestinian Confrontation* 32 (Issue Brief IB 81090, Aug. 10, 1982).

Governments negotiated a cease-fire between the Government of Israel and the PLO which became effective on July 24, 1981.[29] No written text of the agreement has been revealed and it is probable, consequently, that it was oral. At the time the cease-fire was announced, Ambassador Habib and Prime Minister Begin had just met following a meeting of the Israel Cabinet.[30] According to the *New York Times*, each then made "a one sentence announcement":

"I have today reported to President Reagan," Mr. Habib said, "that as of 13:30 hours local time July 24, 1981, all hostile military action between Lebanese and Israeli territory in either direction will cease."

Mr. Begin said, "Ladies and gentlemen of the press, the Government of Israel endorsed the statement just made to you by Mr. Philip Habib, the emissary of the President of the United States."[31]

Thereafter, the PLO interpreted the agreement as being applicable only to the area of the Israeli–Lebanese border referred to by Mr. Habib.[32] This is the area in southern Lebanon where the PLO maintained organized military forces under its control. Following Mr. Habib's trip to the Middle East from February 26 to March 9, 1982, Israel claimed that "the cease-fire included attacks against Israeli positions launched from Jordan, Syria, or other areas"[33] and also included any attacks in the occupied territories of the West

---

29. *Id.*

30. *New York Times*, July 25, 1981, p. 1, col. 6, cont. p. 4, cols. 3–6 at p. 4, col. 5.

31. *Id.* at p. 4, cols. 5–6.

32. *Supra* note 28 at 34.

33. *Id.*

Bank and Gaza.[34] The subsequent Israeli interpretation, as expressed by its representative in the Security Council on July 6, 1982, was that it was applicable to attacks by the PLO on any Jew which took place anywhere in the world.[35] The Israeli interpretation is based upon the assumed validity of the claim of "the Jewish people" as a transnational nationality entity which is legally linked to the State of Israel.[36] This claim, however, is not accepted in international law which acknowledges the legal relationship between an individual and the state of his normal and regular nationality status.[37] There is no valid doctrine in the present international law which ties all members of any particular religion to any national state with both rights and responsibilities involved in the claimed allegiance.

The United States interpretation of the cease-fire agreement was expressed by State Department spokesman Dean Fischer during the March 18, 1982 press briefing:

> The cessation of hostilities pertains to all hostile military activity from Lebanon into Israel and vice versa. Therefore, any hostile action originating from Lebanon, but going through Syria and Jordan into Jordan [sic] would be a violation of the ceasefire.

---

34. The relevant law applicable to the occupied territories, however, is found in the Geneva POW and Civilians Conventions, both of 1949, and a bilateral cease-fire could not supersede these treaties even if it had provisions which attempted to do so. These Conventions do not prohibit acts of resistance against the occupant. Geneva POW Convention, 75 U.N.T.S. 135, 6 U.S.T. & O.I.A. 3316; Geneva Civilians Convention, 75 U.N.T.S. 287, 6 U.S.T. & O.I.A. 3516.

35. *Provisional Verbatim Record of the 2,375th Security Council Meeting*, S/PV 2375, pp. 8–33 at 28–33 (6 June 1982).

36. Mallison, "The Zionist-Israel Juridical Claims to Constitute 'the Jewish People' Nationality Entity and to Confer Membership in It: Appraisal in Public International Law," 32 *Geo. Wash. L. Rev.* 983–1075 (1964).

37. The U.S. Department of State rejected the "Jewish people" claim as a valid concept of international law in the letter from Assistant Secretary of State Talbot of April 20, 1964 to Dr. Elmer Berger, Executive Vice President of the American Council for Judaism. 8 Whiteman, *Digest of Int'l Law* 34–35 (1967).

The same would apply to an Israeli action from Israel into Lebanon transiting international waters or foreign territories.[38]

The U.S. view appears to be inconsistent with the Israeli view that the agreement applied worldwide and within the occupied territories. In an address to the Israeli National Defense College on August 8, 1982 Prime Minister Begin indicated significant differences between the U.S. and Israeli interpretations:

> Even Philip Habib [the U.S. negotiator of the July 24, 1981 cease-fire] interpretated the agreement ending acts of hostility as giving them freedom to attack targets beyond Israel's borders. We have never accepted this interpretation. Shall we permit Jewish blood to be spilled in the Diaspora? Shall we permit bombs to be planted against Jews in Paris, Rome, Athens or London? Shall we permit our ambassadors to be attacked?[39]

A report from Israel appearing in the *New York Times* of February 10, 1982 stated that Israel had drawn up plans for a large-scale invasion of Lebanon but would not attack except in response to a PLO provocation.[40] The article, cleared by the Israeli military censor, reported that there were differences of opinion within the Government of Israel as to what would constitute adequate provocation. The article stated:

> As described here, Mr. Sharon's plan would be directed against the PLO in an effort to deal a decisive, crippling blow to its military employment in southern Lebanon.[41]

A Reuters' dispatch appearing in the *New York Times* on February 26, 1982 reported:

---

38. U.S. Dept. State Press Briefing, March 18, 1982 at 13–14.
39. *Jerusalem Post*, Int'l Ed., Aug. 22–28, 1982, p. 14, cols. 1–5, at col. 5.
40. *New York Times*, Feb. 10, 1982, p. A1, cols. 2–3.
41. *Id.* at col. 3.

Israel's new Ambassador to the United States warned today that Israel could be forced to take military action in southern Lebanon, declaring "I would almost say it's a matter of time."[42]

A report from Beirut appearing in the *Christian Science Monitor* on March 18, 1982 described a series of Israeli military operations across the international boundary into southern Lebanon. The article stated:

Israeli forces appear to have launched a campaign of "brinkmanship shadowboxing" in an attempt to bait the Palestinians into provoking a confrontation in southern Lebanon.

This is the view held by Western diplomats and neutral UN officials here, who say the latest series of Israeli provocations may be an effort to justify an attack the Israelis cannot otherwise afford to make because of unprecedented international pressure.[43]

It also reported that:

UN officials are angered to the point of publicizing recent incidents, hoping it will check the provocation. At the same time, they praise the PLO's "unusual restraint."[44]

On February 16, 1982 the United Nations Secretary-General issued a special report on the UNIFIL which stated, *inter alia*:

The encroachments established in the UNIFIL area of deployment by the *de facto* forces, which are supported and supplied by Israel, have not been removed, and violations of Lebanon's territorial integrity have also continued.[45]

---

42. *Id.*, Feb. 26, 1982, p. All, col. 4.

43. *Christian Sci. Monitor*, Mar. 18, 1982, p. 12, cols. 1–3 at col. 1.

44. *Id.* at col. 2.

45. *Special Report, supra* note 27, at 1, Doc. S/14869 (16 Feb. 1982).

The report also pointed out that it was a strong recommendation of the force commander, Lieutenant-General Callaghan of Ireland, supported fully by the Lebanese Government, that the size of the UNIFIL should be increased by no less than 1,000 troops in order to enhance its ability to carry out its responsibilities pursuant to Security Council resolution 425.[46] On June 10, 1982 the Secretary-General issued a report on UNIFIL covering the period from December 11, 1981 to June 3, 1982. He provided detailed information on the military operations in southern Lebanon. The main points raised by him were:

> The *de facto* forces continued to maintain encroachments in the UNIFIL area of deployment at Bayt Yahun, Blate, Ett Taibe, Rshaf and on Hill 880 near AtTiri. UNIFIL made intensive efforts, including repeated contacts with the Israeli authorities, to have these provocative positions removed. However, the necessary co-operation was not forthcoming.[47]
>
> * * * *
>
> IDF [Israel Defense Forces] activities in the UNIFIL area of operation continued unabated. UNIFIL and UNTSO raised the matter repeatedly with the Israeli authorities.[48]
>
> * * * *
>
> There were violations of Lebanese air space by Israeli aircraft and of Lebanese waters by Israeli naval vessels. UNIFIL observed 130 air violations and 62 sea violations in December 1981, 285 air violations and 53 sea violations in January 1982, 121 air violations and 54 sea violations in February, 187 air violations and 97 sea violations in March, 368 air violations and 59 sea violations in

---

46. *Id.* at 2.
47. *Report, supra* note 27, p. 10, para. 40, Doc. S/15194 (10 June 1982).
48. *Id.*

April, and 302 air violations and 59 sea violations in May.

During the period under review, various UNIFIL positions and personnel came under close fire by IDF. Seventeen such incidents were reported. Those incidents as well as the repeated violations of Lebanese territory were strongly opposed.[49]

On April 21, 1982 one Israeli soldier was killed by a land mine in the area controlled by the *de facto* forces.[50] Within hours, Israeli aircraft bombed areas along the Lebanese coast for a period of about two hours in supposed retaliation. This was a major breach in the cease-fire of July 24, 1981 and the PLO did not retaliate.[51] The Secretary-General also reported that on May 9, 1982 Israeli aircraft again attacked targets in Lebanon and that later that day UNIFIL observed rockets fired from Palestinian positions into northern Israel.[52] This Palestinian response is the only reference to a PLO military response, or indeed to any PLO military action across the Lebanese border against Israel, during the period of the report. The casualties from this particular Israeli bombing were listed as 16 killed and 56 wounded. No Israeli casualties or damage were reported from the PLO response.[53]

Thus the evidentiary record as supplied by the UN forces on the scene shows that during the preceding nine months the PLO did in good faith adhere to the terms of the cease-fire except for the shelling on May 9. There had been no PLO response to the carrying out of Israeli "training maneuvers" with tanks and live ammunition on Lebanese soil near PLO positions, actions called "intensive, excessive and provocative" by UN observers in their official reports.[54]

---

49. *Id.* at 11, para. 46.

50. *Id.* at para. 45.

51. *New York Times*, April 22, 1982, p. 14, col. 4.

52. *Supra* note 47, p. 11, para. 50.

53. *Wash. Post*, May 10, 1982, p. A1, cols. 2–3 at col. 2.

54. Quoted by Robin Wright in "Israeli 'provocations' in southern Lebanon fail to goad PLO – so far," *Christian Sci. Monitor*, March 18, 1982, p. 12, col. 1.

C. THE ATTACK-INVASION

The incident awaited by Israel occurred on June 3, 1982 when the Israeli Ambassador to Great Britain was critically wounded in an assassination attempt.[55] Israel immediately accused the PLO and the PLO denied responsibility, stating through its London representative that the attack served Israeli interests and not Palestinian ones.[56] The British authorities arrested two Jordanians and an Iraqi and charged them with the crime.[57] An intensive Israeli aerial "reprisal" was already underway by the evening of June 5 when the British representative stated at the United Nations that the attack had in fact been carried out by members of an anti-PLO Arab group, one of whom carried a "hit list" which included the PLO London representative.[58] For two days Israel carried out the heaviest and most sustained air attacks on Lebanon since the July 17, 1981 attack.[59] The PLO responded to this with an artillery and rocket attack on the Galilee area of northern Israel in which, according to Israeli accounts, one person was killed.[60]

---

55. *Wash. Post*, June 5, 1982, p. A1, col. 1. The more basic considerations which led to the attack-invasion are considered in Sheila Ryan, "Israel's Invasion of Lebanon: Background to the Crisis," *Journal of Palestine Studies*, Vol. 11, No. 4 and Vol. 12, No. 1 (combined issue Nos. 44 & 45) p. 23 (Summer and Fall, 1982).

A careful chronology of the attack-invasion, consistent with the facts upon which the present text is based, is Carole Collins, "Chronology of the Israeli Invasion of Lebanon, June–August 1982," *id.* pp. 135–92.

56. *Wash. Post, supra* note 55, p. A22, cols. 1–2 at col. 2.

57. *Id.*, June 6, 1982, p. A30, cols. 5–6.

58. *Provisional Verbatim Record of the 2,374th Security Council Meeting*, S/PV. 2374, p. 11 (5 June 1982). Prime Minister Thatcher affirmed this. *Wash. Post*, June 8, 1982, p. A1, col. 4, cont. p. A11, cols. 3–6 at p. A11, col. 6. On June 9, the Associated Press reported that a statement delivered to its Beirut offices signed with a name used by followers of Abu Nidal claimed responsibility for the attack on the Israeli Ambassador in London. Abu Nidal was expelled from the PLO in the early 1970s and was condemned to death by it in 1978. *Wash. Post*, June 10, 1982, p. A24, col. 3.

59. *Wash. Post*, June 5, 1982, p. A1, cols. 3–4, cont. p. A24, cols. 1–6, at col. 4.

60. *Id.* at p. A24, col. 3.

Then on June 6 the massive Israeli attack-invasion into Lebanon began and within a week it was estimated that 10,000 people were killed or wounded.[61] The majority of the victims were Palestinian and Lebanese civilians. Some refugee camps, particularly in the south, were completely destroyed. A number of towns and cities were reduced in large measure to rubble. There were PLO offices, ammunition dumps or other facilities in some of the population centers (just as there are Israeli military facilities in Tel Aviv) but there was no attempt to limit the destruction to such facilities.[62] Their superior offensive weapons allowed the Israelis also to knock out the Syrian surface to air missiles in the Bekaa Valley and many Syrian aircraft.[63] By June 9 the attack-invasion had reached the outskirts of Beirut.

II. Aggression and Self-Defense in the World Legal Order

A. THE INTERNATIONAL LAW CRITERIA

The maintenance of public order is the most basic task of any legal system whether municipal or international. The responsibility of a municipal order is to exercise effective community control over domestic violence. By analogy, the responsibility of the world legal order is to exercise effective community control of violence and coercion by national states and other subjects of international law. The world legal order protects the values of all states and of all peoples in promoting peaceful procedures and deterring aggression.

---

61. The textual paragraph is based on numerous, consistent, and cumulative press reports. *E.g.*, "Agony of the Innocents: For Lebanon's civilians, death and suffering are the victors," *Time* magazine, June 28, 1982, pp. 20–21 at p. 20, col. 3; *Wash. Post*, June 11, 1982, p. A1, col. 5, cont. p. A19, cols. 1–2 at p. A19, col. 2; *New York Times*, June 13, 1982, p. 12, cols. 5–6 at col. 6.

62. *E.g.*, *Wash. Post*, June 12, 1982, p. A1, col. 5, cont. p. A20, cols. 1–4, at p. A1, col. 5.

63. "Into the Wild Blue Electronically," *Time* magazine, June 21, 1982, p. 20, col. 2.

1. THE UNITED NATIONS CHARTER FRAMEWORK

The world legal order is set forth in article 2(3) and (4), and article 51 of the United Nations Charter. These articles provide a codification of the pre-existing customary law concerning aggression and self-defense. Article 2(3) states:

> All members shall settle their international disputes by peaceful means in such a manner that international peace and security are not endangered.

Paragraph 4 of the same article contains the prohibition upon aggression:

> All members shall refrain in their international relations from the threat or use of force against the territorial integrity or political independence of any state, or in any other manner inconsistent with the purposes of the United Nations.

Article 51 of the Charter incorporates the customary law of self-defense in the following words:

> Nothing in the present Charter shall impair the inherent right of individual or collective self-defense if an armed attack occurs ... .

These articles taken together comprise a minimum order. It is minimum in the sense that it protects only the primary interest in freedom from aggression and the right of self-defense as a sanction.[64] An optimum order, in contrast, includes minimum order and a consensual and nondiscriminatory environment in which individuals may achieve their values or interests.

Article 51 is sometimes interpreted as restricting the "inherent right" of self-defense to situations where an armed attack has in fact taken place. If this interpretation is accepted, anticipatory self-defense is illegal *per se*. The

---

64. McDougal & Feliciano, *Law and Minimum World Public Order* 121–24 and *passim* (1961).

negotiating history at the San Francisco Conference reveals that article 51 was intended to incorporate the entire customary law or "inherent right" of self-defense.[65] This comprehensive incorporation of the customary law includes reasonable and necessary anticipatory self-defense since this is an integral part of the customary law. This negotiating history governs the meaning of the article in each of the five official languages of the Charter. The French text which uses the broad term "aggression armée," encompassing the conception of "armed attack" but not limited to it, is a more accurate reflection of the negotiating history than is the English text if the latter is read out of the context of the negotiations.

2. THE UNITED NATIONS DEFINITION OF AGGRESSION

The League of Nations considered the question of defining aggression as early as 1923 in connection with the preparation of a draft Treaty of Mutual Assistance which was abandoned in 1924 for lack of agreement.[66] In 1933 the Soviet Union submitted a detailed proposal listing acts demonstrating aggression at the London Disarmament Conference.[67] This subsequently formed the basis of the Litvinov–Politis definition adopted by the Committee for Security Questions of that Conference and was incorporated in bilateral agreements between the U.S.S.R. and eleven other states.[68]

The framers of the United Nations Charter left the application of "any threat to the peace, breach of the peace, or act of aggression" to the appraisal of the Security Council. Subsequently, when the General Assembly considered the desirability of the formulation of a definition of aggression, various objections were raised.[69] One view was that a definition which would cover all kinds of aggression would

---

65. 12 *U.N. Conference on Int'l Organization* 680 (1945).

66. C. L. Brown-John, "The 1974 Definition of Aggression: A Query," 15 *Can. Y.B. Int'l L.* 301 (1977).

67. 5 Whiteman, *supra* note 37, at 729–31 (1965).

68. *Id.* at 735–36.

69. The textual paragraph is based in part upon *Definition of Aggression,* U.N. Pub. No. OPI/550 (July, 1975).

be rendered very difficult by the changing techniques of modern warfare and that a definition might, by its omissions, encourage an aggressor or delay action by the Security Council. In addition, those opposed to a definition were concerned about the types of aggression covered including whether or not the definition should concern itself with "indirect aggression." Some concerns were expressed about the doctrine of proportionality, but these were resolved. From an historical perspective, the proportionality doctrine has long been established in customary law and is incorporated in the "inherent right" of self-defense in article 51 of the United Nations Charter.

One of the academic critics of defining aggression, Professor Julius Stone, has conceived the task as "finding a definition of aggression clear and precise enough for certain and automatic applications to all future situations."[70] He has also deplored "the impossibility of containing the unceasing struggle for a minimal justice in international relations within the straitjacket of precise formulae for the definition of aggression."[71] If it is conceived in this manner, he accurately regards the task of definition as impossible.[72] His criticism, however, is based upon a misunderstanding of the function of legal principles, rules and definitions. Their function is not to displace human decision-makers in the Security Council or elsewhere by predetermining particular decisions. It is rather to provide the agreed upon community standards which implement in a more detailed manner the basic criteria of the Charter. It should be obvious that the intelligence and integrity of human decision-makers are required to apply any definition to a particular factual situation. Professor Stone, however, appears to have adhered to the elements of his earlier position even after the General Assembly adopted the Definition of Aggression.[73]

---

70. J. Stone, *Aggression and World Order: A Critique of United Nations Theories of Aggression* 10 (1958).

71. *Id.* at 12.

72. *Id.* and *passim.*

73. Stone, "Hopes and Loopholes in the 1974 Definition of Aggression," 71 *Am. J. Int'l L.* 224 (1977); Stone, *Conflict Through Consensus: United Nations Approaches to Aggression, passim* (1977).

After agreement was reached in the drafting committee, the completed text of the Definition was adopted by the General Assembly on December 14, 1974 by consensus as resolution 3314 (XXIX).[74] There was neither the intention nor the authority to modify the wording or meaning of the Charter, and this is enunciated in article 6 of the Definition. The purpose was to provide a more detailed formulation of community criteria than appears in the articles of the Charter.

Article 1 of the Definition states that:

Aggression is the use of armed force by a State against the sovereignty, territorial integrity or political independence of another State, or in any other manner inconsistent with the Charter of the United Nations ... .

The last quoted clause concerning inconsistency with the Charter is particularly important. Since the Charter recognizes the rights of peoples[75] as well as states, aggression by a state against a people is also in violation of article 1.

Article 2 of the Definition provides:

The first use of armed force by a State in contravention of the Charter shall constitute *prima facie* evidence of an act of aggression although the Security Council may, in conformity with the Charter, conclude that a determination that an act of aggression has been committed would not be justified in the light of other relevant circumstances, including the fact that the acts concerned or their consequences are not of sufficient gravity.

Article 3 lists certain actions which qualify as acts of aggression. These include, *inter alia,* the invasion by the armed forces of another state; the bombardment by the armed forces of a state against the territory of another state;

---

74. *29 U.N. GAOR, Supp. 31* at 142, Doc. A/9631.
75. *U.N. Charter,* Preamble, arts. 1(2), 55, 73, 76, 80(1).

the blockade of the ports or coasts of a state; and a state allowing a second state to use the first state's territory for an aggression on a third one. Consistent with the customary law, article 3 states that its provisions are applicable "regardless of a declaration of war." Article 4 points out that the prior enumeration of acts is not exhaustive. The Nuremberg Principles[76] concerning the criminal nature of aggression and the illegality of any territorial acquisition resulting from aggression are incorporated in article 5. Article 7 provides that nothing in the Definition prejudices the right to self-determination as enunciated in the Charter and in the Declaration on the Principles of International Law Concerning Friendly Relations and Co-operation among States;[77] and article 8 sets forth the principle that all the provisions of the Definition are interrelated. It is significant that there was no negative vote on this Definition which constitutes the most authoritative formulation of community criteria concerning the prohibition upon aggression.

3. THE LEGAL REQUIREMENTS FOR SELF-DEFENSE

The international law which sets forth the criteria for self-defense, and distinguishes it from aggression, has been enunciated and developed by the community of states over a considerable period of time. The objective of these legal doctrines is to ensure freedom from coercion and to protect the inclusive interests or values of all states and peoples in promoting peaceful settlement of international disputes and deterring acts of aggression.

The customary law prescribes the use of peaceful procedures, if they are available, as the first basic require-ment of self-defense. The second is an actual necessity as opposed to a sham or pretense, for the use of force in

---

76. U.N. General Assembly resolution 95 (I) (1946) recognized by consensus the principles of international law of the Charter and Judgment of the International Military Tribunal at Nuremberg. These principles were codified by the International Law Commission. [1950] *Y.B. Int'l L. Comm.*, Vol. 2, pp. 374–80.

77. G.A. Res. 2625 (XXV), *25 U.N. GAOR, Supp. 28*, at 121–24 Doc. A/8028 (24 Oct. 1970).

responding coercion, and the third is proportionality in responding coercion.[78] Necessity traditionally has been formulated in narrow and restrictive terms. The policy reason for this apparently has been to avoid an open-ended conception of self-defense which might be employed as a screen for aggression. If the first two requirements for self-defense have been met, and the circumstances require resort to a defensive response involving armed force, the principle of proportionality specifies that the response must be proportional to the character and amount of the initiating coercion.

There are several subsidiary criteria for appraisal of particular aspects of a claimed self-defense situation which give more precise content to the requirements of peaceful procedures, necessity, and proportionality. These include a factual description of the participants, an appraisal of their objectives in terms of their inclusive or exclusive character and whether or not they involve a conservation or extension of values, as well as the relative consequentiality of the values to be protected.[79] These factors must be evaluated favorably before a military action may be appraised as lawful self-defense.

4. ANTICIPATORY SELF-DEFENSE

The legal criteria concerning self-defense include reasonable and necessary anticipatory self-defense. Anticipatory self-defense is regarded as a highly unusual and exceptional matter which may only be employed when the evidence shows a threat of imminent armed attack and the necessity to act is overwhelming.[80] The requirements of necessity and proportionality have always been applied with more rigor to

---

78. The textual paragraph is based, in part, on *supra* note 64 at Chap. 3. As a practical matter, peaceful procedures are usually more available in the situation of anticipatory self-defense.

79. *Id.* at 167–90.

80. See *e.g.*, 12 Whiteman, *Digest of Int'l Law* 47 (1971). The doctrine of anticipatory self-defense was examined in the *Judgment* in 1 Trial of the Major War Criminals Before the Internatinal Military Tribunal at Nuremberg 205–09 (1947). [Hereafter cited as I.M.T.]

a claim of anticipatory self-defense than to a claim of defense against an armed attack.[81]

One of the leading instances in which the legal principle of anticipatory self-defense, which is a part of the "inherent right" referred to in article 51 of the Charter, has been applied is the famous *Caroline* incident[82] which involved a steamer of that name employed in 1837 to transport personnel and equipment from United States territory across the Niagara River to Canadian rebels on Navy Island and then to the mainland of Canada. The British Government (then the sovereign in Canada) apparently expected that the United States Government would stop the military assistance to the rebels, but the latter did not do so and the *Caroline* remained as a threat to Canada. Thereafter, British troops crossed the Niagara River into the territory of the United States and, after a conflict in which at least two United States nationals were killed, they set the *Caroline* afire and it was wrecked on Niagara Falls. Following the attack on the vessel, the troops immediately returned to Canada without any further military action in the United States. In the ensuing controversy, Great Britain rested its case on the basis of reasonable and necessary anticipatory self-defense. The United States did not deny that circumstances might exist in which Great Britain lawfully could invoke such self-defense, but denied that they existed in this situation. The controversy was terminated, nevertheless, following a British diplomatic apology, but significantly without any British assumption of legal responsibility for the deaths of the two Americans, the wounding of others, and the destruction of the *Caroline*. The absence of further legal claim by the United States should be interpreted as tacit acquiescence in the lawfulness of the British action.

The *Caroline* incident is best known for Secretary of State Webster's formulation of the requirements of self-defense as involving a "necessity of self-defence, [which is] instant, overwhelming, leaving no choice of means, and no moment

---

81. *Supra* note 64 at 231.
82. 2 Moore, *Digest Int'l Law* 409–14 (1906).

for deliberation."[83] The quoted wording concerning "no choice of means, and no moment for deliberation" is misleading since, where an actual necessity exists, international law requires a state invoking anticipatory self-defense to go through a process of deliberation resulting in the choice of lawful, that is, proportional, means of responding coercion. In the actual facts of the incident, the British responding coercion was a choice of means which was proportional to the threat posed by the ship.

A more recent incident which is relied upon in customary law arose during the Second World War.[84] Following the Vichy French Government's armistice with Germany in June 1940, many vessels of the French Navy took refuge in Alexandria in Egypt, Oran in French North Africa, or Martinique in the West Indies. In early July, the British presented the French naval commander in each of these locations with proposals setting forth alternatives concerning the disposition of French naval vessels, any one of which was designed to prevent them from coming under German control. The first and preferred proposal was that the French naval vessels join with the Royal Navy in continuing the war against Germany. The second alternative involved the complete demilitarization of the French vessels so that they would be of no use to Germany. The third alternative, which the British emphasized would only be used with great reluctance if the first two were rejected, was that Great Britain would attack and sink the vessels. At Alexandria and Martinique the French naval commanders accepted the second alternative. At Oran the first two alternatives were rejected and after further fruitless negotiations, British naval and air forces attacked and sank or severely damaged the French warships.

If a realistic appraisal is made of the grim realities of the situation confronting Great Britain, the British attack on the warships of its former ally and accompanying incursions into

---

83. Mr. Webster to Mr. Fox, April 24, 1841, 29 *Brit. & Foreign State Papers* 1129 at 1138 (1840–1841).

84. 1 *Oppenheim's International Law* 303 (8th ed., Lauterpacht, 1955).

French territorial waters and airspace were justified as anticipatory self-defense. Very little other than British naval and air power stood between the victorious German armies and successful invasion of the United Kingdom. Acquisition of major elements of the French Navy would probably have made a German invasion possible. The applicable principles of international law did not require the British to defer action until after the French warships were incorporated into the German Navy. Respected international legal authority has appraised the British action as lawful anticipatory self-defense.[85]

The Cuban Missile Crisis of 1962 provides an example of anticipatory self-defense in a nuclear context.[86] As in the two previous instances, the facts were clear, but in this case they were revealed by photographic evidence of intercontinental missile sites being emplaced in Cuba. It will be recalled that when Ambassador Stevenson made them available, these photographs were decisive in changing the climate of opinion, first in the United Nations Security Council and later in the world community. The missiles and the launching sites were being emplaced in secret and in the face of Soviet diplomatic assurances that no offensive weapons would be placed in Cuba. Because prior diplomatic discussions emphasizing United States opposition to the emplacement of any offensive weapons in Cuba had in fact failed to prevent their positioning, and because of a perceived pressure of time in stopping the emplacement, no further diplomatic efforts were considered feasible. Among the alternative recommendations which were presented to President Kennedy was the proposal to bomb the missile sites. Some international lawyers thought that this would be fully justified in law because of the great danger to the entire Western Hemisphere caused by this Soviet attempt to drastically

---

85. *Id*.

86. Mallison, "Limited Naval Blockade or Quarantine-Interdiction: National and Collective Defense Claims Valid Under International Law," 31 *Geo. Wash. L. Rev.* 335–98 (1962).

upset the nuclear balance of power.[87] President Kennedy, however, in invoking national self-defense on October 22, selected a limited naval blockade or quarantine-interdiction as the method to prevent the introduction of further offensive weapons and to bring about the removal of those present. This method permitted the use of diplomatic means at the United Nations and elsewhere and ultimately resulted in the Kennedy–Khrushchev agreement which terminated the missile crisis and led to the withdrawal of the missiles from Cuba.

In appraising whether or not each of the legal requirements had been met in the United States invocation of anticipatory self-defense, it is highly significant that on October 23rd the Organ of Consultation of the Organization of American States invoked collective self-defense on behalf of the Inter-American community. The regional decision-makers dealt with the same fact situation which the United States had dealt with on the previous day and came to the same conclusion that an actual necessity for anticipatory self-defense existed.[88] The Organ of Consultation also approved the specific measures undertaken by the United States, and by the time the limited naval blockade or quarantine-interdiction was ended, there were ships from a number of Latin-American navies participating in the enforcement of the blockade.[89]

The severely limited military measures employed by the United States amounted to the least possible use of the military instrument of national policy. If it had not been successful, somewhat more coercive use of military power could be justified under international law. The legal consequence of the restricted use of military force is that the proportionality test in even its most rigorous and extreme form was easily met.[90] In addition to the approval of the

---

87. Former Secretary of State Acheson was one such lawyer. R. F. Kennedy, *Thirteen Days: A Memoir of the Cuban Missile Crisis* 37–38 (Signet ed., 1979).

88. *Supra* note 86 at 378–79.

89. *Id.* at 392–94.

90. *Id.* at 394.

United States measures by the Organization of American States, the measures also met with wide approval within the United Nations.

B. APPRAISAL OF GOVERNMENT OF ISRAEL CLAIMS UNDER THE CRITERIA OF INTERNATIONAL LAW

1. CLAIMS OF THE GOVERNMENT OF ISRAEL TO LAWFUL SELF-DEFENSE

Dr. Blum, the Israeli Permanent Representative at the United Nations, at the meeting of the Security Council on June 6, 1982 specifically claimed that the Government of Israel attack-invasion was justified as lawful self-defense in the following statement:

> It thus becomes imperative for the Government of Israel to exercise its legitimate right of self-defence to protect the lives of its citizens and to ensure their safety.[91]

On the same day, the Government of Israel through Dr. Blum also invoked anticipatory self-defense to "deter" future "terrorism":

> Faced with intolerable provocations, repeated aggression and harassment, Israel has now been forced to exercise its right of self-defence to arrest the never-ending cycle of attacks against Israel's northern border, to deter continued terrorism against Israel's citizens in Israel and abroad, and to instil the basic concept in the minds of the PLO assassins that Jewish life will never again be taken with impunity.[92]

Since the attack-invasion announced as directed against the PLO has violated the territorial integrity of Lebanon, it is appropriate to also consider Dr. Blum's statement claiming

---

91. *Provisional Verbatim Record of the 2,375th Security Council Meeting,* S/PV.2375, pp. 8–33, at 17 (6 June 1982). [Provisional Verbatim Records are cited hereafter as S/PV.]

92. *Id.* at 33.

Lebanese responsibility for the alleged threat to Israel. He stated concerning Lebanon on June 5:

> If Lebanon is either unwilling or unable to prevent the harbouring, training and financing of PLO terrorists openly operating from Lebanese territory with a view to harassing Israel, Israelis and Jews world-wide, then Lebanon surely must be prepared to face the risk of Israel's taking the necessary countermeasures to stop such terrorist operations.[93]

In connection with this claim against Lebanon, it is important to consider the Government of Israel's prior actions there including, *inter alia*, its support of the *de facto* forces in the south and right-wing militias in the north[94] and its consistent frustration of the United Nations peace-keeping efforts (including those through UNIFIL).[95] This has resulted in a large measure of Israeli responsibility for the ineffectiveness of the Lebanese Government.

2. THE REQUIREMENT OF PEACEFUL PROCEDURES

In the event of an actual armed attack of sufficient gravity upon a state, there is no juridical requirement that it resort to peaceful procedures. The lawfulness of its responding coercion need only be appraised under the criteria of necessity and proportionality. If it should be determined that there was no armed attack upon Israel, then it had an obligation to use peaceful procedures in good faith before

---

93. S/PV.2374, pp. 27–30 at 30 (5 June 1982).

94. Re the *de facto* forces, see the text accompanying note 26. The *New York Times* reported on June 17, 1980 that Israel has given more than one billion dollars to the Christian militias in Lebanon. p. 1, cols. 1–2,. cont. p. A8, cols. 3–6 at col. 4. Re the connection between Israel and the Phalange, see also Loren Jenkins, "Phalangist Ties to Massacre Detailed," *Wash. Post*, Sept. 30, 1982, p. 1, cols. 2–4, cont. p. A38, cols. 1–6 at col. 6 where it is stated that during the Lebanese civil war the Gemayal militia (Phalange) was sent to Israel for training under Mossad (Israeli international secret service) and the Israeli Army.

95. See the text accompanying *supra* note 27.

resorting to coercive measures.

During the winter and spring of 1981–1982 there were press reports of complaints by Israel to the United States concerning a claimed PLO military build-up in southern Lebanon,[96] and on June 6 in the Security Council meeting Dr. Blum referred to "months of cautioning and warnings."[97] During the same period of time there were concurrent reports of an Israeli build-up near the Lebanese border.[98] In the context of the events which have taken place, it is not possible that the Israeli "cautioning and warnings" can be appraised as meeting the requirement of peaceful procedures. In contrast, Lebanon had used peaceful procedures in February, 1982 in asking the Security Council to obtain Israeli "total and unconditional withdrawal" from Lebanon.[99]

On June 5 and 6 opportunities were provided to the Government of Israel to use peaceful procedures. The Secretary-General of the United Nations reported to the Security Council on June 5 concerning the fact situation. He described eight intensive Israeli air raids on and around Beirut on June 4, and stated that the targets included a Palestinian refugee camp near Beirut on the road to the airport, the Sabra refugee camp, and the area of the Sports Stadium adjacent to it.[100] A large number of refugees from the southern part of Lebanon were camping in the Sports Stadium. He also pointed out that there were heavy exchanges of gunfire in southern Lebanon with the PLO and the Lebanese National Movement on one side and the Israeli armed forces and the *de facto* forces of Major Haddad on the other. He added that he had urged the parties to the conflict "to restore and maintain the cease-fire that had generally held since 24 July 1981."[101]

---

96. *E.g.*, *New York Times*, Dec. 5, 1981, p. 26, col. 6.

97. *Supra* note 91 at 33.

98. The U.S. State Dept. had concerns about Israeli military movements near the Lebanese border. See *e.g.*, *New York Times* April 10, 1982, p. 1, col. 4.

99. S/PV 2331, pp. 6–10, at 8–10 (23 Feb. 1982).

100. *Supra* note 93, pp. 6–7, at 6.

101. *Id.* at 7.

The Secretary-General reported to the Security Council on the evening of June 6 pursuant to its call in resolution 508 for a cease-fire no later than 0600 hours local time on Sunday, 6 June 1982. He stated that following the adoption of resolution 508 on June 5, the PLO "reaffirmed its commitment to stop all military operations across the Lebanese border."[102] The Permanent Representative of Israel, however, informed the Secretary-General on June 5 at 2300 hours New York time (0600 on June 6, Beirut time) that "Israeli reactions were in exercise of its right of self-defense" and that resolution 508, adopted on the previous day, would be brought to the attention of the Israeli Cabinet.[103] The Secretary-General further reported that subsequent to the scheduled time of the cease-fire Mr. Arafat had informed him that:

> [I]n spite of heavy Israeli air-strikes after the scheduled time of the cease-fire, he had given orders to all PLO units to withhold fire for a further specified period.[104]

These events had taken place prior to the invasion by Israeli ground forces. UNIFIL reported approximately 110 Israeli air strikes which were observed to take place between 0624 and 1435 hours local time on June 6.[105]

Dr. Blum also expressed the attitude of his government toward the Security Council on June 6:

> When is this Council galvanized into action? When Israel, after years of unparalleled restraint finally resorts to the exercise of its right of self-defence, the fundamental and inalienable right of any State, which is also recognized by the United Nations Charter as the inherent right of Members of this Organization. In order to save a terrorist organization from well-deserved and

---

102. S/PV. 2375, pp. 2–7 at p. 3 (6 June 1982).
103. *Id.*

104. *Id.*

105. *Id.* at 4–5.

> long-overdue retribution, this Council is con-
> vened in emergency meetings, urgent meetings
> and every conceivable form of extraordinary
> session.[106]
>
> * * * *
>
> Given the parliamentary situation in this Orga-
> nization and the constellation within this Council,
> Israel cannot expect this body even to deplore
> PLO barbarism against Israel's civilian popula-
> tion, let alone take any steps with a view to
> curbing that barbarism.[107]

These views appear to indicate that the Government of Israel
would not use peaceful procedures through the United
Nations. The Israeli failure to respond affirmatively to the
calls for a cease-fire combined with its concurrent continuation of air strikes and the initiating of the attack-invasion
amounted to a rejection of the opportunity to use peaceful
procedures and thus a failure to comply with this requirement of law.

3. THE REQUIREMENT OF ACTUAL NECESSITY FOR RESPONDING
COERCION

(a)   Armed Attack
Even though the PLO is a recognized public body and
a national liberation movement representing the people of
Palestine[108] and not a state, it is restricted by the customary
law of self-defense which is termed "inherent right" in article
51 of the United Nations Charter. Consequently, if there
were an armed attack by the PLO against the State of Israel,
assuming that the attack was of "sufficient gravity," to use
the language of the United Nations Definition of Aggression, it would justify defensive measures by the State of

---

106. *Id.* at 16.

107. *Id.* at 17.

108. The authoritative analysis of the legal status of the PLO is Kassim, "The
Palestine Liberation Organization's Claim to Status: A Juridical Analysis
Under International Law," 9 *Denver J. Int'l L. & Policy* 1 (1980).

Israel. There is, however, no evidence of an armed attack of any degree of gravity by the PLO. The only PLO use of military force across the Lebanon border against Israel subsequent to the July 24, 1981 cease-fire and prior to the June, 1982 Israeli invasion, according to the UNIFIL report, was PLO responding coercion on May 9 which has been described.[109]

It is also appropriate to enquire as to whether or not the claims made by the Government of Israel through Dr. Blum concerning incidents elsewhere actually constitute an armed attack on Israel by the PLO. Dr. Blum summarized these claims in the Security Council on June 6 as follows:

> [E]ven in the relatively short period of time which has elapsed since the July 1981 agreement on cessation of hostilities, the total of dead and wounded at the hands of the PLO has steadily mounted to a point where it now reaches 17 dead and 241 wounded in a total of 141 terrorist acts all of them originating from terrorist bases inside Lebanon.[110]

Concerning the 17 stated to have been killed, he provided 15 specific examples which included eight Israeli Jews, seven of whom were apparently killed in Israel, and an Israeli diplomat killed in France.[111] He also referred to seven Jews killed in foreign countries including Austria and Belgium, and in West Berlin, none of whom were stated to be Israeli citizens.[112] Concerning the seven Israeli Jews stated to be killed in Israel, Dr. Blum said that four were killed on April 22, 1979 and three on April 6, 1980 (both times prior to the cease-fire).[113] The assumption of PLO responsibility in all instances is made without proof being provided. Concerning the Jews outside of Israel, it is also made without the

---

109. See the text accompanying *supra* notes 52, 53.

110. *Supra* note 102 at 12–15.

111. *Id.* at 11.

112. *Id.*

113. *Id.* at 9–11.

concurrence of the local police authorities in the assumption that the PLO was responsible. The inclusion by Dr. Blum of attacks on non-Israeli Jews outside the State of Israel is consistent with "the Jewish people" nationality claims advanced by the Israeli Government.[114] The Government of Israel has no legal authority to intervene diplomatically on behalf of Jews who are not Israeli nationals. Mr. Maksoud, the Permanent Observer of the League of Arab States, was the only speaker in the Security Council on June 6 who responded specifically to these claims by Dr. Blum. He stated:

> I am sure that the Jews of the United States, of the United Kingdom, of France, of the Soviet Union, of all the countries in the world reject Israel's claim to be the spokesman for all the Jews in the world and the protector of their rights.[115]

Even if the Jews killed in foreign countries were Israeli nationals, the responsibility for their protection is with the host countries. The Government of Israel would only be entitled to intervene diplomatically if that protection fell below the international law standard.[116] The international law concerning armed attack and aggression relates directly to actions which pose so much danger to the basic interests of a state, including the maintenance of its independence, that the state is justified in using responding military coercion in self-defense. If there were persuasive evidence that the PLO was responsible for all the attacks upon Jews outside Israel, such attacks still could not amount to an armed attack against the State of Israel. To suggest that several isolated attacks on Jews by unidentified assailants in Europe present such a danger to the State of Israel is to attempt to trivialize the international law doctrines which deal with actions of great consequentiality endangering the continued existence of a state. Since there was no armed attack against Israel, there

---

114. See the text accompanying *supra* notes 35–37.

115. *Supra* note 102, pp. 57–62 at 61.

116. *Supra* note 84 at 686–89.

cannot be an actual necessity for responding coercion.

After referring to "the cessation of hostilities on the Lebanese border [which] went into effect on 24 July 1981," Dr. Blum continued:

> Violations of the cessation of hostilities began almost immediately and have continued un-abated, culminating most recently in the attempted assassination of Ambassador Argov in London.[117]

Dr. Blum specifically accused the PLO of responsibility for the attack on Ambassador Argov in this and other statements. Even if the PLO had been proven, contrary to the facts provided by Scotland Yard,[118] responsible for this shooting, it still would not amount to an armed attack on the State of Israel according to the standards of international law. It is well known that United States ambassadors have been attacked in some countries and, on occasion, killed. On no occasion has the United States Government regarded this as an attack on the United States.

(b) Anticipated Armed Attack

Since no actual armed attack or aggression by the PLO upon Israel is involved in the fact situation, it is important to determine whether there existed evidence that any such armed attack was imminent. The striking disparity which the military action showed between the capability of the PLO in southern Lebanon and the Israeli armed forces makes improbable the existence of any credible evidence which might reasonably have led Israel to believe that massive responding coercive measures were necessary to prevent an

---

117. *Supra* note 35 at 28–30.

118. See the text accompanying *supra* note 58.

anticipated armed attack.[119] In addition, the consistent refusal of the PLO to respond to Israeli provocations in southern Lebanon (with the one exception) in the several months prior to the Israeli air attacks of June 4, 1982 indicates a PLO effort to avoid a military confrontation with Israel.

Along with including reference to the " Jewish people" nationality claim in his assertion of the Israeli right to lawful self-defense, Dr. Blum also stated the anticipatory self-defense claim as covering "Israel's citizens in Israel and abroad" and "Jewish life" generally.[120] In evaluating any invocation of anticipatory self-defense, the threatened harm must not only be anticipated, but it must be imminent. The *Caroline* and Oran incidents and the Cuban Missile Crisis,[121] already considered as examples of internationally accepted anticipatory self-defense, each involved the factually ascertained capability of significant military means being used in the immediate or near future. In the first two incidents the probability of armed attack in the near future necessitated the use of a coercive military response. Because the Cuban Missile Crisis involved a lesser degree of the probability of armed attack in the immediate or near future, even though a nuclear capability was being created, the United States response in anticipatory self-defense did not involve the direct coercive use of armed force but rather a quarantine-interdiction or limited naval blockade.

In striking contrast to the factual clarity and the militarily

---

119. Analysts at the International Institute for Strategic Studies (London) classify Israel as the fourth strongest military power after the United States the Soviet Union, and China. *Jerusalem Post*, Int'l Ed., Aug. 8–14, 1982, p. 3 cols. 1–3 at col. 1.

> The war in Lebanon was neither necessary nor inevitable. Ever the Likud Government does not pretend that this was a war t defend and preserve Israel's existence. And Ze'ev Shiff, th respected military correspondent of "Ha'aretz" reports that a of the weapons that we captured are barely enough to arm on PLO division.

Shenker, "Why Didn't We Prevent This War?," *New Outlook* (Tel Aviv Aug.–Sept. 1982, pp. 31–35 at 31, col. 1.

120. *Supra* note 110 at 33. See the text accompanying *supra* notes 36, 37.

121. *Supra* notes 82, 84 and 86.

significant threats posed by these three widely accepted customary law incidents, the alleged PLO threat claimed by Israel was unsupported by convincing evidence and was relatively minor in character. Israeli plans for a large-scale invasion were reported months prior to the actual event and substantiated by Prime Minister Begin's assertion that they awaited only a "clear provocation."[122] Such long-term planning for an alleged defensive measure indicates that the claimed threat was not perceived to be imminent. Moreover, after the event, Mr. Begin, in an address on August 8, 1982 to the Israeli National Defense College, said that the Lebanese invasion "does not really belong to the category of wars of no alternative."[123] He stated that it was in response to attacks on civilians and added: "True, such actions were not a threat to the existence of the state."[124] In plain words, he admitted thereby that it was not a war of self-defense. Claims such as those advanced by Israel have not provided sufficient grounds for the legal conclusion of actual necessity in responding to an anticipated armed attack in the past and cannot do so now.

The German attack-invasion of Norway on April 9, 1940 presents an analogy to the Israeli attack-invasion of June 6, 1982. Both involved the attempt to find legal justification in the doctrine of anticipatory self-defense. The detailed German plans, like the Israeli ones, were made over at least a period of several months prior to implementation. The claim made by defendants before the International Military

---

122. *New York Times*, Jan. 21, 1982, p. 1, col. 1.

Further evidence of long-term Israeli military preparations for the attack-invasion is the admission by Defense Minister Sharon of a secret visit which he made to Beirut in January, 1982 to reconnoiter the city for a possible Israeli assault. *New York Times*, August 13, 1982, p. 4, cols. 1–6 at col. 3. Such reconnaissance of the Lebanese capital also raises doubts as to the Israeli claim that their drive into Beirut was not their intention early in the invasion.

123. "The Choice of War: Prime Minister Menachem Begin explains here why Israel decided to a launch Operation Peace for Galilee," *Jerusalem Post*, Int'l Ed., Aug. 22–28, 1982, p. 14, cols. 1–5, at col. 5.

124. *Id*. See "In the Name of Truth," editorial in *New Outlook* (Tel Aviv) Aug.–Sept. 1982, at p. 5, col. 1 criticizing false statements by the Government of Israel concerning the attack-invasion of June, 1982.

Tribunal at Nuremberg (I.M.T.) was that the German military action was necessary as a defensive measure to forestall a British invasion of Norway. The official diary of the German Naval Operations Staff, however, indicated that this was not the actual perception of German naval officials. An entry of March 23, 1940 records:

> A mass encroachment by the English into Norwegian territorial waters ... is not to be expected at the present time.[125]

Other entries indicated a similar perception. The Judgment of the I.M.T. applied the criteria of the *Caroline* incident and stated, *inter alia:*

> It was further argued that Germany alone could decide, in accordance with the reservations made by many of the Signatory Powers at the time of the conclusion of the Kellogg–Briand Pact, whether preventive action was a necessity, and that in making her decision her judgment was conclusive. But whether action taken under the claim of self-defense was in fact aggressive or defensive must ultimately be subject to investigation and adjudication if international law is ever to be enforced.[126]

The International Military Tribunal also considered and rejected the claim that the invasion of Denmark was justified as self-defense and concluded that:

> In the light of all the available evidence it is impossible to accept the contention that the invasion of Denmark and Norway were defensive, and in the opinion of the Tribunal they were acts of aggressive war.[127]

---

125. 1 I.M.T. 208.

126. *Id.*

127. *Id.* at 209.

Israel, like Germany, made the claim that it alone could decide whether its military response was necessary. This was not done in words alone, but by the considered action of the Israeli Cabinet on June 6, 1982 in ordering the implementation of the plan for the attack-invasion in the face of unanimous disapproval by the Security Council.[128]

4. THE REQUIREMENT OF PROPORTIONALITY IN RESPONDING DEFENSIVE MEASURES

Since Israel has not met the requirements of either good faith use of peaceful procedures or of actual necessity for responding coercion, it is not necessary to inquire as to the proportionality of the attack-invasion. It may, nevertheless, be useful to consider whether this requirement has been met. The proportionality doctrine appraises the character of responding coercion. The responding measures must be proportional, both in kind and amount, to the character of the threat which is claimed to justify anticipatory self-defense. In what are probably the most important words of Secretary of State Webster in the *Caroline* incident, he stated the requirement of proportionality in these terms: "Nothing unreasonable or excessive [is permitted], since the act, justified by the necessity of self-defense, must be limited by that necessity and kept clearly within it."[129]

Professors McDougal and Feliciano have enunciated the fundamental character of the principle:

> [T]he principle of proportionality is seen as but one specific form of the more general principle of economy in coercion and as a logical corollary of the fundamental community policy against change by destructive modes. Coercion that is grossly in excess of what, in a particular context, may be reasonably required for conservation of values against a particular attack, or that is obviously irrelevant or unrelated to this purpose,

---

128. *Supra* note 102, pp. 8–33 at 33.

129. *Supra* note 83.

itself constitutes an unlawful initiation of coercive
or violent change.[130]

It is unfortunate to have to deal with human casualties as
a statistical matter. Nevertheless, it is necessary to respond to
Mr. Blum's undocumented statistical claims before the
Security Council citing the 17 alleged victims of the PLO.[131] If
Israel's extended interpretation of the cease-fire were
accepted for purposes of analysis, the statistics on Palestinian
and Lebanese victims of Israeli attacks, wherever they
occurred, must also be considered on the same basis. During
the time span from the cease-fire through June 3, 1982 one
PLO diplomat was killed in Rome by unknown assailants,[132]
16 Palestinian civilians (including at least 11 teenagers and
one eight-year-old) were killed by Israeli soldiers or settlers in
the West Bank or Gaza,[133] and at least 39 Palestinians and
Lebanese were killed in Israeli air attacks on Lebanon.[134] In
contrast to the Jewish casualties claimed by Mr. Blum where
no evidence of PLO responsibility was produced, all of the
Palestinian (with the exception of the diplomat in Rome) and
Lebanese casualties were clearly caused by Israeli armed
forces or by settlers armed by the Government of Israel. In
addition to these earlier reported victims, there were
thousands of civilian casualties, both Lebanese and Pales-

---

130. *Supra* note 64 at 241–44.

131. Notwithstanding Mr. Blum's claims, the *New York Times* reported the
killing of only three Israelis during the period from the July 24, 1981 ceasefire
through June 3, 1982 when Ambassador Argov was attacked: 2 soldiers – one
in Gaza (*New York Times*, March 26, 1982, p. 4, col. 1) and one in south
Lebanon (*Id.*, April 22, 1982, p. 1, col. 6) – and one Israeli diplomat in Paris
(*Id.*, April 4, 1982, p. 3, col. 1).

132. *Wash. Post,* Oct. 10, 1981, p. A20, col. 1.

133. *New York Times,* Dec. 8, 1981, p. 6, col. 3; *id.*, March 21, 1982, p. 1, col. 6;
id., March 23, 1982, p. 1, col. 3; *id.*, March 25, 1982, p. 1, col. 2; *id.*, April 9,
1982, p. 10, col. 4; *id.*, April 12, 1982, p. 1, col. 3; *id.*, April 14, 1982, p. 9, col. 1;
id., April 17, 1982, p. 3, col. 1; *id.*, April 30, 1982, p. 3, col. 1; *id.*, May 5, 1982,
p. A3, col. 4.

134. At least 23 on April 21 (*Wash. Post,* April 22, 1982, p. 1, col. 6), and 16 on
May 9 (*Id.*, May 10, 1982, p. A1, col. 2).

tinian, reported since the Israeli attack-invasion began on June 4, 1982.[135]

During the Security Council consideration of the events beginning June 5, 1982, no member of the Council and no speaker who was invited to make a statement to the Council supported the view that the Israeli actions met the criteria of proportionality. Ireland (one of the non-permanent members of the Council) spoke to the issue through its Permanent Representative, Mr. Dorr. On June 5, in the context of the Israeli air attacks but before the beginning of the ground invasion, Mr. Dorr expressed his and his government's deep sympathy over the attack on Ambassador Argov who was accredited concurrently as Ambassador to Ireland. He then continued:

> But we see no justification for, and no correspondence, no relation, between that outrage and the large-scale Israeli raids on the Lebanese capital.
>
> According to reports, scores of people have been killed in those raids. This was an indiscriminate attempt at retribution. It was on a massive scale and it has killed many who can have had no knowledge of, and no connexion, and indeed no sympathy, with whatever group or individuals planned the attack on the Ambassador.[136]

On June 8, after the massive character of the attack-invasion had become clear, Mr. Dorr returned to the subject of proportionality:

> Where is the correspondence, where is the sense of proportion?
>
> I do not know exactly the total number of lives lost in attacks on Israel across its borders, or in attacks on Israeli citizens elsewhere over recent years. But I am very sure that the total of lives lost and casualties suffered in all such attacks over

---

135. *Supra* note 61 and accompanying text.

136. *Supra* note 93, pp. 11–12 at 12.

recent years is less than the deaths and injuries caused by the recent major Israeli air attacks on Beirut. Yet we are talking now about a war in which these air raids in turn are merely one aspect of a larger attack on Lebanon.[137]

On June 18 Mr. Dorr reemphasized the importance of the proportionality issue.[138] Dr. Blum was the only person present who expressed a view inconsistent with that of the Irish representative. He characterized Mr. Dorr's statement as "Yet another expression of his well-known tendency to adopt a blinkered, selective, one-sided and lopsided position on the matter before us, as well as on other issues affecting my country."[139]

In summary, this Israeli military action, which according to the Secretary-General initially consisted of "more than two mechanized divisions with full air and naval support,"[140] cannot possibly be appraised as a proportional response to the incidents claimed by Dr. Blum as the justification for the attack-invasion. Neither the customary law nor the provisions of the United Nations Charter nor any other juridical source could provide legal authority for the Israeli military actions. Even the application of the most liberal formulation of the requirement of proportionality would fail to find that it has been satisfied.

C. THE CHARACTER OF THE ATTACK-INVASION UNDER THE JURIDICAL CRITERIA

The Government of Israel may not successfully invoke the claim of lawful self-defense unless it meets each of the three established criteria which have been considered. Since it has not met any one of the three, it follows, *a fortiori*, that the attack-invasion must be an act of aggression. There are further reasons which also compel this conclusion.

---

137. S/PV. 2377, pp. 11–13 at 12.

138. S/PV. 2379, pp. 6–13 at 7 (18 June 1982).

139. *Id.*, pp. 46–61 at 58–60.

140. *Supra* note 102, pp. 2–7 at 6.

The relevant claims and counter-claims which have been considered took place in the context of the adoption of Security Council resolution 508 on June 5 and of Security Council resolution 509 on June 6.[141] The final preambular paragraph in resolution 508 reaffirmed and supported the statement made by the President and members of the Security Council on June 4, 1982 and the "urgent appeal" issued by the Secretary-General on June 4, 1982. Both of these statements were intended to prevent the Israeli attack-invasion which began on June 6. In the first operative paragraph of resolution 508 the Council:

> *Calls upon* all the parties to the conflict to cease immediately and simultaneously all military activities within Lebanon and across the Lebanese–Israeli border and no later than 0600 hours local time on Sunday, 6 June 1982.

The second operative paragraph asks member states to use their influence to achieve a cessation of hostilities, and the third and final operative paragraph asks the Secretary-General to "undertake all possible efforts" to ensure implementation and compliance with the resolution.

Security Council resolution 509 was adopted on June 6 after it had become clear beyond any possible doubt that Israel had commenced its attack-invasion. In the first operative paragraph the Security Council stated that it:

> *Demands* that Israel withdraw all its military forces forthwith and unconditionally to the internationally recognized boundaries of Lebanon.

The second operative paragraph demanded that the terms of operative paragraph 1 of resolution 508 be strictly observed by all parties. The third operative paragraph called upon the parties to communicate their acceptance of the present resolution to the Secretary-General within twenty-four hours.

---

141. More complete documentation for S.C. Res. 508 *U.N. SCOR, Thirty-seventh Year* 5; S. C. Rees 509, *id* at 6.

It will be recalled that the PLO responded affirmatively to the Security Council's call for the cease-fire enunciated in resolution 508, but that the Government of Israel did not.[142] This provides further evidence, if any should be required, of the aggressive character of the attack-invasion. Since it also was "the first use of armed force by a State in contravention of the Charter" it is a *prima facie* act of aggression as enunciated in article 2 of the United Nations Definition of Aggression.[143]

Resolution 509 was drawn in careful and understated terms so as not to bring about a negative vote by the United States and thus block Security Council action. While the United States Government had demonstrated willingness to vote for the basic principles enunciated in resolutions 508 and 509, it was not willing to even consider, much less to adopt, enforcement measures which were indispensable to stop the attack-invasion. The Spanish draft resolution of June 8, 1982 in a preambular paragraph took note of "The two positive replies to the Secretary-General of the Government of Lebanon and the Palestine Liberation Organization ...". The first and fifth draft operative paragraphs provided that the Security Council:

> 1. *Condemns* the non-compliance with resolutions 508 (1982) and 509 (1982) by Israel ... .
>
> 5. *Demands* that within six hours all hostilities must be stopped in compliance with Security Council resolutions 508 (1982) and 509 (1982) and decides, in the event of non-compliance, to meet again to consider practical ways and means in accordance with the Charter of the United Nations.

The intervening operative paragraphs urged compliance with the Hague Regulations of 1907 and repeated the demand concerning Israeli military withdrawal as well as reiterating adherence to the cease-fire enunciated in para-

---

142. *Supra* notes 102–104 and accompanying text.

143. The text accompanying *supra* note 75.

graph 1 of resolution 508. When the vote was taken, all of the members of the Council voted in favor except for the United States which voted against.[144] The massive character of the military action was evident for all to see on June 8, and following the United States negative vote the Government of Israel continued its military operations.

One of the criteria of the customary law which is used to appraise military action as either defensive or aggressive is whether it reflects the inclusive values of the world community or only the exclusive values of a particular state or public body.[145] The inclusive values of the world community in stopping the attack-invasion and returning to peaceful procedures have been set forth authoritatively in Security Council resolutions 508 and 509. The attack-invasion was in no way consistent with those common interests or values and it, at most, reflected the exclusive perceived interests of the Government of Israel. However, it is appropriate to question whether this promotes *bona fide* Israeli interests as opposed to the implementation of the Zionist militarism and expansionism manifested by the Israeli political elite.[146] That which is most urgently needed by the State of Israel and Israelis is the same thing which is most urgently needed by other states and peoples in the Middle East. It is the achievement of a genuine peace based upon justice for all of the peoples of the area and a termination of the continuing conflict situation perpetrated by the policies of the Government of Israel.

It is also necessary, using the same customary law criteria, to inquire as to whether the claimant to self-defense is conserving its existing values or seeking to extend its values at the expense of others.[147] One of the most basic

---

144. *Supra* note 137, at pp. 8–10. Zeev Shiff [military editor of *Ha'aretz*], "The Green Light," *Foreign Policy*, no. 50, p. 73 (1983) sets forth the evidence leading to his conclusion of United States acquiescence in the attack-invasion.

145. McDougal & Feliciano, *supra* note 64 at 182–83.

146. See S. Tillman, *American Interests in the Middle East*, Chap. 3, "Israel: The Politics of Fear" (1980).

147. *Supra* note 145 at 181–82.

elements in the law of self-defense is that it only authorizes a defender to preserve its existing values and not to acquire those of any enemy even if the enemy is characterized as the attacker in the particular military context.[148] This principle is reflected in Security Council resolution 242 in which "the inadmissibility of the acquisition of territory by war" is emphasized.[149] Because of the absence of either an armed attack or the threat of one against Israel, the extension of its military power and political control throughout southern Lebanon demonstrates aggressive rather than defensive action. Some thoughtful critics have pointed out that the attack-invasion is not a meaningful method to conserve the legitimate Israeli interest in protecting the inhabitants of the Galilee from attack across the Lebanese border. Mr. Anthony Lewis, writing on June 7, 1982 stated:

> To protect Israelis in the Galilee from rockets and shells is essential. But the best method of doing so is the one that US envoy Philip Habib negotiated last July: a cease-fire between Israel and the P.L.O. In terms of keeping northern Israel free of artillery attacks, that arrangement has been astonishingly successful.
>
> * * * *
>
> In short, the cease-fire kept the Galilee safe until Israel bombed Lebanon. The argument that aggressive new military action was needed to keep the rockets out turns reality upside-down.[150]

Repeated Government of Israel official statements have declared that Israel does "not covet a square inch of Lebanese soil."[151] It should also be pointed out that the original Israeli justification only claimed the freedom to establish a 25-mile

---

148. R. Y. Jennings, *The Acquisition of Territory in International Law*, Chap. 4, "Title and Unlawful Force (1963)"

149. *22 U.N. SCOR*, pp. 8–9 (22 Nov. 1967).

150. *New York Times*, June 7, 1982, p. A19, cols. 5–6 at col. 5.

151. Moshe Arens (Israeli Ambassador to the US), "What We Want in Lebanon," *Wash. Post*, June 11, 1982, p. A15, cols. 1–3, at col. 2.

zone in southern Lebanon so that the Galilee would be free from artillery and rocket attacks.[152] Promptly thereafter, the Israeli military forces went far beyond that limit and soon were at the outskirts of Beirut and then in the city.

In addition, the fact that the Government of Israel has been in southern Lebanon either directly or indirectly through the *de facto* forces since 1978[153] tends to diminish the credibility of the official statements concerning the limited character of the operation and the further assurances concerning early withdrawal. It is also relevant to recognize that the earlier Zionist and Israeli statements concerning the lack of territorial ambitions have proven to be false. The first was the Zionist Organization/Jewish Agency acceptance of the boundaries provided for the State of Israel under the Palestine Partition Resolution followed by attacks upon Palestinians outside of those boundaries as well as within[154] for a period of time before the claimed "invasion" by the Arab armies. Israeli participation in the tripartite invasion of Egypt of 1956 was originally stated to be only for the purpose of defending against feydaheen attacks.[155] It is well known that only President Eisenhower's stated intention to invoke sanctions compelled Israeli withdrawal in early 1957.[156] The same familiar pattern of initial claims of self-defense followed by territorial aggrandizement was followed in the intense

---

152. *Supra* note 102, pp. 8–33 at 33.

Christopher Walker, "How Peace in Galilee Became the War in Beirut," *The Times* (London), Aug. 14, 1982, p. 8, cols. 2–5 sets forth the inconsistent official explanations and the consistent evidence of long-range planning.

Reserve General Aharon Yariv, former Israeli head of military intelligence and currently Director of the Center for Strategic Studies, Tel Aviv University, said: "I know in fact that going to Beirut was included in the original military plan." *Jerusalem Post*, Int'l Ed., Oct. 3–9, 1982, p. 15, cols. 1–5 at col. 2.

153. The text accompanying *supra* notes 25–27.

154. *E.g.*, the implementation of "Plan D" involving attacks upon Palestinians throughout the Palestine Mandate prior to the "invasion" by the Arab armies is described in Netanel Lorch, *One Long War: Arab Versus Jew Since 1920*, pp. 40–48 under heading "Jewish Forces Take the Initiative" (1976).

155. *E.g.*, Kennet Love, *Suez: The Twice-Fought War* 481 and *passim* (1969).

156. 36 *U.S. Dept. State Bull.*, 387 at 389 (Mar. 11, 1957).

hostilities of June 1967.[157] More recently, the Government of Israel has claimed to annex the Golan Heights and East Jerusalem through municipal law[158] in violation of the fundamental rule of international law prohibiting the acquisition of territory by conquest reflected in Security Council resolution 242.[159] The consistent history just summarized provides convincing evidence of the expansion of Israeli perceived interests or values as opposed to their conservation.

Following the Second World War, the United Kingdom, the United States, the Soviet Union, and the French Republic wrote the Charter of the International Military Tribunal[160] which was subsequently applied in the trial of the major German defendants at Nuremberg. The Charter provided for individual criminal responsibility where evidence indicated the commission of crimes against peace, war crimes, or crimes against humanity. Article 6(A) provided:

> CRIMES AGAINST PEACE: namely, planning, preparation, initiation or waging of a war of aggression, or a war in violation of international treaties, agreements or assurances, or participation in a Common Plan or Conspiracy for the accomplishment of any of the foregoing.

The International Military Tribunal (I.M.T.) considered the basic ideological premises of the Nazi movement including its emphasis on the acquisition of territory by force, its assumption of German racial identification, and its claimed superiority to other races.[161] It then recounted the careful planning and carrying out of aggression in the numerous specific instances in which it occurred. It characterized the seizures of both Czechoslovakia and Austria as acts of

---

157. *Supra* note 155 at 690 and *passim*.

158. Golan Heights Law (Dec. 14, 1981), 21 *Int'l Legal Materials* 214 (1982) [Text provided by Israeli Embassy, Wash. D.C.].

159. The text accompanying *supra* note 149.

160. 1 I.M.T. 10–16.

161. *Id.* at 174–76 and *passim*.

aggression.[162] The attacks-invasions against Poland, Denmark, Norway, Belgium, the Netherlands, Luxembourg, Yugoslavia, and Greece, *inter alia*, were adjudged also to be acts of aggression.[163] The I.M.T. ultimately held that eight members of the German political and military elite were guilty of crimes against the peace.[164]

Justice Robert Jackson, the United States prosecutor at the I.M.T., pointed out in the opening statement for the prosecution that the standards to which German defendants would be held would also be the standards later applied to others.[165] It is therefore appropriate to apply the criteria of the I.M.T. to the actions of the Government of Israel in Lebanon.

As in the situation of the Nazi-German elite, that which is done by the Zionist–Israeli elite is more important than what is said or planned. A plan of aggression, unless it is acted upon, is not an act of aggression. The long prepared Zionist–Israeli plans for aggression against Lebanon were only partially implemented between 1978 and June, 1982. The attack-invasion which began on June 5, 1982 was an act of aggression against both the PLO and the Republic of Lebanon under the existing criteria of international law including the Judgement of the I.M.T.

III. The Humanitarian Law for the Protection of Prisoners of War and Of Civilian Persons and Objects

A. THE HISTORICAL DEVELOPMENT OF THE LAW

International armed conflict has been characterized historically by the extensive destruction of both human and

---

162. *Id.* at 192–98.

163. *Id.* at 198–213.

164. Göring, Hess, Ribbentrop, Keitel, Rosenberg, Raeder, Jodl, and Von Neurath. *Id.* at 366–67.

165. 2 I.M.T. 98–155 at 101.

material values. It is a factual situation of varying degrees of violence conducted by states and other participants including organized resistance movements. The international humanitarian law of armed conflict, traditionally known as the law of war, has been developed by the community of states in order to eliminate, or at least minimize, unnecessary destruction. It is designed to impose limitations upon the kinds and degrees of violence and to the extent that the law is effective, a situation of international armed conflict becomes a system of controlled coercion.

The effective sanctioning and enforcement of the law of armed conflict, like that of other branches of international law and of municipal law, is dependent in large measure for its observance upon the common interests of the participants.[166] The group participants include states and their typically regular armed forces, and organized resistance movements and their typically irregular armed forces. If the law is to be effective in imposing restraints upon these groups, it must provide inducements to bring their individual combatants within the juridical system of rights and duties. The futility of attempting to put irregular combatants outside the law is illustrated by the barbaric methods employed against them during the Second World War by the Nazis and the Japanese militarists. Torture and the death penalty were demonstrated to be failures as deterrent sanctions to prevent resistance by irregular forces.[167]

During the Crusades, Western rulers and armies had contact with the Eastern humanitarianism exemplified by Saladin.[168] They were so unfamiliar with humanitarianism in the context of armed conflict that they initially mistook

---

166. W. T. Mallison, *Studies in the Law of Naval Warfare* 19–22 (U.S. Naval War College, 1966).

167. Mallison & Mallison, "The Juridical Status of Irregular Combatants Under the International Humanitarian Law of Armed Conflict," 9 *Case Western Reserve J. Int'l L.* 39–78, at 41 (1977).

168.   If the taking of Jerusalem were the only fact known about Saladin, it were enough to prove him the most chivalrous and great-hearted conqueror of his own, and perhaps of any age.
S. Lane-Poole, *Saladin and the Fall of the Kingdom of Jerusalem* 234 (1964).

Saladin's compassion for war victims as an indication of military weakness. In contrast, there was little or no influence of humanitarianism in the European wars during the Middle Ages. The Code of Chivalry provided some protection for warriors of high social position, but the code was inapplicable to peasant foot soldiers, civilians, and to enemy personnel of different religious identification.[169]

The origin of the customary law prohibition of direct attack upon the civilian population in the Western world should be credited to Hugo Grotius who, in his famous book, *De Jure Belli ac Pacis*,[170] published in 1625, made the basic distinction between civilians and combatants and recommended humane treatment for prisoners of war.

A more recent historical basis for the contemporary humanitarian law of armed conflict may be found in Lieber's Code (named for its principal author, Professor Francis Lieber of Columbia College, New York) which President Lincoln promulgated to the United States Army as General Order No. 100 in 1863.[171] The Civil War in the United States involved widespread hostilities over a period of four years, and there would have been a much greater destruction of both human and material values if the United States Government had treated every soldier of the armies in rebellion as a traitor under domestic law. In addition, the existence of Lieber's Code encouraged the Confederate forces to adhere to at least the minimal standards of the law of war on the basis of reciprocity and mutuality in observance. The most enduring feature of this Code is that, although it was designed for use in a civil war, it has provided the significant background for the entire modern law of land warfare. Since its provisions included the most enlightened features of the then existing international law of war, it greatly influenced the Brussels Declaration of 1874.

---

169. M. Keen, *The Laws of War in the Late Middle Ages* 82–100 (1965).

170. An English translation is in 2 *Classics of International Law* (Carnegie Endowment for Int'l Peace, Kelsey transl., 1925).

171. Schindler & Toman (eds.), *The Laws of Armed Conflicts: A Collection of Conventions, Resolutions and Other Documents* 3 (1981).

The Brussels Conference of 1874, the first multilateral conference to consider the law of land warfare, met at the invitation of the Russian Czar. The Declaration[172] produced at this Conference has been accorded insufficient attention by most legal scholars because it remained unratified. It comprises, nevertheless, the foundation upon which the modern law of land warfare has been built. Prior to the meeting of the First Hague Conference in 1899, the consensus of the Brussels Conference was widely accepted as the authoritative statement of the customary law on the subject.[173]

Article 9 of the Declaration provided that irregular combatants who meet four conditions are lawful combatants and also provided that they are entitled to prisoner of war status upon capture. Articles 12 and 13 dealt with legal limitations upon the method of injuring the enemy. Article 13(e) forbade "the employment of arms, projectiles, or material calculated to cause unnecessary suffering." Other articles imposed limitations upon sieges and bombardments and provided protections for prisoners as well as for sick and wounded combatants.

The Brussels Declaration was signed by the representatives of all of the states participating in the Conference, but since it was not ratified by their respective governments, it did not become binding as a multilateral treaty. However, it was the basis for Hague Conventions No. II of 1899[174] and No. IV of 1907.[175] Both the 1899 Convention II and the 1907 Convention IV employed a form which included a preamble, a body of the Convention containing important administrative matters, and regulations annexed to the Convention containing the substantive rules of land warfare. These Conventions are considered as embodying the customary

---

172. *Id.* at 25.

173. The Russian circular diplomatic note of Dec. 30, 1898 stated that one of the purposes of the Hague Conference of 1899 was to be " the revision of the declaration concerning the laws and customs of war elaborated in 1874 by the Conference of Brussels, and not yet ratified." *Id.* at 57.

174. *32 U.S. Stat.* 1803, *supra* note 171 at 57–92.

175. *36 U.S. Stat.* 2277, *supra* note 171 at 57–92.

international law binding on all states, whether or not they are parties to the Conventions.[176] Their articles 42 through 56 concern military authority over hostile territory and specifically define occupation. They repeat many of the Brussels provisions concerning protections for the human rights of noncombatants as well as basic protections for prisoners of war, and they also repeat the Brussels criteria for irregular combatants.

During the Second World War, even the limited provisions of Hague Convention No. IV and its Annexed Regulations, along with the customary law, were violated by the practices of both the Nazis and the Japanese militarists. Following the conclusion of that war the International Military Tribunal at Nuremberg[177] and the International Military Tribunal for the Far East at Tokyo[178] were established under Charters which provided for individual criminal responsibility for violations of the conventional and customary law. The major German and Japanese defendants whose guilt was established clearly were subjected to criminal penalties. Other trials involving individual criminal responsibility took place in national courts where the same criteria of international law were applied.[179]

The Geneva Diplomatic Conference of 1949 met in the shadow of those grim events and aimed at preventing the repetition of the horrors which characterized the recent war. The four Geneva Conventions for the Protection of War Victims which were produced are currently effective multilateral agreements with almost as many state-parties as the

---

176. The International Military Tribunal at Nuremberg held that the Hague Regulations were declaratory of the customary law. *Judgment*, 1 I.M.T. 171 at 254 (1947).

177. Trial of the Major War Criminals Before the International Military Tribunal at Nuremberg (42 vols. 1947–1949).

178. Proceedings of the International Military Tribunal for the Far East (Apr. 29, 1946–Apr. 16, 1948) (approx. 50,000 typewritten pages with separate volume for each day of the trial).

179. See, *e.g.*, U.N. War Crimes Comm., Law Reports of Trials of War Criminals (15 vols., 1947–1949). [Hereafter cited as *Rep. U.N. Comm.*]

United Nations. The first two Conventions[180] provide for the protection of sick, wounded, and shipwrecked military personnel, and the third concerns protections for prisoners of war.[181] The fourth, the Geneva Convention for the Protection of Civilian Persons,[182] was an entirely new convention, expanding in great detail the customary law and Hague protections for civilians and specifying a more comprehensive concept of belligerent occupation. The State of Israel and each of the other states which have been parties to the recurring conflicts with it are parties to the four Geneva Conventions of 1949.[183] On three occasions, beginning in 1969, the PLO has officially stated its adherence to the four Geneva Conventions.[184]

---

180. Convention (I) for the Amelioration of the Condition of the Wounded and Sick in Armed Forces in the Field, 75 U.N.T.S. 31, *supra* note 171 at 305; Convention (II) for the Amelioration of the Condition of Wounded, Sick, and Shipwrecked Members of Armed Forces at Sea, 75 U.N.T.S. 85, *supra* note 171 at 333.

181. Convention (III) Relative to the Treatment of Prisoners of War, 75 U.N.T.S. 135, *supra* note 171 at 355.

182. Convention (IV) Relative to the Protection of Civilian Persons in Time of War, 75 U.N.T.S. 287, *supra* note 171 at 427. (Each of these four Geneva Conventions is dated 12 August 1949.)

183. The Government of Israel ratified the four Geneva Conventions of 12 August 1949 on July 6, 1951. *Supra* note 171 at 491. The only reservation made by Israel was concerning its intention to use as its distinctive sign the Red Shield of David rather than one of the signs authorized by article 38 of Geneva Convention I. *Id.* at 506. Lebanon ratified the four Conventions without reservation on April 10, 1951.

184. The first was in a letter of May 6, 1969 from the President of the Palestine Red Crescent Society to the Swiss Federal Political Department (the depositary) in which the adherence was stated to be "on condition of reciprocity." T. Meron [former Legal Adviser of the Israeli Foreign Ministry], *Some Legal Aspects of Arab Terrorists' Claims to Privileged Combatancy* 19 (Sabra Books, Tel Aviv, 1970). This instance and a renewed declaration of December, 1974 are referred to in A. Rosas, *The Legal Status of Prisoners of War* 208 (Helsinki, 1976). On June 7, 1982 the Permanent Observer of the PLO at the United Nations in Geneva sent letters of adherence to the four Geneva Conventions and to Geneva Protocol I Concerning International Armed Conflicts (1977) and to Geneva Protocol II Concerning Non-International Armed Conflicts (1977) to the Swiss Federal Political Department and to the President of the I.C.R.C. Protocols I and II, which are supplementary to the Geneva Conventions of 1949, are in Schindler & Toman, *supra* note 171, at 551 and 619 respectively.

B. THE GENEVA PRISONERS OF WAR CONVENTION (1949)

1. THE LEGAL CRITERIA FOR COMBATANTS

The criteria for the juridical status of privileged combatants which entitles the individual to exercise violence lawfully and to have the privileged status of prisoners of war (POW) if captured, were first set forth in the Brussels Declaration[185] and then repeated in Hague Conventions II and IV concerning land warfare. They were incorporated by reference without amplification into the Geneva Prisoners of War Convention of 1929[186] which provided a more detailed body of rules concerning the treatment of POWs after capture than did the brief articles of the Hague Regulations on the same subject. The POW Convention written at Geneva in 1949 went far beyond this in specifying a comprehensive body of rules governing the treatment of POWs and also developed the law concerning the juridical status of privileged irregular combatants by, *inter alia,* including organized resistance movements.

The inhabitants of many of the states overrun by the German and Japanese armies during the Second World War continued military resistance through irregular or partisan forces which employed guerrilla methods of warfare. Such irregulars were typically executed upon capture without regard to whether or not they complied with article 1 of the Hague Regulations.[187] The International Committee of the Red Cross (ICRC) attempted with great persistence, but with little success, to obtain the privileged status of POWs for those irregulars who met the Hague criteria.[188] The Geneva Diplomatic Conference of 1949 met with a full awareness that

---

185. *Supra* note 172.

186. 118 U.N.T.S. 343, 47 *U.S. Stat.* 2021, *supra* note 171 at 271.

187. *U.S. v. Ohlendorf* ("The Einsatzgruppen Case"), 4 US Trials of War Crims. 1 (1949).

188. J. Pictet (ed.), *Commentary on the Geneva Prisoners of War Convention of 1949*, 53 (Int'l Comm. of the Red Cross, 1960) [Hereafter cited as *I.C.R.C. Commentary.* It consists of 4 volumes with one for each Convention.]

the organized resistance movements had fought on the side of the Allied Powers. In both the Conference and in the preparatory work leading to it there was a strong disposition to expand the privileged status of irregulars beyond that enunciated in the Hague Regulations.

At the Diplomatic Conference of 1949 a British delegate proposed that the criteria which the Hague Regulations laid down for irregulars be made specifically applicable to regulars of an unrecognized government or authority covered by article 4A (3).[189] However, Committee II of the Diplomatic Conference did not deem it necessary to state expressly that these criteria were applicable to such regular armed forces because the matter of applicability to all regulars was so well established in customary law that a treaty provision would have been superfluous.[190] There was no suggestion that it was necessary to provide specifically that the four criteria apply to regulars of recognized governments covered by article 4A (1). The result was to retain, and to rely upon, the customary law application to regulars of recognized and unrecognized governments and authorities of the same criteria which applies to irregulars. Article 4 also provides that POW status is extended to those specified persons "who have fallen into the power of the enemy," thereby using a broader term than "captured" which was used in the Geneva POW Convention of 1929.[191] It was sometimes contended during the Second World War that where regulars surrendered in mass they had not been "captured" and consequently it was not legally required to accord them POW status.

The introductory wording of article 4A(2) concerning irregulars goes beyond article 1 of the Hague Regulations. It characterizes privileged combatants who do not comprise a

---

189. 2A *Final Record of the Diplomatic Conference of Geneva of 1949*, 414 (Swiss Fed. Pol. Dept., undated) [The *Final Record* comprises 4 volumes numbered 1, 2A, 2B and 3 and is cited hereafter as *Geneva Rec.*].

190. The Report of Committee II to the Plenary Assembly of the Conference. 2A *Geneva Rec.* 559, at 561–62.

191. *Supra* note 186, art. 1.

part of the regular armed forces as members of "other militias and members of other volunteer corps, including those of organized resistance movements." The inclusion of "organized resistance movements" is based upon the experience of the Second World War and accords authority and status for such movements which are similar or analogous to the wartime model.[192] The broad language which is made applicable to these resistance movements, "operating in or outside their own territory, even if this territory is occupied," provides a comprehensive geographical area of operations for such movements which was not included in the Hague Regulations.

(a) The Requirement of Organization
The requirement of membership in an "organized" resistance movement is explicit in the first traditional provision concerning a responsible military commander and is implicit in the other three. Its inclusion in additional wording which introduces the other provisions should be interpreted as indicating a special emphasis on the principle that irregulars or partisans should be organized in belligerent groups which better facilitate their compliance with the other conditions of the article. This basic principle had been accepted prior to the Diplomatic Conference in the agreement of the Conference of Government Experts "that the first condition preliminary to granting prisoners-of-war status to partisans was their forming a body having a military organization."[193]

The substantive requirement that resistance movements be "organized" is met by the most rudimentary elements of a military organization. Thus, a corporal's squad on detached duty meets the requirement. In the same way, a few

---

192. The Report of Committee II to the Diplomatic Conference stated that the problem of organized resistance movements was solved by assimilating them to militias and corps of volunteers not "forming part of the armed forces" of a state party to the conflict as specified in article 4A(1). This resulted in placing them in article 4A(2). 2A *Geneva Rec.* 559 at 562. The Committee concluded: "There is therefore an important innovation involved which has become necessary as a result of the experience of the Second World War." *Id.*

193. 3 *I.C.R.C. Commentary* 58.

irregulars who were part of a larger military unit broken through the exigencies of combat will qualify. A single individual separated from his organized unit retains his status as a member of the organized body even though he is unable to rejoin any part of that body before he is captured.

(b) The Requirement of "Belonging to a Party to the Conflict"
The clearest feature of the requirement of "belonging" in article 4A(2) is that it does not mean subordination to state control because if it did, it would merely repeat the terms of article 4A(1) concerning irregulars which are part of regular armed forces. Article 4A(1) repeats the protection afforded under article 1 of the Hague Regulations for such irregulars including, for example, the Allied "commandos" of the Second World War. Their "belonging" to a state party to the conflict in this sense is clear.

The relationship of the irregular forces under article 4A(2) is more complicated. The *I.C.R.C. Commentary* states:

> It is essential that there should be a *de facto* relationship between the resistance organization and the party to international law which is in a state of war, but the existence of this relationship is sufficient. It may find expression merely by tacit agreement, if the operations are such as to indicate clearly for which side the resistance organization is fighting.[194]

The reference to "the party to international law" is to a subject of international law which has status as a state or an authority (public body), and this requirement of "belonging," meaning association, may be met by a loose relationship with either. An example of such an association is the French Forces of the Interior and their relationship with the Free French authority prior to July 15, 1944, at which time they came under the command of Allied regular armies under General Eisenhower.[195] They were protected by article

---

194. *Id.* at 57.
195. *Id.*

1 of the Hague Regulations as irregulars both while acting without state authorization and later when they were associated with the Allied armies. If the present POW Convention had been applicable, the French Forces of the Interior would have come under article 4A(2) until July 15, 1944 and after that time they would have come under 4A(1).

The term "a Party to the conflict," which is somewhat ambiguous standing alone, may be better understood by reference to the context in which it is used. It appears in other articles of the POW Convention in contexts in which, in order to effectuate the purposes of the Convention, it includes authorities such as the stated "organized resistance movements." The term "High Contracting Parties" which appears in articles 1 through 3 does not appear in article 4. It is used once in the common article 1 and twice in the common article 2 to refer to the state parties to the Convention. It is used in the same way at the beginning of the common article 3 concerning internal conflicts or civil wars. At the outset of that article, a different phrase, "Party to the conflict," is used to refer to all of the parties to the internal conflict. In addition to the legitimate government, this must necessarily include the revolutionaries whose military forces are typically organized as irregular groups. In some internal conflicts a revolutionary group may have a regular army structure, such as the Confederate States Army in the Civil War in the United States. In others this may not be the case. The last paragraph of article 3 uses "the Parties to the conflict" to refer to all such parties in a factual sense by providing that the application of the humanitarian provisions shall not affect their legal status. Since the legal status of states is usually not in dispute, this must refer to the status of revolutionary parties.

The next use of "a Party to the conflict" is in article 4A(1). Since this subsection deals with regular armed forces, the context which is thus provided indicates that the term here refers, at least as the norm, to state parties to the conflict. It refers to recognized state parties because subsection 4A(3) deals with regular forces of an unrecognized government or public authority. The term "a Party to the conflict" again appears in article 4A(2) in which the factual reference is to the irregular movements as parties to the conflict by linking them to operations "in or outside their own territory, even if this territory is occupied." This interpretation of the movement as a party is supported by the experience of the Second World War upon which article 4A(2) is based. Marshal Tito's Yugoslav partisan forces had allegiance to their own organized resistance movement which was a party to international law and to the international conflict.[196] They were not associated with any state-party to the conflict until their successes against the German Army made it militarily advantageous to the Allied Powers to develop a relationship with them. They not only rejected any suggestion of relationship with the Royal Government of Yugoslavia in exile, but were at the end of the war the creators of the contemporary Socialist Federal Republic of Yugoslavia.

Article 4A(3) of the POW Convention includes as privileged combatants:

> Members of regular armed forces who profess allegiance to a government or an authority not recognized by the Detaining Power.

This provision must be interpreted "in the light of the actual case which motivated its drafting," that of the regular armed forces of General de Gaulle "which were under the authority of the French National Liberation Committee."[197] After 1940, they continued the armed struggle against Germany contrary to the terms of the Vichy French–German Armistice agreement of that year. That armistice expressly provided that French nationals who continued to bear arms against the German forces would not be considered as privileged combatants who were entitled to the protection of the laws of war. The German Government, however, subsequently acknowledged the privileged status of these forces and regarded them as "fighting for England."[198] Even if General de Gaulle's forces did not "profess allegiance" to a government (they expressly opposed the Vichy French Government) the Free French constituted a public authority (not a

---

196. *Supra* note 167 at 54.

197. 3 *I.C.R.C. Commentary* 62.

198. *Id.* at 63.

government in exile), recognized by many states but not by Germany, to which they professed allegiance. An analagous situation today would entitle such combatants to the same privileged treatment as POWs as other regulars. Thus article 4A(3) requires a relationship between regular armed forces and a public body party to the conflict as an alternative to that with a state party set forth in article 4A(1). The relationship requirement for irregular forces set forth in article 4A(2) is clearly not intended to be more demanding than that for regulars in 4A(3).

At the 1949 Diplomatic Conference in Geneva, the views of those who wished to impose additional requirements upon irregulars were rejected.[199] The basic criteria for irregulars remained the same as that in article 9 of the Brussels Declaration and article 1 of the Hague Regulations of 1899 and 1907, neither of which required state authorization or subjection to orders from regular army headquarters. The original Russian Government's draft of article 9 at Brussels had provided that irregulars must be subject to orders from regular army headquarters, but this provision was widely opposed and omitted in the final text. The most recent edition of *Oppenheim's International Law* by Professor Lauterpacht provides a succinct summary of the change in legal status of irregular forces before and after the Franco-Prussian War of 1870:

> Very often the armed forces of belligerents consist throughout the war of their regular armies only; but it happens frequently that irregular forces take part. Of such irregular forces two different kinds are to be distinguished – first, such as are authorised by the belligerents; and secondly, such as are acting on their own initiative, and on their own account, without special authorisation. Formerly, it was a recognised rule of International Law that only the members of authorised irregular forces enjoy the privileges due to the members of the armed forces of

---

199. *Supra* note 190 at 562.

belligerents; . .... But according to Article 1 of the Hague Regulations this rule is now obsolete. Its place is taken by the rule that irregulars enjoy the privileges due to members of the armed forces of the belligerents, although they do not act under authorisation ... .[200]

Article 4A(2) increased the preexisting category of irregulars by specifically including "organized resistance movements" based on the experience of the Second World War. The interpretation of "a Party to the conflict" which is consistent with the Brussels and Hague criteria is that it makes a broad factual reference under which the organized resistance movement may be its own party to the conflict. This interpretation also makes the word "belonging" in the English text more accurate because organized resistance forces can clearly "belong" to their own movement which is a party to the conflict.[201] Such forces cannot "belong," in the sense of subordination and control, to a state-party to the conflict and remain under the protection of article 4A(2). If state control existed, the protection would be afforded by article 4A(1).

(c) The Requirement of Responsible Military Command
This provision and the ensuing three are the same traditional requirements of article 9 of the Brussels Declaration and article 1 of the Hague Regulations. The requirement limits privileged status to those irregulars who are a part of a belligerent group with a command structure which has responsibility for the actions of its members. It is not necessary that a commander be a regular army officer or be commissioned by a government. The U.S. Army Manual, *The Law of Land Warfare*, declares that "State recognition, however, is not essential and an organizaton may be formed spontaneously and elect its own officers."[202] The main

---

200. 2 *Oppenheim's International Law* 256–57 (7th ed., Lauterpacht, 1952).

201. The equally authoritative French text of art. 4A(2) uses the somewhat less specific word, "appartenant."

202. Field Manual 27–10, *The Law of Land Warfare*, p. 27, para. 64 (1956).

purpose for having a "responsible commander" is to provide for reasonable assurance of adherence by irregulars to the fundamental requirement of compliance with the laws of war. It is thought that a somewhat effective sanction exists by making the commander "responsible for his subordinates." Although there is no stated limitation upon the responsibility of the commander, the requirement should be interpreted so as to effectuate its major purpose. While the dividing line cannot be fixed in advance so as to cover all possible fact situations, some of the clearer ones can be identified. If subordinates attack noncombatant targets in a military operation, the commander is responsible. If a subordinate commits an isolated murder for his own personal objectives while not subject to the control of the commander, the latter is not responsible. Command must be exercised in the preparation and execution of military operations, but not at all times without exception.

In the post-Second World War war crimes trials, the defense of superior orders was available to subordinates in some situations. In general, it was not treated as a bar to the conviction of a subordinate for executing an illegal order, but, dependent upon all the circumstances, it was considered in mitigation of punishment.[203] It should be apparent that unless some effect is given to the defense of superior orders, each subordinate is invited to determine the legality of orders for himself with destructive consequences for the discipline which is an inseparable part of military command. There is no doubt that the commander who issues illegal orders is responsible for them.[204]

---

203. McDougal & Feliciano, *Law and Minimum World Public Order*, 690–99 (1961); Parks, "Command Responsibility for War Crimes," 62 *Mil. L. Rev.* 1 (1973).

204. *Trial of Kurt Meyer*, "The Abbaye Ardenne Case," 4 Rep. U.N. Comm. 97 (Can. Mil. Ct., Aurich, Germany, 1945); *Trial of Baba Masao*, 11 Rep. U.N. Comm. 56 (Austl. Mil. Ct., Rabaul, 1947); *Trial of Wilhelm Von Leeb*, "The German High Command Trial," 12 Rep. U.N. Comm. 1 (U.S. Mil. Trib., Nuremberg, 1948). The cited cases deal with regular army commanders but it is unlikely that a significantly different standard would be applied to irregular commanders.

(d) The Requirement of a Fixed Distinctive Sign

Article 4A(2) (b) prescribes "having a fixed distinctive sign recognizable at a distance." This distinctive sign requirement for the irregular is analagous to the wearing of a uniform by a regular. The requirement is designed to allow privileged status to those combatants who are distinguishable in appearance from the civilian population. The sign must nominally be "fixed," but it is widely agreed that the requirement is met by an armband, an insignia, or, for example, a distinctive headgear or coat.[205] The requirement that the sign be "recognizable at a distance" is rather vague since there is no specification of such obvious questions as to what distance, by whom, and in what circumstances. The distinctive sign of irregulars, like the uniform of regulars, need only be worn during military operations. Such operations should be reasonably construed as including deployments which are preliminary to actual combat.

(e) The Requirement of Open Arms

The purpose of the requirement of "carrying arms openly," like the requirement of a distinctive sign, is to prevent irregulars, at the risk of forfeiting their privileged status as prisoners of war upon capture, perfidiously misleading the enemy by concealing their own identity.[206] The conditions of "open arms" and "distinctive sign" emphasize the necessity that irregulars distinguish themselves as combatants during their operations against the enemy. The *I.C.R.C. Commentary* states that the requirements that arms be carried "openly" means that the "enemy must be able to recognize partisans as combatants in the same way as regular armed forces, whatever their weapons."[207] Similarly, it cannot be interpreted to mean that irregulars are under an obligation to carry their arms more openly than do regular soldiers.[208] The open arms requirement, like that of the distinctive sign, is only applicable during military operations.

---

205. *Supra* note 202.

206. *Supra* note 200 at 430.

207. 3 *I.C.R.C. Commentary* 61.

208. *Id*.

(f) *The Requirement of Compliance with the Laws and Customs of War*

(1) Analysis of the Requirement

This requirement is an expression of the fundamental concept which constitutes the basis for the whole body of the law of armed conflict. Unless hostilities "are to degenerate into a savage contest of physical forces freed from all restraints," the laws and customs of war must continue to be observed in all relevant circumstances.[209] This requirement prescribes that irregulars, like regulars, are bound to conform in the conduct of their operations to the recognized standards of the international humanitarian law.

While it is clear that the present requirement includes each of the preceding criteria of article 4A(2), its full ambit is not defined with precision. The *I.C.R.C. Commentary* recognizes that "the concept of the laws and customs of war is rather vague and subject to variations as the forms of war evolve."[210] In spite of the problem of "vagueness," however, there exist at least some criteria for judging the lawfulness of the particular actions of irregular combatants and for holding the perpetrators of illegitimate acts of warfare criminally responsible for their behavior. The U.S. Army, *Law of Land Warfare*, provides a representative description of such conduct considered violative of the laws and customs of war by especially warning against:

> employment of treachery, denial of quarter, maltreatment of prisoners of war, wounded and dead, improper conduct toward flags of truce, pillage, and unnecessary violence and destruction.[211]

These acts would, of course, be equally violative of law if committed by regular forces. In either case they would be punishable as war crimes as opposed to common crimes

---

209. *Supra* note 200 at 218.

210. *Supra* note 207.

211. *Supra* note 202 at p. 28, para. 64.

under municipal criminal law.

A further explanation of the basic character of the condition of adhering to the laws and customs of war is provided in the *I.C.R.C. Commentary:*

> Partisans [irregulars] are . . . required to respect the Geneva Conventions *to the fullest extent possible.* In particular, they must conform to international agreements as those which prohibit the use of certain weapons (gas). In all their operations, they must be guided by the moral criteria which, in the absence of written provisions, must direct the conscience of man; in launching attacks, they must not cause violence and suffering disproportionate to the military result which they may reasonably hope to achieve. They may not attack civilians or disarmed persons and must, in all their operations, respect the principles of honour and loyalty *as they expect their enemies to do.*[212]

The last italicized clause of the statement implies the consequences of a belligerent state's persistent and demonstrable disregard of the rules of international law. As a practical matter in obtaining enforcement of the laws and customs of war by resistance movements "operating in or outside their own territory," observance of the doctrines by state-parties to the conflict is important in establishing conditions for mutuality and reciprocity which promote similar observance by irregulars. In addition, the state-parties to the 1949 Geneva Conventions have unilateral obligations, not contingent upon mutuality, including the common article 1 requirement "to respect and to ensure respect" for the Conventions. Since resistance movements were not, as such, represented at Geneva in 1949, it is fatuous to expect them to adhere to the laws and customs of war in situations where there are violations by the states which wrote and adopted the rules.

---

212. *Supra* note 207. (Emphasis added.)

The humanitarian treatment of prisoners of war in contemporary conflict situations is an appropriate subject for concern. It is clear that the state-parties to the 1949 POW Convention are bound to carry out all of the very detailed administrative arrangements concerning the protection and care of POWs which appear in the 143 articles of the Convention. It would require a considerable departure from reality to expect irregular forces to meet the same requirements in the treatment of POWs in their hands. A provision of the draft POW Convention prepared by the I.C.R.C. stated that irregulars, in addition to the four criteria first formulated in the Brussels Declaration, must also "treat nationals of the Occupying Power who fall into their hands in accordance with the provisions of the present Convention."[213] This provision was deleted by the Diplomatic Conference because of an unwillingness to impose additional criteria beyond the four traditional ones. The outcome is a recognition of the realities with which irregular forces and their POWs are confronted. One should not, however, reach the opposite conclusion and believe that prisoners are at the mercy of irregular forces. At the minimum, fundamental humanitarian treatment must be accorded to prisoners in the hands of irregulars.

It is necessary to consider briefly the applicability of each of the six criteria of article 4A(2) to the group and to its individual members. Each of the six criteria is imposed upon the irregular group as an entity. According to the widely accepted view, if the group does not meet the first three criteria (organization; association with a factual party to the conflict, either a state or a public body; and military command), the individual member cannot qualify for privileged status as a POW.[214] The last three criteria (distinctive sign, open arms, and adhering to the laws and customs) must be met by most of the members of the group to entitle the individual member to privileged status.[215] The

---

213. Draft art. 3(6) (b). 1 *Geneva Rec.* 73, 74.

214. *Supra* note 167 at 62.

215. See the text accompanying *infra* note 235.

individual may not be denied POW status except by the decision of a properly qualified court which meets the criteria of the POW Convention.[216] Because of both the need to bring irregulars within the legal system and the humanitarian purpose of the applicable law, state officials may not lightly reach the conclusion that most of the members of an irregular group do not comply with the last three criteria.

(2) Situations Where Reprisals Are Applicable

The Geneva Conventions for the Protection of War Victims of 1949 have prohibited all reprisals against POWs, civilians, and militarily ineffective combatants, that is, those who are wounded, sick, or shipwrecked.[217] This leaves reprisals still applicable to effective combatant forces. The U.S. Army, *Law of Land Warfare*, provides the following definition:

> Reprisals are acts of retaliation in the form of conduct which would otherwise be unlawful, resorted to by one belligerent against enemy personnel or property for acts of warfare committed by the other belligerent in violation of the law of war, for the purpose of enforcing future compliance with the recognized rules of civilized warfare.[218]

Reprisals may be lawfully invoked, *inter alia*, where irregular or regular armed forces are responding to prior violations of the laws and customs of war by the opposing belligerent.[219]

2. APPLICATION OF THE LAW CONCERNING POWS TO THE FACT SITUATION IN LEBANON

(a) Denial of POW Status

On July 18, 1982 the Government of Israel Ministry of Foreign

---

216. Art. 5(2).

217. Conv. I: art. 46; Conv. II: art. 47; Conv. III: art. 13(3); Conv. IV: art. 33(3). The four Conventions are cited fully in *supra* notes 180–82.

218. *Supra* note 202 at p. 177, para. 497(a). The same source in para. 497(b) stresses that reprisals should not be resorted to in a hasty and ill-considered manner. See, F. Kalshoven, *Belligerent Reprisals, passim* (1971).

219. *Re Christiansen*, [1948] An. Dig. Int'l L. Cases 412 at 413 (Netherlands Special Court, War Criminals, 1948).

Affairs conducted a briefing and distributed a statement entitled "The Israeli Operation in Lebanon: Legal Aspects." It stated, *inter alia:*

> From the outset of the operation, Israel declared to the International Committee of the Red Cross, that it will apply, as appropriate, the four Geneva Conventions. Accordingly, both during and since the hostilities, Israel has duly applied those conventions.[220]

Another portion of the statement involved the according of prisoner of war status. It stated that Syrian Army regulars would be given such status.[221] No mention was made of Lebanese Army regulars or Lebanese militias. The statement also made no specific mention of Palestinian regular forces such as those comprising the Palestine Liberation Army.[222] It denies POW status to all Palestinian forces by providing:

> The PLO and its associated terror groups do not fall within any of the categories formulated in the Convention regarding persons entitled to the status of prisoners-of-war. They are not "regular armed forces" and do not constitute an "organized resistance movement belonging to a party to the conflict" (Article 4A).[223]

---

220. Israel Ministry of Foreign Affairs, Information Division, Briefing No. 342 at p. 4.

221. *Id*.

222. The Palestine Liberation Army, which consists of regular troops, operates under the authority of the PLO Executive Committee. See the organization chart in H. Sharabi, *Palestine Guerrillas: Their Credibility and Effectiveness* 45 (Georgetown, 1970).

223. *Supra* note 220. This characterization is not consistent, however, with some Israeli statements. For example:

> Sharon [Israeli Defense Minister] said military intelligence experts were "astounded" to discover the extent of the P.L.O. conventional military apparatus in eastern Lebanon. He said that in the territory covered by the Israeli Army, the Palestinians had 15,000 to 20,000 regular troops and 40,000 irregulars.

Wash. Post, June 12, 1982, p. A1, col. 6, cont. p. A20, cols. 5–6, at col. 6. The former chief of military intelligence, Aharon Yariv, stated that "Fatah had units organized in battalions and brigades." *Jerusalem Post*, Int'l Ed., Oct. 3–9, 1982, p. 15, cols. 1–5, at col. 1.

Reports in the press confirm this decision of the Government of Israel not to accord the privileged status to captured Palestinian combatants. For example, an article by William Claiborne printed in the *Washington Post* as early as June 13, 1982 quoted an Israeli Army command source as stating: "They are terrorists. We don't refer to them as prisoners-of-war."[224] The same source then was stated to have listed the four traditional Brussels–Hague–Geneva criteria applicable to irregulars entitled to POW status, and the Claiborne article continued:

> While some of the criteria may be arguable, a military source said, the guerrillas clearly have not conducted their operations in accordance with the laws and customs of war.[225]

Also, according to the same article:

> Although Army officials declined to acknowledge it, refusal to grant internationally recognized prisoner-of-war status to the guerrillas apparently is the result of a political decision stemming from a reluctance of Israeli officials to recognize the Palestine Liberation Organization as a legitimate armed force.[226]

Another indication of the Government of Israel's juridical position was reported in an article by James Feron in the *New York Times* of August 26, 1982.[227] This article states that in the negotiations which led to the PLO departure from Beirut, Israel demanded that the PLO release Israeli POWs which it was holding,[228] but there was no comparable agreement requiring the release of Palestinian combatants

---

224. *Wash. Post*, June 13, 1982, p. A25, cols. 1–3, at col. 1.

225. *Id.* at col. 3.

226. *Id.* at cols. 2–3.

227. *New York Times*, Aug. 26, 1982, p. A1, col. 1, cont. p. A14, cols. 1–6.

228. *Id.* at p. A14, col. 4.

captured by the Israeli Army.[229] The reason given for this by an Israeli Government official was that Israel had rejected the concept of reciprocity because the Palestinians were holding soldiers while the Israelis were holding civilians.[230] The following analysis was attributed by Mr. Feron to Mr. Alan Baker, the Assistant Legal Adviser of the Israeli Foreign Ministry:

> He said that the Syrian soldiers in west Beirut, roughly a third of those trapped there in the fighting, "are entitled to the privileges of prisoners of war, but not the terrorists."[231]

Mr. Feron explained that "Israelis use the word 'terrorists' to refer to the Palestinian guerrillas."[232] The analysis then continued:

> Mr. Baker said that the third Geneva Convention did, in fact, have a category "concerning militias, but they have to belong to a party to the conflict and follow four rules: carry arms openly, operate under a fixed command, wear uniforms and follow the rules and customs of war."
>
> "The PLO," he said, "does not fulfill those requirements, especially following the laws and customs of war." He cited "hijacking, taking actions against civilians and avoiding military activities" as examples.[233]

---

229. *Id.* These statements are consistent with the ultimate agreement entitled, "Plan for the Departure from Lebanon of the PLO Leadership, Offices, and Combatants in Beirut", art. 21 (Aug. 19, 1982). On 20 August President Reagan announced the assent of Lebanon, The United States, France, Italy, Israel and the PLO to this agreement. The agreement and a portion of its context is in U.S. Dept. State, Bureau of Public Affairs, *Lebanon: Plan for the PLO Evacuation From West Beirut* (Current Policy Pub. No. 415, August 1982).

230. *Supra* note 227 at p. A14, col. 4.

231. *Id.*

232. *Id.*

233. *Id.* Mr. Baker's words quoted in the first paragraph indicate confusion concerning military command and "fixed distinctive sign" (not a uniform).

While in the views attributed above to an Israeli military source, "some of the criteria may be arguable," the principal Israeli claim is that the Palestinian armed forces (principally irregulars) have not conducted "their operations in accordance with the laws and customs of war."[234] Such a claim must be appraised under the established law which is stated succinctly in *The Law of Land Warfare*:

> This condition [compliance with law] is fulfilled if most of the members of the body observe the laws and customs of war, notwithstanding the fact that the individual member concerned may have committed a war crime.[235]

Although in the past there have been incidents involving a small number of PLO combatants, as well as dissident Palestinian groups, in clear violation of the laws and customs of war including attacking civilians and hijacking aircraft, no credible evidence has shown that the majority of the thousands of Palestinian combatants have engaged in such conduct. If the Israeli argument that the actions of a small minority disentitles the majority to POW status were accepted, the consistent massive and continuing Israel Defense Force violations of the laws and customs of war in Lebanon as well as in actions against Palestinians in the other occupied territories would likewise disentitle every captured Israeli soldier to POW status.[236] The PLO, nevertheless, has accorded this privileged status to Israelis captured in Lebanon.[237]

No Israeli statement of intention concerning denial of POW status to Lebanese irregulars fighting on the same side as the Palestinian irregulars is known to exist. However, the

---

234. *Supra* note 224, p. A25, at col. 3.

235. *Supra* note 202, at p. 28, para. 64.

236. Further examples of the evidence concerning Israeli violations are considered in the remainder of this study.

237. An article by Mr. Loren Jenkins headlined, "PLO Demands Israel Supply List of its Prisoners" reported eight Israeli POWs being held by the PLO. *Wash. Post*, Sept. 9, 1982, p. A29, cols. 2–5. Thus far there has been no list of Palestinian POWs supplied to the PLO.

media reports of treatment accorded to all irregulars by Israel does not suggest any distinction between Lebanese and Palestinians.[238] Lebanese irregulars are, of course, entitled to POW status upon the same criteria applicable to other irregulars under article 4A(2).

Article 4A(6) of the POW Convention expressly provides POW status for civilians "who on the approach of the enemy spontaneously take up arms to resist the invading forces" and this fits the situation of those civilians, whether Lebanese or Palestinian, who attempted to resist the Israeli invasion of Lebanon. The only requirements applicable to them are that "they carry arms openly and respect the laws and customs of war." It is no more necessary for them to be under the direction and control of a state party to the conflict than it is for regulars under article 4A(3) or for irregulars under 4A(2).

The POW Convention provides specifically for the procedure to be followed concerning persons whose status is in doubt. Its article 5(2) states:

> Should any doubt arise as to whether persons, having committed a belligerent act and having fallen into the hands of the enemy, belong to any of the categories enumerated in Article 4, such persons shall enjoy the protection of the present Convention until such time as their status has been determined by a competent tribunal.

In the draft wording prepared by the International Committee of the Red Cross, the last four words read "by some responsible authority."[239] This wording was thought to be subject to abuse and therefore the 1949 Diplomatic Conference in Geneva substituted the requirement of "a competent tribunal."

Article 84(2) provides:

> In no circumstances whatever shall a prisoner of war be tried in a court of any kind which does

---

238. *E.g., Wash. Post,* July 28, 1982, p. A1, cols. 2–4 cont. p. A16, cols. 3–5.

239. Draft art. 4(2), 1 *Geneva Rec.* 73 at 74.

not offer the essential guarantees of independence and impartiality as generally recognized, and, in particular, the procedure of which does not afford the accused the right and means of defence provided for in article 105.

A report by Edward Cody from "Sidon, Israeli-Occupied Lebanon" printed in the *Washington Post* on June 22, 1982 states:

Israeli soldiers scouring the occupied Lebanese countryside have rounded up between 5,000 and 6,000 Palestinians and are holding them in internment camps in Lebanon and Israel.[240]

* * *

Eventually some may be brought to trial under an Israeli law that allows the government to prosecute PLO members – even if they joined outside Israel – as members of a hostile organization. Justice Minister Moshe Nissim has appointed two special tribunals to weigh the question.[241]

If these individuals are entitled to POW status, the conduct of such trials would be in violation of the requirements of the POW Convention. If they are civilians, any trial of them must conform to the requirements of the Civilians Convention and trial under such a statute would not do so.

In summary, the Government of Israel's denial of POW status to those entitled to it during the invasion of Lebanon is a flagrant violation of the Hague Regulations applicable in the Second World War, which is still recognized treaty law and which has become binding customary law. In the trial of the major German defendants before the International Military Tribunal at Nuremberg and in the subsequent war crimes trials, Germans were convicted of war crimes because of the denial of POW status to partisans (irregulars) who

---

240. *Wash. Post*, June 22, 1982, p. A14, cols. 1–4, at col. 1.

241. *Id.* at col. 4.

were entitled to it under article 1 of the Hague Regulations of 1907.[242] Under the criteria of the Hague Regulations which were applied in those cases, Israeli defendants would be equally guilty of war crimes, and today convictions would be even more certain because irregular combatants now enjoy increased protection as a result of the amplified wording of article 4A(2) of the 1949 Geneva POW Convention.[243]

(b) Violation of the Required Standard of Treatment of POWs and Civilian Detainees

Since the Government of Israel has made no distinction between its treatment of POWs and civilian detainees, the facts of both situations must be treated together. According to the Red Cross *Commentary* on the Civilians Convention, whatever the category of the detained persons:

> Every person in enemy hands must have some status under international law: he is either a prisoner of war and as such, covered by the Third Convention, a civilian covered by the Fourth Convention, or again, a member of the medical personnel of the armed forces who is covered by the First Convention. *There is no* intermediate status; nobody in enemy hands can be outside the law.[244]

Articles 12 to 15 of the POW Convention provide the basic criteria which must be followed in the protection of POWs.

---

242. *E.g.*, the conviction of Field Marshal Keitel. 1 I.M.T. 171 at 289–91; *Trial of Carl Bauer*, 8 Rep. U.N. Comm. 15 (Permanent Mil. Tribunal, Dijon, 1945).

243. In *Military Prosecutor v. Kassem*, 42 Int'l L. Rep. 470 (Israeli Military Court, Ramallah, 1969), Palestinian irregulars were denied POW status and convicted under Israeli municipal law. The case is criticized in *supra* note 167 at 71–72 and by Professor Georg Schwarzenberger in "Human Rights and Guerrilla Warfare," 1 *Israel Y.B. Human Rts.* 246, 249–50 (1951) who points out that the Israeli court did not adhere to the interpretive principle requiring humanitarian conventions to be liberally interpreted to achieve their protective purposes.

244. 4 *I.C.R.C. Commentary* 51. The same source points out that irregulars who do not meet the criteria of art. 4A(2) of the POW Convention are protected persons under the Civilians Convention. *Id.* at 50.

Article 12 provides, *inter alia*, that POWs are in the care of the capturing government and states that, "Irrespective of the individual responsiblities that may exist, the Detaining Power is responsible for the treatment given them."[245] Article 13 expressly prohibits reprisals against POWs and provides, *inter alia*:

> Prisoners of war must at all times be humanely treated. Any unlawful act or omission by the Detaining Power causing death or seriously endangering the health of a prisoner of war in its custody is prohibited and will be regarded as a serious breach of the present Convention.[246]

Article 14 requires respect in all circumstances for the persons and the honor of prisoners and includes special protection for women. Article 15 provides for necessary medical attention and this means, at the least, the standard of medical care usually provided in the captor's armed forces. These standards apply to the protection of POWs in the hands of irregulars as well as regular forces, as a part of the obligation of the parties to the conflict to obey the laws and customs of war. Articles 27 through 34 of the Civilians Convention provide analagous protections for civilians.

Jonathan C. Randal stated in an article in the *Washington Post* on July 28, 1982:

> For more than a month after Israel began taking prisoners in Lebanon, it declined to authorize customary prison visits by the International Committee of the Red Cross, causing the ICRC to set aside its traditional discretion and to drop public hints indicating its displeasure. The Israelis later yielded and the visits were allowed.[247]

It was pointed out that the I.C.R.C. representative was permitted into Ansar prison camp beginning on July 18 and

---

245. Art. 12(1).

246. Art. 13(1).

247. *Supra* note 238 at p. A1, col. 4.

that on July 22, "for the first time in its association with the Arab–Israeli conflict stretching back to the late 1940s," the I.C.R.C. took the initiative to interrupt the visits.[248] In keeping with the tradition of public discretion, no reason was stated for the interruption. The visits were resumed on July 26 after a more satisfactory arrangement had apparently been made.[249]

Mr. William Claiborne reported in the *Washington Post* on June 13, 1982 that: "Israeli Army trucks filled with handcuffed and blindfolded prisoners have been seen leaving Lebanon for undisclosed sites in Israel."[250] Numerous other press reports stated the same essential facts.[251] There have been no press reports concerning treatment accorded to the prisoners upon their arrival at the "undisclosed sites in Israel," but the facts that are known from the accounts of a few individuals who have been released show that the treatment falls far below the required standard.

Dr. Chris Giannou, a Canadian surgeon serving with the Palestine Red Crescent Society (PRCS) in Lebanon, provided some of the relevant facts in testimony presented to the Subcommittee on Europe and the Middle East of the U.S.

---

248. *Id*. at p. A16, cols. 3–4. The grim conditions in Ansar, including reports of beatings and torture, and hooded informers identifying suspects in Sidon are reported by Ms. Trudy Rubin under the heading, "'What will happen to the detainees is a political question,' Israelis say." *Christian Sci. Monitor*, Aug. 5, 1982, p. 12, cols. 1–4, cont. p. 13, col. 1. One Israeli official was quoted concerning the prisoners: "They are 100 per cent terrorists." *Id*. at p. 12, col. 1.

249. *Supra* note 238 at p. A16, col. 4.

250. *Supra* note 224 at p. A25, col. 3.

251. *E.g.*, *New York Times*, Aug. 27, 1982, p. A14, cols. 4–6, at col. 5; *The Guardian* (London), Sept. 7, 1982, p. 6, col. 1; *Christian Sci. Monitor*, Aug. 5, 1982, p. 12, cols. 1–4 at col. 3:

> Israel permits no access to Palestinians detained in Israel. (United Nations peacekeeping forces stationed near Tyre report still seeing busloads of blindfolded prisoners moving south to Israel.)

House of Representatives Committee on Foreign Affairs on July 13, 1982.[252] He was serving as Medical Director of the Nabatieh Hospital and was temporarily working in Sidon, Lebanon at the time of the Israeli invasion. He testified, *inter alia*, that the entire male population of Sidon "which had crossed Israeli lines to get out of the zone of hostilities" was paraded by the Israeli Army past hooded informers, and those who were denounced had a marking placed on their back.[253] In this way between 4,000 and 5,000 men were arrested including Dr. Giannou, "two Norwegian colleagues, and the entire male medical staff of the PRCS in Sidon."[254] Dr. Giannou was detained in Sidon from June 13 to June 16 and then, until his release on June 20, he was detained in the Megiddo (Armageddon) Prison in the north of Israel. He stated that in Sidon 500 to 600 prisoners were confined at one time in a convent schoolyard under difficult conditions including hands being bound, stifling heat, and food and water in short supply. He saw and heard "savage and indiscriminate beatings of the prisoners by the forty Israeli guards";[255] and he stated that a prisoner who called out for water would be subject to particular physical violence. Dr. Giannou pointed out that he and two other Europeans (the Norwegian members of the PRCS medical facility) were not beaten but that the "darker-skinned Arabs, Africans, and Asians" were beaten most severely.[256] This is a flagrant

---

252. *United States Policy Toward Lebanon – Relief and Rehabilitation Assistance,* Hearings Before the Committee on Foreign Affairs and the Subcommittee on Europe and the Middle East, 97th Cong., 2nd Sess. 106–13 (1982).

Dr. Giannou also testified before the "International Commission to Enquire into Reported Violations of International Law by Israel During its Invasion of the Lebanon" chaired by Sean MacBride and composed of Professor Richard Falk, Dean Kader Asmal, Dr. Brian Bercusson, Professor Geraud de la Pradelle, and Professor Stefan Wild. *Israel in Lebanon: The Report of the International Commission,* 239–41 (London, 1983) (hereafter cited as *MacBride Comm.*).

253. House Foreign Affairs Hearings, *supra* note 252 at 110.

254. *Id.*

255. *Id.* at 111.

256. *Id.* at 112.

violation of article 16 of the POW Convention which is a reaction to the discriminatory practices of the Nazis. It prohibits adverse distinctions "based on race, nationality, religious beliefs or political opinions, or any other distinction founded on similar criteria." He also recounts being a witness to prisoners being beaten to death.[257] Some of these events took place in the presence of the Israeli military governor of Sidon, Colonel Arnon Amozer, and other Israeli Army officers.[258] He indicated that some Israeli guards did attempt to stop the beatings but were unsuccessful.

Dr. Giannou's testimony was corroborated by his two Norwegian colleagues who worked with the PRCS, Dr. Steinar Berge and Mr. Oyind Moller. They were with Dr. Giannou in the schoolyard in Sidon and a report of their experiences, translated by the Norwegian Foreign Ministry, was distributed by them during their visit to the United States. The Canadian and Norwegian Embassies in Washington refuted the claim made by the Israeli Embassy that their respective nationals were held because they were connected with European terrorist organizations.[259]

Articles 129 and 130 of the POW Convention are similar to the corresponding articles concerning grave breaches of the Civilians Convention.[260] Article 129 provides that the parties to the Convention agree to enact necessary domestic legislation "to provide effective penal sanctions for persons

---

257. *Id.*

258. *Id.*

259. The official statement of the Norwegian Embassy issued to the press on July 21, 1982, read:

> The Royal Norwegian Embassy hereby confirms that Dr. Steinar Berge and Mr. Oyind Moller were working as *bona fide* health workers in full agreement with the Lebanese Government at the time when they were arrested by Israeli officials. No explanation for their detention has been given by Israeli authorities. The Norwegian Government categorically rejects the accusations made by the Israeli Embassy in Washington, D.C. to the effect that the two Norwegian citizens should have connections to European terrorist organizations.

The analagous Canadian statement appears in House Foreign Affairs Hearings, *supra* note 252, at 321.

260. Arts. 146 and 147 of the Civilians Convention.

committing, or ordering to be committed, any of the grave breaches of the present convention defined in the following Article."[261] It also provides that the parties are obligated to search for and to bring to trial persons suspected of committing such grave breaches.[262] Article 130 provides in full:

Grave breaches to which the preceding Article relates shall be those involving any of the following acts, if committed against persons or property protected by the Convention: wilful killing, torture or inhuman treatment including biological experiments, wilfully causing great suffering or serious injury to body or health, compelling a prisoner of war to serve in the forces of the hostile Power, or wilfully depriving a prisoner of war of the rights of fair and regular trial prescribed in this Convention.

The facts recounted by Dr. Giannou, Dr. Berge, and Mr. Moller indicate that officers and other members of the Israeli armed forces have committed the grave breaches specified in article 130 by carrying out acts, *inter alia*, of "wilful killing, torture, or inhuman treatment." These acts constitute war crimes when committed against those entitled to POW status and crimes against humanity when committed against civilian persons.[263] In addition to the individual responsibility of those persons carrying out the acts and those who ordered them, the Government of Israel is itself responsible under general principles of international law[264] as well as under article 131 of the POW Convention and article 148 of the Civilians Convention. The "grave breaches" articles of the Conventions are designed to deter inhumane treatment of the kind that has taken place in Lebanon and Israel. If

---

261. Art. 146(1).

262. Art. 146(2).

263. *Judgment*, 1 I.M.T. 171 at 226–38.

264. *E.g.*, I. Brownlie, *Principles of Public International Law*, *passim* and Chap. 18 entitled, "The Responsibility of States" (1966).

deterrence is not successful, the secondary purpose is to provide punishment for those who are responsible.

C. THE GENEVA CONVENTIONS CONCERNING THE PROTECTION OF WOUNDED AND SICK COMBATANTS AND OF CIVILIAN PERSONS AND OBJECTS

1. THE SCOPE OF PROTECTIONS UNDER THE CONVENTIONS

The conflict situation in Lebanon has involved matters which come under the protections of both the Geneva Convention for the Amelioration of the Condition of the Wounded and Sick in Armed Forces in the Field (Convention I, known as the "Land Warfare Convention")[265] and the Convention Relative to the Protection of Civilian Persons in Time of War (Convention IV, known as the "Civilians Convention")[266] of August 12, 1949. In particular, the protections afforded to wounded and sick combatants and civilians and to the medical personnel and facilities involved in their care must be considered together because both types of wounded and sick have been treated without distinction in the limited medical facilities which were available. The special protections for civilian persons and civilian objects, of course, come under the law of the Civilians Convention.

It is of particular significance that the common article 2 of all four Geneva Conventions of 1949 was designed to make each Convention applicable broadly to international conflict situations. The first paragraph in article 2 provides in part:

> [T]he present Convention shall apply to all cases of declared war or of any other armed conflict which may arise between two or more of the High Contracting Parties, even if the state of war is not recognized by one of them.

This new provision goes beyond the historically well-established situation of "all cases of declared war" and encompasses "any other armed conflict" which may arise

---

265. 75 U.N.T.S. 31; Schindler & Toman, *supra* note 171, at 305.

266. 75 U.N.T.S. 287; Schindler & Toman, *supra* note 171, at 427.

between the parties "even if the state of war is not recognized by one of them." The change brought about by this carefully considered provision is that these Conventions apply to the facts of international armed conflict and are in no way dependent on the existence of a supposed technical "state of war."

The second paragraph of article 2 prescribes:

> The Convention shall also apply to all cases of partial or total occupation of the territory of a High Contracting Party, even if the said occupation meets with no armed resistance.

Thus the former requirement of a militarily effective occupation found in Hague Conventions II (1899)[267] and IV (1907)[268] as a prerequisite to the application of the legal protections has been eliminated and this results in more comprehensive application of each of the Conventions. There is no longer a distinction between the invasion phase and the establishment of a belligerent occupation regime as there was under the Hague law. The *I.C.R.C. Commentary* on the Civilians Convention states:

> Even a patrol which penetrated into enemy territory without any intention of staying there must respect the Convention in its dealings with the civilians it meets.[269]

One of the principal purposes of the humanitarian law is to protect noncombatants (civilians) as well as disabled combatants from the more destructive consequences of armed conflict. Civilians are usually defined as individuals who are not members of the armed forces and who do not participate in military operations. Civilians who need protection in international conflict situations fall into two categories: those who are living in territory which, while not under the control of an enemy, is subject to attack by an

---

267. *Supra* note 174.

268. *Supra* note 175.

269. 4 *I.C.R.C. Commentary* 60.

enemy state, and those who are living under belligerent occupation. The Civilians Convention of 1949 affords protections to both categories.

The distinction between the civilian population and combatants which began with Grotius and was reflected in Lieber's Code was further advanced in the unratified Brussels Declaration.[270] Provisions of Hague Conventions II (1899) and IV (1907), like the Brussels Declaration, contain the prohibition against forcing the inhabitants of occupied territory to take any part in military operations against their own country or to swear allegiance to the hostile power, as well as the provisions concerning the protection of family honor and rights, lives and property, and religious convictions and practices. They also have provisions forbidding pillage and collective penalties. The Geneva Civilians Convention of 1949 sets forth much more detailed provisions for the protection of noncombatants.

The Geneva Convention for the Amelioration of the Condition of the Wounded in Armies in the Field of 22 August 1864[271] was the first multilateral treaty which provided protection for wounded military personnel as well as for military hospitals and their personnel. Later Geneva Conventions of 6 July 1906 and 27 July 1929[272] provided more detailed rules. The presently effective standards for the protection of medical facilities and personnel for combatants are in the Geneva Land Warfare Convention of 1949. Article 12(1) of this Convention prescribes comprehensive protection for wounded and sick military personnel who must "be protected and respected in all circumstances." Article 13 states: "The present Convention shall apply to the wounded and sick belonging to the following categories" and it then sets forth in identical words the six sub-divisions of article 4A of the POW Convention. The consequence is that Conven-

---

270. Schindler & Toman, *supra* note 171, at 25.

271. *Id.* at 213.

272. Both of these Conventions are entitled "Convention for the Amelioration of the Condition of the Wounded and Sick in Armies in the Field." The 1906 Convention is in *id.* at 213; the 1929 Convention is in *id.* at 257.

tion I applies, *inter alia*, to the wounded and sick of regular armed forces of both recognized government (subdivision 1) and unrecognized government or authority (subdivision 3) parties to the conflict and to irregular armed forces including those of an organized resistance movement which is a party to the conflict (subdivision 2), and to wounded and sick inhabitants of a non-occupied territory who, "on the approach of the enemy, spontaneously take up arms to resist the invading forces" (subdivision 6).

2. PROTECTION OF WOUNDED AND SICK COMBATANTS AND OF CIVILIANS AND MEDICAL PERSONNEL AND FACILITIES
   Article 19(1) of Convention I provides:

> Fixed establishments and mobile medical units of the Medical Service may in no circumstances be attacked, but shall at all times be respected and protected by the Parties to the conflict. Should they fall into the hands of the adverse Party, their personnel shall be free to pursue their duties, as long as the capturing Power has not itself ensured the necessary care of the wounded and sick found in such establishments and units.

Article 24 restates the principle that military medical personnel (as well as chaplains) "shall be respected and protected in all circumstances." There are correlative provisions for the protection of wounded and sick civilians and for their medical facilities and personnel which are found in articles 13 through 26 of Convention IV. Its article 13 specifically states the breadth of coverage of these articles to be "the whole of the populations of the countries in conflict." Article 20(1) provides:

> Persons regularly and solely engaged in the operation and administration of the civilian hospitals including the personnel engaged in the search for, removal and transporting of and caring for wounded and sick civilians, the infirm and maternity cases, shall be respected and protected.

Since Palestine Red Crescent Society (PRCS) facilities in

Lebanon were used to care for both combatants and civilians, they were protected under both the Land Warfare and the Civilians Conventions. PRCS medical personnel are protected by article 24 of the Land Warfare Convention if they are regarded as military medical personnel and by article 20(1) of the Civilians Convention if they are classified as civilian medical personnel. As medical personnel, they must come under the protection of one of these two Conventions.

Dr. Giannou, who has been quoted previously, testified:

> I have been a witness to the entire male staff of the PRCS medical team in Sidon and Nabatieh being taken into custody, prevented from continuing their medical duties and being treated as ordinary prisoners without any respect to their person. The PRCS, once one of the main institutions for medical services in South Lebanon with 3 hospitals, numerous out-patient clinics and a center for mentally retarded children, and occupational rehabilitation . . . no longer exists there.[273]

In the same testimony, specific reference was made to the treatment of PRCS medical personnel:

> One Palestinian, Dr. Nabil, was at one point hung by his hands from a tree and beaten. An Iraqi surgeon, Dr. Mohammed Ibrahim was beaten by several guards viciously, and left to lie in the sun with his face buried in the sand. Other surgeons and doctors were also beaten: Dr. Ahmed Soubra, a Lebanese; Drs. Saifeddin, Mohammad Iman and Shafiq El-Islam, Bangladeshi nationals.[274]

The report of a French commission of lawyers[275] who

---

273. House Foreign Affairs Hearings, *supra* note 252, at 109–10.

274. *Id.* at 111–12.

275. Report on the mission carried out in Israel 18–25 July 1982 at the request of the Center for Information on the Status of Palestinian and Lebanese Prisoners, Displaced and Missing Persons, Paris, France. The mission consisted of Dr. Geraud de la Pradelle (Professor of Law, Univ. of Paris) and four others. [Translation from the French by Ms. Anne Richardson, law student at George Washington University.]

went to Lebanon to investigate the situation contained this statement, among others, about medical personnel:

> The Commission has been told that the Israeli Army, at Tyre and Sidon, broke into banks, confiscated account records and tracked down individuals who had been paid salaries from the PLO accounts. This applied particularly to nurses and workers employed in Palestinian hospitals. According to several witnesses, these interrogations were particularly brutal.[276]

The immunity of both civilian and military hospitals from direct attack is a specific application of the prohibition of direct attack on noncombatants which is firmly established in customary law. The protection of hospitals, however, is regarded as so important that particular provision is made for them. Analagous protection to that of article 19(1) of the Land Warfare Convention is provided by article 18(1) of the Civilians Convention which states:

> Civilian hospitals organized to give care to the wounded and sick, the infirm and maternity cases, may in no circumstances be the object of attack, but shall at all times be respected and protected by the Parties to the conflict.

According to one physician at Bar Bir (Barbir) Hospital, "every hospital in Beirut has been shelled."[277] There are specific reports concerning attacks on Acre Hospital, Gaza Hospital, Baber (Barbir) Hospital and the Islamic Asylum, Triumph Hospital, and the American University Hospital.[278]

Ms. Robin Wright reported in the *Sunday Times* (London) under the heading "The Horror Shelling of a Defenceless

---

276. *Id.* at 2.

277. *New York Times*, Aug. 13, 1982, p. 4, col. 6.

278. *MacBride Comm.*, *supra* note 252, at 150; *Wash. Post*, June 22, 1982, p A14, col. 1; *Philadelphia Inquirer*, June 30, 1982, p. 10–A, col. 1; *Wash. Post* Aug. 5, 1982, p. A28, col. 2; *Time* magazine, Aug. 16, 1982, p. 10, col. 1, and p. 12, col. 3.

Hospital," the continuing Israeli attacks upon the Dan al Ajaza Ismalia Hospital in West Beirut.[279] The article states that the patients in the hospital "are a mixture of senile geriatric patients, mentally retarded adults, and children with mental problems."[280] Hospital officials stated that more than 800 rockets and shells hit the hospital or its vicinity in one two-and-a-half hour attack.[281] A later article in the *Sunday Times Magazine* (London), under the heading "Beirut: Madness Heaped Upon Madness," consisted of both text and pictures concerning the same hospital.[282] The text stated, *inter alia*, that the hospital "had been established in Beirut for 30 years and was flying a red cross and a white flag from its roof."[283] After pointing out that the nearest PLO post was a half mile away, it continued: "The hospital was attacked with artillery, rocket and naval fire."[284] Another article on the same hospital in the *Washington Post* pointed out that most of the children suffered from advanced malnutrition and some had starved to death as a result of lack of adequate care and supplies due to the Israeli siege.[285] This Israeli action of blocking supplies essential to the care of the civilian population, including shipments by the International Committee of the Red Cross (I.C.R.C.),[286] is a violation of article 23 of the Civilians Convention which allows the free passage of medical and hospital supplies intended for civilian use.

The provisions of the Civilians Convention and of the Land Warfare Convention which have been considered indicate clearly that the states which wrote and agreed to the Conventions gave a high priority to the protection of wounded and sick individuals, whether combatants or civilians, as well as of all medical personnel and facilities.

---

279. *Sunday Times* (London), July 4, 1982, p. 8, cols. 6–7.

280. *Id*. at col. 6.

281. *Id*. at col. 7.

282. *Sunday Times Magazine* (London), Aug. 15, 1982, pp. 14–19.

283. *Id*. at 15.
284. *Id*.

285. *Wash. Post*, Aug. 11, 1982, p. A17, cols. 1–3.

286. *E.g.*, *Christian Sci. Monitor*, Aug. 13, 1982, p. 13, cols. 1–4.

These provisons manifest an intention to go beyond the basic immunity of noncombatants by providing special protections so as to leave no doubt as to the applicable law concerning wounded and sick persons and medical personnel and facilities. The facts recounted here constitute violations of the quoted provisions of Conventions I and IV and in addition they constitute "grave breaches" under the common articles of each Convention.[287]

3. PROTECTION OF CIVILIANS AND THEIR PROPERTY

Articles 27 through 34 of the Civilians Convention are stated to have a broad application to the territories of the parties to the conflict as well as to occupied territories. Article 27 is one of the most fundamental provisions of the Convention since it establishes the principle of respect for the human person and the inviolable character of the elementary rights of individual men and women. This article provides in its first paragraph:

> Protected persons are entitled, in all circumstances to respect for their persons, their honour, their family rights, their religious convictions and practices, and their manners and customs. They shall at all times be humanely treated and shall be protected especially against all acts of violence or threats thereof and against insults and public curiosity.

The third paragraph of the same article prohibits "any adverse distinctions being made among protected persons and in particular those based on race, religion, or political opinion." This is similar to the prohibition of discriminations in article 16 of the POW Convention.

On September 18, 1982 the *Washington Post* carried a headline across the top of its first page which read: "Israelis Hunt Palestinian Sympathizers in Beirut: Christian Forces Join in Search."[288] The article by Mr. Loren Jenkins stated that

---

287. Conv. I: arts. 49–51; Conv. IV: arts. 146–49.

288. *Wash. Post*, Sept. 18, 1982, p. A1, cols. 4–6, cont. p. A11, cols. 1–3.

two days after the Israeli Army drove into Moslem West Beirut, the search for Palestinian sympathizers started. It continued:

> Israel did not rely only on the tanks and troops of its regular army. Plainclothes security agents, carrying lists of suspects, led squads of soldiers through the streets in search of presumed enemies to interrogate.[289]

This selecting of victims on the prohibited basis of political opinion later led to the deployment of right-wing Christian militiamen (known locally as the "Kataeb" or Phalange) through Israeli armed forces into the Shatila and Sabra refugee camps[290] which resulted in what later became known as the massacre of Palestinian civilians.[291]

Article 27 of the Civilians Convention, along with article 16 of the POW Convention, was also violated by the racial discriminations pointed out by Dr. Giannou's testimony concerning the greater brutality of treatment accorded to darker-skinned prisoners in the detention places where he was a witness.[292]

Article 29 of the Civilians Convention provides in full:

> The Party to the conflict in whose hands protected persons may be, is responsible for the treatment accorded to them by its agents, irrespective of any individual responsibility which may be incurred.

It should be mentioned that this article is not limited to the High Contracting Parties but makes a factual reference to all parties to the conflict, whether states, organized resistance movements, or others. This article repeats for the benefit of civilians the protection given by article 12 of the POW Convention to prisoners of war.

---

289. *Id.* at p. A1, col. 5.

290. *Wash. Post*, Sept. 19, 1982, p. A1, cols. 4–6, cont. p. A18, cols. 1–2.

291. Subsec. III F *infra*, entitled "The Crime of Genocide."

292. The text accompanying *supra* note 256.

The Government of Israel is the party to the conflict responsible for protected persons wherever its armed forces are in belligerent occupation. It is responsible directly for its own actions or omissions, and it is also responsible for the acts of its agents as specified in article 29. In Lebanon this includes, *inter alia,* responsibility for the acts of the Phalange militia and the acts of Major Haddad's *de facto* forces.[293]

Marvine Howe reported on August 18, 1982 in the *New York Times,* under the headline "Lebanese in Occupied South Say Israelis Give Free Rein to Lawless Militias," that "the Israelis have neutralized the very force they said they wanted to strengthen, the regular Lebanese Army."[294] Reference was made to bombing regular army barracks as well as occupying headquarters and seizing arms from Lebanese regulars.[295] There were several incidents reported of Major Haddad's *de facto* forces acting in a lawless manner including the burning and sacking of a Palestinian refugee camp which had been substantially destroyed during the Israeli attack.[296] The article also stated:

> The Israeli-backed Lebanese Christian militia of Maj. Saad Haddad today seized a kindergarten used by Palestinian and other Moslem children.[297]
>
> * * * *
>
> The kindergarten had already had its troubles, receiving six direct artillery hits during the Israeli attack on the Ain Helweh camp. Later Christian militiamen of the Lebanese Phalangist Party seized the school's bus, a gift from the United Nations Children's Fund, and took much of the furniture, kitchen equipment and even toys, which had been donated by Danish and Swedish groups.[298]

---

293. See, *e.g.,* E. Cody, "Israelis Encourage Irregular Forces," *Wash. Post,* July 2, 1982, p. A24, cols. 1–3.

294. *New York Times,* Aug. 18, 1982, p. 6, cols. 1–6.

295. *Id.* at cols. 1–2.

296. *Id.* at col. 3.

297. *Id.* at col. 1.

298. *Id.* at col. 5.

Lawless acts by the Phalangist militia and by Major Haddad's *de facto* forces are not a new development. For example, the *New York Times* published an Associated Press account on March 6, 1981 which stated, *inter alia:*

> The State Department said today that it had confirmed reports that the leader of an independent army in Lebanon was threatening to shell the town of Sidon unless the Lebanese Government paid him $5 million in ransom.
>
> A State Department spokesman, William J. Dyess, said the United States was "deeply concerned and appalled" by what he called a "criminal" act by Maj. Saad Haddad, a former officer of the Lebanese Army.[299]

The prohibition upon terrorism, also firmly established in customary law, has been codified in article 33 of the Civilians Convention. It provides concerning protected civilian persons: "Collective penalties and likewise all measures of intimidation or of terrorism are prohibited." There are many types of terrorism which have been directed at the civilians in Lebanon who are protected by the Convention. Article 33 also adds a prohibition upon reprisals "against protected persons and their property." Consequently, any kind of terrorism which is directed at civilians may not be justified on the ground that it is a claimed reprisal to a prior unlawful act of the opposing party to the conflict.

The immunity of noncombatants from direct attack is one of the most fundamental rules of the international law of armed conflict. It is almost universally accepted as binding customary law. Professor Lauterpacht has set forth the principle this way:

> Nevertheless it is in that prohibition, which is a clear rule of law, of intentional terrorization – or destruction – of a civilian population as an avowed or obvious object of attack that lies the last vestige of the claim that war can be legally regulated at all.

---

299. *New York Times,* March 6, 1981, p. A5, cols. 4–6.

Without that irreducible principle of restraint there is no limit to the licence and depravity of force.[300]

This basic rule is reflected in the United States Air Force official publication, *International Law – The Conduct of Armed Conflict and Air Operations*.[301] It states under the heading, "General Restrictions on Aerial Bombardment: Principle of Immunity of Civilians":

The civilian population and individual civilians enjoy general protection against dangers arising from military operations. To give effect to this protection, the following specific rules must be observed.

(a) The civilian population as such, as well as individual civilians, shall not be made the object of attack. Acts or threats of violence which have the primary object of spreading terror among the civilian population are prohibited.

(b) Civilian objects shall not be made the object of attack. Civilian objects are all objects which are not military objectives. In case of doubt whether an object which is normally dedicated to civilian purposes, such as a house or other dwelling or a school, is being used to make an effective contribution to military action, it shall be presumed not to be so used.[302]

One of the most characteristic features of the Israeli attack-invasion of June–August 1982 was the use of the massive fire power of its armed forces in target area attacks and in attacks specifically directed at civilian targets such as the refugee camps and hospitals.[303] The reports concerning

---

300. "The Problem of the Revision of the Law of War," 29 *Brit. Y.B. Int'l L.* 360, 369 (1952).

301. U.S.A.F. Pamphlet 110–31 (1976).

302. *Id.* at para. 5–3.

303. *E.g.*, *Int'l Herald Tribune*, Aug. 13, 1982, p. 1, cols. 1–6.

attacks upon civilians and civilian objects are numerous and only a few examples will be considered in the ensuing analysis.

All accounts agree that there were a large number of civilians killed and wounded in the Israeli military attack upon Sidon on the coast of Lebanon, south of Beirut.[304] Mr. Eric Pace reported in the *New York Times* on June 17, 1982 in an article headed "In Sidon, 80 More Bodies for a Vast Bulldozed Pit."[305] The 80 additional bodies were stated to be Lebanese citizens.[306] The article continued:

> In a patch of open land in the battle-scarred center of Sidon, 200 yards from the Israeli military government headquarters, a dusty bulldozer was spreading dirt over the bodies of civilians in a pit 60 yards long, 10 to 15 yards wide and up to 15 feet deep.[307]

> * * * *

> At the military headquarters, housed in a labor union building, the Israeli civil affairs administrator for Sidon, Maj. Arnon Mozer, estimated that the Lebanese civilian death toll in Sidon was 400 at most. He indicated that the plan was to bury them in the pit.[308]

Mr. Jonathan Randal reported from Sidon in the *Washington Post* on June 19, 1982 under the headline, "Sidon's Dead are still Uncounted."[309] The article stated:

---

304. Even the lowest estimation, that of Israel, is substantial. The Israeli Foreign Ministry announced on June 22 that there were 400 civilians killed and 1,500 wounded in Sidon alone. *New York Times*, June 23, 1982, p. A8, cols. 2–4 at col. 3.

305. *New York Times*, June 17, 1982, p. A21, cols. 1–5.

306. *Id.* at col. 1.

307. *Id.* at cols. 2–3.

308. *Id.* at cols. 3–4.

309. *Wash. Post*, June 19, 1982, p. A1, col. 2, cont. p. A21, cols. 1–6.

No one has yet bothered to identify the dead in the basement of the secondary school in Qanaya neighborhood. Still entombed in their makeshift shelter that failed when Israeli bombs fell here last week, they have been dusted with white disinfectant and are swarming with flies.

Nor has anyone counted the corpses in this or other smaller mass graves around the city. Lying in the 50-by-30 foot space beneath the school there are anywhere from 100, according to neighbors, to 260, according to Sidon doctors.

Most of the dead apparently were women and children who had fled their homes at Tyre, 22 miles to the south along the coast, when the Israelis invaded Lebanon June 8.[310]

During and after the invasion of southern Lebanon, various press reports indicated the inadequacy of Israeli claimed attempts to minimize the widespread destruction of civilian human and material values. For example, Ms. Trudy Rubin reported in the *Christian Science Monitor* on July 15, 1982 under the headline "Largest Palestinian Camp Now a 'Wasteland of Rubble'" concerning the Ain Hilweh (Sweet Spring) camp which was the largest Palestinian refugee camp in Lebanon with at least 25,000 residents.[311] The article stated that Israeli military officials insisted that they warned civilians by loudspeaker and air dropped pamphlets to leave before the final attack on the camp and that they delayed the attack in an attempt to negotiate its surrender.[312] The Israeli claim that they "had no alternative " but to bomb and shell the camp prior to the entry of tanks and other military vehicles was disputed by surviving residents of the camp who stated that the bombing continued while the leaflets were being dropped.[313] Israeli military sources said that the

---

310. *Id.* at p. A1, col. 2.
311. *Christian Sci. Monitor*, July 15, 1982, p. 13, cols. 1–3.
312. *Id.* at col. 1.
313. *Id.* at col. 2.

methods of attack employed resulted in "few casualties" to themselves.[314]

The *Jerusalem Post* International Edition of August 15, 1982 carried an article concerning the Rashidiye camp based on the findings of an Israeli academician, Dr. Zvi Lanir of the Tel Aviv University Center for Strategic Studies.[315] The article reported that the Israeli armed forces had not only destroyed the military infrastructure of the PLO "but also a very extensive socio-economic system which had supported the bulk of the Palestinian population there."[316] Dr. Lanir pointed out that an effective concrete shelter was beyond the means of most residents of the Rashidiye Camp but that it was "increasingly necessary as IDF [Israel Defense Forces] attacks on PLO bases in and around Rashidiye became more common."[317] The article stated that the PLO undertook to build shelters for the residents of the camp,[318] and it continued:

> A visit to Rashidiye reveals that one in every three houses has, in fact, been destroyed, ostensibly because it contained what the IDF escort describes as a "bunker." Lanir draws attention to the curious unwillingness of the IDF to recognize that there was an authentic need for shelters in the camp, and even though some of them may indeed have contained weapons or even explosives, the primary purpose of most of them was clearly to protect civilians when the camp came under bombardment.
>
> The provision of the best medical care available and the construction of shelters were clearly high-priority projects for the PLO in the camps.[319]

---

314. *Id.*

315. *Jerusalem Post*, Int'l Ed., Aug. 15–21, 1982, p. 12, cols. 1–5, cont. p. 13, cols. 1–5.

316. *Id.* at p. 12, col. 1.

317. *Id.* at col. 5.

318. *Id.*

319. *Id.*

Dr. Lanir was also reported to state that the approximately 9,000 men being held at the Ansar prison camp as "terrorists" have as many as 60,000 civilian relatives in the area and that these people "are becoming increasingly hostile to Israel, as they fail to understand why their menfolk are still being held."[320] The article continued by pointing out the hazardous situation of Palestinian civilians:

> The danger of a massacre of the Palestinian population in South Lebanon should not be dismissed, Lanir warns – and if it ever occurs, those who survived would provide the breeding ground for a Palestinian liberation movement that, born of desperation, might be even worse than the PLO.[321]

A sense of realism concerning the early bombing of Beirut can be achieved from reading a dispatch by Jonathan C. Randal of June 10 which was published in the *Washington Post* the next day.[322] He described June 10 as "the most intensive air bombardment to date against Beirut."[323] His report referred to attacks on civilian objects and persons:

> In one sequence of bombing runs, observed from the hills above the airport, the warplanes hit a Datsun car depot, the Pepsi-Cola bottling plant, a farm equipment warehouse and a tin can factory just to the east of the runways where four jetliners were parked.
>
> Later, the Israeli aircraft bombed refugee camps at Bourj el Brajneh and Chatila Sabra, the guerrilla office near the Arab University and a previously spared neighborhood less than 200 yards from the dividing line between the Moslem and Christian sections of the city.[324]

---

320. *Id.* at p. 13, cols. 4–5.

321. *Id.* at col. 5.

322. "Waves of Israeli Jets Bomb Lebanon's Besieged Capital," *Wash. Post* June 11, 1982, p. A1, cols. 5–6, cont. p. A19, cols. 1–5.

323. *Id.* at p. A1, col. 1.

324. *Id.* at col. 2.

During the negotiations leading to the evacuation of the Palestinian armed forces from Beirut, Mr. Robert Fisk reported from the scene in *The Times* (London) on August 13, 1982 under the headline: "Beirut shudders under 10–hour aerial attack." The article stated, *inter alia:*

> In 10 hours of non-stop air raids, the Israelis poured high explosive bombs on to the two Palestinian camps in west Beirut yesterday in an apparent attempt to destroy them before Palestinian guerrillas begin to evacuate the city.[325]
>
> * * * *
>
> If the Israeli air attacks were predictable, their ferocity was unexpected. For much of the day . . . fighter-bomber aircraft flew only 100 ft. over the rooftops, unloading hundreds of tons of high explosives.[326]

Article 31 of the Civilians Convention broadly prohibits "physical or moral coercion" against protected persons and, in particular, any such coercion which is designed "to obtain information from them or from third parties." Article 17 of the POW Convention contains a similar protection against physical or moral coercion for the purpose of obtaining information. According to numerous on the scene press reports, one of the principal purposes of Israeli conducted interrogations of prisoners was to obtain information concerning the identities of the "Palestinian sympathizers" who were hunted throughout southern Lebanon and in west Beirut.[327]

Like several other provisions of the Civilians Convention, article 32 is a reaction to the practices particularly

---

325. *The Times* (London), Aug. 13, 1982, p. 4, cols. 1–3, at col. 1.

326. *Id.*

> Israeli forces attacking West Beirut have battered the city's small Jewish community, shelled its only synagogue and sent dozens of Jewish families fleeing for safety . . . .

Wash. Post, Aug. 12, 1982, p. A25, cols. 4–5 at col. 5.

327. The text accompanying *supra* notes 288 and 289.

associated with the Nazis and reflects a determination to avoid their repetition. It provides in full:

> The High Contracting Parties specifically agree that each of them is prohibited from taking any measure of such a character as to cause the physical suffering or extermination of protected persons in their hands. This prohibition applies not only to murder, torture, corporal punishment, mutilation and medical or scientific experiments not necessitated by the medical treatment of a protected person, but also to any other measures of brutality whether applied by civilian or military agents.

According to its terms, this is a unilateral obligation undertaken by each of the state parties to the Convention including the State of Israel. In spite of the narrow wording of the provision as based upon the agreement of "the High Contracting Parties," the basic prohibition upon "murder, torture," and "any other measures of brutality" must be interpreted as also being applicable to all factual parties to the conflict in order to effectuate the humanitarian purpose of the Convention. The actions of the Government of Israel and its agents which have been amply documented include, *inter alia*, acts of murder, torture, and corporal punishment.[328]

The prohibition on pillage (or looting) is firmly established in customary law and it is codified in article 33(2) of the Civilians Convention: "Pillage is prohibited." The *Washington Post* on September 29, 1982 carried an article by Mr. Loren Jenkins which gave the details of a long list of thefts, as well as destruction of the property which was not taken, and the spreading of feces in both residences and business establishments by the Israeli Army.[329] Many residents of Beirut complained of the theft or irreparable damage to items such as artifacts which were irreplaceable.[330] Mr. Salim Salam, the

---

328. *E.g.*, the text accompanying *supra* notes 252–59.

329. *Wash. Post*, Sept. 29, 1982, p. A15, cols. 1–2.

330. *Id*. at col. 2.

managing director of Middle East Airlines, reported massive thefts of its properties during the time that the Israeli Army was in control of Beirut International Airport. The items, *inter alia*, included the entire computer reservations system, six minibuses, four Land Rovers, as well as numerous smaller items including aircraft mechanics' tools.[331] Mr. Jenkins corroborated the facts concerning the spreading of feces in a Beirut mosque.[332] In another article, the Beirut reporter of Agence France Presse, Mr. Xavier Baron, wrote that several apartments including his own in the Hamra district of west Beirut had been ransacked "and the only people who had access were Israeli troops."[333]

The properties of the Palestine Liberation Organization were given particular attention. The offices of the PLO were ransacked with valuables and records stolen.[334] The PLO Research Center, a publisher of academic works in English and Arabic, was stripped of everything in it including irreplaceable manuscripts and its 25,000-volume library.[335] Dr. Sabri Jiryis, the Director of the Center, estimated material losses at $1.5 million.[336]

Reference has previously been made to truckloads of blindfolded and handcuffed Palestinian and Lebanese men being transported to unknown destinations in the State of Israel.[337] Among the men so transported there were probably substantial numbers of Palestinian and Lebanese civilians. If even one civilian was included, it would be a violation of article 49(1) of the Civilians Convention which provides that:

Individual or mass forcible transfers, as well

---

331. *Id.* at col. 1.

332. *Id.*

333. *Supra* note 329 at col. 2

334. *New York Times*, Oct. 1, 1982, p. A8, cols. 5–6.

335. *Id.* at col. 5.

336. *Id.* The cumulative destruction was a violation of the Hague Convention for the Protection of Cultural Property in the Event of Armed Conflict of May 14, 1954 to which Israel became a party on October 3, 1957. The Convention appears in Schindler & Toman, *supra* note 171, at 661.

337. The text accompanying *supra* notes 250–51.

as deportations of protected persons from occupied territory to the territory of the Occupying
Power, or to that of any other country, occupied or
not, are prohibited, regardless of their motive.

The second paragraph of the same article provides that the
occupying power may undertake the partial or total evacuation of the population of a particular area if the security of the
population or imperative military reasons require that it be
done. Even then, such transfers may not take protected
civilians outside the occupied territory unless it is impossible
to care for them adequately in the occupied territory. It is also
provided that: "Persons thus evacuated shall be transferred
back to their homes as soon as hostilities in the area in
question have ceased."[338] It is clear that the Israeli deportation of civilians into Israel is not permitted by any of the
exceptions which are set forth in the article.

Following the destruction of the Ain Hilweh camp in
southern Lebanon, Yaacov Gravinsky, an assistant to Israeli
Cabinet Minister Jaacov Meridor, who was supervising the
Israeli relief aid for Lebanon, said that the refugees were
being denied tents for temporary shelter "because this would
turn into a 'permanent' solution."[339] The United Nations
Relief and Works Agency (UNRWA), which is responsible
for the refugees, says about 35,000 persons in the Sidon and
Tyre area are homeless.[340] The subsequent Israeli decision to
permit the tents was stated to have come after weeks of
negotiations with UNRWA.[341] According to the report of Mr.
Edward Walsh in the *Washington Post* on August 27, 1982,
Cabinet Minister Meridor stressed that this was merely a
"temporary solution" and "Israel remains determined to see
the camps dismantled and the refugees dispersed ... ."[342]

---

338. Art. 49(2).

339. *Supra* note 311 at p. 13, col. 3.

340. *Id.*

341. *Wash. Post*, Aug. 27, 1982, p. A1, cols. 2–3 at col. 2.

342. *Id.* at cols. 2–3.

There have been a number of claims concerning casualty figures for the attack-invasion. An article in the *New York Times* on June 23, 1982 referred to inconsistent casualty figures concerning particular areas:

> Israel's Foreign Ministry announced today that a total of 460 to 470 civilians had been killed and 1,600 wounded in fighting in southern Lebanon, excluding Beirut, for which the Israelis have no casualty figures.[343]
>
> The head of the Red Cross delegation in Beirut, Francesco Noseda, said June 12 that his organization had estimated the number of people killed in Sidon alone had reached as high as 1,500. He said the estimates of the number of homeless in southern Lebanon were as high as 600,000.[344]

There were also inconsistent casualty figures for the entire attack-invasion. The *Washington Post* on September 3, 1982 quoted the independent Beirut newspaper, *An Nahar*, as listing a total of 48,000 with 17,825 killed and 30,203 wounded.[345] A total figure of 2,000 casualties with most stated to be military was attributed to Israeli Defense Minister Sharon.[346] An unidentified relief official was quoted as stating that studies by his organization indicated "that about 80 per cent of the injured were civilian and only 20 per cent military."[347] Whatever the figure of civilian casualties is ultimately determined to be, those casualties which are due to direct attack upon concentrations of civilians, civilian objects, hospitals and medical personnel, have been the result of violations of the applicable provisions of international law. The reports of the contemporary factual events upon which this analysis is based are fully supported by the

---

343. *Supra* note 304 at p. A8, col. 1.

344. *Id.* at col. 2.

345. *Wash. Post*, Sept. 3, 1982, p. A22, cols. 1–3 at col. 1.

346. *Id.* at col. 2.

347. *Id.* at col. 3.

findings of the International Commission chaired by Sean MacBride.[348]

D. INTERNATIONAL LAW LIMITATIONS UPON WEAPONS

1. THE LEGAL CRITERIA CONCERNING WEAPONS

The prohibitory rules concerning weapons should be considered in the broader context of the basic principles limiting the conduct of hostilities. These principles are military necessity and humanity. Military necessity permits a party to the conflict to apply that degree and kind of regulated force, not otherwise prohibited by the law, required for the partial or complete submission of an enemy.[349] The closely related principle of humanity prohibits the employment of any kind or degree of force which is not necessary to achieve a lawful military objective.[350] Both basic principles protect important value interests of the world community. Until war and hostilities are abolished, the basic principles reflect the interest of states in conducting war or hostilities (at least for defensive purposes), but in conducting them with the least possible destruction of human and material values. It is wanton and unreasonable destruction which is made illegal by the principles of military necessity and humanity. The application of either principle as if the other did not exist would result in unbalanced decision. It is essential to apply each principle in the light of the other if the common interests of states are to be honored. From this perspective, each principle may be usefully conceived as an element of a larger composite principle which may be formulated as the minimization of the unnecessary destruction of human and material values.[351]

---

348. *MacBride Comm.*, *supra* note 252 at 51–65, 68–76.

349. U.S. Air Force Pamphlet 110–31, *International Law – The Conduct of Arm-Conflict and Air Operations*, para. 1–3(a) (1) (1976).

350. *Id.* at para. 1–3(a) (2). The legal principle of humanity is supported b the military principle of economy of force. W. T. Mallison, *Studies in the Law Naval Warfare* 20 (U.S. Naval War College, 1966).

351. McDougal & Feliciano, *Law and Minimum World Public Order* 530 (1961

A determination of what is excessive destruction must be made by reference to the doctrine of proportionality as it is applied to combat situations. Proportionality, in this sense, postulates that there must be a reasonable relationship between the lawful destructiveness of the weapon and its ancillary or collateral effects as set forth in the principles of military necessity and humanity.[352] Its prohibited ancillary effects include both excessive killing and wounding of enemy combatants and of civilians as an incident to the lawful attacks on the military targets. The concept of proportionality is difficult to apply to borderline situations because the comparisons involved are between decidedly different values. The specific context attempts to assess the relative weights to be given to innocent human lives as opposed to military efficiency in achieving a particular military objective. The practical, but unfortunate, result of this is that in most borderline situations some destruction of civilian values is usually accepted as lawful. However, the utility of the proportionality doctrine is demonstrated by its application in relatively extreme situations such as where the ancillary destruction of civilian values is so great as to be obviously disproportionate to the military objective sought. It is in this type of context that the doctrine is useful in prohibiting such unreasonable or unnecessary destruction of human and material values.

A basic distinction exists between the juridical status of a weapon itself and the uses to which the weapon is put.[353] Customary law or treaties make some weapons illegal *per se*, and this has the result of prohibiting their use under any circumstances. In addition, any weapon may be used in an unlawful manner such as by directing it at civilians rather than at lawful military objectives. It is important to be aware that the doctrine of proportionality has no relevance to situations where civilians are made direct objects of attack. The unequivocal rule prohibiting direct attacks upon civilians in any circumstances is applicable.

---

352. *Id.* at 241–44.

353. W. T. Mallison, *supra* note 350 at 156.

The principal treaty law on the subject of weapons is in the Hague Regulations of 1907[354] which are now binding customary law. Many of the 1907 Regulations simply repeat the 1899 Hague Regulations with occasional minor changes in words, and some of them were probably customary law when they were written in 1899.[355]

Article 22 of both the 1899 and 1907 Regulations provides: "The right of belligerents to adopt means of injuring the enemy is not unlimited." Article 23 of the 1907 Regulations sets forth more specific prohibitions concerning weapons under this general guideline of article 22. The relevant provisions of article 23 state:

> In addition to the prohibitions provided by special Conventions, it is especially forbidden –
> a. To employ poison or poisoned weapons;
> b. To kill or wound treacherously individuals belonging to the hostile nation or army;
> * * * *
> e. To employ arms, projectiles, or material calculated to cause unnecessary suffering ... .

These provisions are indentical with the similarly numbered provisions of the 1899 Regulations except that the last clause of paragraph "e" reads "material of a nature to cause superfluous injury" in the 1899 Regulations. In the situation where a lawful military objective is attacked, articles 22 and 23 together prohibit excessive incidental or collateral injury to military personnel and civilians.

Weapons which have been made illegal *per se* by customary law without regard to the uses to which they may be put include projectiles filled with glass, plastic, or other materials which are undetectable through the use of medical procedures.[356] Such weapons are also in violation of subsec-

---

354. 36 *U.S. Stat.* 2277, Schindler & Toman, *supra* note 171, at 57–92.

355. 2 *Oppenheim's International Law* 340 (7th ed., Lauterpacht, 1952).

356. See Swedish Working Group Study, *Conventional Weapons: Their Deployment and Effects From Humanitarian Aspect* 165 (Swedish Foreign Affairs Ministry, 1973).

tions "b" and "e" of article 23 because of their characteristics involving treachery and causing unnecessary suffering. Other examples of weapons which are similarly prohibited are booby traps disguised as harmless objects such as mechanical pencils or pens, watches, and various kinds of trinkets and toys. These weapons embody a treacherous form of attack on both enemy combatants and civilians. In addition, they are designed to cause indiscriminate as well as unnecessary suffering to those who are victimized by them. Booby traps appearing to be trinkets or toys are particularly offensive because children are their most likely victims. The official U.S. Air Force Manual states that "mines in the nature of booby traps are frequently unlawfully used" and includes in this category:

> portable booby traps in the form of fountain pens, watches and trinkets which suggest treachery and unfairly risk injuries to civilians likely to be attracted to the objects.[357]

2. APPLICATION OF THE CRITERIA CONCERNING WEAPONS

The legality of two particular weapons widely used in the attack-invasion of Lebanon must be questioned under the principles set forth in both the customary and the treaty law. These are the cluster bombs and the phosphorous incendiary bombs. While such weapons used against a military target under certain conditions may not be illegal *per se*, the legality of their use in an indiscriminate attack on a heavily populated area must be examined under the relevant criteria.

Cluster bombs are a type of unit in which hundreds of smaller bombs are packed into a cannister dropped from aircraft.[358] Mr. Robert Fisk described an attack by cluster bombs in *The Times* of London on August 13, 1982:

---

357. *Supra* note 349 at para. 6–6(d).

358. See "Cluster Bombs: How They Work", *MacBride Comm.* 230–37 containing description and diagrams. See also "How a Cluster Bomb Works," *New York Times*, June 20, 1982, p. A12, cols. 1–4.

By late afternoon, the Israeli jets were drop-
ping bombs never previously seen over such
heavily residential districts, projectiles that
streaked from the aircraft and exploded at 50 ft.
intervals in the sky in clouds of smoke, apparently
spraying smaller bombs in a wider arc around.
Most of these weapons were dropped in the
district of Corniche Mazraa, the boulevard that
runs from the museum – where Israeli tanks are
positioned – through the heart of West Beirut.[359]

A report in the *Christian Science Monitor*, on July 20, 1982,
stated that:

The effective coverage area for a single CBU is
reported by James Dunnican in "How to Make
War: A Comprehensive Guide to Modern Warfare" to be 50 meters wide by 200 meters long.
Therefore they are difficult to deliver with pin-
point accuracy in areas where military targets are
close to civilian populations.[360]

An article in the *Philadelphia Inquirer* entitled "Israel
criticized for use of indiscriminate bombs" reports several
examples of the effects of these bombs on children and other
civilians.[361] Dr. Ammal Shamma, Chief of Pediatrics at Barbir
Hospital in Beirut, is an American of Lebanese birth trained
at Johns Hopkins University. She acted as Head of Emergency Services during the attack on Beirut. She is quoted as
saying in reference to the victims of cluster bombs:

"So many amputations. I have never seen it so
bad. The number of people who lose limbs, the
number of bodies that come in in pieces. We've
had children literally brought in in pieces. It's the

---

359. *The Times* (London), Aug. 13, 1982, p. 4, col. 2.

360. *Christian Sci. Monitor*, July 20, 1982, p. 1, col. 1, cont. p. 8, cols. 1–3 at col.
3. "CBU" refers to cluster bomb units.

361. *Philadelphia Inquirer*, June 30, 1982, p. 1–A, cols. 1–3, cont. p. 10–A, cols.
1–4.

most hideous group of injuries I've ever seen in my career."[362]

Concern over possible misuse of U.S.-supplied cluster bombs against civilians in the 1978 Israeli invasion into Lebanon is reported to have resulted in a special agreement whereby Israel pledged not to use the weapons except in full-scale wars in defense of Israeli territory and against organized armies.[363] Another source stated that the weapons would only be used "against fortified military positions."[364] An article in the *New York Times* of June 30, 1982 reports that while the agreement itself is secret, "United States officials said today that Israel had agreed in 1978 not to use American-made cluster bomb units except in combat with 'two or more Arab states' ... ."[365] The special provisions governing the supply of these weapons indicate United States awareness of the unique destructiveness and potentially devastating effect they can have when used in an area inhabited by civilians. A Pentagon spokesman is quoted as saying that, "the United States is opposed to the use of any weapons that 'kill indiscriminately,' which would characterize them as 'terror weapons'".[366] Concurrent with numerous reports by foreign correspondents on the scene that Israel had used cluster bombs against heavily populated areas in the 1982 attack-invasion, Israeli Major General Aharon Yariv denied such use: "They were not used against civilians. I mean areas where there were concentrations of civilians."[367] An article in the *Christian Science Monitor* of October 8, 1982 stated that:

---

362. *Id.* at p. 10–A, col. 1.

363. *Christian Sci. Monitor*, July 20, 1982, p. 1, col. 1, cont. p. 8, cols. 1–2, at col. 1.

364. *Wash. Post*, June 28, 1982, p. A15, col. 5.

365. *New York Times*, *supra* note 358 at A12, col. 1.

366. *Supra* note 361, p. 10–A, col. 4.

367. *Wash. Post*, June 28, 1982, p. A15, col. 5.

> Mr. Shai of the Israeli Embassy [Washington,
> D.C.] says that Israel used CBUs in Lebanon as
> "an antipersonnel weapon."
>
> "It doesn't do anything to buildings or tanks,"
> he says. "But it does do a lot to people."[368]

As a result of the evidence of the Israeli use of this weapon in
areas of Lebanon with heavy concentrations of civilians,
President Reagan suspended shipment of such ammunition
to Israel following a secret review stated to concern violations
of the agreements under which the weapons were supplied.
Mr. John Goshko reported in the *Washington Post* of July 28,
1982:

> Although Israel has denied it broke agreements
> restricting use of the U.S.-supplied cluster units,
> the still-secret review is understood to have
> concluded that some violations did occur.[369]

It is clear that a number of basic principles of international law have been violated by the use of this weapon in the
attacks on populated areas. The weapon is indiscriminate, it
causes injuries which are excessive in relation to any possible
military objective that might be accomplished by its use, and
it was directed at areas where the main impact was on
civilians.

A similar conclusion has been reached by the International Commission chaired by Sean MacBride:

> The Commission concludes on the evidence
> before it that there was extensive use of frag-
> mentation weapons [the term used by the Com-
> mission to refer to cluster bombs] in areas where
> there was and is a high concentration of civilians;
> that in light of the widespread impact and
> destructive effects of these weapons, and in some
> cases, their delayed-action nature, indiscriminate

---

368. *Christian Sci. Monitor*, Oct. 8, 1982, p. 5, col. 2.

369. "Reagan Bans Indefinitely Cluster Shells for Israel," *Wash. Post*, July 28,
1982, p. A16, cols. 5–6, at col. 5.

death and injury to combatants and civilians occurred. The Commission concludes that this use of fragmentation weapons by the IDF was contrary to the principle of discrimination and was thus a violation of the laws of war.[370]

The other weapon which should be specifically examined is the phosphorous incendiary bomb which again, while probably not illegal against specific military targets, violates international law when used against a heavily populated area. *The Times* of London, in an article entitled "Robert Fisk reports on Israel's use of phosphorous bombs in Beirut," describes this weapon:

> Phosphorous shells and bombs are regarded as routine ammunition in most western armies, which use the projectiles as artillery markers or smokescreens. However, their use is generally confined to open battlefields, and three protocols agreed at a 1980 United Nations convention in Geneva contain broad restrictions on the use of incendiary weapons against military objectives located in residential areas of towns and cities.[371]

The reference here is to the three weapons protocols of 1980. These protocols were negotiated with the participation of military experts and representatives of all the major military powers.[372] Protocol III requires that civilians not be attacked by incendiary weapons.[373] It is a modern codification reflecting the customary law prohibiting attacks on civilians as well as the treaty law of the Hague Regulations of 1907

---

370. *MacBride Comm., supra* note 252 at 97.

371. *The Times* (London), Aug. 2, 1982, p. 8, cols. 2–5 at cols. 3–4.

372. The State of Israel and the United States were represented.

373. "Protocol III on Prohibitions or Restrictions on the Use of Incendiary Weapons" in Final Report of the U.N. Conference on the Use of Certain Conventional Weapons Which May be Deemed to be Excessively Injurious or to Have Indiscriminate Effects, A/CONF. 95/15 at pp. 16–17 (27 Oct. 1980). None of the three Protocols has been ratified thus far by Israel or the United States, but both states are bound by the customary law reflected in them.

forbidding the use of weapons which cause unnecessary suffering.

An article in the *Christian Science Monitor* on August 19, 1982 reported:

> In west Beirut, phosphorous shells and bombs have crashed into the main street, Hamra, hitting banks, local newspapers, and foreign news offices. They have plowed into two hospitals, a Red Cross building, and hundreds of apartments.[374]

> * * * *

> Those used in the city have crashed into areas where Palestinian civilians had taken refuge, such as Hamra.[375]

> * * * *

> They say that without the proper [medical] supplies, the only way to stop the burning is either to cut the burning tissue away or amputate. No one here has supplies.[376]

> * * * *

> Relief workers are reporting an unusually high incidence of amputations in west Beirut – particularly, they say, among civilians.[377]

> * * * *

> "Usually war is on the battlefield," Dr. Russli [a Canadian born Norwegian physican with experience in Cambodia] said. "Seventy percent of my patients are civilians."[378]

There are numerous other press reports of the injuries created by the phosphorous burns which cannot be extinguished and continue to burn the victim. For example, an

---

374. *Christian Sci. Monitor*, Aug. 19, 1982, p. 3, cols. 1–4 at col. 2.

375. *Id.*

376. *Id.* at col. 3.

377. *Id.*

378. *Id.* at col. 4.

article by Loren Jenkins in the *Washington Post* of August 20, 1982 under the headline "Beirut Phospohorus Victim: 'I Felt I Was Suddenly on Fire'" reported:

> The wounds are distinctive and much harder to treat than ordinary burns, the doctors say, in part because phosphorus sticks to the skin and can burn for hours. It cannot be extinguished by water, which causes a chemical reaction that makes the wound burn more. Like the Aytawi family [described in detail in an earlier part of the article], victims often arrive at the hospital with smoke still pouring out of their bodies from internal burns as well as skin injuries.[379]

Even if this weapon is not illegal *per se*, since its accepted use is as a flare or marker in an open area, its use as an anti-personnel weapon in a heavily populated area with the resulting extreme injuries to civilians must be characterized as illegal.

The International Commission, after examining the Israeli use of these weapons, stated:

> The Commission concludes on the evidence before it that the IDF did shell Beirut extensively using phosphorus shells in areas where there was a high concentration of civilians; that the incendiary effects of these shells on civilian objects and particularly on the civilian population was considerable. The Commission therefore finds that the use of these incendiary weapons by the IDF was contrary to the principle of discrimination and is a violation of the laws of war.[380]

The United States Air Force Manual states:

> International law does not require that a weapon's effects be strictly confined to the

---

379. *Wash. Post*, Aug. 20, 1982, p. A1, cols. 3–4 at col. 4.

380. *MacBride Comm.* 99.

military objectives against which it is directed, but it does restrict weapons whose foreseeable effects result in unlawful disproportionate injury to civilians or damage to civilian objects.[381]

* * * *

In particular, the potential capacity of fire to spread must be considered in relation to the rules protecting civilians and civilian objects . . . . For example, incendiary weapons should be avoided in urban areas to the extent that other weapons are available and effective. Additionally, incendiary weapons must not be used so as to cause unnecessary suffering.[382]

This analysis based upon the customary and treaty law makes it clear that the use of two of the weapons (cluster bombs and phosphorus shells) employed by the Israeli military in Lebanon, including in the attack on the city of Beirut, was contrary to international law.

The International Commission has reached the same conclusion. Its report states:

The Commission is of the view that, on the evidence, the horrific extent and nature of these wounds and death inflicted by these weapons was unnecessary; and that there are limits which humanity places on the use of weapons causing human suffering of the types described. The Commission concludes that the use by the IDF of fragmentation weapons [cluster bombs] and phosphorus shells in the urban centres of civilian population of Lebanon violated the international legal principle of humanity in the conduct of war.[383]

There are also reports of children's toys and other

---

381. *Supra* note 349 at para. 6–3(c).

382. *Id*. at para. 6–6(c).

383. *MacBride Comm*. 103.

attractive objects containing explosives which injure or maim.[384] In addition to violating the prohibition against treacherous weapons, these objects appear to be part of an attempt to terrorize the population, contrary to the prohibition of the use of terror against the civilian population in the Geneva Civilians Convention,[385] and to place extra stress on medical facilities which were seriously damaged and handicapped from the beginning of the attack-invasion. These conditions are described, *inter alia,* in an article entitled "Young Victims of a Savage War" by Pat McDonnell, appearing in *The Middle East* magazine:

> The exhausted hospital director, Dr. Ibrahim Alway, said the hospital had 400 patients, 80 per cent of whom were civilians. His staff had treated victims of booby-trapped toys, napalm, phosphorous and cluster bombs.[386]

It is clear that booby-trapped toys and trinkets are illegal *per se.*

E. THE CRIME OF GENOCIDE

1. THE ELEMENTS OF THE CRIME

The question of whether or not the Israeli attacks on the Palestinians during the summer and fall of 1982, including Israeli implication in the Beirut massacre, constitutes an act of genocide has been raised and must be addressed. The matter was raised specifically in the United Nations General Assembly where, while accepting the decision not to act on the proposal that the credentials of the State of Israel be

---

384. Pat McDonnell, "Young Victims of a Savage War," *The Middle East,* No. 95, pp. 28–29 (Sept. 1982). The *Christian Sci. Monitor,* Nov. 2, 1982, p. 1, col. 4, cont. p. 7, cols. 2–3 cites military experts as saying that unexploded cluster bomblets are a particular hazard to children because they appear to be toys. The article reports a number of specific cases of such injuries and deaths to children.

385. *Supra* note 182, art. 33(1).

386. *The Middle East, supra* note 384.

rejected, a group of 50 countries submitted a collective written reservation in a letter to the General Assembly on October 26, 1982.[387] Among the matters included in the letter was the "crime of genocide" which it said had been committed against the Palestinians.

The Convention on the Prevention and Punishment of the Crime of Genocide[388] was drafted following the Second World War. During that War, the Nazis, in addition to individual acts of murder, killed groups of people selected on the basis of their national, ethnic, racial or religious indentification. The International Military Tribunal acted on the postulate that such killing of groups was in violation of pre-existing law and that the perpetrators incurred individual criminal responsibility.[389] The drafters of the Convention were motivated by a desire to prevent mass killings in the future.

The second, third, and fourth articles of the Convention state the elements of the crime of genocide:

> Art. 2. In the present Convention, genocide means any of the following acts committed with intent to destroy, in whole or in part, a national ethnical, racial or religious group, as such:
> (a) Killing members of the group;
> (b) Causing serious bodily or mental harm to members of the group;
> (c) Deliberately inflicting on the group conditions of life calculated to bring about its physical destruction in whole or in part;

---

387. U.N. Press Release WS/1099, Oct. 29, 1982, p. 3.

388. 78 U.N.T.S. 277, Schindler & Toman, *supra* note 171, at 171.

389. The Charter of the International Military Tribunal at Nuremberg defined crimes against humanity as, *inter alia*, "murder, extermination, enslavement, deportation, and other inhumane acts committed against any civilian population, before or during the war." Charter of the International Military Tribunal art. 6(c) in 1 I.M.T. 10 at 11. The Judgment of the Tribunal held that mass murders within the definition had taken place and those defendants who had participated in them directly or indirectly were adjudged to be guilty. *Id.* at 232–38.

(d) Imposing measures intended to prevent births within the group;

(e) Forcibly transferring children of the group to another group.

Art. 3. The following acts shall be punishable:
(a) Genocide;
(b) Conspiracy to commit genocide;
(c) Direct and public incitement to commit genocide;
(d) Attempt to commit genocide;
(e) Complicity in genocide.

Art. 4. Persons committing genocide or any of the other acts enumerated in Article 3 shall be punished, whether they are constitutionally responsible rulers, public officials or private individuals.

The Convention was approved by General Assembly resolution 260A(III) of December 9, 1948[390] and entered into force on January 12, 1951. Both Lebanon and Israel are parties to it. In its Advisory Opinion of May 28, 1951[391] the International Court of Justice stated that the Genocide Convention was "adopted for a purely humanitarian and civilizing purpose" and that:

In such a convention the contracting States do not have any interests of their own; they merely have, one and all, a common interest, namely the accomplishment of those high purposes which are the *raison d'être* of the Convention.[392]

There are two elements involved in the definition of the crime of genocide. The first is the commission of certain acts, and the second is the requisite state of mind defined as the "intent to destroy, in whole or in part," a particular

---

390. *3 U.N. GAOR, Part I, Annex*, p. 494, Doc. A/760.

391. *Reservations to the Convention on Genocide*, [1951] I.C.J. Reps.15.

392. *Id*. at 23.

identifiable group. The ancillary killings of disproportionate numbers of Palestinian and Lebanese civilians as part of combat operations is contrary to the international law regarding the protection of civilians[393] and may come within the meaning of article 2(a) of the Genocide Convention which refers to the killing of members of a national, ethnical, racial or religious group as such. The reported brutal treatment of detained persons[394] constitutes the "serious bodily or mental harm" referred to in paragraph (b), and the calculated destruction of homes and facilities necessary for the survival of the civilian population[395] may be characterized as deliberately creating the group conditions for the physical destruction referred to in paragraph (c). In addition, one of the results of imprisoning substantially the entire Palestinian adult male population in Lebanon could be interpreted to be to "prevent births within the group" which is referred to in paragraph (d). While each of these actions involves violations of the humanitarian law concerning protected civilian persons and prisoners of war, they may also be referred to as acts of genocide if the requisite intent to destroy a particular group in whole or in part is shown.

2. THE APPLICATION OF THE LAW

On September 15, 1982 Israel moved its troops into West Beirut in violation of its undertaking not to do so.[396] It was claimed that the purpose of this action was to maintain public order and security following the assassination of Lebanese President-elect Bashir Gemayal in East Beirut which was

---

393. Sec. III C *supra*.

394. See the text accompanying notes 252–258.

395. See secs. III C2 and 3 *supra*.

396. Agreement between Lebanon, the United States, France, Italy, and the PLO entitled "Plan for the Departure from Lebanon of the PLO Leadership, Offices, and Combatants in Beirut," Aug. 19, 1982, U.S. Dept. of State, Bureau of Public Affairs, Current Policy No. 415 (Aug. 1982). Art. 2 provides in full: "A cease-fire in place will be scrupulously observed by all in Lebanon." On Sept. 18, 1982, after learning of the massacre in the refugee camps, President Reagan issued a statement which said, *inter alia*, "[W]e were assured that Israeli forces would not enter West Beirut." *Wash. Post*, Sept. 19, 1982, p. A16, col. 3.

under Israeli military occupation. According to Israeli Defense Minister Sharon, this claim was "only a 'smoke screen' to hide Israel's real intention – the destruction of the remaining Palestinian guerrillas thought still to be in the city."[397]

The grim events of Thursday, Friday, and Saturday, September 16, 17, and 18, 1982 in which at least several hundred[398] helpless civilian women, children and elderly people were slaughtered in the Sabra and Shatila refugee camps brought the issue of genocide sharply into focus. The facts indicate that these people were murdered because they were Palestinians.[399] Mr. Zeev Shiff, the military correspondent of the independent Israeli newspaper, *Ha'aretz*, wrote:

> A war crime has been committed in the refugee camps of Beirut. The Falangists executed hundreds or more women, children and old people. What happened was exactly what used to happen in the pogroms against the Jews. It is not true that these atrocities came to our attention only on Saturday afternoon, after foreign correspondents had filed reports on them from Beirut, as is claimed by Israeli spokesmen.[400]

Mr. Shiff points out that his own personal experience in Beirut on those days shows clearly that there was Israeli knowledge of and implication in the events.[401]

---

397. Edward Walsh, "Israeli Army Under Siege: Questions Surrounding Massacre Strain Credibility," *Wash. Post*, Sept. 26, 1982, p. A21, cols. 1–3 at col. 2. There has been no evidence of the presence of Palestinian combatants in the Beirut refugee camps.

398. The Lebanese Government placed the number killed at "nearly 2000." *Christian Sci. Monitor*, Oct. 14, 1982, p. 2, cols. 2–3, at col. 3.

399. The hatred of the Phalangists and other ultra-rightist militias toward Palestinians is described in "Phalangist Ties to Massacre Detailed" by Loren Jenkins, *Wash. Post*, Sept. 30, 1982, p. 1, cols. 2–4, cont. p. A38, cols. 1–6. See also Loren Jenkins, "Unprotected Palestinians Live in Fear," *Wash. Post*, Sept. 22, 1982, p. A1, cols. 1–2, cont. p. A18, cols. 1–4.

400. "War Crime in Beirut," *Ha'aretz*, Sept. 20, 1982 translated in *Israeli Mirror* (London), Sept. 22, 1982, pp. 1–2.

401. *Id.* at 2.

The International Committee of the Red Cross (ICRC) issued a press release on the massacre on September 18, 1982. It stated in part:

> ICRC DELEGATES IN BEIRUT HAVE RE-PORTED THAT HUNDREDS OF CHILDREN, ADOLESCENTS, WOMEN AND OLD PEOPLE HAVE BEEN KILLED IN THE CHATILA QUAR-TER OF BEIRUT, THEIR CORPSES LYING SCAT-TERED IN THE STREETS.
>
> THE ICRC HAS ALSO ASCERTAINED THAT WOUNDED PATIENTS HAVE BEEN MUR-DERED IN THEIR HOSPITAL BEDS, WHILE OTHER PATIENTS AND DOCTORS HAVE BEEN ABDUCTED.
>
> * * * *
>
> THE ICRC SOLEMNLY APPEALS TO THE INTERNATIONAL COMMUNITY TO INTER-VENE TO PUT AN IMMEDIATE STOP TO THE INTOLERABLE MASSACRE PERPETRATED IN BEIRUT ON WHOLE GROUPS OF PEOPLE AND TO ENSURE THAT THE WOUNDED AND THOSE WHO TREAT THEM BE RESPECTED AND PROTECTED AND THAT THE BASIC RIGHT TO LIVE BE OBSERVED.
>
> FOR YOUR INFORMATION, ICRC HAS RE-MINDED THE ISRAELI GOVERNMENT THAT, WHOEVER THE AUTHORS OF THESE CRIMES ARE, IT IS THE RESPONSIBILITY OF THE ISRAELI ARMED FORCES ACCORDING TO THE HAGUE AND GENEVA CONVENTIONS, TO TAKE ALL MEASURES TO INSURE PUBLIC ORDER AND SAFETY AND TO PROTECT CIVI-LIANS AGAINST ACTS OF VIOLENCE IN THE TERRITORIES WHICH THEY CONTROL.[402]

---

402. I.C.R.C. Press Release No. 1450, Sept. 18, 1982.

Under the customary law expressed in Hague Convention IV Respecting the Laws and Customs of War on Land,[403] the responsibility of the belligerent occupant for acts taking place within the occupied territory is established. Article 3 of the text of this Convention provides: "It [the belligerent occupant] shall be responsible for all acts committed by persons forming part of its armed forces." Article 29 of the Geneva Civilians Convention[404] provides in comprehensive terms that the party to the conflict responsible for protected persons (in the present situation, it is the belligerent occupant) "is responsible for the treatment accorded to them by its agents."

As stated by the International Commission, it is clear that:

> [T]he residents of the camps were "protected persons" within the meaning of Geneva Convention IV and Israel as an Occupying Power was under a special obligation to prevent the commission of "outrages" against them.[405]

The question of whether or not the Israeli leadership had the "intent," which is an essential element in the crime of genocide, should be determined judicially. Widely accepted legal definitions of "intent" and related concepts are:

> Intent: A mental attitude which can seldom be proved by direct evidence, but must ordinarily be proved by circumstances from which it may be inferred.[406]

> Constructive intent: Exists where one should have reasonably expected or anticipated a particular result.[407]

---

403. *Supra* note 354.

404. 75 U.N.T.S. 287, Schindler & Toman, *supra* note 171 at 427.

405. *MacBride Comm.* 163.

406. *Black's Law Dictionary* 727 (rev. 5th ed. 1979).

407. *Id.* at 284.

Constructive knowledge: If one by exercise of reasonable care should have known a fact, he is deemed to have had constructive knowledge of such fact.[408]

Using these definitions as criteria, it is necessary to consider the factual circumstances from which Israeli intent may be inferred. It is clear that the Israeli Government made the decision to allow the Phalangists, who were known to have carried out prior attacks involving substantial killing of Palestinian civilians, to enter the camps.[409] In the words of Defense Minister Sharon, the intended role of these units was to "comb out and mop up terrorists."[410] In testimony before the Israeli Commission of Inquiry[411] investigating responsibility for the massacre, Defense Minister Sharon was quoted as stating:

"I want today, in my name and on behalf of the entire defense establishment, to say that no one foresaw – nor could have foreseen – the atrocities committed in the neighbourhoods of Sabra and Shatila."[412]

---

408. *Id.*

409. The decision was made by the Prime Minister, the Minister of Defense and the Chief of Staff. *Kahan Report* 13. The *Kahan Report* is cited fully in note 413 *infra*. Re known militia hatred of Palestinians, see *supra* note 395. See also *MacBride Comm.* 179–80.

410. *Supra* note 397 at p. A21, col. 3.

411.   The Sept. 19 Cabinet meeting produced a defiant statement charging that it was a "blood libel" to suggest that Israel had any responsibility for the massacre. Ten days later, under intense domestic and international pressure, Begin agreed to the creation of the inquiry board.

Edward Walsh, "Begin Tells Probe Phalangist Killings Weren't Expected," *Wash. Post*, Nov. 9, 1982, p. A1, col. 5, cont. p. A12, cols. 1–4, at cols. 3–4.

412. *Wash. Post*, Oct. 26, 1982, p. A1, col. 5, cont. p. A13, cols. 1–5, at p. A1, col. 5.

"No one even imagined or spoke of or worried about this [a massacre], and I begin with myself."[413]

He also testified that he had "anticipated civilian casualties" but not on the mass basis that actually took place.[414] In addition, he claimed that he first learned of "widespread civilian casualties in the refugee camps" at about 2100 hours on Friday, September 17,[415] which was about twenty-four hours after the Phalangist militia had entered the camps. He stated that at the same time he learned that Lieutenant General Rafael Eitan, the Chief of Staff, and Major General Amir Drori, the northern area field commander, had ordered the Phalangists to leave the camps by 0500 hours the next morning and that he considered this a "reasonable" amount of time.[416] Eyewitness accounts stated that most of the killings took place Friday night and Saturday morning after the order to halt the operation had been given.[417] No reasons have been advanced for the delay of several hours after the killings were known to have started other than that it was a "reasonable" time.

According to a report in the *Washington Post* on September 20, 1982, the radio station of the Israel Defense Force (IDF) announced early on Friday, September 17 that it had been decided on the previous day to send the Phalangist militia into the Beirut refugee camps to carry out "purging operations."[418] The British Broadcasting Corporation monitored the broadcast by IDF correspondent, Arad Mir, and quoted him as saying:

---

413. *Id*. at p. A13, col. 4. *The Commission of Inquiry into the Events at the Refugee Camps in Beirut: Final Report* (Authorized Transl., 1983) (hereafter cited as *Kahan Report*) summarizes this statement of Sharon at 44 and 67. The Commission was composed of President of the Supreme Court Yitzak Kahan, Justice of the Supreme Court Aharon Barak, and Major General (Res.) Yona Efrat.

414. *Wash. Post, supra* note 412 at p. A1, col. 5.

415. *Id*. at p. A13, col. 1.

416. *Id*. at col. 2.

417. *Id*.

418. *Wash. Post*, Sept. 21, 1982, p. A14, col. 6.

> "The intention is that the IDF will not operate tonight to purge the areas of Sabra and Shatila and the nearby refugee camps."
> "It was decided to entrust the Phalanges with the mission to carry out these purging operations."
> "The IDF today completed the encirclement of West Beirut. The forces are now controlling all the main crossroads and roads in the city, and only houses inside the various neighborhoods remain to be purged."[419]

The International Commission summarized Israeli participation in the massacre:

> The Israeli media exposed the following: the militias passed through the Israeli lines on the west side of the camps; IDF-Phalange radio contact continued throughout the operation; the IDF supplied the Phalangists with maps of the camps; the IDF assisted with flares and, within hours of the entry of the Phalange, Israeli HQ was informed that the operation was proceeding in a way inconsistent with the IDF's declared guidelines and alleged purposes.[420]

Additional evidence of Israeli participation from which intent may be inferred was supplied in the testimony before the Israeli Commission of Inquiry on November 7 by Brigadier General Amos Yaron who was the commander of all Israeli forces in the Beirut area and whose immediate superior was Major General Drori.[421] The main points of General Yaron's public testimony have been summarized by Mr. Edward Walsh in the *Washington Post*:

> Despite reports of civilian casualties, the Israeli Army allowed Lebanese Christian militia

---

419. *Id.*

420. *MacBride Comm.* 173.

421. *Wash. Post*, Nov. 8, 1982, p. A1, col. 5, cont. p. A17, cols. 4–6.

units in the Sabra and Shatila refugee camps of West Beirut to bring in fresh troops and restock their ammunition supplies during the second day of the massacre, a senior Israeli Army officer said today.

Brig. Gen. Amos Yaron, the commander of all Israeli forces in the Beirut area, said he authorized the resupply and troop rotation operation even after he and a superior, Maj. Gen. Amir Drori, had become uneasy about the militiamen's behavior and initially had ordered a halt to the militia units' activities in the camps.[422]

The Israeli Commission of Inquiry found that after

it became known to Brigadier General Yaron [late on Thursday, September 16] that the Phalangists were perpetrating acts of killing which went beyond combat operations, and were killing women and children as well, . . . he was satisfied with reiterating the warning to the Phalangists' liaison officer and to Elie Hobeika not to kill women and children: but beyond that he did nothing to stop the killing.[423]

The legal significance of this finding is that it provides additional factual basis indicating Israeli complicity which would be a punishable offense under article 3(e) of the Genocide Convention.

Israeli tactical assistance facilitating the massacre is further indicated by their providing illumination for the Phalange units, as described by Edward Walsh in the *Washington Post* on September 26:

Thursday evening, the Phalange units began entering the refugee centers under the illumination provided by flares fired from Israeli mortars

---

422. *Id.* at p. A1, col. 5.

423. *Kahan Report, supra* note 413 at 93.

and dropped from Israeli planes. According to a report by Michael Elkins of the British Broadcasting Corp., Phalangist commanders were in radio contact with Israeli liaison officers outside the camps "and called in a request for flares."

A short time later, Israeli soldiers on the ground began to encounter hysterical Palestinian women running from the refugee neighborhoods and telling of a massacre going on inside. These accounts were relayed to officers and presumably transmitted along the chain of command.[424]

The danger to Palestinian civilians after the departure of Palestinian combatants was foreseen by all parties involved. Don Oberdorfer reported in the *Washington Post* on July 11, 1982 that in the negotiations leading to the withdrawal of the combatants the PLO "made involvement of an international force one of its negotiating demands."[425] He also stated that "the PLO is concerned about their family members' security as well as that of many thousands of other Palestinian civilians after the guerrillas' departure."[426] The likelihood of danger to the Palestinian civilians was taken into consideration during the negotiations for the PLO departure, and it was dealt with in the ensuing agreement of August 29, 1982 between Lebanon, the United States, France, Italy, Israel, and the PLO.[427] As set forth in this agreement, entitled "Plan for the Departure from Lebanon of the PLO Leadership, Offices and Combatants in Beirut," the United States provided guarantees concerning the "Palestinian noncombatants left behind in Beirut, including the families of those who have departed." The guarantee stated:

---

424. *Supra* note 397 at p. A22, col. 1.

425. *Wash. Post*, July 11, 1982, p. A24, cols. 1–2 at col. 1.

426. *Id.*

427. The Agreement is cited in *supra* note 396.

> The United States will provide its guarantees
> on the basis of assurances received from the
> Government of Israel and from the leadership of
> certain Lebanese groups with which it has been in
> touch.[428]

The Lebanese Government also provided guarantees "on the basis of having secured assurances from armed groups with which it has been in touch."[429]

The testimony of Major General Drori before the Israeli Commission, as reported in the *Washington Post* on November 1, 1982, demonstrates that some Israelis were also concerned about the danger to Palestinian civilians. He stated:

> [H]e and other Israeli officers privately feared that
> mass killing of civilians would result from the
> decision to send Lebanese Christian Phalangist
> militia units into the Palestinian refugee camps of
> West Beirut.[430]

Given these facts, it is difficult to believe that the Israeli authorities were not aware of the probability of a massacre of Palestinian civilians when they sent in the Phalange militia. If intent is to be inferred from circumstances, and constructive intent exists where one should have reasonably expected or anticipated a particular result, there are plausible grounds for accusations of genocide against those Israeli officials who fall into the Genocide Convention categories in article 3(b), conspiracy to commit genocide, and (e), complicity in genocide. The Report of the International Commission states:

---

428. *Id.* at art. 4(3).

429. *Id.* at art. 4(2).

430. Edward Walsh, "Israeli Says He Feared Massacre: General's Testimony Conflicts With Sharon's," *Wash. Post*, Nov. 1, 1982, p. A1, col. 5, cont. p. A19, cols. 1–3 at p. A1, col. 5. *Kahan Report* states at p. 90 that Gen. Drori's knowledge of the Phalange "based on his constant contact with them" showed that he was aware that "the Phalangists were liable to act in an uncontrolled way." See also *MacBride Comm.* 172–79.

The massacres that took place at Sabra and Chatila in September 1982 can be described as genocidal massacres, and the term "complicity in genocide" is wide enough to establish the responsibility of Israel for these acts.[431]

In addition to the basic responsibility of the belligerent occupant under Hague Convention IV[432] and the Civilians Convention,[433] there is individual criminal responsibility for the Phalange perpetrators and those who acted in complicity with them under article 4 of the Genocide Convention.[434] Both Israel and Lebanon, as state-parties to this Convention, were required to enact legislation "to provide effective penalties for persons guilty of genocide or any of the other acts enumerated in article 3."[435] Such persons are to be tried by either a competent domestic tribunal or by an agreed upon international penal tribunal.[436]

F.   GRAVE BREACHES OF THE CIVILIANS CONVENTION

Even if it is determined that the facts do not show commission of the crime of genocide, it is clear that killings have taken place which must be appraised under the grave breaches provisions of the 1949 Civilians Convention. Articles 146 to 148 of this Convention are analogous to the grave breaches provisions of the POW Convention[437] but are

---

431. "Majority Note on Genocide and Ethnocide," *MacBride Comm.* 194 at 196.

432. *Supra* note 354.

433. *Supra* note 404.

434. *Supra* note 388.

435. *Id.* at art. 5.

436. *Id.* at art. 6.

437. Arts. 129–31. Protocol Additional to the Geneva Conventions of 12 August 1949 and Relating to the Protection of Victims of International Armed Conflicts (Protocol I) of 8 June 1977, Schindler & Toman, *supra* note 171 at 551, contains arts. 11, 85 and 86 concerning grave breaches which are supplementary to those in the Geneva Conventions. Protocol I contains considerable customary law which binds Israel although it is not a party to the Protocol.

directed specifically to the dangers faced by civilians.

Article 146, like article 129 of the POW Convention, requires state-parties to enact necessary legislation "to provide effective penal sanctions for persons committing, or ordering to be committed," any of the grave breaches as defined by article 147. Article 146 also requires state-parties to bring such persons to trial. Article 147 defines grave breaches and provides in full:

> Grave breaches to which the preceding Article relates shall be those involving any of the following acts, if committed against persons or property protected by the present Convention: wilful killing, torture or inhuman treatment, including biological experiments, wilfully causing great suffering or serious injury to body or health, unlawful deportation or transfer or unlawful confinement of a protected person, compelling a protected person to serve in the forces of a hostile Power, or wilfully depriving a protected person of the rights of fair and regular trial prescribed in the present Convention, taking of hostages and extensive destruction and appropriation of property, not justified by military necessity and carried out unlawfully and wantonly.

Article 148 is identical to article 131 of the POW Convention and it codifies the customary law principle of state financial responsibility for violations of law and applies it specifically to violations of article 147 by state-parties to the Conventions. In the context of the protection of civilians, article 148 should be considered along with article 29 of the Civilians Convention which provides in full:

> The Party to the conflict in whose hands protected persons may be, is responsible for the treatment accorded to them by its agents, irrespective of any individual responsibility which may be incurred.

It is significant that article 29 places obligations upon parties to the conflict rather than only upon state-parties and is not limited to situations involving grave breaches. The grave breaches provisions are supplemented by article 149, common to all the Conventions,[438] which provides for an inter-governmental fact-finding inquiry to be initiated by the state-parties.

Although no such inter-governmental inquiry has been instituted, the International Commission chaired by Sean MacBride has issued a report following a careful investigation of the facts.[439] In addition, under intense internal and international pressure, the Israeli Cabinet on September 28 asked for the establishment of a Commission of Inquiry in accordance with the 1968 domestic Commission of Inquiry Law,[440] and the Commission was established, with Justice Kahan as chairman, to examine the facts concerning responsibility for the massacres at Sabra and Shatila refugee camps.[441]

The Israeli Commission's Final Report makes a sharp distinction between "direct responsibility" which it placed upon the Phalange, and the "indirect responsibility" of the Israeli political and military leadership.[442] The evidence presented established the danger, and even the probability, of a massacre of the Palestinian civilians in the camps.[443] Because of this, the Commission determined that what actually happened was foreseeable and that the Israeli leadership was indirectly responsible even if it did not intend the result "and merely disregarded the anticipated danger."[444] The Israeli Commission is to be commended for placing at least this limited, or "indirect" responsibility on the Israeli political and military leadership. At the political level, the principal blame was placed upon Minister of Defense Sharon and the Commission found that he bears

---

438. Conv. I, art. 52; Conv. II, art. 53; Conv. III, art. 132.

439. A full citation to the MacBride Comm. Report is in *supra* note 252.

440. *Kahan Report* 1. The statute is in 23 Israel Laws (auth. transl.) 32 (1968).

441. A full citation to the Kahan Comm. Report is in *supra* note 413.

442. *Kahan Report* 48.

443. *Id.* at 27, 60, 67–69, and *passim*.

444. *Id.* at 54–60.

personal responsibility for not taking necessary steps to avert the foreseen danger and to terminate the massacre.[445] They also found the Chief of Staff, Lieutenant General Eitan,[446] and Major General Drori[447] and Brigadier General Yaron[448] were guilty of not foreseeing the danger and not acting to terminate the killings once they had started.

The Commission's only reference to the applicable international law was its refusal to determine that parts of Lebanon, including west Beirut and the refugee camps, were occupied territory according to the criteria of international law[449] in spite of the common article 2 of the four Geneva Conventions for the Protection of War Victims which specifies that each Convention "shall also apply to all cases of partial or total occupation of the territory of a High Contracting Party." In addition, article 29 of the Civilians Convention establishes the responsibility of the occupying power for treatment accorded to protected persons by its agents. It is clear that the Palestinian civilians in the Sabra and Shatila camps were protected persons within the meaning of the Geneva Civilians Convention.[450] The evidence before the Commission which is referred to repeatedly in its Report establishes that the Phalange was not merely an agent of the Government of Israel in some generalized sense, but that it was under IDF command control.[451] Even if there had been only a loose agency relationship between the Government of Israel and the Phalange, the Government of Israel would still be responsible for the maintenance of public order and safety as the

---

445. *Id*. at 67–71.

446. *Id*. at 74–80.

447. *Id*. at 89–92.

448. *Id*. at 93–96.

449. *Id*. at 54.

450. See *MacBride Comm*. at 163.

451. *Kahan Report* 8, 10, 20, 24, and *passim*. From time to time, but not during the massacre, the Phalange was directed by the Israeli Mossad [Institute for Intelligence and Special Projects]. *Id*. at 7–8.

belligerent occupant under the basic principles of international law.[452]

The Commission's findings cannot be regarded as complying with the grave breaches requirements of the Civilians Convention. No inquiry was made concerning the extent to which the facts brought out by the testimony before the Commission concerning IDF command control and the provision of support and assistance throughout the massacre constituted responsibility for any of the specifically enumerated grave breaches in article 147. Even if it should be contended that Israel has a statute which meets the requirements of article 146 by providing penal sanctions for persons "ordering to be committed" the specified grave breaches, the Commission made no suggestion that appropriate criminal prosecutions be undertaken. Such prosecution should not only involve the Israeli military personnel whom the Commission found to be "indirectly responsible," but also the officers and members of the Phalange militia who participated in the massacre.

The Government of Lebanon has initiated an inquiry which appears to be only *pro forma*. It has thus far produced no known findings and is not expected to produce any significant ones because of the reported links between the Phalangist movement and some elements in the Government of Lebanon.[453]

In addition to the criminal liabilities of individuals, the Civilians Convention specifies further responsibilities. Under article 148, state-parties are responsible for grave breaches committed in violation of article 147. In the situation of occupied territory, the responsible party is the belligerent occupant rather than the sovereign. Since Lebanon was only the nominal sovereign where the massacre took place, it would have at most a secondary responsibility for what occurred. Because the Sabra and Shatila camps were within the area of Beirut occupied by the Israeli Army at the time of

---

452. Hague Conv. IV, Annexed Regs., *supra* note 175, art. 43.

453. Loren Jenkins, "In Lebanon, Massacre is Hushed Up," *Wash. Post*, Dec. 24, 1982, p. A1, cols. 4–6, cont. p. A8, cols. 1–4.

the massacre, the Government of Israel had the primary legal responsibility.

There is also a serious question of the responsibility of the United States Government. The agreement concerning the departure of PLO combatants from Beirut of August 19, 1982[454] was designed, *inter alia*, to prevent the commission of crimes which would constitute grave breaches as defined in article 147. If the agreement had been honored, the massacre would not have taken place. In the agreement the United States provided its "guarantees," *inter alia*, on the basis of "assurances" received from the Government of Israel.[455] In a letter from Ambassador Habib, the Personal Representative of the President of the United States, to the Prime Minister of Lebanon (to avoid the appearance of communicating directly to the PLO) it was stated:

> I would also like to assure you that the United States government fully recognizes the importance of these assurances from the government of Israel and that my government will do its utmost to ensure that these assurances are scrupulously observed.[456]

There is at least reasonable doubt as to whether the protests which were made over the Israeli entrance into west Beirut constitute compliance with the undertakings made by the United States.[457]

---

454. *Supra* note 396.

455. The negotiating history of the Agreement of Aug. 19, 1982 which demonstrates clearly the United States undertaking in four documents to guarantee "the 'security of the camps' where Palestinian civilians lived" is set forth in the *Wash. Post*, Nov. 13, 1982, p. A1, col. 6, cont. p. A14, cols. 1–3, and p. A15, cols. 1–3.

456. M. Viorst, "America's Broken Pledge to the PLO," *Wash. Post*, Dec. 19, 1982, p. C1, cols. 1–5, cont. p. C2, cols. 1–6, at col. 1.

The protection of civilians on a nondiscriminatory basis is dependent upon the implementation of the existing sanctions provisions of the applicable international conventions. The failure to invoke these sanctions in the case of particular grave breaches can become a precedent for further destruction of civilian human and material values.

---

457. See the reports of United States official knowledge when the massacre was taking place in W. Blitzer, "Officials Say U.S. Had Early Word Massacre," *Jerusalem Post*, Int'l Ed., Feb. 6–12, 1983, p. 10, cols. 4–5. See th appraisal of the Israeli move into West Beirut in J. C. Harsch, "A Trail Deceit," *Christian Sci. Monitor*, Sept. 28, 1982, p. 22, col. 1.

Chapter 8

The Solution of the Palestine Problem within the World Legal Order

I. The Source of the Problem

The rise of Zionist nationalism must be seen as a process with both political and juridical aspects which began to take its present political form at the Zionist Congress of 1897 in Basle, Switzerland.[1] From that time until the present, Zionism has been a political and secular movement which has used the religion of Judaism for its purposes.[2] Although the Zionists' objectives were frustrated by the Balfour Declaration, they nevertheless claimed a legal right to a "national home" and transformed that claim to one for a national state in Palestine. Concurrently there was a parallel juridical effort to constitute in international law a transnational nationality entity under which all those nationals of any state who meet the Zionist criteria for "Jews" become automatic members of "the Jewish people."[3] These claims to constitute "the Jewish people" have been advanced in many contexts ranging from political

---

1. The textual paragraph is documented in *supra* Chaps. 1 and 2.

2. The basic incompatibility between Judaism and Zionism was articulated in a conference in Washington, D.C., U.S.A., May 6 and 7, 1983, entitled, "Judaism or Zionism: What Difference for the Middle East?" sponsored by American Jewish Alternatives to Zionism (of New York) and the International Organization for the Elimination of all Forms of Racial Discrimination (of London).

3. These criteria are set forth in Feinberg, "The Recognition of the Jewish People in International Law," *Jewish Yearbook Int'l L.*, 1 (1948).

pronouncements to the domestic law decisions of Israeli courts.[4] Prior to the establishment of the State of Israel, the Zionist Organization/Jewish Agency was the main political instrument for the implementation of Zionist objectives. These objectives were pursued without regard to the rights of the indigenous Moslem, Christian and Jewish Palestinians.

During the period of the British Mandate, 1922 to 1948, the British Government made some efforts to maintain basic Palestinian rights while promoting or permitting the Zionist "national home."[5] When the inevitable conflict occurred between the Zionist immigrants with their political objectives and the native inhabitants who saw their rights under the League of Nations Mandate being frustrated, the British Government was no longer able to cope with the situation. It asked the General Assembly of the United Nations, as the successor to the Assembly of the League of Nations, to assume the responsibility for Palestine. The ensuing Partition Resolution which was adopted by the United Nations General Assembly authorized two independent states in Palestine and provided for an international regime for the City of Jerusalem. The State of Israel was proclaimed under the authority of this plan following the British withdrawal in 1948, but the "Arab State" was not established and the Palestinians, supported by the Arab governments, claimed that the partitioning of their country in opposition to the will of the majority of its inhabitants was a violation of their right of self-determination.

The State of Israel was admitted to membership in the United Nations by the General Assembly decision of May 11, 1949[6] on the basis of its undertakings to comply with the obligations imposed by the Charter and to honor the provisions of General Assembly resolutions 181 concerning partition and 194 concerning return or compensation for the

---

4. *E.g., Rufeisen v. Minister of Interior* (the "Brother Daniel" Case), 16 P 2428 (1962) translated in Select Judgments of the Supreme Court of Isra (Special vol.) at 1 (F. Landau, ed., Ministry of Justice of Israel, 1971).

5. The textual paragraph is documented in *supra* Chap. 3.

6. G.A. Res. 273 (III).

refugees. These undertakings have not been carried out.[7] During the years 1949 to 1967, the right of return of individual Palestinians, firmly established in customary law, was re-affirmed in consistent resolutions of the General Assembly, but neither it nor the alternative right of compensation has been implemented.[8] While denying compensation to the Palestinians, the Zionist Organization/Jewish Agency, acting on behalf of the Government of Israel, negotiated the Luxembourg Agreement of 1953 providing for massive financial "compensation" to the State of Israel from the Federal Republic of Germany for the property of Jews confiscated by the Nazis.[9]

After 1967 the relationship between the State of Israel and the community of states acting through the United Nations changed significantly and Israel attempted to minimize its reliance on the Partition Resolution as a basis for its lawful existence.[10] Following the intense hostilities and extensive military occupations of June 1967, the Security Council, in resolution 242, called for Israeli withdrawal only from territories occupied in 1967 and it thereby appeared to give juridical recognition to the pre-June 1967 *de facto* boundaries of the State of Israel which were considerably in excess of those set forth in the Partition Resolution. The post-1967 resolutions of the General Assembly recognized the Palestinians as a people and reaffirmed their national right of self-determination, including the right to constitute a state, which had been established earlier in the League of Nations Covenant, the Mandate for Palestine, and the Palestine Partition Resolution. The post-1967 resolutions of both the General Assembly and the Security Council have called for Israeli withdrawal from territories occupied since 1967 including East Jerusalem.[11]

---

7. See H. Cattan, *Palestine and International Law* 252-55 (2nd ed., 1976).

8. See the documentation in *supra* Chap. 4.

9. The text of the Luxembourg Agreement is in J. Grossman, *Germany's Moral Debt: The German–Israel Agreement* 37 (1954).

10. The textual paragraph is documented in *supra* Chap. 4.

11. *Supra* Chap. 5.

One aspect of the history of Israel as a Zionist state may be accurately described as the consistent use of military methods to achieve territorial expansion. This policy, including the establishment of exclusivist "Jewish people" settlements manned by armed settlers in the occupied territories, is consistent with the expansion which began in 1947 immediately following the acceptance by the Zionist Organization/Jewish Agency of the boundaries specified in the Palestine Partition Resolution. Settlements in occupied territories are prohibited unequivocally by articles 49(1) and (6) of the Geneva Civilians Convention as well as by the applicable long-established customary law.[12] By persisting in the settlements policy designed to acquire territory through the creation of facts, the State of Israel is perpetuating the basic conflict with the Palestinian people.

The attack on the Palestinian people and the invasion of Lebanon in the summer of 1982 must be evaluated in the context of the overall territorial objectives of the State of Israel. The invasion of Lebanon is integrally connected to the policy in the territories occupied in 1967. The destruction of the PLO, which was a major motivation of the attack-invasion into Lebanon, has been seen by then Defense Minister Sharon and others as being essential for Israel's implementation of its objectives in the West Bank and Gaza Strip. Mr. Sharon stated in June, 1982:

> The bigger the blow is and the more we damage the PLO infrastructure in Lebanon, the more the Arabs in the West Bank and Gaza will be ready to negotiate with us. . . . I am convinced that the echo of this campaign is reaching into the house of every Arab family in [the West Bank] and Gaza.[13]

---

12. *Supra* Chap. 6.

13. Interview in *Time* magazine, June 21, 1982, p. 19. (Brackets in original.) The June 7, 1981 attack on the Iraqi nuclear reactor must also be appraised in the larger context. See Mallison & Mallison, "The Israeli Aerial Attack of June 7, 1981 Upon the Iraqi Nuclear Reactor: Aggression or Self-Defense?", 15 *Vanderbilt J. Transnat. L.* 417 (1982).

Seen in this larger context, it is clear that the resolution of the conflict in Lebanon must be linked to a solution of the larger Palestine problem. The principal victims of the attack-invasion of the summer of 1982 have been Arab civilians, whether Lebanese or Palestinian. This is not a new factual development. All of the armed conflicts conducted by the State of Israel have been carried out in Arab countries inhabited by Arab civilians, and the civilians have always been the principal victims of these armed attacks.[14]

In the same way, the violations of the humanitarian law, some of which have been documented in this study,[15] are part of the larger pattern of systematic violation of law. It is this pattern of violation of the applicable international law, rather than the establishment of the State of Israel under the authority of the United Nations, that is the basic source of the Palestine problem. Zionist leaders have, on occasion, expressed themselves with commendable candor. For example, Prime Minister Ben Gurion stated:

> Why should the Arabs make peace? If I was an Arab leader I would never make terms with Israel. That is natural: we have taken their country ... . They only see one thing: we have come here and stolen their country. Why should they accept that?[16]

After his retirement from public office, Mr. Ben Gurion recognized the necessity of a compromise peace based upon the recognition of Palestinian rights and declared that all of the occupied territories except Jerusalem should be evacuated by Israel.[17]

---

14. *Problems of Protecting Civilians Under International Law in the Middle East Conflict*, Hearing Before the Subcommittee on International Organizations and Movements of the U.S. House of Representatives Foreign Affairs Committee, 93rd Cong., 2nd Sess. at p. 2 Prof. Mallison, at p. 11 Mr. Richardson of American Near East Refugee Aid, at p. 33 Prof. Shahak of the Hebrew University of Jerusalem (April 4, 1974).

15. See *supra* Chap. 7.

16. Quoted in N. Goldmann, *The Jewish Paradox* 99 (1978).

17. *Id.* at 100.

The late Moshe Sharett was the first foreign minister and the second prime minister of the State of Israel. Since his death his carefully written and thoughtful diary, not intended for publication, has been published in Israel and more recently portions of it have become available in the United States.[18] He recounts numerous Israeli military incursions which he states were misrepresented as acts of self-defense. His diary states:

> What shocks and worries me is the narrow-mindedness and the short-sightedness of our military leaders. They seem to presume that the State of Israel may – or even must – behave in the realm of international relations according to the laws of the jungle.[19]

Dr. Nahum Goldmann, subsequent to his retirement as president of the World Zionist Organization, became a critic of Israeli policy and practice and has strongly recommended that Israel assume a neutral status in order to assure its future as a state. In an important statement, he wrote:

> Israel is increasingly isolated politically and faces a growing danger of losing the support of world public opinion. The greatest threat to Israel today is not Arab arms and the lack of financial means but the slow erosion of world sympathy, particularly among the progressive nations that have always supported Israel.[20]

---

18. L. Rokach, *Israel's Sacred Terrorism: A Study Based on Moshe Sharett's "Personal Diary" and Other Documents* (1980).

19. *Id*. at 21.

20. "True Neutrality for Israel", *Foreign Policy*, no. 37, p. 133 at 140–41 (1979–80).

II. The Proposals to Solve the Problem and Achieve Peace in Palestine

A. PLANS ADVANCED OUTSIDE OF THE UNITED NATIONS

A number of peace plans have been advanced. Many of them, like Secretary of State Rogers' plan of December 9, 1969, do little more than reaffirm a commitment to Security Council resolution 242 of November 22, 1967 and its basic principle of "the inadmissibility of the acquisition of territory by war."[21] The Rogers Plan added that the only variations in the pre-June 1967 boundaries which should be permitted were insubstantial ones required for the mutual security of states in the region.

The Camp David Agreements of September 17, 1978[22] were also stated to be subject to Security Council Resolution 242. The Egyptian component of Camp David has resulted in the withdrawal of Israel from the Sinai, and, most important of all, a separate peace between Israel and its strongest Arab military opponent. The Palestinian component of Camp David involved a plan of "autonomy" for the Palestinians to be negotiated by others than the recognized representative of the Palestinian people and subject to Israeli veto. The Camp David Agreements, like other agreements entered into by the State of Israel, have been subjected to unilateral Israeli interpretation. The one advanced here is that the Agreement on the West Bank and Gaza provides autonomy for the inhabitants of the area and not for the territory.[23] Even the limited "autonomy" involving an "elected self governing authority in the West Bank and Gaza" included in this plan

---

21. The Rogers Plan is considered in S. P. Tillman, *The United States in the Middle East: Interests and Obstacles* 232–33 (1982).

22. The texts of the Agreements appear in "The Camp David Summit" (U.S. Dept. State. Pub. 8954, Sept. 1978).

23. Prime Minister Begin's statement to the Knesset that "We never agreed to autonomy for the territories but only for the inhabitants," is quoted in Tillman, *supra* note 21 at 32.

has not been brought into existence.

Following the failure of the Camp David "peace process" to produce a peaceful or just settlement, the members of the European Economic Community issued what came to be known as the "Venice Declaration" on June 13, 1980.[24] It endorsed Palestinian self-determination and called for the association of the Palestine Liberation Organization in the peace process. While condemning the Israeli settlements policy in the occupied territories, it reaffirmed the commitment to Israel's right to exist. On June 29, 1982 the European Economic Community issued the "Brussels Declaration"[25] in which they vigorously condemned the Israeli attack-invasion of June 1982 and pointed out that Israel could not obtain security by using force and creating "faits accomplis" but that it can find security by satisfying the legitimate aspirations of the Palestinian people. The Declaration stated that the Palestinian people should have "the opportunity to exercise their right of self-determination, with all that this implies." The call for the association of the Palestine Liberation Organization with the negotiations was reaffirmed.

The Saudi Peace Plan, enunciated by Crown Prince Fahd on August 7, 1981,[26] was based upon Security Council resolution 242 and other resolutions of the United Nations. It called for Israeli withdrawal from all the Arab territories occupied in 1967, including Arab Jerusalem but without mention of West Jerusalem, for the removal of Israeli settlements established in the Arab territories since 1967, and for the establishment of an independent Palestinian State with East Jerusalem as its capital. By affirming the right of all states in the region to live in peace, it included pre-June 1967 Israel. The result was the implicit recognition of the State of Israel within those boundaries.

President Reagan's Peace Plan of September 1, 1982[27] also

---

24. The Venice Declaration is considered in Tillman, *supra* note 21 at 35–36.

25. The text is in the *New York Times*, June 30, 1982, p. A12, cols. 1–6.

26. Copy provided by courtesy of the Saudi Arabian Embassy, Wash., D.C.

27. "A New Opportunity for Peace in the Middle East" (U.S. Dept. State Current Policy no. 417, Sept. 1, 1982).

reaffirmed Security Council Resolution 242 and stressed its application to all fronts. It further called for an immediate cessation of the creation of new Israeli settlements, expressed opposition to annexation or permanent control of the West Bank and Gaza by Israel, and stated that while the United States will not support the establishment of an independent Palestinian State, it is important to deal justly with the Palestinians. President Reagan stated that this could be achieved through Palestinian self-government in the West Bank and Gaza in association with Jordan.

The Arab Summit Conference at Fez, Morocco issued a declaration on September 9, 1982[28] which specified principles for the settlement of the Arab–Israeli conflict. Like the Saudi Peace Plan, it was consistent with Security Council resolution 242 and General Assembly resolution 3236 in calling for both Israeli withdrawal from the territories occupied since 1967 and the exercise of Palestinian self-determination and independence in the West Bank and the Gaza Strip under the leadership of the Palestine Liberation Organization. Like the Saudi Peace Plan, the Fez Declaration recognizes Israel within its pre-June 1967 boundaries by implication.

B. THE ZIONIST-ISRAEL PLAN

The Zionist plan for Palestine, initiated in the Basle Program, has been implemented since 1948 by the Zionist Organization/ Jewish Agency in cooperation with the Government of Israel under the leadership of the Labor Party starting in 1948 and the Likud Party since 1977.[29] The Begin Plan of 1977[30] concerning Palestinian "autonomy", the Drobles Plan of 1979[31] concerning settlements, and the attack-invasion of Lebanon in June, 1982 are among its more recent manifesta-

---

28. The text is in the *Wash. Post*, Sept. 10, 1982, p. A21, col. 1.

29. See *supra* Chap. 2 concerning the integral relationship between the Zionist Organization/Jewish Agency and the Government of Israel.

30. The text is in the *New York Times*, Dec. 29, 1977, p. A8, cols. 1–3 and in D. H. Ott, *Palestine in Perspective*, Appendix at 153–57 (1980).

31. See the text of *supra* Chap. 6 at note 33.

tions. In addition to retaining the land within Israel's pre-1967 boundaries, it now includes, at the least, Israeli present military control and later sovereignty over all of Mandatory Palestine including the West Bank and Gaza.[32] It also includes the Golan Heights of Syria and probably continuing indirect or direct control of southern Lebanon.[33] This plan violates the basic premise of Security Council resolution 242 prohibiting the acquisition of territory by war and is inconsistent with any peace plan which requires even the most modest recognition of the rights of the Palestinian people. It is predicated upon the false assumption that Israeli self-determination must be achieved by the frustration of Palestinian self-determination. Consequently, if it is a peace plan in any sense, it is a unilaterally imposed military settlement in violation of the applicable international law. It is more likely, however, to be a plan for perpetuation of the conflict.[34] The Zionist plan is different from all the others in one significant respect: it is the only one which is being implemented.

C. THE TWO-STATE SOLUTION OF THE WORLD COMMUNITY ACTING THROUGH THE UNITED NATIONS

The central feature of the two-state solution for Palestine is that it is based on fundamental legal principles which have

---

32. See, *e.g.*, "West Bank: Plans for Piece-Meal Annexation", *Kol Ha'ir*, Feb. 16, 1982, translated in *Israeli Mirror* (London) no. 594, Feb. 2, 1982 at p. 1.

33. Israel's strategic interests, however, are stated to be much broader than its immediate territorial objectives.

> [B]eyond the Arab countries in the Middle East, the Mediterranean and the Red Sea, Israel's sphere of strategic interest must be broadened to include in the '80s countries such as Turkey, Iran and Pakistan, and regions such as the Persian Gulf and Africa, particularly the countries of North and Central Africa.

"Israel's Strategic Problems in the '80s", Speech of Defense Minister Sharon at the Institute of Strategic Studies, Tel Aviv University, Dec. 14, 1981, p. 9 [Text provided by courtesy of Tel Aviv University].

34. See the careful appraisal of the Begin Plan in D. H. Ott, *supra* note 30, *passim*.

not been varied since the adoption of the Palestine Partition Resolution of 1947.[35] It is also based on compromise in the sense that the Palestinian people's undoubted right to self-determination as the overwhelming majority of the population of the country in 1947 has now been limited by the introduction of Israeli self-determination within Palestine. The pre-June 1967 boundaries of the State of Israel appear to have received the assent of the community of states acting through the United Nations.[36] Consequently, the boundaries of the state in which Palestinian self-determination is to be exercised are those of Mandatory Palestine outside of the lawfully established boundaries of the State of Israel which would probably be its pre-June 1967 boundaries subject to minor variations.[37]

The recommendations of the General Assembly Committee on the Exercise of the Inalienable Rights of the Palestinian People are based on the two-state solution.[38] These recommendations were endorsed by the General Assembly at its thirty-first regular session in 1976 by a large majority of states and since that time have been re-endorsed with increasing majorities.[39] In General Assembly resolution 37/86A of December 10, 1982 the General Assembly again endorsed the report of this Committee and only two states, Israel and the United States, voted in opposition. This resolution also emphasized the necessity for the implementation of the recommendations. General Assembly resolution 37/86C of the same date recalled General Assembly resolution 36/120C

---

35. Mallison & Mallison, *An International Law Analysis of the Major United Nations Resolutions Concerning the Palestine Question*, Chap. 4 and *passim* (United Nations Doc. #ST/SG/SER.F/4, 1979).

36. See the text of *supra* Chap. 4 at notes 79, 80.

37. *Supra* Chap. 4, Sec. II D.

38. See the text of *supra* Chap. 4 at notes 82, 83. The recommendations of the Committee are in "Report of the Committee on the Exercise of the Inalienable Rights of the Palestinian People", 37 *U.N. GAOR, Supp. No. 35* (A/37/35), at 21 (1982).

39. G.A. Res. 31/20 of Nov. 24, 1976 recorded 90 in favor, 16 against and 30 abstentions; G.A. Res. 37/86A of Dec. 10, 1982 recorded 119 in favor, 2 against and 21 abstentions.

of December 10, 1981 in which it was decided to convene an International Conference on the Question of Palestine for a comprehensive effort to seek ways and means to enable the Palestinian people to attain and to exercise their rights. This resolution, adopted with only the votes of Israel and the United States in opposition, also called upon member states to contribute to the achievement of Palestinian rights and their implementation through participation in the Conference and the regional preparatory meetings preceding it.

General Assembly resolution 37/86D, also adopted on December 10, 1982, provided that the General Assembly:

> *Reaffirms once again* that a comprehensive, just and lasting peace in the Middle East cannot be established without the unconditional withdrawal of Israel from the Palestinian and other Arab territories occupied since 1967, including Jerusalem, and without the exercise and attainment by the Palestinian people of its inalienable rights in Palestine in accordance with the principles of the Charter and the relevant resolutions of the United Nations.

This explicit provision which requires the withdrawal of the State of Israel only from the Arab territories occupied since the intense hostilities, of June, 1967, is consistent with previous resolutions of the General Assembly, as well as Security Council Resolution 242, and it provides further indication that Palestinian self-determination is not to impinge upon Israeli self-determination within the pre-June 1967 borders of Israel. Canada and Costa Rica joined Israel and the United States in providing the negative votes on this resolution.

A principal feature of the two-state solution to the Palestine problem is the interdependence of Israeli and Palestinian national rights. Both are grounded upon the Palestine Partition Resolution and the unvarying reaffirmation of its legal principles by the world community acting through the United Nations. This method of law-making by the consensual actions of states over a period of time is the same way that customary law has been made throughout history.

III. The Urgent Necessity for Enforcement of the World Legal Order

The basic provisions of Security Council Resolution 242 are included in each of the proposed solutions except the Zionist–Israel one. The resolution calls for the withdrawal of Israel to its pre-1967 borders, the "termination of all claims or states of belligerency," and the "acknowledgement of the sovereignty, territorial integrity and political independence of each state in the area." The particular plan which has the maximum legal authority is the one adopted through the United Nations because it is the solution supported by the overwhelming majority of the world community. The other plans which incorporate many of the major features of the two-state plan provide additional support for it. The consistent resolutions of the United Nations beginning with the Palestine Partition Resolution have provided the basis for peace with as much justice as can be attained in this imperfect world. It is now imperative to enforce this plan. The Israeli attack on the Palestinian people and invasion of Lebanon in the summer of 1982 is further evidence that the Zionist–Israel aggression will continue until international action is taken to stop it. With each act of aggression it becomes more difficult to implement the world community legal solution to the problem.[40]

The world legal order must, at the very least, protect peoples and states from coercion and aggression.[41] Such an order is prescribed by the United Nations Charter requirement of peaceful methods of dispute settlement[42] combined with its prohibition upon "the threat or use of force against the territorial integrity or political independence of any state, or in any other manner inconsistent with the Purposes of the

---

40. J. Reddaway, "The Future of Jerusalem," in *"Seek Peace, and Ensue It"*: *Selected Papers on Palestine and the Search for Peace* 127 (Council for the Advancement of Arab–British Understanding, 1982).

41. The world legal order is considered systematically in M. S. McDougal and Associates, *Studies in World Public Order* (1960).

42. United Nations Charter, art. 2(3).

43. *Id.*, art. 2(4).

United Nations."[43] The Secretary-General of the United Nations wrote in 1983:

[O]ur most urgent goal is to reconstruct the Charter concept of collective action for peace and security so as to render the United Nations more capable of carrying out its primary function.[44]

The Charter also contains the complementary provision which authorizes the use of force only for defensive purposes.[45] The enforcement of the United Nations legal order system will free Palestinians and Israelis alike from the terror and responding violence to which they have been subjected for decades.[46]

If there is any single point that has been made most clearly in the world community dealings with the State of Israel and Zionist nationalism over a period of more than three decades, it is that there will be no solution of the Palestine problem until effective sanctions are applied to the Government of Israel. The main authority to apply sanctions is allocated to the Security Council and its action may be blocked by the negative vote of a single permanent member.[47] The General Assembly may not act while the Security Council is exercising its functions under the Charter concerning any dispute or situation.[48] The General Assembly, nevertheless, may act when the Council is blocked by a great power negative vote. The first time that the General Assembly acted in such a context was during the Korean War in 1950 when the Soviet Union blocked action by the Security Council. Under the leadership of the United States, the General Assembly adopted the famous Uniting for Peace

---

44. J. Perez de Cuellar, *Report of the Secretary-General on the Work of the Organization* 6 (1982).

45. *Supra* note 42, art. 51.

46. Both the Israeli state terror and the Palestinian responding violence are described and analyzed in D. Hirst, *The Gun and the Olive Branch: The Roots of Violence in the Middle East* (1977). Primary authority on the state terror is in Rokach, *supra* note 18.

47. *Supra* note 42, art. 27(3).

48. *Id.*, art. 12(1).

Resolution on November 3, 1950[49] by more than the two-thirds majority required by the Charter for important questions.[50] Thereafter, pursuant to subsequent resolutions of the Assembly, the community of states took effective enforcement action. This method is still available under the Charter and it can be used to overcome a negative vote by any permanent member of the Council.

The application of sanctions to enforce the world community consensus concerning Palestine is indispensable. No organized community, domestic or international, can achieve even a minimum legal order without the ability and the will to use the necessary coercion to obtain it. The essential element is that coercion must be in the responsible hands of the community and not in the hands of a militaristic and expansionist state. The central point was made by J. W. Fulbright some time ago when he wrote:

> The crucial distinction is not between coercion and voluntarism, but between duly constituted force applied through law . . . and the arbitrary coercion of the weak by the strong.[51]

One of the objections that will be made to this recommendation for the application of adequate sanctions is that it is an "imposed settlement."[52] This objection should be clearly understood both in its explicit meaning and in its implication. Its explicit meaning is that an imposed settlement by the world community under law is opposed. Its unexpressed but necessary implication is that the existing imposed settlement by the military power of the Government of Israel is condoned. It is remarkable that this position applies only to the Israeli–Palestinian conflict. It overlooks

---

49 G.A. Res. 377A (V), 5 U.N. GAOR, Supp. 20 (A/1775), pp. 10–12.

50. *Supra* note 42, art. 18(2).

51. J. W. Fulbright, *The Crippled Giant*, 108 (Vintage Books, 1972).

52. *E.g.*, the opposition to such a settlement, as applied to Israel, expressed by Acting U.S. Ambassador to the United Nations, W. J. Vanden Heuvel, in the Emergency Special Session of the General Assembly on Palestine on July 24, 1980. 80 *U.S. Dept. State Bull.* 67 (Sept., 1980).

the highly successful imposition of a settlement on Japan in the years following the end of the Second World War. It also fails to mention the imposed settlement in Europe at the end of the same war. One of the most successful imposed settlements in history was the peace which the Congress of Vienna imposed on France beginning in 1815.[53] The justice involved in that settlement, including the protection of legitimate French national interests, resulted in less coercion being required than would otherwise have been necessary. Both justice and coercion are typically required in peace settlements and where justice is used less, coercion must be used more.[54] The absence of elementary justice in the military settlement now imposed upon Palestine leads to the great and increasing use of coercion.

Although sanctions which do not have the participation of the United States would not be sufficiently effective, it may be hoped that the combination of world community pressure and the increasing economic drain of support for Israel on the United States[55] will bring it back to the principled position taken by President Eisenhower when Israel refused to withdraw from Suez in response to the United Nations demand in 1957. President Eisenhower said:

> This raises a basic question of principle. Should a nation which attacks and occupies foreign territory in the face of United Nations disapproval be allowed to impose conditions on its own withdrawal?
> If we agree that armed attack can properly achieve the purpose of the assailant, then I fear we will have turned back the clock of international

---

53. H. A. Kissinger, *A World Restored: Metternich, Castlereagh and the Problems of Peace, 1812–1822* (Sentry ed., undated).

54. S. P. Tillman, *supra* note 21, Chap. 7 entitled "Conclusion: On Peace and How to Get It" (1982).

55. Report of the Comptroller General of the United States, *U.S. Assistance to the State of Israel*, GAO/ID–83–51 (June 24, 1983) concludes that Israel will request substantial increases in the multi-billion dollar aid received from the United States unless there is an enduring peaceful settlement in the Middle East.

order. We will, in effect, have countenanced the use of force as a means of settling international differences and through this gaining national advantages.[56]

* * * *

The United Nations must not fail. I believe that – in the interests of peace – the United Nations has no choice but to exert pressure upon Israel to comply with the withdrawal resolutions.[57]

Israel withdrew following the clear statement that the United States would support sanctions.

Because of the continuing Israeli economic crisis, largely caused by the militarization of its foreign policy and its domestic society, there is every reason to believe that economic sanctions would be successful in achieving Israeli compliance with the relevant United Nations resolutions.[58] Such sanctions would immediately raise a new hope in Israel on the part of those patriotic and enlightened Israeli citizens who have been urging their government to enter into a peaceful settlement. In the unlikely event that the economic sanctions were unsuccessful, military sanctions are available under the United Nations Charter. It is necessary to emphasize that sanctions must be conceptualized and applied as a comprehensive process, starting with persuasive measures and leading to increasingly coercive ones, rather than as a group of isolated and unrelated episodes.[59]

It is also imperative that the world community enforce the application of the customary and treaty humanitarian law. The state-parties to the four Geneva Conventions of 1949 for the Protection of War Victims have agreed in the common article 1 to not only respect, but to "ensure respect" for the

---

56. 36 *U.S. Dept. State Bull.* 387 at 389 (Mar. 11, 1957).

57. *Id.* at 390.

58. *U.N. Charter* arts. 39–50 provide for sanctions.

59. The past performance and the present potential of such sanctions by the world community are analyzed in M. S. McDougal and F. P. Feliciano, *Law and Minimum World Public Order*, Chap. 4 entitled, "Community Sanctioning Process and Minimum Order" (1961).

Conventions. Consequently, where one state-party is in violation, the others are also in violation unless they take energetic measures to bring the violator into compliance. The grave breaches provisions of the Geneva Conventions and the precedent of the International Military Tribunal at Nuremberg provide existing legal authority for enforcement.

The alternative to enforcement of the law is to accept an international system based upon the use of military power outside the law. Such a system is the antithesis of a just and stable peace and requires the entire world community to live under the cloud of impending nuclear catastrophe. In addition to removing this threat, the effective application of the relevant law in the Middle East will result in first the conservation and then the development of the human and material resources of all the peoples of the area through the achievement of peace based upon international law and the world legal order.

Appendices

Appendix 1

The Basle Program
August 1897

The aim of Zionism is to create for the Jewish people a home in Palestine secured by public law.

In order to attain this object the Congress adopts the following means:

1. The systematic promotion of the settlement of Palestine with Jewish agriculturists, artisans, and craftsmen.

2. The organisation and federation of all Jewry by means of local and general institutions in conformity with the local laws.

3. The strengthening of Jewish sentiment and national consciousness.

4. Preparatory steps for the procuring of such Government assents as are necessary for achieving the object of Zionism.

Appendix 2*

Balfour Declaration, November 2nd, 1917

Foreign Office,
November 2nd, 1917.

Dear Lord Rothschild,

    I have much pleasure in conveying to you, on behalf of His Majesty's Government, the following declaration of sympathy with Jewish Zionist aspirations which has been submitted to, and approved by, the Cabinet.

    'His Majesty's Government view with favour the establishment in Palestine of a national home for the Jewish people, and will use their best endeavours to facilitate the achievement of this object, it being clearly understood that nothing shall be done which may prejudice the civil and religious rights of existing non-Jewish communities in Palestine, or the rights and political status enjoyed by Jews in any other country".

    I should be grateful if you would bring this declaration to the knowledge of the Zionist Federation.

(signature)

* Reproduced from the records and with the permission of the Controller of Her Majesty's Stationery Office.

Appendix 3

Successive Drafts and Final Text of the Balfour Declarati

Zionist Draft July, 1917	Balfour Draft August, 1917	Milner Draft August, 1917
1. His Majesty's Government accepts the principle that Palestine should be reconstituted as the national home of the Jewish people.	His Majesty's Government accept the principle that Palestine should be reconstituted as the national home of the Jewish people	His Majesty's Gover accepts the principl every opportunity sh afforded for the est ment of a home f Jewish people in Pal
2. His Majesty's Government will use its best endeavours to secure the achievement of this object and will discuss the necessary methods and means with the Zionist Organization.	and will use their best endeavours to secure the achievement of this object and will be ready to consider any suggestions on the subject which the Zionist Organization may desire to lay before them.	and will use its be deavours to facilita achievement of this and will be ready to c any suggestions on t. ject which the Zioni nizations may desir before them.

Milner–Amery Draft 4 October 1917	Final Text 31 October, 1917
His Majesty's Government views with favour the establishment in Palestine of a national home for the Jewish race	His Majesty's Government view with favour the establishment in Palestine of a national home for the Jewish people
and will use its best endeavours to facilitate the achievement of this object, it being clearly understood that nothing shall be done which may prejudice the civil and religious rights of existing non-Jewish communities in Palestine or the rights and political status enjoyed in any other country by such Jews who are fully contented with their existing nationality (and citizenship).	and will use their best endeavours to facilitate the achievement of this object, it being clearly understood that nothing shall be done which may prejudice the civil and religious rights of existing non-Jewish communities in Palestine or the rights and political status enjoyed by Jews in any other country.

(Note: words in parentheses added subsequently.)

Appendix 4

State of Israel – The Law of Return

4 ISRAEL LAWS 114 (1950) AS AMENDED IN 1954 AND 1970

1. Every Jew has the right to immigrate to this country.

2. (a) Immigration shall be by immigrant's visa.

(b) An immigrant's visa shall be given to every Jew who has expressed his desire to settle in Israel, unless the Minister of the Interior is satisfied that the applicant –

> (1) is engaged in an activity directed against the Jewish people; or
>
> (2) is liable to endanger public health or the security of the State; or
>
> (3) is a person with a criminal past liable to endanger public welfare.

3. (a) A Jew who comes to Israel and subsequently expresses his desire to settle may, whilst still in Israel, receive an immigrant's certificate.

(b) The exceptions set out in section 2(b) shall also apply to the grant of an immigrant's certificate, provided that a person shall not be considered as endangering public health on account of an illness contracted after his arrival in Israel.

4. Every Jew who immigrated to this country before the commencement of this Law and every Jew born in the country, whether before or after the commencement of this Law, is in the same position as one who immigrated under this Law.

4A. (a) The rights of a Jew under this Law, the rights of an immigrant under the Nationality Law, 1952 and the rights of an immigrant under any other legislation are also granted to the child and grandchild of a Jew, to the spouse of a Jew and to the spouse of the child and grandchild of a Jew – with the exception of a person who was a Jew and willingly changed his religion.

(b) It makes no difference whether or not the Jew through whom a right is claimed under sub-section (a) is still alive or whether or not he has immigrated to this country.

(c) The exceptions and conditions appertaining to a Jew or an immigrant under or by virtue of this Law or the legislation referred to in sub-section (a) shall also apply to a person claiming any right under sub-section (a).

4B. For the purpose of this Law, "a Jew" means a person born to a Jewish mother or converted to Judaism and who is not a member of another religion.

5. The Minister of the Interior is charged with the implementation of this Law and may make regulations as to any matter relating to its implementation and as to the grant of immigrants' visas and certificates to minors up to the age of 18.

Regulations regarding sections 4A and 4B require the approval of the Constitution, Law and Justice Committee of the Knesset.

Appendix 5

State of Israel
World Zionist Organization – Jewish Agency (Status) Law

7 ISRAEL LAWS 3 (1952)

1. The State of Israel regards itself as the creation of the entire Jewish people, and its gates are open, in accordance with its laws, to every Jew wishing to immigrate to it.

2. The World Zionist Organization, from its foundation five decades ago, headed the movement and efforts of the Jewish people to realize the age-old vision of the return to its homeland and, with the assistance of other Jewish circles and bodies, carried the main responsibility for establishing the State of Israel.

3. The World Zionist Organization, which is also the Jewish Agency, takes care as before of immigration and directs absorption and settlement projects in the State.

4. The State of Israel recognizes the World Zionist Organization as the authorized agency which will continue

to operate in the State of Israel for the development and settlement of the country, the absorption of immigrants from the Diaspora and the coordination of the activities in Israel of Jewish institutions and organizations active in those fields.

5. The mission of gathering in the exiles, which is the central task of the State of Israel and the Zionist Movement in our days, requires constant efforts by the Jewish people in the Diaspora; the State of Israel, therefore, expects the cooperation of all Jews, as individuals and groups, in building up the State and assisting the immigration to it of the masses of the people, and regards the unity of all sections of Jewry as necessary for this purpose.

6. The State of Israel expects efforts on the part of the World Zionist Organization for achieving this unity; if, to this end, the Zionist Organization, with the consent of the Government and the approval of the Knesset, should decide to broaden its basis, the enlarged body will enjoy the status conferred upon the World Zionist Organization in the State of Israel.

7. Details of the status of the World Zionist Organization – whose representation is the Zionist Executive, also known as the Executive of the Jewish Agency – and the form of its cooperation with the Government shall be determined by a Covenant to be made in Israel between the Government and the Zionist Executive.

8. The Covenant shall be based on the declaration of the 23rd Zionist Congress in Jerusalem that the practical work of the World Zionist Organization and its various bodies for the fulfilment of their historic tasks in Eretz-Israel requires full cooperation and coordination on its part with the State of Israel and its Government, in accordance with the laws of the State.

9. There shall be set up a committee for the coordination of the activities of the Government and Executive in the spheres in which the Executive will operate according to the Covenant; the tasks of the Committee shall be determined by the Covenant.

10. The Covenant and any variation or amendment thereof made with the consent of the two parties shall be published in *Reshumot* and shall come into force on the day of publication, unless they provide for an earlier or later day for this purpose.

11. The Executive is a juristic body and may enter into contracts, acquire, hold and relinquish property and be a party to any legal or other proceeding.

12. The Executive and its funds and other institutions shall be exempt from taxes and other compulsory Government charges, subject to such restrictions and conditions as may be laid down by the Covenant; the exemption shall come into force on the coming into force of the Covenant.

Appendix 6

Covenant Between the Government of Israel (Hereafter the Government) and The Zionist Executive called also the Executive of the Jewish Agency (hereafter the Executive)

Entered into this day, in accordance with the Zionist Organization – Jewish Agency Status Bill, 1952.

1. The following are the functions of the Zionist Executive as included in this Covenant:

The organizing of immigration abroad and the transfer of immigrants and their property to Israel; co-operation in the absorption of immigrants in Israel; youth immigration; agricultural settlement in Israel; the acquisition and amelioration of land in Israel by the institutions of the Zionist Organization, the Keren Kayemeth Leisrael and the Keren Hayesod; participation in the establishment and the expansion of development enterprises in Israel; the encouragement of private capital investments in Israel; assistance to cultural enterprises and institutions of higher learning in Israel; the mobilization of resources for financing these activities; the co-ordination of the activities in Israel of Jewish institutions and organizations acting within the limits of these functions by means of public funds.

2. Any activity carried out in Israel by the Executive or on its behalf for the purpose of carrying out the said functions, or part of them, shall be executed in accordance with the laws of Israel and the regulations and administrative instructions

in force from time to time, which govern the activities of the governmental authorities whose functions cover, or are affected by, the activity in question.

3. In the organizing of immigration and the handling of immigrants, the Executive shall act on the basis of a plan agreed on with the Government or authorized by the Co-ordinating Board (see para. 8). Immigrants will require visas according to the Law of the Return 5711–1950.

4. The Executive shall, in agreement with the Government, co-ordinate the activities in Israel of Jewish institutions and organizations which act within the limits of the Executive's functions.

5. The Executive may carry out its functions itself or through its existing institutions or those which it may establish in the future, and it may also enlist in its activities the co-operation of other institutions in Israel, with the proviso that it may not delegate any of its functions or rights under the Covenant without the agreement of the Government, and shall not authorize any body or institution to carry out its functions, in whole or in part, except after prior notification of the Government.

6. The Executive shall be responsible for the mobilization of the financial and material resources required for the execution of its functions, by means of the Keren Hayesod, the Keren Kayemeth Leisrael and other funds.

7. The Government shall consult with the Executive in regard to legislation specially impinging on the functions of the Executive before such legislation is submitted to the Knesset.

8. For the purpose of co-ordinating activities between the Government and the Executive in all spheres to which this Covenant applies, a Co-ordinating Board shall be established (hereafter called the Board). The Board shall be composed of an even number of members, not fewer than four, half of whom shall be members of the Government appointed by it, and half of whom shall be members of the Executive appointed by it. The Government and the Executive shall be entitled from time to time to replace the members of the Board by others among their members.

9. The Board shall meet at least once a month. It may appoint sub-committees consisting of members of the Board

and also of non-members. The Board shall from time to time submit to the Government and the Executive reports of its deliberations and recommendations. Except as stated above, the Board shall itself determine the arrangements for its sessions and deliberations.

10. The Government must see to it that its authorized organs shall provide the Executive and its institutions with all the permits and facilities required by law for activities carried out in accordance with this Covenant for the purpose of carrying out the Executive's functions.

11. Donations and legacies to the Executive or any of its institutions shall be exempt from Inheritance Tax. All other problems connected with the exemption of the Executive, its Funds and its other institutions, from payment of taxes, customs and other obligatory governmental imposts shall be the subject of a special arrangement between the Executive and the Government. This arrangement shall be formulated in an annex to this Covenant within eight months, as an inseparable part thereof, and shall come into force as from the date of signature of this Covenant.

12. All proposals for alterations or amendments to this Covenant, or any addition thereto, must be made in writing, and no alteration or amendment of this Covenant, or addition thereto, shall be made except in writing.

13. Any notification to be sent to the Government shall be sent to the Prime Minister, and any notification to be sent to the Executive shall be sent to the Chairman of the Executive in Jerusalem.

14. This Covenant shall come into force on the date of signature.

IN WITNESS WHEREOF, etc.
SIGNED – Jerusalem
     July 26, 1954
              FOR THE GOVERNMENT

MOSHE SHARITT,
Prime Minister
FOR THE ZIONIST EXECUTIVE

BERL LOCKER

DR. NAHUM GOLDMANN
CHAIRMEN

Annex A

The Chairman   Jerusalem, July 26, 1954
Zionist Executive
The Jewish Agency
Jerusalem

Dear Mr. Chairman,

I have the honour to inform you of the Government's decision that any administrative order that may be in force from time to time in regard to investigations, searches and detentions in Government offices shall apply also to the Executive and its institutions as defined in the Covenant entered into this day between the Government of Israel and the Zionist Executive.

You have agreed, and the Government has taken note, that the Zionist Executive will not maintain in Israel judicial or investigative machinery of its own, except in compliance with the laws of the State and in constant co-ordination with the Attorney-General of the Government of Israel.

Yours sincerley,
(sgd.)
Prime Minister

Annex B

The Chairman   Jerusalem, July 26, 1954
Zionist Executive
The Jewish Agency
Jerusalem

Dear Mr. Chairman,

I have the honour to inform you of the Government's decision that in the order of precedence at official ceremonies the Chairmen of the Zionist Executive and the Chairman of the Zionist General Council will immediately follow the Members of the Government; Members of the Zionist Executive will be equal in precedence to Members of the Knesset, and Members of the Zionist General Council will immediately follow Members of the Knesset.

Yours sincerely,
(Sgd.)
Prime Minister

Annex C
The Jewish Agency, P.O.B. 92, Jerusalem

The Prime Minister   July 26, 1954
Jerusalem

Dear Mr. Prime Minister,

We have the honour to acknowledge the receipt of your letter in which you inform us of the Government's decision that any administrative order that may be in force from time to time in regard to investigations, searches and detentions in Government offices shall apply also to the Executive and its institutions as defined in the Covenant entered into this day between the Government of Israel and the Zionist Executive.

We hereby confirm that the Zionist Executive has agreed not to maintain in Israel judicial or criminal investigative machinery of its own, unless approved by the Government, and that any such machinery will function in constant co-ordination with the Attorney-General of the Government of Israel.

Yours sincerely,
(sgd.)
Chairmen of the Executive

Appendix 7

Appendix to the Covenant Between
the Government and the Executive
of the Jewish Agency 1

In accordance with section 11 of the Covenant between the Government of Israel (hereinafter "the Government") and between the Executive of the Jewish Agency for Israel (hereinafter "the Executive") made on 25 Tammuz 5714 (26 July, 1954), as amended, this Appendix was signed this day:

1. In this Appendix – "The Executive" – includes the Jewish National Fund and Keren Hayesod – United Israel Appeal.

2. The Executive shall be exempt from taxes and the other government mandatory payments that are specified hereafter subject to such limitations and conditions as follows:

437

(a) From municipal property tax under the Municipal Property Tax Ordinance 1940, and from agricultural property tax under the Agricultural Property Tax Ordinance, 1942, for all property that is not leased thereby and was not given to another party in any manner whatsoever.

(b) From fees under the Land Transfer (Fees) Regulation 5716–1956 and under the Cooperative Houses Regulations, 5713–1953.

(c) From land appreciation tax under the Land Appreciation Tax Law, 5709–1949.

(d) From the tax under the War Damage Compensation Tax Law, 5711–1951, with respect to those properties of the Executive that were not leased and not given to another party in any manner whatsoever, and in respect whereof the Executive requests the exemption thereof from the tax. If the Executive requests an exemption for any property as aforesaid, it will not be entitled to compensation in respect of such property from the fund under the War Damage Compensation Law, as is set out in the War Damage Compensation Tax (Payment of Damages) Regulations 5713–1953.

(e) From compulsory loans under the Compulsory Loan Law, 5713–1953.

(f) From registration fees and capital fees under sections 1(1), 1(2), 1(3), 1(8), 1(9) and 1(10) of the Companies (Fees) Order 5713–1953, provided:

(i) that the exemption from the fee as aforesaid in respect of a company having a share capital shall apply only with respect to that portion of the fee which bears the same ratio to the total fee as is the ratio of the fraction of the share capital attributable to the Executive in respect whereof such fee is paid to the entire sum of the said share capital.

(ii) that the aforesaid exemption from the fee in respect of a company that does not have a share capital shall apply only to that portion of the fee the amount whereof is equal to the amount of the fee divided by the number of members for whom the fee is paid and multiplied by the number of members who are entitled to the exemption under this Appendix.

1. Yalkut Pirsumim 549, 5717 (1.8.1957), p. 1204.
2. Amendment: Yalkut Pirsumim: 595, 5718 (17.4.1958) (17.4.1958) p. 831.

(g) (i) From purchase tax under the Purchase Tax Law, 5712–1952 – in respect of merchandise to the Executive the tax rate wherefor exceeds 10%, and in respect of the importation of all merchandise, provided that the merchandise is designated for the execution of its duties;

(ii) From customs duties under the Customs Tariff and Exemptions Ordinance, 1937 – in respect of all merchandise imported by the Executive for development purposes and in respect whereof the Executive has notified the Director of Customs at the time of application for a licence to import the said merchandise, or if the merchandise does not require an import licence – prior to the order, of the import of the merchandise.

(iii) With reference to merchandise in respect whereof an exemption has been given under this section and which the Executive has transferred to another party or which has been transferred for a different use or purpose other than that wherefor an exemption was granted, the Executive shall be liable for payment of the tax commencing from the time of the transfer.

(h) From income tax and company profits tax, under the Income Tax Ordinance, 1947, and from any other tax imposed on income – with respect to all income of the Executive; provided that the exemption shall not apply to income from dividends or interest on debentures paid to the Executive by a company which deals in trade, works or any enterprise unless such company deals in trade, works or any enterprise designed for settling the land or absorption of immigrants.

(i) From stamp duty under the Stamp Duty Ordinance – with respect to the following documents:

(1) Debentures issued by the Executive in respect whereof stamp duty applies under item 26 of the Schedule to the Stamp Duty Ordinance, when a guarantee for their redemption is secured by guarantee of the State of Israel;

(2) The transfer of all stocks and shares in respect whereof stamp duty applies under item 37(c) of the Schedule to the Stamp Duty Ordinance and in respect whereof the Executive in transferee;

(3) Receipts given by the Executive;

(4) Guarantees under item 27 of the said Schedule when

the guaranteed party is the Executive or guarantees given by the Executive when the guaranteed party is a body supported by the Executive.

(j) From licence fees under the Transport Ordinance in respect of all vehicles of the Executive which are not private motor vehicles as defined in the Transport Ordinance.

3. (a) The exemptions granted to the Executive under sections 2(a), 2(b), 2(c), 2(d), 2(e) and 2(i) (1) shall also be granted to Himanutah Company Ltd.

(b) Himanutah Company Ltd. will be exempt from income tax, company profits tax, and from other taxes imposed upon income, with respect to income received by it from its real estate transactions.

4. The exemptions under this Appendix are supplementary to exemptions under any other law and do not detract therefrom.

IN WITNESS WHERE OF the parties have signed in Jerusalem on this day of 20 of Tammuz 5717 (19 July, 1957).

Nahum Goldman   David Ben-Gurion
The Zionist Executive   The Government of Israel

Appendix 8

30 *Israel Laws* 43

World Zionist Organisation – Jewish Agency
for Israel (Status) (Amendment) Law, 5736–1975**

1.   In the World Zionist Organisation – Jewish Agency for
Israel (Status) Law, 5713–1953[2]) (hereinafter referred to as
"the principal Law"), the following section shall be inserted
after section 2:
"2A. The Jewish Agency for Israel is an independent
voluntary association consisting of the World Zionist
Organisation and other organisations and bodies. It
operates in the State of Israel in fields chosen by it with
the consent of the Government.".

2.   Section 3 of the principal Law shall be replaced by the
following section:
"3. The World Zionist Organisation and the Jewish
Agency for Israel take care of immigration as before and
conduct absorption and settlement projects in the
State.".

3.   In section 4 of the principal Law, the words "the World
Zionist Organisation as the authorised agency which will
continue to operate" shall be replaced by the words "the
World Zionist Organisation and the Jewish Agency for Israel
as the authorised agencies which will continue to operate".

4.   The following section shall be inserted after section 6 of
the principal Law:
"6A. The provisions of sections 5 and 6 shall apply
mutatis mutandis to the Jewish Agency for Israel.".

5.   Section 7 of the principal Law shall be replaced by the
following section:
"7. Details of the status of the World Zionist Organisation and the Jewish Agency for Israel and the form of
their cooperation with the Government shall be determined by Covenants to be made in Israel between the
Government and each of these two bodies.".

Amendment of section 8.

6.　In section 8 of the principal Law –

(1) the words "with the World Zionist Organisation" shall be inserted after the words "the Covenant";

(2) the subsection mark "(a)" shall be inserted after the figure "8" and the following subsection shall be added after subsection (a):

"(b)　The Covenant with the Jewish Agency for Israel shall provide for full cooperation and coordination on its part with the State of Israel and its Government in accordance with the laws of the State.".

Replacement of section 9.

7.　Section 9 of the Law shall be replaced by the following section:

"9.　Two committees shall be set up for the coordination of activities between the Government and the World Zionist Organisation and the Jewish Agency for Israel in the spheres in which each of them is to operate according to the Covenant made with it. The tasks of the committees shall be determined by the Covenants.".

Amendment of section 10.

8.　In section 10 of the principal Law, the words "The Covenant and any variation or amendment thereof" shall be replaced by the words "The Covenants and any variation or amendment thereof.".

Replacement of section 11.

9.　Section 11 of the principal Law shall be replaced by the following section:

"11. The World Zionist Organisation and the Jewish Agency for Israel are juristic persons and may enter into contracts, acquire, hold and relinquish property and be parties to any legal or other proceedings.".

Amendment of section 12.

10. In section 12 of the principal Law, the words "The Executive and its funds and other institutions" shall be replaced by the words "The World Zionist Organisation and the Jewish Agency for Israel and their respective funds and other institutions".

Change of title.

11. The principal Law shall be renamed the World Zionist Organisation and Jewish Agency for Israel (Status) Law, 5713–1952.

Commencement.

12. This Law shall have effect from the 28th Sivan, 5731 (21st June, 1971).

YITZCHAK RABIN
Prime Minister

Appendix 9

Basic Law: Jerusalem, Capital of Israel, 5740–1980*

1. Jerusalem united in its entirety is the capital of Israel.

2. Jerusalem is the seat of the President of the State, the Knesset, the Government and the Supreme Court.

3. The Holy Places shall be protected from desecration and any other violation and from anything likely to violate the freedom of access of the members of the different religions to the places sacred to them or their feelings with regard to those places.

4. (a) The Government shall diligently persist in the development and prosperity of Jeruslaem and the welfare of its inhabitants, by the appropriation of special resources, including a special annual grant to the Jerusalem Municipality (Capital City Grant) with the approval of the Finance Committee of the Knesset.

(b) Jerusalem shall be given particular priority in the activities of the State's authorities for the development of the city in the financial and economic spheres and in other areas.

(c) The Government shall constitute a special body or bodies for the implementation of this Section.

(Passed by the Knesset on July 30, 1980)

---

* Reproduction from the text supplied by the Embassy of Israel, Washington, DC.

Appendix 10

Israel: Law on Golan Heights*

[December 14, 1981]
Golan Heights Law – 5742/1981

1. The law, jurisdiction and administration of the State shall apply to the Golan Heights, as described in the appendix.

2. This law shall become valid on the day of its passage in the Knesset.

3. The Minister of the Interior shall be charged with the implementation of this law, and he is entitled, in consultation with the Minister of Justice, to enact regulations for its implementation and to formulate in regulations transitional provisions and provisions concerning the continued application of regulations, orders, administrative orders, rights and duties which were in force on the Golan Heights prior to the application of this law.

---

*   Reproduced from the text provided to *International Legal Materials* by the Embassy of Israel at Washington, D.C.

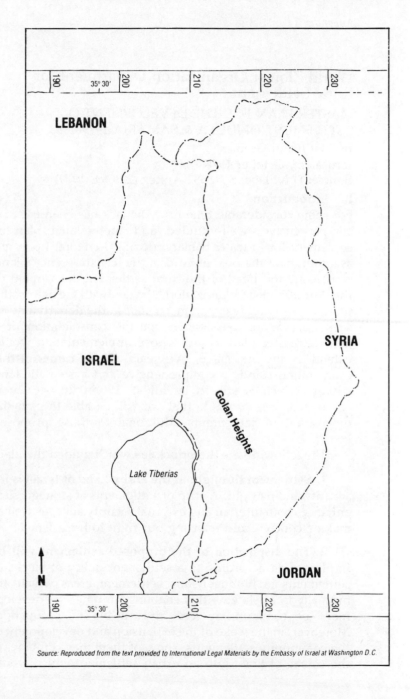

LEBANON

ISRAEL

SYRIA

Golan Heights

Lake Tiberias

N

JORDAN

Source: Reproduced from the text provided to International Legal Materials by the Embassy of Israel at Washington D.C.

Appendix 11

World Zionist Organization Department for Rural Settlement

MASTER PLAN FOR THE DEVELOPMENT OF
SETTLEMENT IN JUDEA & SAMARIA 1979–1983
by Matityahu Drobles
Jerusalem, October 1978
Source: U.N. Doc. S./13582 Annex (22 Oct. 1979)

I. Introduction

For some considerable time now the lack has been felt of a comprehensive, well-founded and professional plan of settlement for Judea & Samaria (J&S). Therefore, upon my assumption of the post of head of the Jewish Agency's land settlement and head of the rural settlement department of the World Zionist Organization, I began, with the help of the first-rate and highly experienced staff in the department, to seek out various possibilities for the consolidation of a general master plan in J&S whose implementation would extend, in the first stage, five years. At the center of this examination stands a comprehensive and systematic land survey, which is still in its midst. When the survey is completed, it is probable that we will be able to plan the disposition of settlements additional to those proposed below.

The following are the principles which guided the plan:

1. Settlement throughout the entire Land of Israel is for security and by right. A strip of settlements at strategic sites enhances both internal and external security alike, as well as making concrete and realizing our right to Eretz-Israel.

2. The disposition of the proposed settlement will be implemented according to a settlement policy of blocks of settlements in homogeneous settlement areas which are mutually interrelated – this enabling, in time, the development of common services and means of production. Moreover, in the wake of the expansion and development of the community settlements, some of them may combine, in the course of time, into an urban settlement which would consist of all the settlements in that particular bloc. Only in four instances was there no choice but to propose the establishment of an isolated settlement in an area, due to territorial and land limitations at the site.

3. The disposition of the settlements must be carried out not only *around* the settlements of the minorities, but also *in between them*, this in accordance with the settlement policy adopted in Galilee and in other parts of the country. Over the course of time, with or without peace, we will have to learn to live *with* the minorities and *among them*, while fostering goodneighborly relations – and they with us. It would be best for both peoples – the Jewish and the Arab – to learn this as early as possible, since when all is said and done the development and flowering of the area will be to the benefit of *all* the residents of the land. Therefore the proposed settlement blocs are situated as a strip surrounding the (Judea & Samaria) ridge – starting from its western slopes from north to south, and along its eastern slopes from south to north: both *between* the minorities population and *around* it.

4. New settlements will be established only on State-owned land, and not on private Arab-owned land which is duly registered. We should ensure that there is no need for the expropriation of private plots from the members of the minorities. This is the chief and outstanding innovation in this master plan: *all* the areas proposed below as sites for the establishment of new settlements have been meticulously examined, their location precisely determined, and all of them are without any doubt State-owned – this according to the preliminary findings of the fundamental and comprehensive land survey now being carried out.

5. The location of the settlements was determined following a thorough examination of the various sites with respect to their being suitable and amenable to settlement, taking into account topographical conditions, land-preparation possibilities, etc.

6. In order to create as broad a disposition as possible and to establish settlements which will excel in a high quality of life, we suggest that the majority of the settlements in J&S be established from the outset as community settlements. In addition to these, a number of agricultural and combined settlements will be established at locations where there are suitable means for production. The settlers' employment will be mainly in industry, tourism and services, with a minority engaging in intensive agriculture.

* * * *

As is known, it is the task of the land settlement department to initiate, plan and implement the settlement enterprise according to the decisions of the Government and of the joint Government–World Zionist Organization Committee for Settlement. I hope and believe that this plan – which is based on experience, professional know-how, surveys and planning, all of which are aimed at ensuring effective implementation – will in fact be approved, and soon, by these bodies.

It must be borne in mind that it may be too late tomorrow to do what is not done today. I believe that we should encourage and direct the tendency which exists today of moving from city to country, because of the quality of life which characterizes rural settlement. This will enable us to bring about the dispersion of the population from the densely populated urban strip of the coastal plain eastward to the presently empty areas of J&S. There are today persons who are young or young in spirit who want to take up the challenge of national goals and who want to settle in J&S. We should enable them to do so, and sooner is better.

Upon the approval of the plan proposed herein, the land settlement department will devote itself to drawing up a detailed plan for the development of settlement in J&S – including a timetable for the establishment of the proposed settlements – and the same applies for the thickening and development of the existing settlements and those now under construction. We must also ensure, from the State and WZO budgets, the required investments for realizing and executing this task.

* * * *

According to the plan here presented, *46 new settlements* in J&S will be added within five years, which at the end of that period will be inhabited by *16,000 families*, this at an investment of *IL32 billion*. In the first year of the plan's execution the number of families in the new settlements will total, according to the plan, 5,000 at an investment of *IL10 billion;* this the annual investment in each of the plan's four remaining years will be *IL5.5 billion.*

With respect to the thickening of the existing settlements and those under construction, an additional 11,000 families at the end of five years is proposed, at an investment of *IL22 billion.* For the first year of the thickening project, a total of 3,000 additional families is proposed, which will necessitate an investment of IL6 billion in that year. Therefore, the annual investment in each of *this project's four remaining years will be IL4 billion.

Altogether, then after five years there will be added in J&S – in the proposed settlements, the existing ones and those under construction – *27,000 families,* this necessitating an overall investment of *IL54 billion.* In the first year of the project's implementation *8,000 families* will be added at an investment of *IL16 billion.* Thus the annual overall investment in each of the remaining four years will be *IL9.5 billion.*

This investment is absolutely essential and is a condition for the execution of a paramount national mission.

II. Disposition of the Settlements

REIHAN BLOC

It is proposed to establish a new settlement in this bloc – Reihan B – to go up west of the village of Arakah. This will be a settlement based on agriculture and industry, and which will have after one year 50 families, and within five years 100 families.

There are presently two settlements in this bloc: Reihan (which it is proposed to thicken by adding 50 families in the first year and 100 by the end of five years); and Mei-Ami (an additional 80 families). In addition, there are already plans for establishing in this bloc the settlements of Mei-Ami B and Barkai B, with each of them to have 50 families at the end of the first year and 100 families at the end of five years.

The Reihan Bloc settlements will be moshavim (smallholders' collective settlement) based on a combination of agriculture and industry.

MAARAV BLOC

Here it is proposed to establish four new agricultural settlements which will constitute a strip descending from north to south on the border of the green line, with the farming areas to lie west of that line. Each of the four settlements will have 50 families in the first Year and 100 families within five years. Maarav A will go up southeast of Kafin village; Maarav B will be southeast of Baka-al-Gharbiyeh; Maarav C would be east of Kibbutz Bahan (and south of Maarav B); and Maarav D is slated for east of Tulkarm.

The Maarav Bloc settlements will be linked by a new national highway parallel to the Nahal Iron road, which will pass by Baka-al-Gharbiyeh and continue to Kfar Sava.

DOTAN REGION

At this stage just one site has been found for settling this bloc: the Mirka junction, which overlooks the Dotan Valley. Here it is proposed that a large community settlement be established, to be called Dotan, to be inhabited after the first year of the project's implementation by 150 families and after five years by 500 families.

SLA'IT BLOC

Two settlements already exist in this bloc: Sla'it and Zur-Natan. For the two of them together it is proposed that another 100 families be added in the first year and 200 families at the end of five years.

SHOMRON BLOC

Here it is proposed that two new community settlements be established: Maaleh Nahal (north of the village of Bourkah), and Maaleh Nahal B on Jabl Yazzid (east of Malleh Nahal). Each of these two settlements will be populated by 100 families in the first year and by 300 families after five years. To date two settlements have been established in this bloc: Sanour and Shomron. For each, it is proposed to add 50 families in the first year and 200 families within five years.

KEDUMIM BLOC

In addition to the already existing settlement of Kedumim (to which it is proposed to add 50 families in the first year and 200 by the end of five years), it is proposed to establish another three community settlements, to be based on industry and intensive agriculture: Kedumim B, at a site located at "Imam Ali" (north of Kedumim)*; Kedumim C, at Ras-a-Bayyad (southeast of Kedumim); Kedumim D, at a site on A-Ras (south of the village of Tal). Each of these settlements will have 100 families in the first year and 300 families at the end of five years.

The Shomron and Kedumim Blocs will be linked by an electricity grid which today ends at the town of Anabtah. This line will be extended to the Shomron settlement and from there will be set up to the rest of the settlements in the two Blocs.

The water supply system for the settlements in these two Blocs will be based on local well-drillings. There are today two drillings, at Kedumim and at Beit Abba. Should the need arise (and in accordance with the detailed plan to be drawn up and implemented in the future) the drilling of additional wells in these areas should be considered.

KARNEI SHOMRON BLOC

Here it is proposed to establish four new community settlements: Karnei Shomron B (south of Karnei Shomron), Karnei Shomron C (east of Karnei Shomron), Karnei Shomron D (southeast of Karnei Shomron C) and Karnei Shomron E (east of Karnei Shomron C). Each of these settlements will have 100 families in the first year and 300 families after five years.

With respect to the urban settlements in this Bloc – Karnei Shomron and Elkana – it is proposed to add 200 families to each of them in the first year, and 800 families each by the end of five years.

---

* A gravesite which is sacred to Muslims, located 3.5 kms. southeast of Sha'ar Hagai, named after Imam Ali, a holy man who appears in a famous Arab legend. – RM.

ARIEL BLOC

In this Bloc the urban settlement of Ariel (Haris) has already been established, which it is proposed to thicken by adding 260 families in the first year of the plan's execution and 1,500 families by the end of five years. This settlement lies on the Samaria transverse road, which links the center of the country with the Jordan Rift.

In addition to this urban settlement it is proposed to establish a new community settlement: Ariel B, at the site located at Hirbet a-Shelal (west of Ariel), which is planned to have 100 families by the end of its first year and 300 families five years later.

NEVEH-ZUF BLOC

In addition to the already existing community settlement of Neveh-Zuf (to which it is proposed to add another 50 families in the first year and 200 after five years), it is proposed to establish in this bloc, three new community settlements: Neveh-Zuf B, at Hirbet Rushniyeh (southwest of Neveh-Zuf), Neveh-Zuf C (north of Neveh-Zuf) and Neveh-Zuf D (northeast of Neveh-Zuf) – the later two near Kafr Ayin. Each of these three settlements will, according to the plan, have 100 families in the first year and 300 families within five years.

Neveh-Zuf already has an electric line hookup. The water supply will be from the direction of Bir-Zeit, from the Ramallah water line.

MODIIM BLOC

Four settlements – on both sides of the green line – already exist here, united within the Modiim regional council. For the settlements of Shilat, Kfar Ruth and Mevoh Modiim, an additional 20 families each is proposed for the first year and 80 families within five years. For Mevoh Horon the figures are 50 families and 150 families within five years. Also planned for this area is the settlement of Matityahu, which is expected to be inhabited by 100 families in the first year and 300 families five years later.

In addition to these existing and planned settlements it is proposed to establish, on Hill 386, a new community settlement, Matityahu B (west of the village of IBil'in). This settlement will be populated by 100 families after one year and by 300 families after five years.

GIVON BLOC

Two settlements exist in this area: Beit Horon (a community settlement for which 200 or more families are proposed within five years) and Givon, which was originally slated as an urban settlement but which, it is proposed – due to land limitations there – be a community settlement to which 150 families will be added within five years. Instead, it is proposed to establish, on a hill north of Givon, a new urban settlement, Givon B, to be inhabited by 500 families in the first year and by 3,000 families after five years. It is also proposed to establish, west of Givon B, a new community settlement, Givon C, where 100 families would live at the end of the first year and 300 after five years.

ETZION BLOC (GUSH ETZION)

Six settlements already exist here: Rosh Tzurim (where an additional 30 families would come within five years), Elon Shvut (an additional 100 families within five years), Kfar Etzion (20 more families), Elazar (another 15 families), Migdal Oz (another 70 families within five years) and Tekoah (which it is proposed become an urban settlement because of its relative distance from the other Etzioin Bloc settlements), which would have another 200 families within one year and 800 families after five years. Planned for this Bloc is the settlement of Haforit, to be based on agriculture and industry (50 families in the first year and 100 at the end of five years).

There was a suggestion to establish an urban settlement – Efrat – at a site located south of Bethlehem, but ground conditions there do not enable such extensive development, so it is proposed that this be a community settlement. In addition to Efrat 5 it is proposed to establish another four community settlements in this Bloc: Etzion B, in the Beit Fajr Forest (between Migdal Oz and Kfar Etzion), Etzion C, at Givat Hamukhtar (west of Kfar Etzion), Elazar B, at Sheikh Abdallah Ibrahim (northeast of Elazar) and Nahalim (west of

Nahlin village). Each of the five settlements mentioned would have 100 families in the first year and 300 families five years later.

This new disposition of Etzion Bloc settlements will form a territorial continuity with the settlements of the Adulam District. (The Adulam District lies between Beit Shemesh and Beit Goubrin. – RM).

TARKUMYAH REGION

East of the village of Tarkumyah (which lies northwest of Hebron), in the Tarkumyah forest, it is proposed to establish a large community settlement, Tirat-Horesh, which is slated for 150 families within a year of its establishment and for 400 families five years later. For its services the settlement will rely on the Etzion Bloc settlements to the north, or, alternatively, on the settlements of the Mount Hebron slopes to the west and the south.

ADORAYIM BLOC

Here, two settlements can be established: at the Dorah junction, east of Sikha village, it is proposed to establish a community settlement to be based on a combination of agriculture and industry. To be called Adorayim, the settlement would have 100 families within one year and 300 families within five years. It is also proposed to establish a new agricultural settlement, Eiton (near Tel Eiton), where 50 families would live within the first year and 100 families after five years.

YATIR BLOC

Here, too, settlements would be established on both sides of the green line which together would constitute one unified bloc. There are in this area two settlements at present: Yatir (Ardon) and Lutsifer. For each of them an additional 100 families is proposed for the first year and 300 within five years. Also planned for this area is an agricultural settlement, Kramim (50–100 families).

In addition to these three settlements it is proposed to establish another five new community settlements to be based on agriculture, industry and tourism: Raveh (at the Rahaveh police station site, northeast of Kramim), Yatir B, Yatir C, Yatir D (all three of them northeast of Yatir), Susiya (at the site of the ancient synagogue northeast of Samua). Each of these five settlements would have 100 families in the first year and 300 families five years later.

It should be noted that at the impressive site of the ancient synagogue, as well as at Yatir and environs a tourist project could be set up which would provide employment to many families in the area.

AMOS REGION

In the area of Rujm-a-Nakah (between Nahal Amos and Nahal Arugot, northeast of Hebron) it is proposed to establish a large community settlement to be called Amos. It would have 150 families in its first year and 400 families at the end of five years.

This settlement, along with others to be established to its east, could form a territorial continuity with the settlements planned for the Dead Sea shoreline, including the already existing Mitzpeh Shalem. It is proposed that the Amos Region settlements be linked with Tekoah and with the Etzion Bloc settlements by means of a Judean transverse road to be paved from east to west, extending to the settlements of the Mount Hebron slopes and the Adulam District.

ADUMIM BLOC

The temporary settlement of Maaleh-Adumim already exists here, along with its adjacent industrial zone. The permanent urban settlement is now under construction at a site near Aizariyah, just outside Jerusalem, and where an additional 300 families would take up residence in the first year and 1,500 families within five years. Also in the area is the settlement of Mitzpeh Jericho, for which an additional 100 families is proposed in the first year of the plan and 300 after five years.

In addition to these two settlements it is proposed to establish a series of three new settlements which will form a territorial continuity with the Beil-El Bloc settlements to the north: Pe'era (Maaleh Adumim B, near Air Farah), which is to be a large community settlement based mainly on tourism and holidaying, to be inhabited by 150 families in the first year and 400 families five years later; Maaleh Adumim C, north of Pe'era; and still further north Maaleh Adumim D – the latter two being community settlements meant to be inhabited by 300 families each within five years.

BEIT-EL BLOC

Four community settlements have already been established in this Bloc: Beit-El (where it is proposed to add 400 families within five years), Ofra (an additional 300 families), Rimonim and Kohav HaShahar (for each of which it is proposed to add 300 families within five years). East of Kohave HaShahar it is proposed to establish a new community settlement, Kohav HaShahar B, to be inhabited by 100 families within one year and by 300 families within five years.

EPHRAIM BLOC

New settlements to go up in this Bloc will form a territorial continuity with the Jordan Rift settlements. At present there are three settlements in this area, Gitit, Maaleh Ephraim and Mevoh Shiloh. It is proposed to establish a new community settlement, Mevoh Shiloh B, west of Mevoh Shiloh, which would have 100 families in the first year and 300 families at the end of five years.

SHILOH BLOC

Two community settlements have already been established here: Shiloh and Tapuah (it is proposed to add 300 families to each of them within five years of the project's implementation).

Another three community settlements could be established in this area, with each of them having 100 families in their first year and 300 families five years later: Shiloh B, at the Batan Hiluah site (west of Shiloh), Shiloh C, at the Jabl Batan site (northwest of Shiloh B) and Shiloh D, on Jabl Rawat (northeast of Shiloh C).

ELON MOREH REGION

In this area, southeast of Nablus, on Jabl Rujaib, it is proposed to establish a large community settlement, Elon Moreh, to be inhabited by 400 families within five years of its establishment.

NAHAL TIRZAH REGION

Near Nahal Tirzah, on Jabl Thayur, it is proposed to establish a large community settlement (400 families within five years) called Tirzah.

III. Employment and Economic Branches in Settlements

Employment and the economic basis of the residents in J&S will be in accordance with the nature of the settlement and the surrounding area.

In the *urban settlements* some 60% of the families will be employed in industry, handicrafts, holidaying & tourism, and the rest in services and work outside the settlement. In the towns close to Jerusalem the proportion of those employed in outside work will be higher.

In the *community settlements* the economic basis in the development state will be as follows: about 50% of the families will earn their living from industry and handicrafts; about 12% from capital-based intensive agriculture; about 25% from outside work; and about 13% from local services.

The *agricultural* and the *combined settlements* will be based on agricultural baranches (mainly intensive, depending on the means for production in the area), as well as on industry, handicrafts and tourism. Some of the settlers will engage in local and regional services.

IV. Services and Social Integration

The regional services in education, health, culture, etc. will be planned and set up already in the first stage of the plan's execution, in each bloc, in one of the bloc's central settlements. Their preparation as early as possible will prove a boon to the settlers in the new settlements.

Social Integration: The detailed planning of the settlements will be carried out along with the formation of settlement core groups and their organization in anticipation of settlement. The absorption unit in the land settlement department will draw up an action framework in the sphere of the social absorption of the settlers (new immigrants and veterans) through coordination with the land settlement movements and other social bodies.

V. Investment Required to Execute the Plan

The overall investment for executing the five-year plan (proposed new settlements plus thickening of existing settlements and of those under construction) is IL54 billion, of which IL16 billion would be needed in the first year to activate the plan and IL9.5 billion in each of the four ensuing years. The calculation for investment is based on the additional families which, by the plan, would take up residence in J&S – 27,000 in the five years. The average investment for settling one family totals (in prices of July 1978 – sic) IL2 million, as follows: (All figures are in thousands of pounds) –

Infrastructure (roads, electricity, sewerage, etc.)	150
Temporary housing	150
Permanent housing (including public buildings)	600
Water sources	100
Means of production	900
Miscellaneous	100
Total investment per family	2,000

NOTE: The investment for a rural settlement is higher than that for the establishment of an urban settlement. The above calculation, of *IL2 million per family*, reflects the *average* investment per family in urban and rural settlement.

Appendix 12

General Assembly Resolution 181
29 November 1947 [in part]

PLAN OF PARTITION WITH ECONOMIC UNION

Part I
Future constitution and government of Palestine

B. STEPS PREPARATORY TO INDEPENDENCE

10. The Constituent Assembly of each State shall draft a democratic constitution for its State and choose a provisional government to succeed the Provisional Council of Government appointed by the Commission. The constitutions of the States shall embody chapters 1 and 2 of the Declaration provided for in section C below and include *inter alia* provisions for:

(a) Establishing in each State a legislative body elected by universal suffrage and by secret ballot on the basis of proportional representation, and an executive body responsible to the legislature;

(b) Settling all international disputes in which the State may be involved by peaceful means in such a manner that international peace and security, and justice, are not endangered;

(c) Accepting the obligation of the State to refrain in its international relations from the threat or use of force against the territorial integrity or political independence of any State, or in any other manner inconsistent with the purposes of the United Nations;

(d) Guaranteeing to all persons equal and non-discriminatory rights in civil, political, economic and religious matters and the enjoyment of human rights and fundamental freedoms, including freedom of religion, language, speech and publication, education, assembly and association;

(e) Preserving freedom of transit and visit for all residents and citizens of the other State in Palestine and the

City of Jerusalem, subject to considerations of national security, provided that each State shall control residence within its borders.

* * * *

C. DECLARATION

A declaration shall be made to the United Nations by the provisional government of each proposed State before independence. It shall contain *inter alia* the following clauses:

GENERAL PROVISION

The stipulations contained in the declaration are recognized as fundamental laws of the State and no law, regulation or official action shall conflict or interfere with these stipulations, nor shall any law, regulation or official action prevail over them.

* * * *

CHAPTER 2

Religious and minority rights

1. Freedom of conscience and the free exercise of all forms of worship, subject only to the maintenance of public order and morals, shall be ensured to all.

2. No discrimination of any kind shall be made between the inhabitants on the ground of race, religion, language or sex.

3. All persons within the jurisdiction of the State shall be entitled to equal protection of the laws.

4. The family law and personal status of the various minorities and their religious interests, including endowments, shall be respected.

5. Except as may be required for the maintenance of public order and good government, no measure shall be taken to obstruct or interfere with the enterprise of religious or charitable bodies of all faiths or to discriminate against any representative or member of these bodies on the ground of his religion or nationality.

6. The State shall ensure adequate primary and secondary education for the Arab and Jewish minority, respectively, in its own language and its cultural traditions.

The right of each community to maintain its own schools for the education of its own members in its own language, while conforming to such educational requirements of a general nature as the State may impose, shall not be denied or impaired. Foreign educational establishments shall continue their activity on the basis of their existing rights.

7. No restriction shall be imposed on the free use by any citizen of the State of any language in private intercourse, in commerce, in religion, in the Press or in publications of any kind, or at public meetings.[1]

8. No expropriation of land owned by an Arab in the Jewish State (by a Jew in the Arab State)[2] shall be allowed except for public purposes. In all cases of expropriation full compensation as fixed by the Supreme Court shall be paid previous to dispossession.

Appendix 13

General Assembly Resolution 2535B
10 December 1969

The General Assembly

Recognizing that the problem of the Palestine Arab refugees has arisen from the denial of their inalienable rights under the Charter of the United Nations and the Universal Declaration of Human Rights,

Gravely concerned that the denial of their rights has been aggravated by the reported acts of collective punishment, arbitrary detention, curfews, destruction of homes and property, deportation and other repressive acts against the refugees and other inhabitants of the occupied territories,

---

1. The following stipulation shall be added to the declaration concerning the Jewish State: "In the Jewish State adequate facilities shall be given to Arabic-speaking citizens for the use of their language, either orally or in writing, in the legislature, before the Courts and in the administration."
2. In the declaration concerning the Arab State, the words "by an Arab in the Jewish State" should be replaced by the words "by a Jew in the Arab State".

Recalling Security Council resolution 237 (1967) of 14 June 1967,

Recalling also its resolution 2252 (ES-V) of 4 July 1967 and its resolution 2452 A (XXIII) of 19 December 1968 calling upon the Government of Israel to take effective and immediate steps for the return without delay of those inhabitants who had fled the areas since the outbreak of hostilities,

Desirous of giving effect to its resolutions for relieving the plight of the displaced persons and the refugees,

1. *Reaffirms* the inalienable rights of the people of Palestine;

2. *Draws the attention* of the Security Council to the grave situation resulting from Israeli policies and practices in the occupied territories and Israel's refusal to implement the above resolutions;

3. *Requests* the Security Council to take effective measures in accordance with the relevant provisions of the Charter of the United Nations to ensure the implementation of these resolutions.

Appendix 14

General Assembly Resolution 2625
24 October 1970 [in part]

DECLARATION ON PRINCIPLES OF INTERNATIONAL LAW CONCERNING FRIENDLY RELATIONS AND CO-OPERATION AMONG STATES IN ACCORDANCE WITH THE CHARTER OF THE UNITED NATIONS

* * * *

The principle of equal rights and self-determination of peoples
By virtue of the principle of equal rights and self-determination of peoples enshrined in the Charter of the United Nations, all peoples have the right freely to determine, without external interference, their political status and to pursue their economic, social and cultural development, and every state has the duty to respect this

right in accordance with the provisions of the Charter.

Every state has the duty to promote, through joint and separate action, realization of the principle of equal rights and self-determination of peoples, in accordance with the provisions of the Charter, and to render assistance to the United Nations in carrying out the responsibilities entrusted to it by the Charter regarding the implementation of the principle, in order:

(a) To promote friendly relations and co-operation among states; and
(b) To bring a speedy end to colonialism, having due regard to the freely expressed will of the peoples concerned;

and bearing in mind that subjection of peoples to alien subjugation, domination and exploitation constitutes a violation of the principle, as well as a denial of fundamental human rights, and is contrary to the Charter.

Every state has the duty to promote through joint and separate action universal respect for and observance of human rights and fundamental freedoms in accordance with the Charter.

The establishment of a sovereign and independent state, the free association or integration with an independent state or the emergence into any other political status freely determined by a people constitute modes of implementing the right of self-determination by that people.

Every state has the duty to refrain from any forcible action which deprives peoples referred to above in the elaboration of the present principle of their right to self-determination and freedom and independence. In their actions against, and resistance to, such forcible action in pursuit of the exercise of their right to self-determination, such peoples are entitled to seek and to receive support in accordance with the purposes and principles of the Charter.

The territory of a colony or other non-self-governing territory has, under the Charter, a status separate and distinct from the territory of the state administering it; and such separate and distinct status under the Charter shall exist until the people of the colony or non-self-governing territory have exercised their right of self-determination in accordance with the Charter, and particularly its purposes and principles.

Nothing in the foregoing paragraphs shall be construed as authorizing or encouraging any action which would dismember or impair, totally or in part, the territorial integrity or political unity of sovereign and independent states conducting themselves in compliance with the principle of equal rights and self-determination of peoples as described above and thus possessed of a government representing the whole people belonging to the territory without distinction as to race, creed or colour.

Every state shall refrain from any action aimed at the partial or total disruption of the national unity and territorial integrity of any other state or country.

* * * *

The principles of the Charter which are embodied in this Declaration constitute basic principles of international law, and consequently [the General Assembly] appeals to all states to be guided by these principles in their international conduct and to develop their mutual relations on the basis of the strict observance of these principles.

Appendix 15

General Assembly Resolution 3089D 7 December 1973

The General Assembly,
Recognizing that the problem of the Palestine Arab refugees has arisen from the denial of their inalienable rights under the Charter of the United Nations and the Universal Declaration of Human Rights,

Recalling its resolution 2535 B (XXIV) of 10 December 1969, in which it reaffirmed the inalienable right of the people of Palestine, and its resolutions 2649 (XXV) of 30 November 1970, 2672 C (XXV) of 8 December 1970, 2787 (XXVI) and 2792 D (XXVI) of 6 December 1971, 2955 (XXVII) of 12 December 1972 and 2963 E (XXVII) of 13 December 1972, in which it recognized, *inter alia*, that the people of Palestine is entitled to the right of self-determination,

Bearing in mind the principle of equal rights and self-determination enshrined in Articles 1 and 55 of the Charter and more recently reaffirmed in the Declaration on Principles of International Law concerning Friendly Relations and Co-operation among States in accordance with the Charter of the United Nations[7] and in the Declaration on the Strengthening of International Security,[8]

1. *Reaffirms* that the people of Palestine is entitled to equal rights and self-determination, in accordance with the Charter of the United Nations;

2. *Expresses once more its grave concern* that the people of Palestine has been prevented by Israel from enjoying its inalienable rights and from exercising its right to self-determination;

3. *Declares* that full respect for and realization of the inalienable rights of the people of Palestine, particularly its right to self-determination, are indispensable for the establishment of a just and lasting peace in the Middle East, and that the enjoyment by the Palestine Arab refugees of their right to return to their homes and property, recognized by the General Assembly in resolution 194 (III) of 11 December 1948, which has been repeatedly reaffirmed by the Assembly since that date, is indispensable for the achievement of a just settlement of the refugee problem and for the exercise by the people of Palestine of its right to self-determination.

---

7.   Resolution 2625 (xxv), annex
8.   Resolution 2734 (xxv)

Appendix 16

General Assembly Resolution 3236
22 November 1974

The General Assembly,

Having considered the question of Palestine,

Having heard the statement of the Palestine Liberation Organization, the representative of the Palestinian people,[14]

Having also heard other statements made during the debate,

Deeply concerned that no just solution to the problem of Palestine has yet been achieved and recognizing that the problem of Palestine continues to endanger international peace and security,

Recognizing that the Palestinian people is entitled to self-determination in accordance with the Charter of the United Nations,

Expressing its grave concern that the Palestinian people has been prevented from enjoying its inalienable rights, in particular its right to self-determination,

Guided by the purposes and principles of the Charter,

Recalling its relevant resolutions which affirm the right of the Palestinian people to self-determination,

1. *Reaffirms* the inalienable rights of the Palestinian people in Palestine, including:

(a) The right to self-determination without external interference;

(b) The right to national independence and sovereignty;

2. *Reaffirms also* the inalienable right of the Palestinians to return to their homes and property from which they have been displaced and uprooted, and calls for their return;

3. *Emphasizes* that full respect for and the realization of these inalienable rights of the Palestinian people are indispensable for the solution of the question of Palestine;

4. *Recognizes* that the Palestinian people is a principal party in the establishment of a just and lasting peace in the Middle East;

5. *Further recognizes* the right of the Palestinian people to regain its rights by all means in accordance with the purposes

and principles of the Charter of the United Nations;

6. *Appeals* to all States and international organizations to extend their support to the Palestinian people in its struggle to restore its rights, in accordance with the Charter;

7. *Requests* the Secretary-General to establish contacts with the Palestine Liberation Organization on all matters concerning the question of Palestine;

8. *Requests* the Secretary-General to report to the General Assembly at its thirtieth session on the implementation of the present resolution;

9. *Decides* to include the item entitled "Question of Palestine" in the provisional agenda of its thirtieth session.

Appendix 17

General Assembly Resolution 3237
22 November 1974

The General Assembly,

Having considered the question of Palestine,

Taking into consideration the universality of the United Nations prescribed in the Charter,

Recalling its resolution 3102 (XXVIII) of 12 December 1973,

Taking into account Economic and Social Council resolutions 1835 (LVI) of 14 May 1974 and 1840 (LVI) of 15 May 1974,

Noting that the Diplomatic Conference on the Reaffirmation and Development of International Humanitarian Law Applicable in Armed Conflicts, the World Population Conference and the World Food Conference have in effect invited the Palestine Liberation Organization to participate in their respective deliberations,

Noting also that the Third United Nations Conference on the Law of the Sea has invited the Palestine Liberation Organization to participate in its deliberations as an observer,

1. *Invites* the Palestine Liberation Organization to participate in the sessions and the work of the General Assembly in

the capacity of observer;

2. *Invites* the Palestine Liberation Organization to participate in the sessions and the work of all international conferences convened under the auspices of the General Assembly in the capacity of observer;

3. *Considers* that the Palestine Liberation Organization is entitled to participate as an observer in the sessions and the work of all international conferences convened under the auspices of other organs of the United Nations;

4. *Requests* the Secretary-General to take the necessary steps for the implementation of the present resolution.

Appendix 18

General Assembly Resolution 35/169E
15 December 1980

The General Assembly,

Recalling and reaffirming its resolutions 2253 (ES-V) of 4 July 1967 and 2254 (ES-V) of 14 July 1967,

Recalling the resolutions of the Security Council relevant to the character and status of the Holy City of Jerusalem, in particular resolutions 252 (1968) of 21 May 1968, 267 (1969) of 3 July 1969, 271 (1969) of 15 September 1969, 298 (1971) of 25 September 1971, 465 (1980) of 1 March 1980, 476 (1980) of 30 June 1980 and 478 (1980) of 20 August 1980,

Reaffirming that the acquisition of territory by force is inadmissible,

Bearing in mind the specific status of Jerusalem and, in particular, the need for protection and preservation of the unique spiritual and religious dimension of the Holy Places in the city,

Expressing its satisfaction at the decision taken by the States which have responded to Security Council resolution 478 (1980) and withdrawn their diplomatic representatives from the Holy City of Jerusalem,

Recalling the Geneva Convention relative to the Protection of Civilian Persons in Time of War, of 12 August 1949,

Deploring the persistence of Israel in changing the physical character, demographic composition, institutional structure and the status of the Holy City of Jerusalem,

Deeply concerned over the enactment of a "basic law" in the Israeli Knesset proclaiming a change in the character and status of the Holy City of Jerusalem, with its implications for peace and security,

1. *Censures* in the strongest terms the enactment by Israel of the "Basic Law" on Jerusalem;

2. *Affirms* that the enactment of the "Basic Law" by Israel constitutes a violation of international law and does not affect the continued application of the Geneva Convention relative to the Protection of Civilian Persons in Time of War, of 12 August 1949, in the Palestinian and other Arab territories occupied since June 1967, including Jerusalem;

3. *Determines* that all legislative and administrative measures and actions taken by Israel, the occupying Power, which have altered or purport to alter the character and status of the Holy City of Jerusalem, and, in particular, the recent "Basic Law" on Jerusalem and the proclamation of Jerusalem as the capital of Israel are null and void and must be rescinded forthwith;

4. *Affirms also* that this action constitutes a serious obstruction to achieving a comprehensive, just and lasting peace in the Middle East;

5. *Decides* not to recognize that "Basic Law" and such other actions by Israel that, as a result of this law, seek to alter the character and status of Jerusalem and calls upon all States, specialized agencies and other international organizations to comply with the present resolution and other relevant resolutions and urges them not to conduct any business which is not in conformity with the provisions of the present resolution and the other relevant resolutions.

Appendix 19

General Assembly Resolution ES-7/8
19 August 1982

The General Assembly,

Having considered the question of Palestine at its resumed seventh emergency special session,

Appalled by the great number of innocent Palestinian and Lebanese children victims of Israel's acts of aggression,

Decides to commemorate 4 June of each year as the International Day of innocent Children Victims of Aggression.

Appendix 20

General Assembly Resolution ES-7/9
24 September 1982

The General Assembly,

Having considered the question of Palestine at its resumed seventh emergency special session,

Having heard the statement of the Palestine Liberation Organization, the representative of the Palestinian people,

Recalling and reaffirming, in particular, its resolution 194 (III) of 11 December 1948,

Appalled at the massacre of Palestinian civilians in Beirut,

Recalling Security Council resolutions 508 (1982) of 5 June 1982, 509 (1982) of 6 June 1982, 513 (1982) of 4 July 1982, 520 (1982) of 17 September 1982 and 521 (1982) of 19 September 1982,

Taking note of the reports of the Secretary-General relevant to the situation, particularly his report of 18 September 1982,

Noting with regret that the Security Council has so far not taken effective and practical measures, in accordance with the Charter of the United Nations, to ensure implementation of its resolutions 508 (1982) and 509 (1982),

Referring to the humanitarian principles of the Geneva Convention relative to the Protection of Civilian Persons in Time of War, of 12 August 1949, and to the obligations arising from the regulations annexed to the Hague Conventions of 1907,

Deeply concerned at the sufferings of the Palestinian and Lebanese civilian populations,

Noting the homelessness of the Palestinian people,

Reaffirming the imperative need to permit the Palestinian people to exercise their legitimate rights,

1. *Condemns* the criminal massacre of Palestinian and other civilians in Beirut on 17 September 1982;

2. *Urges* the Security Council to investigate, through the means available to it, the circumstances and extent of the massacre of Palestinian and other civilians in Beirut on 17 September 1982, and to make public the report on its findings as soon as possible;

3. *Decides* to support fully the provisions of Security Council resolutions 508 (1982) and 509 (1982), in which the Council, *inter alia*, demanded that:

(a) Israel withdraw all its military forces forthwith and unconditionally to the internationally recognized boundaries of Lebanon;

(b) All parties to the conflict cease immediately and simultaneously all military activities within Lebanon and across the Lebanese–Israeli border;

4. *Demands* that all Member States and other parties observe strict respect for the sovereignty, territorial integrity, unity and political independence of Lebanon within its internationally recognized boundaries;

5. *Reaffirms* the fundamental principle of the inadmissibility of the acquisition of territory by force;

6. *Resolves* that, in conformity with its resolution 194 (III) and subsequent relevant resolutions, the Palestinian refugees should be enabled to return to their homes and property from which they have been uprooted and displaced, and demands that Israel comply unconditionally and immediately with the present resolution;

7. *Urges* the Security Council, in the event of continued failure by Israel to comply with the demands contained in resolutions 508 (1982) and 509 (1982) and the present

resolution, to meet in order to consider practical ways and means in accordance with the Charter of the United Nations;

8. *Calls upon* all States and international agencies and organizations to continue to provide the most extensive humanitarian aid possible to the victims of the Israeli invasion of Lebanon;

9. *Requests* the Secretary-General to prepare a photographic exhibit of the massacre of 17 September 1982 and to display it in the United Nations visitors' hall;

10. *Decides* to adjourn the seventh emergency special session temporarily and to authorize the President of the latest regular session of the General Assembly to resume its meetings upon request from Member States.

Appendix 21

Security Council Resolution 242
22 November 1967

The Security Council,

Expressing its continuing concern with the grave situation in the Middle East,

Emphasizing the inadmissibility of the acquisition of territory by war and the need to work for a just and lasting peace in which every State in the area can live in security,

Emphasizing further that all Member States in their acceptance of the Charter of the United Nations have undertaken a commitment to act in accordance with Article 2 of the Charter,

1. *Affirms* that the fulfilment of Charter principles requires the establishment of a just and lasting peace in the Middle East which should include the application of both the following principles:

    (i) Withdrawal of Israel armed forces from territories occupied in the recent conflict;

    (ii) Termination of all claims or states of belligerency and respect for and acknowledgement of the sovereignty, territorial integrity and political independence of every State in the area and their right to live in peace within secure and recognized boundaries free from threats or acts of force;

2. *Affirms further* the necessity

(a) For guaranteeing freedom of navigation through international waterways in the area;

(b) For achieving a just settlement of the refugee problem;

(c) For guaranteeing the territorial inviolability and political independence of every State in the area, through measures including the establishment of demilitarized zones;

3. *Requests* the Secretary-General to designate a Special Representative to proceed to the Middle East to establish and maintain contacts with the States concerned in order to promote agreement and assist efforts to achieve a peaceful and accepted settlement in accordance with the provisions and principles in this resolution;

4. *Requests* the Secretary-General to report to the Security Council on the progress of the efforts of the Special Representative as soon as possible.

Appendix 22

Security Council Resolution 338
15 October 1973

The Security Council

1. *Calls upon* all parties to the present fighting to cease all firing and terminate all military activity immediately, no later than 12 hours after the moment of the adoption of this decision, in the positions they now occupy;

2. *Calls upon* the parties concerned to start immediately after the cease-fire the implementation of Security Council resolution 242 (1967) in all of its parts;

3. *Decides* that, immediately and concurrently with the cease-fire, negotiations shall start between the parties concerned under appropriate auspices aimed at establishing a just and durable peace in the Middle East.

Appendix 23

Security Council Resolution 465
1 March 1980

The Security Council,

Taking note of the reports of the Commission of the Security Council established under resolution 446 (1979) to examine the situation relating to settlements in the Arab territories occcupied since 1967, including Jerusalem, contained in documents S/13450 and Corr. 1 and S/13679,

Taking note also of letters from the Permanent Representative of Jordan (S/13801) and the Permanent Representative of Morocco, Chairman of the Islamic Group (S/13802),

Strongly deploring the refusal by Israel to co-operate with the Commission and regretting its formal rejection of resolutions 446 (1979) and 452 (1979),

Affirming once more that the Fourth Geneva Convention relative to the Protection of Civilian Persons in Time of War of 12 August 1949 is applicable to the Arab territories occupied by Israel since 1967, including Jerusalem,

Deploring the decision of the Government of Israel to officially support Israeli settlement in the Palestinian and other Arab territories occupied since 1967,

Deeply concerned over the practices of the Israeli authorities in implementing that settlement policy in the occupied Arab territories, including Jerusalem, and its consequences for the local Arab and Palestinian population,

Taking into account the need to consider measures for the impartial protection of private and public land and property, and water resources,

Bearing in mind the specific status of Jerusalem and, in particular, the need for protection and preservation of the unique spiritual and religious dimension of the Holy Places in the city,

Drawing attention to the grave consequences which the settlement policy is bound to have on any attempt to reach a comprehensive, just and lasting peace in the Middle East,

Recalling pertinent Security Council resolutions, specifically resolutions 237 (1967) of 14 June 1967, 252 (1968) of 2〕

May 1968, 267 (1969) of 3 July 1969, 271 (1969) of 15 September 1969 and 298 (1971) of 25 September 1971, as well as the consensus statement made by the President of the Security Council on 11 November 1976,

Having invited Mr. Fahd Qawasmeh, Mayor of Al-Khalil (Hebron), in the occupied territory, to supply it with information pursuant to rule 39 of the provisional rules of procedure,

1. *Commends* the work done by the Commission in preparing the report contained in document S/13679;

2. *Accepts* the conclusions and recommendations contained in the above-mentioned report of the Commission;

3. *Calls upon* all parties, particularly the Government of Israel, to co-operate with the Commission;

4. *Strongly deplores* the decision of Israel to prohibit the free travel of Mayor Fahd Qawasmeh in order to appear before the Security Council, and requests Israel to permit his free travel to the United Nations Headquarters for that purpose;

5. *Determines* that all measures taken by Israel to change the physical character, demographic composition, institutional structure or status of the Palestinian and other Arab territories occupied since 1967, including Jerusalem, or any part thereof, have no legal validity and that Israel's policy and practices of settling parts of its population and new immigrants in those territories constitutes a flagrant violation of the Fourth Geneva Convention relative to the Protection of Civilian Persons in Time of War and also constitute a serious obstruction to achieving a comprehensive, just and lasting peace in the Middle East;

6. *Strongly deplores* the continuation and persistence of Israel in pursuing those policies and practices and calls upon the Government and people of Israel to rescind those measures, to dismantle the existing settlements and in particular to cease, on an urgent basis, the establishment, construction and planning of settlements in the Arab territories occupied since 1967, including Jerusalem,

7. *Calls upon* all States not to provide Israel with any assistance to be used specifically in connexion with settlements in the occupied territories;

8. *Requests* the Commission to continue to examine the

situation relating to settlements in the Arab territories occupied since 1967, including Jerusalem, to investigate the reported serious depletion of natural resources, particularly the water resources, with a view to ensuring the protection of those important natural resources of the territories under occupation, and to keep under close scrutiny the implementation of the present resolution;

9. *Requests* the Commission to report to the Security Council before 1 September 1980, and decides to convene at the earliest possible date thereafter in order to consider the report and the full implementation of the present resolution.

Appendix 24

Security Council Resolution 497
17 December 1981

The Security Council,

Having considered the letter of 14 December 1981 from the Permanent Representative of the Syrian Arab Republic contained in document S/14791,

Reaffirming that the acquisition of territory by force is inadmissible, in accordance with the United Nations Charter, the principles of international law, and relevant Security Council resolutions,

1. *Decides* that the Israeli decision to impose its laws, jurisdiction and administration in the occupied Syrian Golan Heights is null and void and without international legal effect;

2. *Demands* that Israel, the occupying Power, should rescind forthwith its decision;

3. *Determines* that all the provisions of the Geneva Convention Relative to the Protection of Civilian Persons in Time of War of 12 August 1949 continue to apply to the Syrian territory occupied by Israel since June 1967;

4. *Requests* the Secretary-General to report to the Security Council on the implementation of this resolution within two weeks and decides that in the event of non-compliance by Israel, the Security Council would meet urgently, and not

later than 5 January 1982, to consider taking appropriate measures in accordance with the Charter of the United Nations.

Appendix 25

Security Council Resolution 508
5 June 1982

The Security Council,

Recalling Security Council resolutions 425 (1978), 426 (1978) and the ensuing resolutions, and more particularly, Security Council resolution 501 (1982),

Taking note of the letters of the Permanent Representative of Lebanon dated 4 June 1982 (S/15161 and S/15162),

Deeply concerned at the deterioration of the present situation in Lebanon and in the Lebanese–Israeli border area, and its consequences for peace and security in the region,

Gravely concerned at the violation of the territorial integrity, independence, and sovereignty of Lebanon,

Reaffirming and supporting the statement made by the President and the members of the Security Council on 4 June 1982 (S/15163), as well as the urgent appeal issued by the Secretary-General on 4 June 1982,

Taking note of the report of the Secretary-General,

1. *Calls upon* all the parties to the conflict to cease immediately and simultaneously all military activities within Lebanon and across the Lebanese–Israeli border and no later than 0600 hours local time on Sunday, 6 June 1982;

2. *Requests* all Member States which are in a position to do so to bring their influence to bear upon those concerned so that the cessation of hostilities declared by Security Council resolution 490 (1981) can be respected;

3. *Requests* the Secretary-General to undertake all possible efforts to ensure the implementation of and compliance with this resolution and to report to the Security Council as early as possible and not later than forty-eight hours after the adoption of this resolution.

Appendix 26

Security Council Resolution 509
6 June 1982

The Security Council,

Recalling its resolutions 425 (1978) of 19 March 1978 and 508 (1982) of 5 June 1982,

Gravely concerned at the situation as described by the Secretary-General in his report to the Council,

Reaffirming the need for strict respect for the territorial integrity, sovereignty and political independence of Lebanon within its internationally recognized boundaries,

1. *Demands* that Israel withdraw all its military forces forthwith and unconditionally to the internationally recognized boundaries of Lebanon;

2. *Demands* that all parties observe strictly the terms of paragraph 1 of resolution 508 (1982) which called on them to cease immediately and simultaneously all military activities within Lebanon and across the Lebanese–Israeli border;

3. *Calls* on all parties to communicate to the Secretary-General their acceptance of the present resolution within 24 hours;

4. *Decides* to remain seized of the question.

Appendix 27

Spanish Draft Security Council Resolution[1]
U.N. Doc. S/15185
8 June 1982

The Security Council,

Recalling its resolutions 508 (1982) and 509 (1982),

---

1. Failed of adoption because of the negative vote of the United States.

Taking note of the report of the Secretary-General (S/15178) of 7 June 1982,

Also taking note of the two positive replies to the Secretary-General of the Government of Lebanon and the Palestine Liberation Organization contained in document S/15178,

1. *Condemns* the non-compliance with resolutions 508 (1982) and 509 (1982) by Israel;

2. *Urges* the parties to comply strictly with the regulations attached to the Hague Convention of 1907;

3. *Reiterates its demand* that Israel withdraw all its military forces forthwith and unconditionally to the internationally recognized boundaries of Lebanon;

4. *Reiterates also its demand* that all parties observe strictly the terms of paragraph 1 of resolution 508 (1982) which called on them to cease immediately and simultaneously all military activities within Lebanon and across the Lebanese–Israeli border;

5. *Demands* that within six hours all hostilities must be stopped in compliance with Security Council resolutions 508 (1982) and 509 (1982) and decides, in the event of non-compliance, to meet again to consider practical ways and means in accordance with the Charter of the United Nations.

Appendix 28

Security Council Resolution 511
18 June 1982

The Security Council,

Recalling its resolutions 425 (1978), 426 (1978), 427 (1978), 434 (1978), 444 (1979), 450 (1979), 459 (1979), 467 (1980), 483 (1980), 488 (1981), 490 (1981), 498 (1981), and 501 (1982),

Reaffirming its resolutions 508 (1982) and 509 (1982),

Having studied the report of the Secretary-General on the United Nations Interim Force in Lebanon (S/15194 and Add. 1 and 2) and taking note of the conclusions and recommendations expressed therein,

Bearing in mind the need to avoid any developments

which could further aggravate the situation and the need, pending an examination of the situation by the Council in all its aspects, to preserve in place the capacity of the United Nations to assist in the restoration of the peace,

1. *Decides* as an interim measure, to extend the present mandate of the Force for a period of two months, that is, until 19 August 1982;

2. *Authorizes* the Force during that period, to carry out, in addition, the interim tasks referred to in paragraph 17 of the Secretary-General's report (S/15194/Add. 2);

3. *Calls on* all concerned to extend full co-operation to the Force in the discharge of its tasks;

4. *Requests* the Secretary-General to keep the Security Council regularly informed of the implementation of resolutions 508 (1982) and 509 (1982) and the present resolution.

Appendix 29

Security Council Resolution 512
19 June 1982

The Security Council,

Deeply concerned at the sufferings of the Lebanese and Palestinian civilian populations,

Referring to the humanitarian principles of the Geneva Conventions of 1949 and to the obligations arising from the regulations annexed to the Hague Convention of 1907,

Reaffirming its resolutions 508 (1982) and 509 (1982),

1. *Calls upon* all the parties to the conflict to respect the rights of the civilian populations, to refrain from all acts of violence against those populations and to take all appropriate measures to alleviate the suffering caused by conflict, in particular, by facilitating the dispatch and distribution of aid provided by United Nations agencies and by non-governmental organizations, in particular, the International Committee of the Red Cross (ICRC);

2. *Appeals* to Member States to continue to provide the most extensive humanitarian aid possible;

3. *Stresses* the particular humanitarian responsibilities of

the United Nations and its agencies, including the United Nations Relief and Works Agency for Palestine Refugees in the Near East (UNRWA), towards civilian populations and calls upon all the parties to the conflict not to hamper the exercise of those responsibilities and to assist in humanitarian efforts;

4. *Takes note* of the measures taken by the Secretary-General to co-ordinate the activities of the international agencies in this field and requests him to make every effort to ensure the implementation of and compliance with this resolution and to report on these efforts to the Council as soon as possible.

Appendix 30

Security Council Resolution 513
4 July 1982

The Security Council,

Alarmed by the continued sufferings of the Lebanese and Palestinian civilian populations in South Lebanon and in West Beirut,

Referring to the humanitarian principles of the Geneva Conventions of 1949 and to the obligations arising from the Regulations annexed to the Hague Convention of 1907,

Reaffirming its resolutions 508 (1982), 509 (1982) and 512 (1982),

1. *Calls* for respect for the rights of the civilian populations without any discrimination and repudiates all acts of violence against those populations;

2. *Calls further* for the restoration of the normal supply of vital facilities such as water, electricity, food and medical provisions, particularly in Beirut;

3. *Commends* the efforts of the Secretary-General and the action of international agencies to alleviate the sufferings of the civilian population and requests them to continue their efforts to ensure their success.

Appendix 31

Security Council Resolution 515
29 July 1982

The Security Council,

Deeply concerned at the situation of the civilian population of Beirut,

Referring to the humanitarian principles of the Geneva Conventions of 1949 and to the obligations arising from the regulations annexed to the Hague Convention of 1907,

Recalling its resolutions 512 (1982) and 513 (1982),

1. *Demands* that the Government of Israel lift immediately the blockade of the city of Beirut in order to permit the dispatch of supplies to meet the urgent needs of the civilian population and allow the distribution of aid provided by United Nations agencies and by non-governmental organizations, particularly the International Committee of the Red Cross (ICRC);

2. *Requests* the Secretary-General to transmit the text of this resolution to the Government of Israel and keep the Security Council informed of its implementation.

Appendix 32

Security Council Resolution 520
17 September 1982

The Security Council,

Having considered the report of the Secretary-General of 1! September 1982 (S/15382/Add.1),

Condemning the murder of Bashir Gemayel, Lebanon' constitutionally selected President-elect, and every effort t disrupt by violence the restoration of a strong, stabl government in Lebanon,

Having listened to the statement by the Permanen Representative of Lebanon,

Taking note of Lebanon's determination to ensure th

withdrawal of all non-Lebanese forces from Lebanon,

1. *Reaffirms* its resolutions 508 (1982), 509 (1982) and 516 (1982) in all their components;

2. *Condemns* the recent Israeli incursions into Beirut in violation of the cease-fire agreements and of Security Council resolutions;

3. *Demands* an immediate return to the positions occupied by Israel before 15 September 1982, as a first step towards the full implementation of Security Council resolutions;

4. *Calls again* for the strict respect for Lebanon's sovereignty, territorial integrity, unity and political independence under the sole and exclusive authority of the Lebanese Government through the Lebanese Army throughout Lebanon;

5. *Reaffirms* its resolutions 512 (1982) and 513 (1982) which call for respect for the rights of the civilian populations without any discrimination and repudiates all acts of violence against those populations;

6. *Supports* the efforts of the Secretary-General to implement Security Council resolution 516 (1982) concerning the deployment of United Nations observers to monitor the situation in and around Beirut and requests all the parties concerned to co-operate fully in the application of that resolution;

7. *Decides* to remain seized of the question and asks the Secretary-General to keep the Council informed on developments as soon as possible and not later than twenty-four hours.

Appendix 33

Security Council Resolution 521
19 September 1982

The Security Council,
Appalled at the massacre of Palestinian civilians in Beirut,
   Having heard the report of the Secretary-General (S/15400),

Noting that the Government of Lebanon has agreed to the dispatch of United Nations Observers to the sites of greatest human suffering and losses in and around that city,

1. *Condemns* the criminal massacre of Palestinian civilians in Beirut;

2. *Reaffirms* once again its resolutions 512 (1982) and 513 (1982) which call for respect for the rights of the civilian population without any discrimination and repudiates all acts of violence against that population;

3. *Authorizes* the Secretary-General as an immediate step to increase the number of United Nations observers in and around Beirut from 10 to 50 and insists that there shall be no interference with the deployment of the observers and that they shall have full freedom of movement;

4. *Requests* the Secretary-General, in consultation with the Government of Lebanon, to ensure the rapid deployment of those observers in order that they may contribute in every way possible within their mandate, to the effort to ensure full protection for the civilian population;

5. *Requests* the Secretary-General as a matter of urgency to initiate appropriate consultations and in particular consultations with the Government of Lebanon on additional steps which the Council might take, including the possible deployment of United Nations forces, to assist that Government in ensuring full protection for the civilian population in and around Beirut and requests him to report to the Council within forty-eight hours;

6. *Insists* that all concerned must permit United Nations observers and forces established by the Security Council in Lebanon to be deployed and to discharge their mandates and in this connexion solemnly calls attention to the obligation on all Member States under Article 25 of the Charter to accept and carry out the decisions of the Council in accordance with the Charter;

7. *Requests* the Secretary-General to keep the Council informed on an urgent and continuing basis.

Appendix 34

Geneva Convention Relative to the Treatment of Prisoners of War 12 August 1949

ARTICLE 4

A. Prisoners of war, in the sense of the present Convention, are persons belonging to one of the following categories, who have fallen into the power of the enemy:

(1) Members of the armed forces of a Party to the conflict, as well as members of militias or volunteer corps forming part of such armed forces.

(2) Members of other militias and members of other volunteer corps, including those of organized resistance movements belonging to a Party to the conflict and operating in or outside their own territory, even if this territory is occupied, provided that such militias or volunteer corps, including such organized resistance movements, fulfil the following conditions:

(*a*) that of being commanded by a person responsible for his subordinates;

(*b*) that of having a fixed distinctive sign recognizable at a distance;

(*c*) that of carrying arms openly;

(*d*) that of conducting their operations in accordance with the laws and customs of war.

(3) Members of regular armed forces who profess allegiance to a government or an authority not recognized by the Detaining Power.

(4) Persons who accompany the armed forces without actually being members thereof, such as civilian members of military aircraft crews, war correspondents, supply contractors, members of labour units or of services responsible for the welfare of the armed forces, provided that they have received authorization from the armed forces which they accompany, who shall provide them for that purpose with an identity card similar to the annexed model.

(5) Members of crews, including masters, pilots and

apprentices, of the merchant marine and the crews of civil aircraft of the Parties to the conflict, who do not benefit by more favourable treatment under any other provisions of international law.

(6) Inhabitants of a non-occupied territory, who on the approach of the enemy spontaneously take up arms to resist the invading forces, without having had time to form themselves into regular armed units provided they carry arms openly and respect the laws and customs of war.

Appendix 35

Geneva Convention Relative to the Protection of Civilian Persons in Time of War 12 August 1949

ARTICLE 47

Protected persons who are in occupied territory shall not be deprived, in any case or in any manner whatsoever, of the benefits of the present Convention by any change introduced, as the result of the occupation of a territory, into the institutions or government of the said territory, nor by any agreement concluded between the authorities of the occupied territories and the Occupying Power, nor by any annexation by the latter of the whole or part of the occupied territory.

ARTICLE 49

(1) Individual or mass forcible transfers, as well as deportations of protected persons from occupied territory to the territory of the Occupying Power or to that of any other country, occupied or not, are prohibited, regardless of their motive.

* * * *

(6) The Occupying Power shall not deport or transfer parts of its own civilian population into the territory it occupies.

486

Appendix 36

Common Articles 1 and 2 of the Four Geneva Conventions of 1949 for the Protection of War Victims

Article 1. The High Contracting Parties undertake to respect and to ensure respect for the present Convention in all circumstances.

Art. 2. In addition to the provisions which shall be implemented in peace-time, the present Convention shall apply to all cases of declared war or of any other armed conflict which may arise between two or more of the High Contracting Parties, even if the state of war is not recognized by one of them.

The Convention shall also apply to all cases of partial or total occupation of the territory of a High Contracting Party, even if the said occupation meets with no armed resistance.

Although one of the Powers in conflict may not be a party to the present Convention, the Powers who are parties thereto shall remain bound by it in their mutual relations. They shall furthermore be bound by the Convention in relation to the said Power, if the latter accepts and applies the provisions thereof.

Appendix 37

95 U.S. Statutes at Large 1526, § 2754. Purposes for which military sales or leases by United States are authorized; report to Congress.

Defense articles and defense services shall be sold or leased by the United States Government under this chapter to friendly countries solely for internal security, for legitimate self-defense, to permit the recipient country to participate in regional or collective arrangements or measures consistent with the Charter of the United Nations, or otherwise to permit the recipient country to participate in collective measures requested by the United Nations for the purpose of maintaining or restoring international peace and security, or for the purpose of enabling foreign military forces in less developed friendly countries to construct public works and to engage in other activities helpful to the economic and social development of such friendly countries. It is the sense of the Congress that such foreign military forces should not be maintained or established solely for civic action activities and that such civic action activities not significantly detract from the capability of the military forces to perform their military missions and be coordinated with and form part of the total economic and social development effort: *Provided,* That none of the funds contained in this authorization shall be used to guarantee, or extend credit, or participate in an extension of credit in connection with any sale of sophisticated weapons systems, such as missile systems and jet aircraft for military purposes, to any underdeveloped country other than Greece, Turkey, Iran, Israel, the Republic of China, the Philippines and Korea unless the President determines that such financing is important to the national security of the United States and reports within thirty days each such determination to the Congress.

As amended Pub. L. 97–113, Title I, § 109 (b) (3), Dec. 29, 1981, 95 Stat. 1526.

Appendix 38

3 U.S. Treaties and Other International Agreements 4985

U.S.–Israel
Mutual Defense Assistance Agreement

Agreement effected by exchange of notes signed at Tel Aviv July 1 and 23, 1952; entered into force July 23, 1952.

The American Ambassador to the Israeli Acting Minister for Foreign Affairs

AMERICAN EMBASSY, TEL AVIV
July 1, 1952

NO. 1
EXCELLENCY:

I have the honor to inform Your Excellency that the Government of Israel has been declared eligible to receive from the Government of the United States of America reimbursable military assistance under the provisions of Section 408 (e) of the Mutual Defense Assistance Act of 1949 (Public Law 329, 81st Congress), as amended. The provisions of these laws and the policy of the United States Government require that certain assurances be received before completing any transactions under Section 408 (e) of the Act.

It is the understanding of the United States Government that the Government of Israel is prepared to accept the following undertakings:

1. The Government of Israel agrees to use any assistance furnished under the Mutual Defense Assistance Act of 1949, as amended, to further the policies and purposes of that Act which are to foster international peace and security within the framework of the Charter of the United Nations through measures which will further the ability of nations dedicated to the principles and purposes of the Charter to participate effectively in arrangements for individual and collective self-defense in support of those purposes and principles. The Government of Israel further agrees to furnish equipment

489

and materials, services, or other assistance, consistent with the Charter of the United Nations, to the United States or to and among other nations eligible for assistance under the Mutual Defense Assistance Act to further the policies and purposes of this Act, as set forth above, and as may be mutually agreed hereafter.

2. *The Government of Israel assures the United States Government that such equipment, materials, or services as may be acquired from the United States* under the provisions of Section 408 (e) of the Mutual Defense Assistance Act of 1949, as amended, *are required for and will be used solely to maintain its internal security, its legitimate self-defense, or to permit it to participate in the defense of the area of which it is a part, or in United Nations collective security arrangements and measures, and that it will not undertake any act of aggression against any other state.*

3. The Government of Israel will not relinquish title to or possession of any equipment and materials, information or services furnished under Section 408 (e) of the Mutual Defense Assistance Act of 1949, as amended, without the consent of the United States Government.

4. The Government of Israel will protect the security of any article, service or information furnished under Section 408 (e) of the Mutual Defense Assistance Act of 1949, as amended.

5. The Government of Israel understands that, prior to the transfer of any item or the rendering of any services, the United States Government retains the right to terminate the transaction.

6. The Government of Israel is prepared to accept terms and conditions of payment for any item or service which may be furnished under the Mutual Defense Assistance Act of 1949, as amended, which are in accord with the provisions of Section 408 (e) (2) of this Act.

I have the honor to propose that this note, together with your reply confirming these assurances, constitute an agreement between the Government of the United States of America and the Government of Israel, effective on the date of your Note.

Accept, Excellency, the renewed assurances of my highest consideration.

MONNETT B. DAVIS

His Excellency
DAVID BEN GURION,
Acting Minister for Foreign Affairs,
Hakirya.

The Israeli Minister for Foreign Affairs to the American Ambassador

MINISTRY FOR FOREIGN AFFAIRS
HAKIRYA, ISRAEL

HAKIRYA, *23rd July, 1952*

SIR:

I have the honor to refer to your note of July 1, 1952, concerning certain assurances and undertakings required from the Israel Government prior to the completion of transactions between the Israel Government and the United States Government under the provisions of Section 408 (e) of the Mutual Defense Assistance Act of 1949, as amended.

The Government of Israel accepts the undertakings and assurances outlined in that note and concurs with proposal that this note, together with your note dated July 1, 1952, referred to above, constitute an agreement covering all transactions for the supply of military assistance under Section 408 (e) of the Mutual Defense Assistance Act of 1949, as amended, between the respective governments, the said agreement to enter into force on the date of this note.

I avail myself of this opportunity to renew to you the assurances of my highest consideration.

M. SHARETT

The Honorable
MONNETT B. DAVIS,
Ambassador of the United States of America,
Tel Aviv.

Appendix 39

Geneva Declaration on Palestine

In pursuance of General Assembly resolutions 36/120 C of 10 December 1981, ES–7/7 of 19 August 1982 and 37/86 C of 10 December 1982, an International Conference on the Question of Palestine was convened at the United Nations Office at Geneva from 29 August to 7 September 1983 to seek effective ways and means to enable the Palestinian people to attain and to exercise their inalienable rights. The conference was opened by the Secretary-General of the United Nations, Javier Pérez de Cuéllar and presided over by the Minister for Foreign Affairs of Senegal, Moustapha Niassé.

1.   The Conference, having thoroughly considered the question of Palestine in all its aspects, expresses the grave concern of all nations and peoples regarding the international tension that has persisted for several decades in the Middle East, the principal cause of which is the denial by Israel, and those supporting its expansionist policies, of the inalienable legitimate rights of the Palestinian people. The Conference reaffirms and stresses that a just solution of the question of Palestine, the core of the problem, is the crucial element in a comprehensive, just and lasting political settlement in the middle East.

2.   The Conference recognizes that, as one of the most acute and complex problems of our time, the question of Palestine – inherited by the United Nations at the time of its establishment – requires a comprehensive, just and lasting political settlement. This settlement must be based on the implementation of the relevant United Nations resolutions concerning the question of Palestine and the attainment of the legitimate, inalienable rights of the Palestinian people including the right to self-determination and the right to the establishment of its own independent State in Palestine and should also be based on the provision by the Security Council of guarantees for peace and security among all States in the region, including the independent Palestinian State, within secure and internationally recognized boundaries. The Conference is convinced that the attainment by the Palesti

nian people of their inalienable rights, as defined by General Assembly resolution 3236 (XXIX) of 22 November 1974, will contribute substantially to the achievement of peace and stability in the Middle East.

3. The Conference considers the role of the United Nations in the achievement of a comprehensive, just and lasting peace in the Middle East to be essential and paramount. It emphasizes the need for respect for, and application of the provisions of the Charter of the United Nations, the resolutions of the United Nations relevant to the question of Palestine and the observance of the principles of international law.

4. The Conference considers that the various proposals, consistent with the principles of international law, which have been presented on this question, such as the Arab peace plan adopted unanimously at the twelfth Arab Summit Conference held at Fez, Morocco, in September 1982, should serve as guidelines for concerted international effort to resolve the question of Palestine. These guidelines include the following:

(a) The attainment by the Palestinian people of its legitimate inalienable rights, including the right to return, the right to self-determination and the right to establish its own independent State in Palestine;

(b) The right of the Palestine Liberation Organization, the representative of the Palestinian people, to participate on an equal footing with other parties in all efforts, deliberations and conferences on the Middle East;

(c) The need to put an end to Israel's occupation of the Arab territories, in accordance with the principle of the inadmissibility of the acquisition of territory by force, and, consequently, the need to secure Israeli withdrawal from the territories occupied since 1967, including Jerusalem;

(d) The need to oppose and reject such Israeli policies and practices in the occupied territories, including Jerusalem, and any *de facto* situation created by Israel as are contrary to international law and relevant United Nations resolutions, particularly the establishment of settlements, as these policies and practices constitute major obstacles to the achievement of peace in the Middle East;

(e) The need to reaffirm as null and void all legislative and administrative measures and actions taken by Israel, the occupying Power, which have altered or purported to alter the character and status of the Holy City of Jerusalem, including the expropriation of land and property situated thereon, and in particular the so-called 'Basic Law' on Jerusalem and the proclamation of Jerusalem as the capital of Israel;

(f) The right of all States in the region to existence within secure and internationally recognized boundaries, with justice and security for all the people, the *sine qua non* of which is the recognition and attainment of the legitimate, inalienable rights of the Palestinian people as stated in paragraph (a) above.

5. In order to give effect to these guidelines, the Conference considers it essential that an international peace conference on the Middle East be convened on the basis of the principles of the Charter of the United Nations and the relevant resolutions of the United Nations, with the aim of achieving a comprehensive, just and lasting solution to the Arab–Israeli conflict, an essential element of which would be the establishment of an independent Palestinian State in Palestine. This peace conference should be convened under the auspices of the United Nations, with the participation of all parties to the Arab–Israeli conflict, including the Palestine Liberation Organization, as well as the United States of America, the Union of Soviet Socialist Republics, and other concerned States, on an equal footing. In this context the Security Council has a primary responsiblity to create appropriate institutional arrangements on the basis of relevant United Nations resolutions in order to guarantee and to carry out the accords of the international peace conference.

6. The International Conference on the Question of Palestine emphasizes the importance of the time factor in achieving a just solution to the problems of Palestine. The Conference is convinced that partial solutions are inadequate and delays in seeking a comprehensive solution do not eliminate tensions in the region.

The above Declaration was adopted by consensus by the International Conference on the Question of Palestine on 7 September 1983.

Appendix 40

Juridical Analysis of Security Council Resolution 242 of 22 November, 1967

Security Council Resolution 242 has been repeatedly referred to as the principal agreed basis for solution of the Middle East conflict and the achievement of peace in the area with as much justice as possible. As it is supplemented by General Assembly Resolution 3236 of November 22, 1974 specifying self-determination for the Palestinian people, it is a key element of the United Nations two-state solution. The Resolution's emphasis upon 'the inadmissibility of the acquistion of territory by war' (which is grounded upon the law of the United Nations Charter as well as the law governing the International Military Tribunal at Nuremberg) is the cardinal principle. It is, nevertheless, limited in its application to those 'territories occupied in the recent conflict.' The then recent conflict was the intense hostilities of June, 1967. According to the authoritative view of Lord Caradon, the principal author of the Resolution, this means:

> It was from occupied territories that the Resolution called for withdrawal. The test was which territories were occupied. That was a test not possibly subject to doubt. As a matter of plain fact East Jerusalem, the West Bank, Gaza, the Golan and Sinai were occupied in the 1967 conflict. it was on withdrawal from occupied territories that the Resolution insisted. [Lord Caradon et al., *U.N. Security Council Resolution 242*, p. 9 (Georgetown Univ., 1981)].

The Resolution also specifies 'secure and recognized boundaries' for every state in the area and Lord Caradon has pointed out that his permits minor variations in the pre-June, 1967 boundaries of the State of Israel which should be specified by an impartial boundary commission.

495

Each of the peace plans consistent with Resolution 242 including the Saudi Peace Plan of August 7, 1981 and the Fez Declaration of September 9, 1982, has accepted the principle of 'secure and recognized boundaries' for every state in the area and thereby recognized Israel within its pre-1967 boundaries. Even the Camp David Agreements of September 17, 1978 are expressly stated to be subject to Resolution 242 'in all its parts.' Camp David is the plan to which Israel has accorded partial acceptance subject to unilateral interpretations which violate the letter and spirit of 242. President Reagan's Peace Plan of September 1, 1982 reaffirmed 242 and emphasized its application to all of the occupied territories. Nevertheless, Israel has frustrated the withdrawal provisions and the United States Government continues to provide the massive military and financial support which permits the State of Israel to remain in all of the occupied territories except the Sinai and to continue the establishment of settlements which are designed to acquire the territories in violation of the cardinal principle of Resolution 242. (The settlements are also in violation of article 49(6) of the Geneva Convention Relative to the Protection of civilian Persons of August 12, 1949.) The Palestine Liberation Organization has objected to the one part of 242 which deals with the people of Palestine as merely a 'refugee problem' in need of a 'just settlement'. This defect is corrected by the specification of the Palestinian people being entitled to the national right of self-determination in General Assembly Resolution 3236.

The basic principles of Security Council Resolution 242 and General Assembly Resolution 3236 are consistent with the key elements of the General Assembly Palestine Partition Resolution 181 of November 29, 1947 and with the law of the United Nations Charter. The contemporary breakdown of the legal order system in Palestine–Israel and the Middle East is caused by the failure to enforce these authoritative United Nations Resolutions. An adequate enforcement process is necessary for the establishment of peace under law which will terminate coercion and violence and bring the benefits to Palestinians and Israelis alike as well as to the Middle East and the world community.

MAP 1

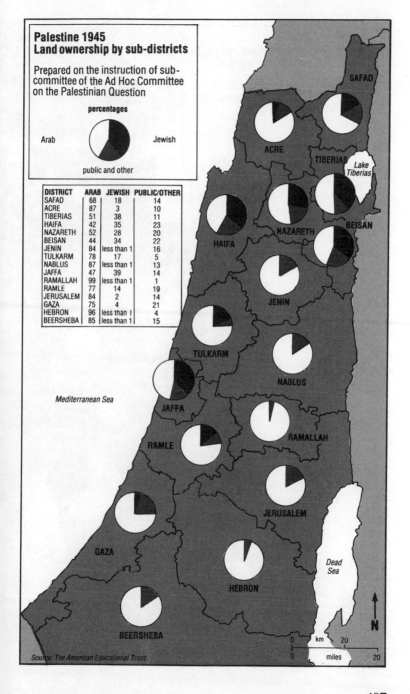

Palestine 1945
Land ownership by sub-districts

Prepared on the instruction of sub-committee of the Ad Hoc Committee on the Palestinian Question

percentages

Arab   Jewish

public and other

DISTRICT	ARAB	JEWISH	PUBLIC/OTHER
SAFAD	68	18	14
ACRE	87	3	10
TIBERIAS	51	38	11
HAIFA	42	35	23
NAZARETH	52	28	20
BEISAN	44	34	22
JENIN	84	less than 1	16
TULKARM	78	17	5
NABLUS	87	less than 1	13
JAFFA	47	39	14
RAMALLAH	99	less than 1	1
RAMLE	77	14	19
JERUSALEM	84	2	14
GAZA	75	4	21
HEBRON	96	less than 1	4
BEERSHEBA	85	less than 1	15

SAFAD

ACRE

TIBERIAS

Lake Tiberias

NAZARETH

BEISAN

HAIFA

JENIN

TULKARM

NABLUS

Mediterranean Sea

JAFFA

RAMLE

RAMALLAH

JERUSALEM

GAZA

HEBRON

Dead Sea

BEERSHEBA

N

km   20

miles   20

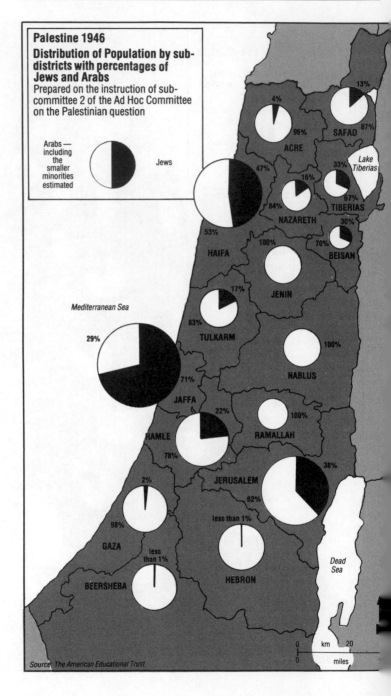

Palestine 1946

Distribution of Population by sub-districts with percentages of Jews and Arabs

Prepared on the instruction of sub-committee 2 of the Ad Hoc Committee on the Palestinian question

Arabs — including the smaller minorities estimated

Jews

Source: The American Educational Trust

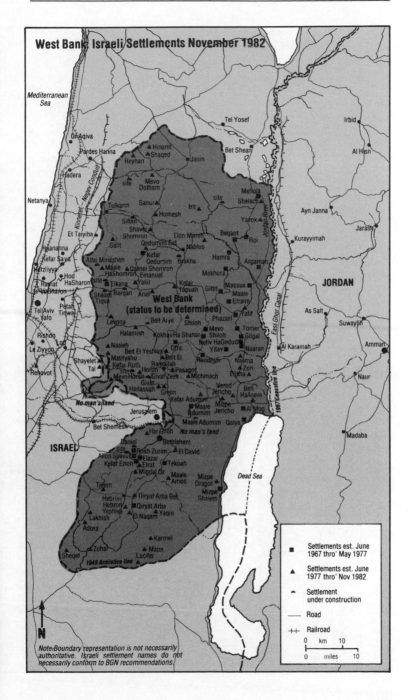

West Bank: Israeli Settlements November 1982

MAP 3

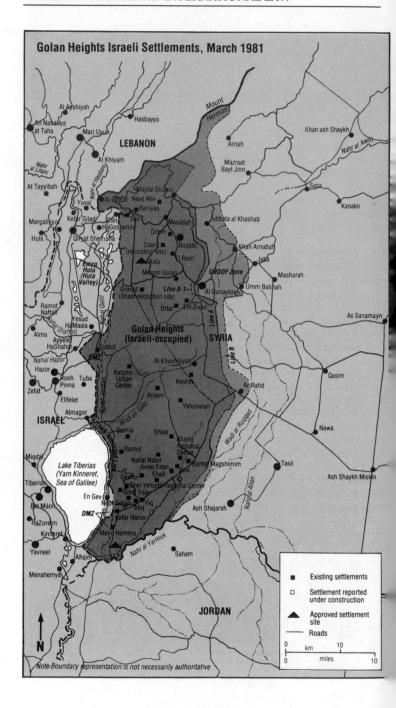

Golan Heights Israeli Settlements, March 1981

MAP 5

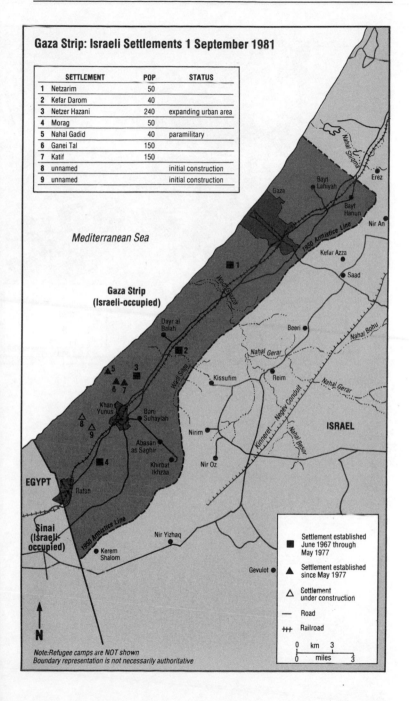

Gaza Strip: Israeli Settlements 1 September 1981

	SETTLEMENT	POP	STATUS
1	Netzarim	50	
2	Kefar Darom	40	
3	Netzer Hazani	240	expanding urban area
4	Morag	50	
5	Nahal Gadid	40	paramilitary
6	Ganei Tal	150	
7	Katif	150	
8	unnamed		initial construction
9	unnamed		initial construction

Mediterranean Sea

Gaza Strip
(Israeli-occupied)

EGYPT

Sinai
(Israeli-occupied)

ISRAEL

Erez

Bayt Lahiyah

Gaza

Bayt Hanun

Nir An

Kefar Azza

Saad

Nahal Shiqma

1950 Armistice Line

Wadi Gaza

Dayr al Balah

Beeri

Nahal Bohu

Nahal Gerar

Kissufim

Reim

Nahal Gerar

Wadi Slite

Khan Yunus

Bani Suhaylah

Nirim

Kinneret – Negev Conduit

Abasan as Saghir

Khirbat Ikhzaa

Nir Oz

Nahal Beson

Rafah

1950 Armistice Line

Nir Yizhaq

Kerem Shalom

Gevulot

■	Settlement established June 1967 through May 1977
▲	Settlement established since May 1977
△	Settlement under construction
—	Road
+++	Railroad

0   km   3
0   miles   3

N

Note: Refugee camps are NOT shown
Boundary representation is not necessarily authoritative

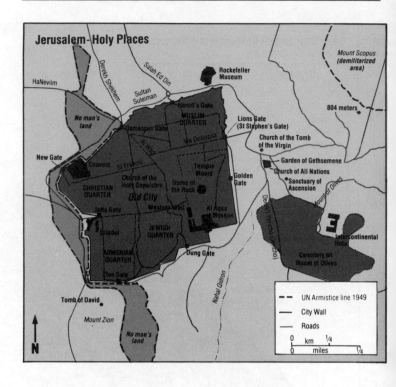

MAP 7

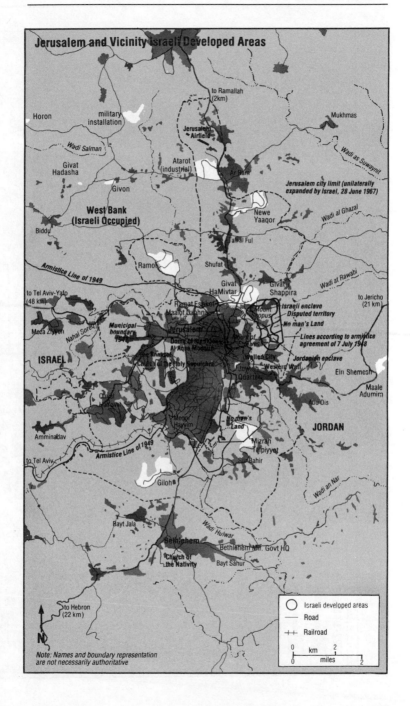

Jerusalem and Vicinity Israeli Developed Areas

Horon

military
installation

to Ramallah
(2km)

Mukhmas

Wadi Salman

Jerusalem
Airfield

Givat
Hadasha

Atarot
(industrial)

Ar Ram

Wadi as Suwaynit

Givon

**West Bank
(Israeli Occupied)**

Jerusalem city limit (unilaterally
expanded by Israel, 28 June 1967)

Newe
Yaaqor

Wadi al Ghazal

Biddu

al al Ful

Armistice Line of 1949

Ramot

Shufat

Wadi at Rawabi

to Tel Aviv-Yafo
(48 km)

Givat
HaMivtar

Givat
Shappira

to Jericho
(21 km)

Nahal Soreq

Municipal
boundary
1967

Ramat Eshkol
Maalot Dafhna

Mount
Scopus

Israeli enclave
Disputed territory
No man's Land

Moza Illiyot

Jerusalem

Mount
of Olives

Lines according to armistice
agreement of 7 July 1948

ISRAEL

Dome of the Rock
Ar Aqsa Mosque

Jordanian enclave

Ein Shemesh

Mea Shearim
Church of the Holy Sepulchre

Walled City

Western Wall

Jewish
Quarter

Maale
Adumim

Givat
HaYovel

Abu Dis

Amminadav

Megor
Hayyim

No man's
Land

JORDAN

to Tel Aviv

Armistice Line of 1949

Mizrah
Talpiyyot

Sur Bahir

Wadi an Nar

Giloh

Bayt Jala

Wadi Hulwar

Bethlehem

Bethlehem Mil. Govt HQ

Church of
the Nativity

Bayt Sahur

to Hebron
(22 km)

N

Note: Names and boundary representation
are not necessarily authoritative

◯	Israeli developed areas
—	Road
++	Railroad

0   km   2
0   miles   2

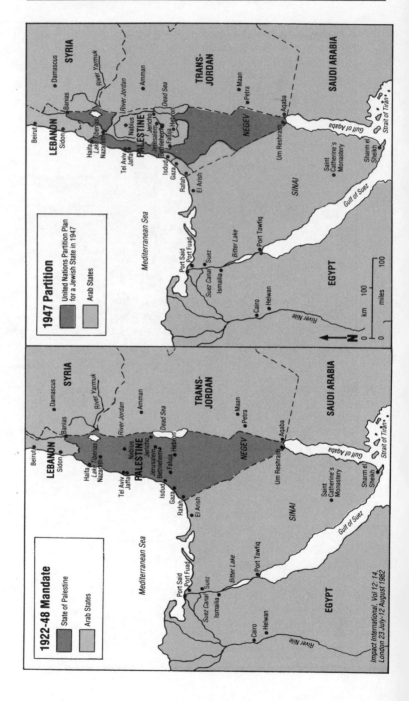

1947 Partition

United Nations Partition Plan for a Jewish State in 1947

Arab States

1922-48 Mandate

State of Palestine

Arab States

Impact International, Vol 12: 14, London 23 July–12 August 1982

504

MAP 9

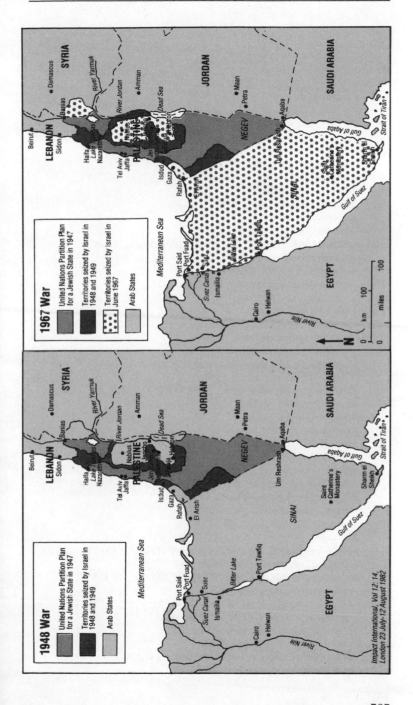

1967 War

United Nations Partition Plan for a Jewish State in 1947

Territories seized by Israel in 1948 and 1949

Territories seized by Israel in June 1967

Arab States

1948 War

United Nations Partition Plan for a Jewish State in 1947

Territories seized by Israel in 1948 and 1949

Arab States

Impact International, Vol 12: 14, London 23 July–12 August 1982

Index

Table of United Nations Resolutions

A General Assembly

95	1946,	*2,296*
106(S-1)	15 May 1947,	*154,155*
181	29 Nov. 1947,	*69,70,159–173,185–187,190,191,*
		193,198, 203,204,206,210–213,216,
		230,231,235,321,408,409,417–420,
		459–461,496,

(Palestine Partition Resolution)

185	26 April 1948,	*211*
186	14 May 1948,	*212*
187	6 May 1948,	*211*
194	11 Dec. 1948,	*178–184,186,212–214,216,408*
217	10 Dec. 1948,	*176,183,190*

(Universal Declaration of Human Rights)

260	9 Dec. 1948,	*389*
273	11 May 1949,	*408*

(Admission of Israel)

303	9 Dec. 1949,	*213,216*
377	3 Nov. 1950,	*150,205,217,420, 421*

(Uniting for Peace Resolution)

513	26 Jan. 1952,	*180–182*
1514	14 Dec. 1960,	*193,194,198*
2252	4 July 1967,	*183,216*
2253	4 July 1967,	*215–217,221–223*
2254	6 July 1967,	*215,217,221–223*
2452	19 Dec. 1968,	*181–183*
2535	10 Dec. 1969,	*181–183,190,198,461,462*
2625	24 Oct. 1970,	*194–196,198,201,202,296,462–464*
2649	30 Nov. 1970,	*198*
2672	8 Dec. 1970,	*190,198,199*
2963	13 Dec. 1972,	*181,183,184*
3070	30 Nov. 1973,	*201*
3089	7 Dec. 1973,	*184,185,199,464,465*
3210	14 Oct. 1974,	*190*
3236	22 Nov. 1974,	*184,185,187,191,200,201,203,415,*
		466,467
3237	22 Nov. 1974,	*201,467,468*
3314	14 Dec. 1974,	*295,296*
3376	10 Nov. 1975,	*187,204*
31/15A/D	23 Nov. 1976,	*186,187*
31/20	24 Nov. 1976,	*417*

32/40B	2 Dec. 1977,	*204*
33/28A	7 Dec. 1978,	*187*
34/90B	12 Dec. 1979,	*275*
35/122A	3 Nov. 1980,	*274*
35/169A/E	15 Dec. 1980,	*205,218,468,469*
ES-7/2	29 July 1980,	*205,217,218*
36/120C/E	10 Dec. 1981,	*219,417,492*
36/147A	16 Dec. 1981,	*275*
ES-7/7	19 Aug. 1982,	*492*
ES-7/8	19 Aug. 1982,	*470*
ES-7/9	24 Sept. 1982,	*470,471*
37/86A/C/D	10 Dec. 1982,	*417,418,492*

B Security Council

73	11 Aug. 1949,	*187*
237	14 June 1967,	*182,183,188*
242	22 Nov. 1967,	*188,203,205,206,220,229,232,244, 275,320, 322,409,413–416,418,419, 472,473,495,496*
252	21 May 1968,	*221–224*
267	3 July 1969,	*222 224*
271	15 Sept. 1969,	*223*
298	25 Sept. 1971,	*223,224*
338	22 Oct. 1973,	*188,473*
425	19 March 1978,	*282,288*
446	22 March 1979,	*225,234*
465	1 March 1980,	*225,226,474–476*
476	30 June 1980,	*226*
478	20 Aug. 1980,	*218,227*
490	21 July 1981,	*283*
497	17 Dec. 1981,	*476,477*
508	5 June 1982,	*305,317–319,477*
509	6 June 1982,	*317–319,478*
511	18 June 1982,	*479,480*
512	19 June 1982,	*480,481*
513	4 July 1982,	*481*
515	29 July 1982,	*482*
520	17 Sept. 1982,	*482,483*
521	19 Sept. 1982,	*483,484*
(draft Spanish Resolution		
	8 June 1982,	*318,478,479)*

Table of Israeli Laws

Table of International Agreements